UNCOVER

SEE FOR YOURSELF

MARK

The Gospel of Mark

John the Baptist prepares the way

1 The beginning of the good news about Jesus the Messiah, the Son of God, ² as it is written in Isaiah the prophet:

> 'I will send my messenger ahead of you,
>   who will prepare your way' –
> ³ 'a voice of one calling in the wilderness,
>   "Prepare the way for the Lord,
>   make straight paths for him." '

⁴ And so John the Baptist appeared in the wilderness, preaching a baptism of repentance for the forgiveness of sins. ⁵ The whole Judean countryside and all the people of Jerusalem went out to him. Confessing their sins, they were baptised by him in the River Jordan. ⁶ John wore clothing made of camel's hair, with a leather belt round his waist, and he ate locusts and wild honey. ⁷ And this was his message: 'After me comes the one more powerful than I, the straps of whose sandals I am not worthy to stoop down and untie. ⁸ I baptise you with water, but he will baptise you with the Holy Spirit.'

The baptism and testing of Jesus

⁹ At that time Jesus came from Nazareth in Galilee and was baptised by John in the Jordan. ¹⁰ Just as Jesus was coming up out of the water, he saw heaven being torn open and the Spirit descending on him like a dove. ¹¹ And a voice came from heaven: 'You are my Son, whom I love; with you I am well pleased.'

¹² At once the Spirit sent him out into the wilderness, ¹³ and he was in the

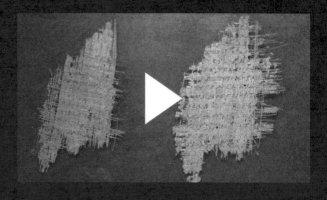

R

Can we trust Mark?
Watch at uncover.org.uk/reliability

wilderness for forty days, being tempted by Satan. He was with the wild animals, and angels attended him.

Jesus announces the good news

[14] After John was put in prison, Jesus went into Galilee, proclaiming the good news of God. [15] 'The time has come,' he said. 'The kingdom of God has come near. Repent and believe the good news!'

Jesus calls his first disciples

[16] As Jesus walked beside the Sea of Galilee, he saw Simon and his brother Andrew casting a net into the lake, for they were fishermen. [17] 'Come, follow me,' Jesus said, 'and I will send you out to fish for people.' [18] At once they left their nets and followed him.

[19] When he had gone a little farther, he saw James son of Zebedee and his brother John in a boat, preparing their nets. [20] Without delay he called them, and they left their father Zebedee in the boat with the hired men and followed him.

Jesus drives out an impure spirit

[21] They went to Capernaum, and when the Sabbath came, Jesus went into the synagogue and began to teach. [22] The people were amazed at his teaching, because he taught them as one who had authority, not as the teachers of the law. [23] Just then a man in their synagogue who was possessed by an impure spirit cried out, [24] 'What do you want with us, Jesus of Nazareth? Have you come to destroy us? I know who you are – the Holy One of God!'

[25] 'Be quiet!' said Jesus sternly. 'Come out of him!' [26] The impure spirit shook the man violently and came out of him with a shriek.

[27] The people were all so amazed that they asked each other, 'What is this? A new teaching – and with authority! He even gives orders to impure spirits and they obey him.' [28] News about him spread quickly over the whole region of Galilee.

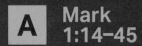

A Mark 1:14–45

Mark wants his readers to be in no doubt about the world-changing significance of what he is claiming about Jesus.

Discuss in Study A // **Page 101**

Jesus heals many

²⁹ As soon as they left the synagogue, they went with James and John to the home of Simon and Andrew. ³⁰ Simon's mother-in-law was in bed with a fever, and they immediately told Jesus about her. ³¹ So he went to her, took her hand and helped her up. The fever left her and she began to wait on them.

³² That evening after sunset the people brought to Jesus all who were ill and demon-possessed. ³³ The whole town gathered at the door, ³⁴ and Jesus healed many who had various diseases. He also drove out many demons, but he would not let the demons speak because they knew who he was.

Jesus prays in a solitary place

³⁵ Very early in the morning, while it was still dark, Jesus got up, left the house and went off to a solitary place, where he prayed. ³⁶ Simon and his companions went to look for him, ³⁷ and when they found him, they exclaimed: 'Everyone is looking for you!'

³⁸ Jesus replied, 'Let us go somewhere else – to the nearby villages – so that I can preach there also. That is why I have come.' ³⁹ So he travelled throughout Galilee, preaching in their synagogues and driving out demons.

Jesus heals a man with leprosy

⁴⁰ A man with leprosy came to him and begged him on his knees, 'If you are willing, you can make me clean.'

⁴¹ Jesus was indignant. He reached out his hand and touched the man. 'I am willing,' he said. 'Be clean!' ⁴² Immediately the leprosy left him and he was cleansed.

⁴³ Jesus sent him away at once with a strong warning: ⁴⁴ 'See that you don't tell this to anyone. But go, show yourself to the priest and offer the sacrifices that Moses commanded for your cleansing, as a testimony to them.' ⁴⁵ Instead he went out and began to talk freely, spreading the news. As a result, Jesus could

no longer enter a town openly but stayed outside in lonely places. Yet the people still came to him from everywhere.

Jesus forgives and heals a paralysed man

2 A few days later, when Jesus again entered Capernaum, the people heard that he had come home. [2] They gathered in such large numbers that there was no room left, not even outside the door, and he preached the word to them. [3] Some men came, bringing to him a paralysed man, carried by four of them. [4] Since they could not get him to Jesus because of the crowd, they made an opening in the roof above Jesus by digging through it and then lowered the mat the man was lying on. [5] When Jesus saw their faith, he said to the paralysed man, 'Son, your sins are forgiven.'

[6] Now some teachers of the law were sitting there, thinking to themselves, [7] 'Why does this fellow talk like that? He's blaspheming! Who can forgive sins but God alone?'

[8] Immediately Jesus knew in his spirit that this was what they were thinking in their hearts, and he said to them, 'Why are you thinking these things? [9] Which is easier: to say to this paralysed man, "Your sins are forgiven," or to say, "Get up, take your mat and walk"? [10] But I want you to know that the Son of Man has authority on earth to forgive sins.' So he said to the man, [11] 'I tell you, get up, take your mat and go home.' [12] He got up, took his mat and walked out in full view of them all. This amazed everyone and they praised God, saying, 'We have never seen anything like this!'

Jesus calls Levi and eats with sinners

[13] Once again Jesus went out beside the lake. A large crowd came to him, and he began to teach them. [14] As he walked along, he saw Levi son of Alphaeus sitting at the tax collector's booth. 'Follow me,' Jesus told him, and Levi got up and followed him.

B **Mark
2:1–22, 3:1–6**

Jesus was exploding the categories and
expectations of his day. By forgiving sins
and welcoming those seen as unholy,
Jesus was doing what only God had the
right to do.

Discuss in Study B // Page 117

¹⁵ While Jesus was having dinner at Levi's house, many tax collectors and sinners were eating with him and his disciples, for there were many who followed him. ¹⁶ When the teachers of the law who were Pharisees saw him eating with the sinners and tax collectors, they asked his disciples: 'Why does he eat with tax collectors and sinners?'

¹⁷ On hearing this, Jesus said to them, 'It is not the healthy who need a doctor, but those who are ill. I have not come to call the righteous, but sinners.'

Jesus questioned about fasting

¹⁸ Now John's disciples and the Pharisees were fasting. Some people came and asked Jesus, 'How is it that John's disciples and the disciples of the Pharisees are fasting, but yours are not?'

¹⁹ Jesus answered, 'How can the guests of the bridegroom fast while he is with them? They cannot, so long as they have him with them. ²⁰ But the time will come when the bridegroom will be taken from them, and on that day they will fast.

²¹ 'No one sews a patch of unshrunk cloth on an old garment. Otherwise, the new piece will pull away from the old, making the tear worse. ²² And no one pours new wine into old wineskins. Otherwise, the wine will burst the skins, and both the wine and the wineskins will be ruined. No, they pour new wine into new wineskins.'

Jesus is Lord of the Sabbath

²³ One Sabbath Jesus was going through the cornfields, and as his disciples walked along, they began to pick some ears of corn. ²⁴ The Pharisees said to him, 'Look, why are they doing what is unlawful on the Sabbath?'

²⁵ He answered, 'Have you never read what David did when he and his companions were hungry and in need? ²⁶ In the days of Abiathar the high priest, he entered the house of God and ate the consecrated bread, which is lawful only for priests to eat. And he also gave some to his companions.'

²⁷ Then he said to them, 'The Sabbath was made for man, not man for the Sabbath. ²⁸ So the Son of Man is Lord even of the Sabbath.'

Jesus heals on the Sabbath

3 Another time Jesus went into the synagogue, and a man with a shrivelled hand was there. ² Some of them were looking for a reason to accuse Jesus, so they watched him closely to see if he would heal him on the Sabbath. ³ Jesus said to the man with the shrivelled hand, 'Stand up in front of everyone.'

⁴ Then Jesus asked them, 'Which is lawful on the Sabbath: to do good or to do evil, to save life or to kill?' But they remained silent.

⁵ He looked around at them in anger and, deeply distressed at their stubborn hearts, said to the man, 'Stretch out your hand.' He stretched it out, and his hand was completely restored. ⁶ Then the Pharisees went out and began to plot with the Herodians how they might kill Jesus.

Crowds follow Jesus

⁷ Jesus withdrew with his disciples to the lake, and a large crowd from Galilee followed. ⁸ When they heard all he was doing, many people came to him from Judea, Jerusalem, Idumea, and the regions across the Jordan and around Tyre and Sidon. ⁹ Because of the crowd he told his disciples to have a small boat ready for him, to keep the people from crowding him. ¹⁰ For he had healed many, so that those with diseases were pushing forward to touch him. ¹¹ Whenever the impure spirits saw him, they fell down before him and cried out, 'You are the Son of God.' ¹² But he gave them strict orders not to tell others about him.

Jesus appoints the Twelve

¹³ Jesus went up on a mountainside and called to him those he wanted, and they came to him. ¹⁴ He appointed twelve that they might be with him and that he might send them out to preach ¹⁵ and to have authority to drive out demons.

¹⁶ These are the twelve he appointed: Simon (to whom he gave the name Peter); ¹⁷ James son of Zebedee and his brother John (to them he gave the name Boanerges, which means 'sons of thunder'), ¹⁸ Andrew, Philip, Bartholomew, Matthew, Thomas, James son of Alphaeus, Thaddaeus, Simon the Zealot ¹⁹ and Judas Iscariot, who betrayed him.

Jesus accused by his family and by teachers of the law

²⁰ Then Jesus entered a house, and again a crowd gathered, so that he and his disciples were not even able to eat. ²¹ When his family heard about this, they went to take charge of him, for they said, 'He is out of his mind.'

²² And the teachers of the law who came down from Jerusalem said, 'He is possessed by Beelzebul! By the prince of demons he is driving out demons.'

²³ So Jesus called them over to him and began to speak to them in parables: 'How can Satan drive out Satan? ²⁴ If a kingdom is divided against itself, that kingdom cannot stand. ²⁵ If a house is divided against itself, that house cannot stand. ²⁶ And if Satan opposes himself and is divided, he cannot stand; his end has come. ²⁷ In fact, no one can enter a strong man's house without first tying him up. Then he can plunder the strong man's house. ²⁸ Truly I tell you, people can be forgiven all their sins and every slander they utter, ²⁹ but whoever blasphemes against the Holy Spirit will never be forgiven; they are guilty of an eternal sin.'

³⁰ He said this because they were saying, 'He has an impure spirit.'

³¹ Then Jesus' mother and brothers arrived. Standing outside, they sent someone in to call him. ³² A crowd was sitting round him, and they told him, 'Your mother and brothers are outside looking for you.'

³³ 'Who are my mother and my brothers?' he asked.

³⁴ Then he looked at those seated in a circle round him and said, 'Here are my mother and my brothers! ³⁵ Whoever does God's will is my brother and sister and mother.'

The parable of the sower

4 Again Jesus began to teach by the lake. The crowd that gathered round him was so large that he got into a boat and sat in it out on the lake, while all the people were along the shore at the water's edge. ²He taught them many things by parables, and in his teaching said: ³'Listen! A farmer went out to sow his seed. ⁴As he was scattering the seed, some fell along the path, and the birds came and ate it up. ⁵Some fell on rocky places, where it did not have much soil. It sprang up quickly, because the soil was shallow. ⁶But when the sun came up, the plants were scorched, and they withered because they had no root. ⁷Other seed fell among thorns, which grew up and choked the plants, so that they did not bear grain. ⁸Still other seed fell on good soil. It came up, grew and produced a crop, some multiplying thirty, some sixty, some a hundred times.'

⁹Then Jesus said, 'Whoever has ears to hear, let them hear.'

¹⁰When he was alone, the Twelve and the others around him asked him about the parables. ¹¹He told them, 'The secret of the kingdom of God has been given to you. But to those on the outside everything is said in parables ¹²so that,

'"they may be ever seeing but never perceiving,
and ever hearing but never understanding;
otherwise they might turn and be forgiven!" '

¹³Then Jesus said to them, 'Don't you understand this parable? How then will you understand any parable? ¹⁴The farmer sows the word. ¹⁵Some people are like seed along the path, where the word is sown. As soon as they hear it, Satan comes and takes away the word that was sown in them. ¹⁶Others, like seed sown on rocky places, hear the word and at once receive it with joy. ¹⁷But since they have no root, they last only a short time. When trouble or persecution comes because of the word, they quickly fall away. ¹⁸Still others, like seed sown among thorns, hear the word; ¹⁹but the worries of this life, the deceitfulness of wealth

and the desires for other things come in and choke the word, making it unfruitful. [20] Others, like seed sown on good soil, hear the word, accept it, and produce a crop – some thirty, some sixty, some a hundred times what was sown.'

A lamp on a stand

[21] He said to them, 'Do you bring in a lamp to put it under a bowl or a bed? Instead, don't you put it on its stand? [22] For whatever is hidden is meant to be disclosed, and whatever is concealed is meant to be brought out into the open. [23] If anyone has ears to hear, let them hear.'

[24] 'Consider carefully what you hear,' he continued. 'With the measure you use, it will be measured to you – and even more. [25] Whoever has will be given more; whoever does not have, even what they have will be taken from them.'

The parable of the growing seed

[26] He also said, 'This is what the kingdom of God is like. A man scatters seed on the ground. [27] Night and day, whether he sleeps or gets up, the seed sprouts and grows, though he does not know how. [28] All by itself the soil produces corn – first the stalk, then the ear, then the full grain in the ear. [29] As soon as the corn is ripe, he puts the sickle to it, because the harvest has come.'

The parable of the mustard seed

[30] Again he said, 'What shall we say the kingdom of God is like, or what parable shall we use to describe it? [31] It is like a mustard seed, which is the smallest of all seeds on earth. [32] Yet when planted, it grows and becomes the largest of all garden plants, with such big branches that the birds can perch in its shade.'

[33] With many similar parables Jesus spoke the word to them, as much as they could understand. [34] He did not say anything to them without using a parable. But when he was alone with his own disciples, he explained everything.

Jesus calms the storm

35 That day when evening came, he said to his disciples, 'Let us go over to the other side.' 36 Leaving the crowd behind, they took him along, just as he was, in the boat. There were also other boats with him. 37 A furious squall came up, and the waves broke over the boat, so that it was nearly swamped. 38 Jesus was in the stern, sleeping on a cushion. The disciples woke him and said to him,

'Teacher, don't you care if we drown?'

39 He got up, rebuked the wind and said to the waves, 'Quiet! Be still!' Then the wind died down and it was completely calm.

40 He said to his disciples, 'Why are you so afraid? Do you still have no faith?'

41 They were terrified and asked each other, 'Who is this? Even the wind and the waves obey him!'

Jesus restores a demon-possessed man

5 They went across the lake to the region of the Gerasenes. 2 When Jesus got out of the boat, a man with an impure spirit came from the tombs to meet him. 3 This man lived in the tombs, and no one could bind him anymore, not even with a chain. 4 For he had often been chained hand and foot, but he tore the chains apart and broke the irons on his feet. No one was strong enough to subdue him. 5 Night and day among the tombs and in the hills he would cry out and cut himself with stones.

6 When he saw Jesus from a distance, he ran and fell on his knees in front of him. 7 He shouted at the top of his voice, 'What do you want with me, Jesus, Son of the Most High God? In God's name don't torture me!' 8 For Jesus had said to him, 'Come out of this man, you impure spirit!'

9 Then Jesus asked him, 'What is your name?'

'My name is Legion,' he replied, 'for we are many.' 10 And he begged Jesus again and again not to send them out of the area.

11 A large herd of pigs was feeding on the nearby hillside. 12 The demons

begged Jesus, 'Send us among the pigs; allow us to go into them.' [13] He gave them permission, and the impure spirits came out and went into the pigs. The herd, about two thousand in number, rushed down the steep bank into the lake and were drowned.

[14] Those tending the pigs ran off and reported this in the town and countryside, and the people went out to see what had happened. [15] When they came to Jesus, they saw the man who had been possessed by the legion of demons, sitting there, dressed and in his right mind; and they were afraid. [16] Those who had seen it told the people what had happened to the demon-possessed man – and told about the pigs as well. [17] Then the people began to plead with Jesus to leave their region.

[18] As Jesus was getting into the boat, the man who had been demon-possessed begged to go with him. [19] Jesus did not let him, but said, 'Go home to your own people and tell them how much the Lord has done for you, and how he has had mercy on you.' [20] So the man went away and began to tell in the Decapolis how much Jesus had done for him. And all the people were amazed.

Jesus raises a dead girl and heals a sick woman

[21] When Jesus had again crossed over by boat to the other side of the lake, a large crowd gathered round him while he was by the lake. [22] Then one of the synagogue leaders, named Jairus, came, and when he saw Jesus, he fell at his feet. [23] He pleaded earnestly with him, 'My little daughter is dying. Please come and put your hands on her so that she will be healed and live.' [24] So Jesus went with him.

A large crowd followed and pressed round him. [25] And a woman was there who had been subject to bleeding for twelve years. [26] She had suffered a great deal under the care of many doctors and had spent all she had, yet instead of getting better she grew worse. [27] When she heard about Jesus, she came up behind him in the crowd and touched his cloak, [28] because she thought, 'If I just touch his

C Mark
5:21–43

People were travelling from far around
to see for themselves what they had
heard about the man, his message and
(most of all) his miracles. Jesus was
clearly reluctant to become famous as a
miracle worker and yet he continued to
heal people.

Discuss in Study C // Page 133

clothes, I will be healed.' [29]Immediately her bleeding stopped and she felt in her body that she was freed from her suffering.

[30]At once Jesus realised that power had gone out from him. He turned round in the crowd and asked, 'Who touched my clothes?'

[31]'You see the people crowding against you,' his disciples answered, 'and yet you can ask, "Who touched me?"'

[32]But Jesus kept looking around to see who had done it. [33]Then the woman, knowing what had happened to her, came and fell at his feet and, trembling with fear, told him the whole truth. [34]He said to her, 'Daughter, your faith has healed you. Go in peace and be freed from your suffering.'

[35]While Jesus was still speaking, some people came from the house of Jairus, the synagogue leader. 'Your daughter is dead,' they said. 'Why bother the teacher anymore?'

[36]Overhearing what they said, Jesus told him, 'Don't be afraid; just believe.'

[37]He did not let anyone follow him except Peter, James and John the brother of James. [38]When they came to the home of the synagogue leader, Jesus saw a commotion, with people crying and wailing loudly. [39]He went in and said to them, 'Why all this commotion and wailing? The child is not dead but asleep.' [40]But they laughed at him.

After he put them all out, he took the child's father and mother and the disciples who were with him, and went in where the child was. [41]He took her by the hand and said to her, '*Talitha koum!*' (which means 'Little girl, I say to you, get up!'). [42]Immediately the girl stood up and began to walk around (she was twelve years old). At this they were completely astonished. [43]He gave strict orders not to let anyone know about this, and told them to give her something to eat.

A prophet without honour

6 Jesus left there and went to his home town, accompanied by his disciples. ² When the Sabbath came, he began to teach in the synagogue, and many who heard him were amazed.

'Where did this man get these things?' they asked. 'What's this wisdom that has been given him? What are these remarkable miracles he is performing? ³ Isn't this the carpenter? Isn't this Mary's son and the brother of James, Joseph, Judas and Simon? Aren't his sisters here with us?' And they took offence at him.

⁴ Jesus said to them, 'A prophet is not without honour except in his own town, among his relatives and in his own home.' ⁵ He could not do any miracles there, except lay his hands on a few people who were ill and heal them. ⁶ He was amazed at their lack of faith.

Jesus sends out the Twelve

Then Jesus went around teaching from village to village. ⁷ Calling the Twelve to him, he began to send them out two by two and gave them authority over impure spirits.

⁸ These were his instructions: 'Take nothing for the journey except a staff – no bread, no bag, no money in your belts. ⁹ Wear sandals but not an extra shirt. ¹⁰ Whenever you enter a house, stay there until you leave that town. ¹¹ And if any place will not welcome you or listen to you, leave that place and shake the dust off your feet as a testimony against them.'

¹² They went out and preached that people should repent. ¹³ They drove out many demons and anointed with oil many people who were ill and healed them.

John the Baptist beheaded

¹⁴ King Herod heard about this, for Jesus' name had become well known. Some were saying, 'John the Baptist has been raised from the dead, and that is why miraculous powers are at work in him.'

¹⁵ Others said, 'He is Elijah.'

And still others claimed, 'He is a prophet, like one of the prophets of long ago.'

¹⁶ But when Herod heard this, he said, 'John, whom I beheaded, has been raised from the dead!'

¹⁷ For Herod himself had given orders to have John arrested, and he had him bound and put in prison. He did this because of Herodias, his brother Philip's wife, whom he had married. ¹⁸ For John had been saying to Herod, 'It is not lawful for you to have your brother's wife.' ¹⁹ So Herodias nursed a grudge against John and wanted to kill him. But she was not able to, ²⁰ because Herod feared John and protected him, knowing him to be a righteous and holy man. When Herod heard John, he was greatly puzzled; yet he liked to listen to him.

²¹ Finally the opportune time came. On his birthday Herod gave a banquet for his high officials and military commanders and the leading men of Galilee. ²² When the daughter of Herodias came in and danced, she pleased Herod and his dinner guests.

The king said to the girl, 'Ask me for anything you want, and I'll give it to you.' ²³ And he promised her with an oath, 'Whatever you ask I will give you, up to half my kingdom.'

²⁴ She went out and said to her mother, 'What shall I ask for?'

'The head of John the Baptist,' she answered.

²⁵ At once the girl hurried in to the king with the request: 'I want you to give me right now the head of John the Baptist on a dish.'

²⁶ The king was greatly distressed, but because of his oaths and his dinner guests, he did not want to refuse her. ²⁷ So he immediately sent an executioner with orders to bring John's head. The man went, beheaded John in the prison, ²⁸ and brought back his head on a dish. He presented it to the girl, and she gave it to her mother. ²⁹ On hearing of this, John's disciples came and took his body and laid it in a tomb.

Jesus feeds the five thousand

³⁰ The apostles gathered round Jesus and reported to him all they had done and taught. ³¹ Then, because so many people were coming and going that they did not even have a chance to eat, he said to them, 'Come with me by yourselves to a quiet place and get some rest.'

³² So they went away by themselves in a boat to a solitary place. ³³ But many who saw them leaving recognised them and ran on foot from all the towns and got there ahead of them. ³⁴ When Jesus landed and saw a large crowd, he had compassion on them, because they were like sheep without a shepherd. So he began teaching them many things.

³⁵ By this time it was late in the day, so his disciples came to him. 'This is a remote place,' they said, 'and it's already very late. ³⁶ Send the people away so that they can go to the surrounding countryside and villages and buy themselves something to eat.'

³⁷ But he answered, 'You give them something to eat.'

They said to him, 'That would take more than half a year's wages! Are we to go and spend that much on bread and give it to them to eat?'

³⁸ 'How many loaves do you have?' he asked. 'Go and see.'

When they found out, they said, 'Five – and two fish.'

³⁹ Then Jesus told them to make all the people sit down in groups on the green grass. ⁴⁰ So they sat down in groups of hundreds and fifties. ⁴¹ Taking the five loaves and the two fish and looking up to heaven, he gave thanks and broke the loaves. Then he gave them to his disciples to distribute to the people. He also divided the two fish among them all. ⁴² They all ate and were satisfied, ⁴³ and the disciples picked up twelve basketfuls of broken pieces of bread and fish. ⁴⁴ The number of the men who had eaten was five thousand.

Jesus walks on the water

⁴⁵ Immediately Jesus made his disciples get into the boat and go on ahead of

him to Bethsaida, while he dismissed the crowd. ⁴⁶After leaving them, he went up on a mountainside to pray.

⁴⁷Later that night, the boat was in the middle of the lake, and he was alone on land. ⁴⁸He saw the disciples straining at the oars, because the wind was against them. Shortly before dawn he went out to them, walking on the lake. He was about to pass by them, ⁴⁹but when they saw him walking on the lake, they thought he was a ghost. They cried out, ⁵⁰because they all saw him and were terrified.

Immediately he spoke to them and said, 'Take courage! It is I. Don't be afraid.' ⁵¹Then he climbed into the boat with them, and the wind died down. They were completely amazed, ⁵²for they had not understood about the loaves; their hearts were hardened.

⁵³When they had crossed over, they landed at Gennesaret and anchored there. ⁵⁴As soon as they got out of the boat, people recognised Jesus. ⁵⁵They ran throughout that whole region and carried those who were ill on mats to wherever they heard he was. ⁵⁶And wherever he went – into villages, towns or countryside – they placed those who were ill in the market-places. They begged him to let them touch even the edge of his cloak, and all who touched it were healed.

That which defiles

7 The Pharisees and some of the teachers of the law who had come from Jerusalem gathered round Jesus ²and saw some of his disciples eating food with hands that were defiled, that is, unwashed. ³(The Pharisees and all the Jews do not eat unless they give their hands a ceremonial washing, holding to the tradition of the elders. ⁴When they come from the market-place they do not eat unless they wash. And they observe many other traditions, such as the washing of cups, pitchers and kettles.)

⁵So the Pharisees and teachers of the law asked Jesus, 'Why don't your

disciples live according to the tradition of the elders instead of eating their food with defiled hands?'

⁶He replied, 'Isaiah was right when he prophesied about you hypocrites; as it is written:

> "These people honour me with their lips,
>> but their hearts are far from me.
> ⁷They worship me in vain;
>> their teachings are merely human rules."

⁸You have let go of the commands of God and are holding on to human traditions.'

⁹And he continued, 'You have a fine way of setting aside the commands of God in order to observe your own traditions! ¹⁰For Moses said, "Honour your father and mother," and, "Anyone who curses their father or mother is to be put to death." ¹¹But you say that if anyone declares that what might have been used to help their father or mother is *Corban* (that is, devoted to God) – ¹²then you no longer let them do anything for their father or mother. ¹³Thus you nullify the word of God by your tradition that you have handed down. And you do many things like that.'

¹⁴Again Jesus called the crowd to him and said, 'Listen to me, everyone, and understand this. ¹⁵Nothing outside a person can defile them by going into them. Rather, it is what comes out of a person that defiles them.'

¹⁷After he had left the crowd and entered the house, his disciples asked him about this parable. ¹⁸'Are you so dull?' he asked. 'Don't you see that nothing that enters a person from the outside can defile them? ¹⁹For it doesn't go into their heart but into their stomach, and then out of the body.' (In saying this, Jesus declared all foods clean.)

²⁰He went on: 'What comes out of a person is what defiles them. ²¹For it is from within, out of a person's heart, that evil thoughts come – sexual immorality, theft,

murder, [22] adultery, greed, malice, deceit, lewdness, envy, slander, arrogance and folly. [23] All these evils come from inside and defile a person.'

Jesus honours a Syro-Phoenician woman's faith

[24] Jesus left that place and went to the vicinity of Tyre. He entered a house and did not want anyone to know it; yet he could not keep his presence secret. [25] In fact, as soon as she heard about him, a woman whose little daughter was possessed by an impure spirit came and fell at his feet. [26] The woman was a Greek, born in Syrian Phoenicia. She begged Jesus to drive the demon out of her daughter.

[27] 'First let the children eat all they want,' he told her, 'for it is not right to take the children's bread and toss it to the dogs.'

[28] 'Lord,' she replied, 'even the dogs under the table eat the children's crumbs.'

[29] Then he told her, 'For such a reply, you may go; the demon has left your daughter.'

[30] She went home and found her child lying on the bed, and the demon gone.

Jesus heals a deaf and mute man

[31] Then Jesus left the vicinity of Tyre and went through Sidon, down to the Sea of Galilee and into the region of the Decapolis. [32] There some people brought to him a man who was deaf and could hardly talk, and they begged Jesus to place his hand on him.

[33] After he took him aside, away from the crowd, Jesus put his fingers into the man's ears. Then he spat and touched the man's tongue. [34] He looked up to heaven and with a deep sigh said to him, *'Ephphatha!'* (which means 'Be opened!'). [35] At this, the man's ears were opened, his tongue was loosed and he began to speak plainly.

[36] Jesus commanded them not to tell anyone. But the more he did so, the more they kept talking about it. [37] People were overwhelmed with amazement. 'He has

done everything well,' they said. 'He even makes the deaf hear and the mute speak.'

Jesus feeds the four thousand

8 During those days another large crowd gathered. Since they had nothing to eat, Jesus called his disciples to him and said, ² 'I have compassion for these people; they have already been with me three days and have nothing to eat. ³ If I send them home hungry, they will collapse on the way, because some of them have come a long distance.'

⁴ His disciples answered, 'But where in this remote place can anyone get enough bread to feed them?'

⁵ 'How many loaves do you have?' Jesus asked.

'Seven,' they replied.

⁶ He told the crowd to sit down on the ground. When he had taken the seven loaves and given thanks, he broke them and gave them to his disciples to distribute to the people, and they did so. ⁷ They had a few small fish as well; he gave thanks for them also and told the disciples to distribute them. ⁸ The people ate and were satisfied. Afterwards the disciples picked up seven basketfuls of broken pieces that were left over. ⁹ About four thousand were present. After he had sent them away, ¹⁰ he got into the boat with his disciples and went to the region of Dalmanutha.

¹¹ The Pharisees came and began to question Jesus. To test him, they asked him for a sign from heaven. ¹² He sighed deeply and said, 'Why does this generation ask for a sign? Truly I tell you, no sign will be given to it.' ¹³ Then he left them, got back into the boat and crossed to the other side.

The yeast of the Pharisees and Herod

¹⁴ The disciples had forgotten to bring bread, except for one loaf they had with

them in the boat. [15] 'Be careful,' Jesus warned them. 'Watch out for the yeast of the Pharisees and that of Herod.'

[16] They discussed this with one another and said, 'It is because we have no bread.'

[17] Aware of their discussion, Jesus asked them: 'Why are you talking about having no bread? Do you still not see or understand? Are your hearts hardened? [18] Do you have eyes but fail to see, and ears but fail to hear? And don't you remember? [19] When I broke the five loaves for the five thousand, how many basketfuls of pieces did you pick up?'

'Twelve,' they replied.

[20] 'And when I broke the seven loaves for the four thousand, how many basketfuls of pieces did you pick up?'

They answered, 'Seven.'

[21] He said to them, 'Do you still not understand?'

Jesus heals a blind man at Bethsaida

[22] They came to Bethsaida, and some people brought a blind man and begged Jesus to touch him. [23] He took the blind man by the hand and led him outside the village. When he had spat on the man's eyes and put his hands on him, Jesus asked, 'Do you see anything?'

[24] He looked up and said, 'I see people; they look like trees walking around.'

[25] Once more Jesus put his hands on the man's eyes. Then his eyes were opened, his sight was restored, and he saw everything clearly. [26] Jesus sent him home, saying, 'Don't even go into the village.'

Peter declares that Jesus is the Messiah

[27] Jesus and his disciples went on to the villages around Caesarea Philippi. On the way he asked them, 'Who do people say I am?'

D **Mark 8:22–33, 9:30–37**

With Jesus' first touch the man was able to see things, but his brain seemed unable to make sense of what he saw. He needed a second touch from Jesus to see things clearly.

Discuss in Study D // Page 149

28 They replied, 'Some say John the Baptist; others say Elijah; and still others, one of the prophets.'

29 'But what about you?' he asked. 'Who do you say I am?'

Peter answered, 'You are the Messiah.'

30 Jesus warned them not to tell anyone about him.

Jesus predicts his death

31 He then began to teach them that the Son of Man must suffer many things and be rejected by the elders, the chief priests and the teachers of the law, and that he must be killed and after three days rise again. 32 He spoke plainly about this, and Peter took him aside and began to rebuke him.

33 But when Jesus turned and looked at his disciples, he rebuked Peter. 'Get behind me, Satan!' he said. 'You do not have in mind the concerns of God, but merely human concerns.'

The way of the cross

34 Then he called the crowd to him along with his disciples and said: 'Whoever wants to be my disciple must deny themselves and take up their cross and follow me. 35 For whoever wants to save their life will lose it, but whoever loses their life for me and for the gospel will save it. 36 What good is it for someone to gain the whole world, yet forfeit their soul? 37 Or what can anyone give in exchange for their soul? 38 If anyone is ashamed of me and my words in this adulterous and sinful generation, the Son of Man will be ashamed of them when he comes in his Father's glory with the holy angels.'

9 And he said to them, 'Truly I tell you, some who are standing here will not taste death before they see that the kingdom of God has come with power.'

The transfiguration

2 After six days Jesus took Peter, James and John with him and led them up

a high mountain, where they were all alone. There he was transfigured before them. ³His clothes became dazzling white, whiter than anyone in the world could bleach them. ⁴And there appeared before them Elijah and Moses, who were talking with Jesus.

⁵Peter said to Jesus, 'Rabbi, it is good for us to be here. Let us put up three shelters – one for you, one for Moses and one for Elijah.' ⁶(He did not know what to say, they were so frightened.)

⁷Then a cloud appeared and covered them, and a voice came from the cloud: 'This is my Son, whom I love. Listen to him!'

⁸Suddenly, when they looked around, they no longer saw anyone with them except Jesus.

⁹As they were coming down the mountain, Jesus gave them orders not to tell anyone what they had seen until the Son of Man had risen from the dead. ¹⁰They kept the matter to themselves, discussing what 'rising from the dead' meant.

¹¹And they asked him, 'Why do the teachers of the law say that Elijah must come first?'

¹²Jesus replied, 'To be sure, Elijah does come first, and restores all things. Why then is it written that the Son of Man must suffer much and be rejected? ¹³But I tell you, Elijah has come, and they have done to him everything they wished, just as it is written about him.'

Jesus heals a boy possessed by an impure spirit

¹⁴When they came to the other disciples, they saw a large crowd around them and the teachers of the law arguing with them. ¹⁵As soon as all the people saw Jesus, they were overwhelmed with wonder and ran to greet him.

¹⁶'What are you arguing with them about?' he asked.

¹⁷A man in the crowd answered, 'Teacher, I brought you my son, who is possessed by a spirit that has robbed him of speech. ¹⁸Whenever it seizes

him, it throws him to the ground. He foams at the mouth, gnashes his teeth and becomes rigid. I asked your disciples to drive out the spirit, but they could not.'

19 'You unbelieving generation,' Jesus replied, 'how long shall I stay with you? How long shall I put up with you? Bring the boy to me.'

20 So they brought him. When the spirit saw Jesus, it immediately threw the boy into a convulsion. He fell to the ground and rolled around, foaming at the mouth.

21 Jesus asked the boy's father, 'How long has he been like this?'

'From childhood,' he answered. 22 'It has often thrown him into fire or water to kill him. But if you can do anything, take pity on us and help us.'

23 ' "If you can"?' said Jesus. 'Everything is possible for one who believes.'

24 Immediately the boy's father exclaimed, 'I do believe; help me overcome my unbelief!'

25 When Jesus saw that a crowd was running to the scene, he rebuked the impure spirit. 'You deaf and mute spirit,' he said, 'I command you, come out of him and never enter him again.'

26 The spirit shrieked, convulsed him violently and came out. The boy looked so much like a corpse that many said, 'He's dead.' 27 But Jesus took him by the hand and lifted him to his feet, and he stood up.

28 After Jesus had gone indoors, his disciples asked him privately, 'Why couldn't we drive it out?'

29 He replied, 'This kind can come out only by prayer.'

Jesus predicts his death a second time

30 They left that place and passed through Galilee. Jesus did not want anyone to know where they were, 31 because he was teaching his disciples. He said to them, 'The Son of Man is going to be delivered into the hands of men. They will kill him, and after three days he will rise.' 32 But they did not understand what he meant and were afraid to ask him about it.

33 They came to Capernaum. When he was in the house, he asked them, 'What

were you arguing about on the road?' ³⁴ But they kept quiet because on the way they had argued about who was the greatest.

³⁵ Sitting down, Jesus called the Twelve and said, 'Anyone who wants to be first must be the very last, and the servant of all.'

³⁶ He took a little child whom he placed among them. Taking the child in his arms, he said to them, ³⁷ 'Whoever welcomes one of these little children in my name welcomes me; and whoever welcomes me does not welcome me but the one who sent me.'

Whoever is not against us is for us

³⁸ 'Teacher,' said John, 'we saw someone driving out demons in your name and we told him to stop, because he was not one of us.'

³⁹ 'Do not stop him,' Jesus said. 'For no one who does a miracle in my name can in the next moment say anything bad about me, ⁴⁰ for whoever is not against us is for us. ⁴¹ Truly I tell you, anyone who gives you a cup of water in my name because you belong to the Messiah will certainly not lose their reward.

Causing to stumble

⁴² 'If anyone causes one of these little ones – those who believe in me – to stumble, it would be better for them if a large millstone were hung round their neck and they were thrown into the sea. ⁴³ If your hand causes you to stumble, cut it off. It is better for you to enter life maimed than with two hands to go into hell, where the fire never goes out. ⁴⁵ And if your foot causes you to stumble, cut it off. It is better for you to enter life crippled than to have two feet and be thrown into hell. ⁴⁷ And if your eye causes you to stumble, pluck it out. It is better for you to enter the kingdom of God with one eye than to have two eyes and be thrown into hell, ⁴⁸ where

　' "the worms that eat them do not die,
　　and the fire is not quenched."

⁴⁹ Everyone will be salted with fire.

⁵⁰ 'Salt is good, but if it loses its saltiness, how can you make it salty again? Have salt among yourselves, and be at peace with each other.'

Divorce

10 Jesus then left that place and went into the region of Judea and across the Jordan. Again crowds of people came to him, and as was his custom, he taught them.

² Some Pharisees came and tested him by asking, 'Is it lawful for a man to divorce his wife?'

³ 'What did Moses command you?' he replied.

⁴ They said, 'Moses permitted a man to write a certificate of divorce and send her away.'

⁵ 'It was because your hearts were hard that Moses wrote you this law,' Jesus replied. ⁶ 'But at the beginning of creation God "made them male and female". ⁷ "For this reason a man will leave his father and mother and be united to his wife, ⁸ and the two will become one flesh." So they are no longer two, but one flesh. ⁹ Therefore what God has joined together, let no one separate.'

¹⁰ When they were in the house again, the disciples asked Jesus about this. ¹¹ He answered, 'Anyone who divorces his wife and marries another woman commits adultery against her. ¹² And if she divorces her husband and marries another man, she commits adultery.'

The little children and Jesus

¹³ People were bringing little children to Jesus for him to place his hands on them, but the disciples rebuked them. ¹⁴ When Jesus saw this, he was indignant. He said to them, 'Let the little children come to me, and do not hinder them, for the kingdom of God belongs to such as these. ¹⁵ Truly I tell you, anyone who will

not receive the kingdom of God like a little child will never enter it.' [16] And he took the children in his arms, placed his hands on them and blessed them.

The rich and the kingdom of God

[17] As Jesus started on his way, a man ran up to him and fell on his knees before him. 'Good teacher,' he asked, 'what must I do to inherit eternal life?'

[18] 'Why do you call me good?' Jesus answered. 'No one is good – except God alone. [19] You know the commandments: "You shall not murder, you shall not commit adultery, you shall not steal, you shall not give false testimony, you shall not defraud, honour your father and mother." '

[20] 'Teacher,' he declared, 'all these I have kept since I was a boy.'

[21] Jesus looked at him and loved him. 'One thing you lack,' he said. 'Go, sell everything you have and give to the poor, and you will have treasure in heaven. Then come, follow me.'

[22] At this the man's face fell. He went away sad, because he had great wealth.

[23] Jesus looked round and said to his disciples, 'How hard it is for the rich to enter the kingdom of God!'

[24] The disciples were amazed at his words. But Jesus said again, 'Children, how hard it is to enter the kingdom of God! [25] It is easier for a camel to go through the eye of a needle than for someone who is rich to enter the kingdom of God.'

[26] The disciples were even more amazed, and said to each other, 'Who then can be saved?'

[27] Jesus looked at them and said, 'With man this is impossible, but not with God; all things are possible with God.'

[28] Then Peter spoke up, 'We have left everything to follow you!'

[29] 'Truly I tell you,' Jesus replied, 'no one who has left home or brothers or sisters or mother or father or children or fields for me and the gospel [30] will fail to receive a hundred times as much in this present age: homes, brothers, sisters,

mothers, children and fields – along with persecutions – and in the age to come eternal life. [31] But many who are first will be last, and the last first.'

Jesus predicts his death a third time

[32] They were on their way up to Jerusalem, with Jesus leading the way, and the disciples were astonished, while those who followed were afraid. Again he took the Twelve aside and told them what was going to happen to him. [33] 'We are going up to Jerusalem,' he said, 'and the Son of Man will be delivered over to the chief priests and the teachers of the law. They will condemn him to death and will hand him over to the Gentiles, [34] who will mock him and spit on him, flog him and kill him. Three days later he will rise.'

The request of James and John

[35] Then James and John, the sons of Zebedee, came to him. 'Teacher,' they said, 'we want you to do for us whatever we ask.'

[36] 'What do you want me to do for you?' he asked.

[37] They replied, 'Let one of us sit at your right and the other at your left in your glory.'

[38] 'You don't know what you are asking,' Jesus said. 'Can you drink the cup I drink or be baptised with the baptism I am baptised with?'

[39] 'We can,' they answered.

Jesus said to them, 'You will drink the cup I drink and be baptised with the baptism I am baptised with, [40] but to sit at my right or left is not for me to grant. These places belong to those for whom they have been prepared.'

[41] When the ten heard about this, they became indignant with James and John. [42] Jesus called them together and said, 'You know that those who are regarded as rulers of the Gentiles lord it over them, and their high officials exercise authority over them. [43] Not so with you. Instead, whoever wants to become great among you must be your servant, [44] and whoever wants to be first must be slave of all.

E

Mark
10:32–52

Many people with power or influence use it to get their own way and end up oppressing others. Jesus has immense power, yet he didn't come so that we could serve him, he came so that he could serve us.

Discuss in Study E // Page 163

⁴⁵ For even the Son of Man did not come to be served, but to serve, and to give his life as a ransom for many.'

Blind Bartimaeus receives his sight

⁴⁶ Then they came to Jericho. As Jesus and his disciples, together with a large crowd, were leaving the city, a blind man, Bartimaeus (which means 'son of Timaeus'), was sitting by the roadside begging. ⁴⁷ When he heard that it was Jesus of Nazareth, he began to shout, 'Jesus, Son of David, have mercy on me!'

⁴⁸ Many rebuked him and told him to be quiet, but he shouted all the more, 'Son of David, have mercy on me!'

⁴⁹ Jesus stopped and said, 'Call him.'

So they called to the blind man, 'Cheer up! On your feet! He's calling you.' ⁵⁰ Throwing his cloak aside, he jumped to his feet and came to Jesus.

⁵¹ 'What do you want me to do for you?' Jesus asked him.

The blind man said, 'Rabbi, I want to see.'

⁵² 'Go,' said Jesus, 'your faith has healed you.' Immediately he received his sight and followed Jesus along the road.

Jesus comes to Jerusalem as king

11 As they approached Jerusalem and came to Bethphage and Bethany at the Mount of Olives, Jesus sent two of his disciples, ² saying to them, 'Go to the village ahead of you, and just as you enter it, you will find a colt tied there, which no one has ever ridden. Untie it and bring it here. ³ If anyone asks you, "Why are you doing this?" say, "The Lord needs it and will send it back here shortly." '

⁴ They went and found a colt outside in the street, tied at a doorway. As they untied it, ⁵ some people standing there asked, 'What are you doing, untying that colt?' ⁶ They answered as Jesus had told them to, and the people let them go. ⁷ When they brought the colt to Jesus and threw their cloaks over it, he sat on it.

8 Many people spread their cloaks on the road, while others spread branches they had cut in the fields. 9 Those who went ahead and those who followed shouted,

> 'Hosanna!'
> 'Blessed is he who comes in the name of the Lord!'
> 10 'Blessed is the coming kingdom of our father David!'
> 'Hosanna in the highest heaven!'

11 Jesus entered Jerusalem and went into the temple courts. He looked around at everything, but since it was already late, he went out to Bethany with the Twelve.

Jesus curses a fig-tree and clears the temple courts

12 The next day as they were leaving Bethany, Jesus was hungry. 13 Seeing in the distance a fig-tree in leaf, he went to find out if it had any fruit. When he reached it, he found nothing but leaves, because it was not the season for figs. 14 Then he said to the tree, 'May no one ever eat fruit from you again.' And his disciples heard him say it.

15 On reaching Jerusalem, Jesus entered the temple courts and began driving out those who were buying and selling there. He overturned the tables of the money-changers and the benches of those selling doves, 16 and would not allow anyone to carry merchandise through the temple courts. 17 And as he taught them, he said, 'Is it not written: "My house will be called a house of prayer for all nations"? But you have made it "a den of robbers".'

18 The chief priests and the teachers of the law heard this and began looking for a way to kill him, for they feared him, because the whole crowd was amazed at his teaching.

19 When evening came, Jesus and his disciples went out of the city. 20 In the morning, as they went along, they saw the fig-tree withered from the roots.

²¹ Peter remembered and said to Jesus, 'Rabbi, look! The fig-tree you cursed has withered!'

²² 'Have faith in God,' Jesus answered. ²³ 'Truly I tell you, if anyone says to this mountain, "Go, throw yourself into the sea," and does not doubt in their heart but believes that what they say will happen, it will be done for them. ²⁴ Therefore I tell you, whatever you ask for in prayer, believe that you have received it, and it will be yours. ²⁵ And when you stand praying, if you hold anything against anyone, forgive them, so that your Father in heaven may forgive you your sins.'

The authority of Jesus questioned

²⁷ They arrived again in Jerusalem, and while Jesus was walking in the temple courts, the chief priests, the teachers of the law and the elders came to him. ²⁸ 'By what authority are you doing these things?' they asked. 'And who gave you authority to do this?'

²⁹ Jesus replied, 'I will ask you one question. Answer me, and I will tell you by what authority I am doing these things. ³⁰ John's baptism – was it from heaven, or of human origin? Tell me!'

³¹ They discussed it among themselves and said, 'If we say, "From heaven," he will ask, "Then why didn't you believe him?" ³² But if we say, "Of human origin" . . .' (They feared the people, for everyone held that John really was a prophet.)

³³ So they answered Jesus, 'We don't know.'

Jesus said, 'Neither will I tell you by what authority I am doing these things.'

The parable of the tenants

12 Jesus then began to speak to them in parables: 'A man planted a vineyard. He put a wall round it, dug a pit for the winepress and built a watchtower. Then he rented the vineyard to some farmers and moved to another place. ² At harvest time he sent a servant to the tenants to collect from them some of the fruit of the vineyard. ³ But they seized him, beat him and sent him

away empty-handed. ⁴ Then he sent another servant to them; they struck this man on the head and treated him shamefully. ⁵ He sent still another, and that one they killed. He sent many others; some of them they beat, others they killed.

⁶ 'He had one left to send, a son, whom he loved. He sent him last of all, saying, "They will respect my son."

⁷ 'But the tenants said to one another, "This is the heir. Come, let's kill him, and the inheritance will be ours." ⁸ So they took him and killed him, and threw him out of the vineyard.

⁹ 'What then will the owner of the vineyard do? He will come and kill those tenants and give the vineyard to others. ¹⁰ Haven't you read this passage of Scripture:

> ' "The stone the builders rejected
> has become the cornerstone;
> ¹¹ the Lord has done this,
> and it is marvellous in our eyes" ?'

¹² Then the chief priests, the teachers of the law and the elders looked for a way to arrest him because they knew he had spoken the parable against them. But they were afraid of the crowd; so they left him and went away.

Paying the poll-tax to Caesar

¹³ Later they sent some of the Pharisees and Herodians to Jesus to catch him in his words. ¹⁴ They came to him and said, 'Teacher, we know that you are a man of integrity. You aren't swayed by others, because you pay no attention to who they are; but you teach the way of God in accordance with the truth. Is it right to pay the poll-tax to Caesar or not? ¹⁵ Should we pay or shouldn't we?'

But Jesus knew their hypocrisy. 'Why are you trying to trap me?' he asked.

'Bring me a denarius and let me look at it.' [16] They brought the coin, and he asked them, 'Whose image is this? And whose inscription?'

'Caesar's,' they replied.

[17] Then Jesus said to them, 'Give back to Caesar what is Caesar's and to God what is God's.'

And they were amazed at him.

Marriage at the resurrection

[18] Then the Sadducees, who say there is no resurrection, came to him with a question. [19] 'Teacher,' they said, 'Moses wrote for us that if a man's brother dies and leaves a wife but no children, the man must marry the widow and raise up offspring for his brother. [20] Now there were seven brothers. The first one married and died without leaving any children. [21] The second one married the widow, but he also died, leaving no child. It was the same with the third. [22] In fact, none of the seven left any children. Last of all, the woman died too. [23] At the resurrection whose wife will she be, since the seven were married to her?'

[24] Jesus replied, 'Are you not in error because you do not know the Scriptures or the power of God? [25] When the dead rise, they will neither marry nor be given in marriage; they will be like the angels in heaven. [26] Now about the dead rising – have you not read in the Book of Moses, in the account of the burning bush, how God said to him, "I am the God of Abraham, the God of Isaac, and the God of Jacob"? [27] He is not the God of the dead, but of the living. You are badly mistaken!'

The greatest commandment

[28] One of the teachers of the law came and heard them debating. Noticing that Jesus had given them a good answer, he asked him, 'Of all the commandments, which is the most important?'

[29] 'The most important one,' answered Jesus, 'is this: "Hear, O Israel: the Lord our God, the Lord is one. [30] Love the Lord your God with all your heart and with

all your soul and with all your mind and with all your strength." [31] The second is this: "Love your neighbour as yourself." There is no commandment greater than these.'

[32] 'Well said, teacher,' the man replied. 'You are right in saying that God is one and there is no other but him. [33] To love him with all your heart, with all your understanding and with all your strength, and to love your neighbour as yourself is more important than all burnt offerings and sacrifices.'

[34] When Jesus saw that he had answered wisely, he said to him, 'You are not far from the kingdom of God.' And from then on no one dared ask him any more questions.

Whose son is the Messiah?

[35] While Jesus was teaching in the temple courts, he asked, 'Why do the teachers of the law say that the Messiah is the son of David? [36] David himself, speaking by the Holy Spirit, declared:

' "The Lord said to my Lord:
  'Sit at my right hand
  until I put your enemies
  under your feet.' "

[37] David himself calls him "Lord". How then can he be his son?' The large crowd listened to him with delight.

Warning against the teachers of the law

[38] As he taught, Jesus said, 'Watch out for the teachers of the law. They like to walk around in flowing robes and be greeted with respect in the market-places, [39] and have the most important seats in the synagogues and the places of

honour at banquets. ⁴⁰ They devour widows' houses and for a show make lengthy prayers. These men will be punished most severely.'

The widow's offering

⁴¹ Jesus sat down opposite the place where the offerings were put and watched the crowd putting their money into the temple treasury. Many rich people threw in large amounts. ⁴² But a poor widow came and put in two very small copper coins, worth only a few pence.

⁴³ Calling his disciples to him, Jesus said, 'Truly I tell you, this poor widow has put more into the treasury than all the others. ⁴⁴ They all gave out of their wealth; but she, out of her poverty, put in everything – all she had to live on.'

The destruction of the temple and signs of the end times

13 As Jesus was leaving the temple, one of his disciples said to him, 'Look, Teacher! What massive stones! What magnificent buildings!'

² 'Do you see all these great buildings?' replied Jesus. 'Not one stone here will be left on another; every one will be thrown down.'

³ As Jesus was sitting on the Mount of Olives opposite the temple, Peter, James, John and Andrew asked him privately, ⁴ 'Tell us, when will these things happen? And what will be the sign that they are all about to be fulfilled?'

⁵ Jesus said to them: 'Watch out that no one deceives you. ⁶ Many will come in my name, claiming, "I am he," and will deceive many. ⁷ When you hear of wars and rumours of wars, do not be alarmed. Such things must happen, but the end is still to come. ⁸ Nation will rise against nation, and kingdom against kingdom. There will be earthquakes in various places, and famines. These are the beginning of birth-pains.

⁹ 'You must be on your guard. You will be handed over to the local councils and flogged in the synagogues. On account of me you will stand before governors and kings as witnesses to them. ¹⁰ And the gospel must first be preached

to all nations. [11] Whenever you are arrested and brought to trial, do not worry beforehand about what to say. Just say whatever is given you at the time, for it is not you speaking, but the Holy Spirit.

[12] 'Brother will betray brother to death, and a father his child. Children will rebel against their parents and have them put to death. [13] Everyone will hate you because of me, but the one who stands firm to the end will be saved.

[14] 'When you see "the abomination that causes desolation" standing where it does not belong – let the reader understand – then let those who are in Judea flee to the mountains. [15] Let no one on the housetop go down or enter the house to take anything out. [16] Let no one in the field go back to get their cloak. [17] How dreadful it will be in those days for pregnant women and nursing mothers! [18] Pray that this will not take place in winter, [19] because those will be days of distress unequalled from the beginning, when God created the world, until now – and never to be equalled again.

[20] 'If the Lord had not cut short those days, no one would survive. But for the sake of the elect, whom he has chosen, he has shortened them. [21] At that time if anyone says to you, "Look, here is the Messiah!" or, "Look, there he is!" do not believe it. [22] For false messiahs and false prophets will appear and perform signs and wonders to deceive, if possible, even the elect. [23] So be on your guard; I have told you everything in advance.

[24] 'But in those days, following that distress,

' "the sun will be darkened, and the moon will not give its light;
[25] the stars will fall from the sky,
and the heavenly bodies will be shaken."

[26] 'At that time people will see the Son of Man coming in clouds with great power and glory. [27] And he will send his angels and gather his elect from the four winds, from the ends of the earth to the ends of the heavens.

28 'Now learn this lesson from the fig-tree: as soon as its twigs get tender and its leaves come out, you know that summer is near. 29 Even so, when you see these things happening, you know that it is near, right at the door. 30 Truly I tell you, this generation will certainly not pass away until all these things have happened. 31 Heaven and earth will pass away, but my words will never pass away.

The day and hour unknown

32 'But about that day or hour no one knows, not even the angels in heaven, nor the Son, but only the Father. 33 Be on guard! Be alert! You do not know when that time will come. 34 It's like a man going away: he leaves his house and puts his servants in charge, each with their assigned task, and tells the one at the door to keep watch.

35 'Therefore keep watch because you do not know when the owner of the house will come back – whether in the evening, or at midnight, or when the cock crows, or at dawn. 36 If he comes suddenly, do not let him find you sleeping. 37 What I say to you, I say to everyone: "Watch!" '

Jesus anointed at Bethany

14 Now the Passover and the Festival of Unleavened Bread were only two days away, and the chief priests and the teachers of the law were scheming to arrest Jesus secretly and kill him. 2 'But not during the festival,' they said, 'or the people may riot.'

3 While he was in Bethany, reclining at the table in the home of Simon the Leper, a woman came with an alabaster jar of very expensive perfume, made of pure nard. She broke the jar and poured the perfume on his head.

4 Some of those present were saying indignantly to one another, 'Why this waste of perfume? 5 It could have been sold for more than a year's wages and the money given to the poor.' And they rebuked her harshly.

⁶'Leave her alone,' said Jesus. 'Why are you bothering her? She has done a beautiful thing to me. ⁷The poor you will always have with you, and you can help them any time you want. But you will not always have me. ⁸She did what she could. She poured perfume on my body beforehand to prepare for my burial. ⁹Truly I tell you, wherever the gospel is preached throughout the world, what she has done will also be told, in memory of her.'

¹⁰Then Judas Iscariot, one of the Twelve, went to the chief priests to betray Jesus to them. ¹¹They were delighted to hear this and promised to give him money. So he watched for an opportunity to hand him over.

The Last Supper

¹²On the first day of the Festival of Unleavened Bread, when it was customary to sacrifice the Passover lamb, Jesus' disciples asked him, 'Where do you want us to go and make preparations for you to eat the Passover?'

¹³So he sent two of his disciples, telling them, 'Go into the city, and a man carrying a jar of water will meet you. Follow him. ¹⁴Say to the owner of the house he enters, "The Teacher asks: where is my guest room, where I may eat the Passover with my disciples?" ¹⁵He will show you a large room upstairs, furnished and ready. Make preparations for us there.'

¹⁶The disciples left, went into the city and found things just as Jesus had told them. So they prepared the Passover.

¹⁷When evening came, Jesus arrived with the Twelve. ¹⁸While they were reclining at the table eating, he said, 'Truly I tell you, one of you will betray me – one who is eating with me.'

¹⁹They were saddened, and one by one they said to him, 'Surely you don't mean me?'

²⁰'It is one of the Twelve,' he replied, 'one who dips bread into the bowl with me. ²¹The Son of Man will go just as it is written about him. But woe to that man who betrays the Son of Man! It would be better for him if he had not been born.'

²² While they were eating, Jesus took bread, and when he had given thanks, he broke it and gave it to his disciples, saying, 'Take it; this is my body.'

²³ Then he took a cup, and when he had given thanks, he gave it to them, and they all drank from it.

²⁴ 'This is my blood of the covenant, which is poured out for many,' he said to them. ²⁵ 'Truly I tell you, I will not drink again from the fruit of the vine until that day when I drink it new in the kingdom of God.'

²⁶ When they had sung a hymn, they went out to the Mount of Olives.

Jesus predicts Peter's denial

²⁷ 'You will all fall away,' Jesus told them, 'for it is written:

> ' "I will strike the shepherd,
>> and the sheep will be scattered." '

²⁸ But after I have risen, I will go ahead of you into Galilee.'

²⁹ Peter declared, 'Even if all fall away, I will not.'

³⁰ 'Truly I tell you,' Jesus answered, 'today – yes, tonight – before the cock crows twice you yourself will disown me three times.'

³¹ But Peter insisted emphatically, 'Even if I have to die with you, I will never disown you.' And all the others said the same.

Gethsemane

³² They went to a place called Gethsemane, and Jesus said to his disciples, 'Sit here while I pray.' ³³ He took Peter, James and John along with him, and he began to be deeply distressed and troubled. ³⁴ 'My soul is overwhelmed with sorrow to the point of death,' he said to them. 'Stay here and keep watch.'

³⁵ Going a little farther, he fell to the ground and prayed that if possible the hour

might pass from him. 36 '*Abba*, Father,' he said, 'everything is possible for you. Take this cup from me. Yet not what I will, but what you will.'

37 Then he returned to his disciples and found them sleeping. 'Simon,' he said to Peter, 'are you asleep? Couldn't you keep watch for one hour? 38 Watch and pray so that you will not fall into temptation. The spirit is willing, but the flesh is weak.'

39 Once more he went away and prayed the same thing. 40 When he came back, he again found them sleeping, because their eyes were heavy. They did not know what to say to him.

41 Returning the third time, he said to them, 'Are you still sleeping and resting? Enough! The hour has come. Look, the Son of Man is delivered into the hands of sinners. 42 Rise! Let us go! Here comes my betrayer!'

Jesus arrested

43 Just as he was speaking, Judas, one of the Twelve, appeared. With him was a crowd armed with swords and clubs, sent from the chief priests, the teachers of the law, and the elders.

44 Now the betrayer had arranged a signal with them: 'The one I kiss is the man; arrest him and lead him away under guard.' 45 Going at once to Jesus, Judas said, 'Rabbi!' and kissed him. 46 The men seized Jesus and arrested him. 47 Then one of those standing near drew his sword and struck the servant of the high priest, cutting off his ear.

48 'Am I leading a rebellion,' said Jesus, 'that you have come out with swords and clubs to capture me? 49 Every day I was with you, teaching in the temple courts, and you did not arrest me. But the Scriptures must be fulfilled.' 50 Then everyone deserted him and fled.

51 A young man, wearing nothing but a linen garment, was following Jesus. When they seized him, 52 he fled naked, leaving his garment behind.

Jesus before the Sanhedrin

⁵³ They took Jesus to the high priest, and all the chief priests, the elders and the teachers of the law came together. ⁵⁴ Peter followed him at a distance, right into the courtyard of the high priest. There he sat with the guards and warmed himself at the fire.

⁵⁵ The chief priests and the whole Sanhedrin were looking for evidence against Jesus so that they could put him to death, but they did not find any. ⁵⁶ Many testified falsely against him, but their statements did not agree.

⁵⁷ Then some stood up and gave this false testimony against him: ⁵⁸ 'We heard him say, "I will destroy this temple made with human hands and in three days will build another, not made with hands." ' ⁵⁹ Yet even then their testimony did not agree.

⁶⁰ Then the high priest stood up before them and asked Jesus, 'Are you not going to answer? What is this testimony that these men are bringing against you?' ⁶¹ But Jesus remained silent and gave no answer.

Again the high priest asked him, 'Are you the Messiah, the Son of the Blessed One?'

⁶² 'I am,' said Jesus. 'And you will see the Son of Man sitting at the right hand of the Mighty One and coming on the clouds of heaven.'

⁶³ The high priest tore his clothes. 'Why do we need any more witnesses?' he asked. ⁶⁴ 'You have heard the blasphemy. What do you think?'

They all condemned him as worthy of death. ⁶⁵ Then some began to spit at him; they blindfolded him, struck him with their fists, and said, 'Prophesy!' And the guards took him and beat him.

Peter disowns Jesus

⁶⁶ While Peter was below in the courtyard, one of the servant-girls of the high priest came by. ⁶⁷ When she saw Peter warming himself, she looked closely at him.

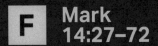 **Mark 14:27–72**

The trial turns on the one question that Jesus breaks his silence to answer. For the first and only time in the Gospel, he gives an undeniably clear answer.

Discuss in Study F // Page 179

'You also were with that Nazarene, Jesus,' she said.

⁶⁸ But he denied it. 'I don't know or understand what you're talking about,' he said, and went out into the entrance.

⁶⁹ When the servant-girl saw him there, she said again to those standing round them, 'This fellow is one of them.' ⁷⁰ Again he denied it.

After a little while, those standing near said to Peter, 'Surely you are one of them, for you are a Galilean.'

⁷¹ He began to call down curses, and he swore to them, 'I don't know this man you're talking about.'

⁷² Immediately the cock crowed the second time. Then Peter remembered the word Jesus had spoken to him: 'Before the cock crows twice you will disown me three times.' And he broke down and wept.

Jesus before Pilate

15 Very early in the morning, the chief priests, with the elders, the teachers of the law and the whole Sanhedrin, made their plans. So they bound Jesus, led him away and handed him over to Pilate.

² 'Are you the king of the Jews?' asked Pilate.

'You have said so,' Jesus replied.

³ The chief priests accused him of many things. ⁴ So again Pilate asked him, 'Aren't you going to answer? See how many things they are accusing you of.'

⁵ But Jesus still made no reply, and Pilate was amazed.

⁶ Now it was the custom at the festival to release a prisoner whom the people requested. ⁷ A man called Barabbas was in prison with the rebels who had committed murder in the uprising. ⁸ The crowd came up and asked Pilate to do for them what he usually did.

⁹ 'Do you want me to release to you the king of the Jews?' asked Pilate, ¹⁰ knowing it was out of self-interest that the chief priests had handed Jesus

over to him. [11] But the chief priests stirred up the crowd to get Pilate to release Barabbas instead.

[12] 'What shall I do, then, with the one you call the king of the Jews?' Pilate asked them.

[13] 'Crucify him!' they shouted.

[14] 'Why? What crime has he committed?' asked Pilate.

But they shouted all the louder, 'Crucify him!'

[15] Wanting to satisfy the crowd, Pilate released Barabbas to them. He had Jesus flogged, and handed him over to be crucified.

The soldiers mock Jesus

[16] The soldiers led Jesus away into the palace (that is, the Praetorium) and called together the whole company of soldiers. [17] They put a purple robe on him, then twisted together a crown of thorns and set it on him. [18] And they began to call out to him, 'Hail, king of the Jews!' [19] Again and again they struck him on the head with a staff and spat on him. Falling on their knees, they paid homage to him. [20] And when they had mocked him, they took off the purple robe and put his own clothes on him. Then they led him out to crucify him.

The crucifixion of Jesus

[21] A certain man from Cyrene, Simon, the father of Alexander and Rufus, was passing by on his way in from the country, and they forced him to carry the cross. [22] They brought Jesus to the place called Golgotha (which means 'the place of the skull'). [23] Then they offered him wine mixed with myrrh, but he did not take it. [24] And they crucified him. Dividing up his clothes, they cast lots to see what each would get.

[25] It was nine in the morning when they crucified him. [26] The written notice of the charge against him read: THE KING OF THE JEWS.

[27] They crucified two rebels with him, one on his right and one on his left.

G Mark 15:16–41

On the cross, Jesus was not only identifying with us in our experiences of pain and loneliness, he was substituting himself for us.

Discuss in Study G // Page 197

[29] Those who passed by hurled insults at him, shaking their heads and saying, 'So! You who are going to destroy the temple and build it in three days, [30] come down from the cross and save yourself!' [31] In the same way the chief priests and the teachers of the law mocked him among themselves. 'He saved others,' they said, 'but he can't save himself! [32] Let this Messiah, this king of Israel, come down now from the cross, that we may see and believe.' Those crucified with him also heaped insults on him.

The death of Jesus

[33] At noon, darkness came over the whole land until three in the afternoon. [34] And at three in the afternoon Jesus cried out in a loud voice, '*Eloi, Eloi, lema sabachthani?*' (which means 'My God, my God, why have you forsaken me?').

[35] When some of those standing near heard this, they said, 'Listen, he's calling Elijah.'

[36] Someone ran, filled a sponge with wine vinegar, put it on a staff, and offered it to Jesus to drink. 'Now leave him alone. Let's see if Elijah comes to take him down,' he said.

[37] With a loud cry, Jesus breathed his last.

[38] The curtain of the temple was torn in two from top to bottom. [39] And when the centurion, who stood there in front of Jesus, saw how he died, he said, 'Surely this man was the Son of God!'

[40] Some women were watching from a distance. Among them were Mary Magdalene, Mary the mother of James the younger and of Joseph, [d] and Salome. [41] In Galilee these women had followed him and cared for his needs. Many other women who had come up with him to Jerusalem were also there.

The burial of Jesus

[42] It was Preparation Day (that is, the day before the Sabbath). So as evening approached, [43] Joseph of Arimathea, a prominent member of the Council, who

was himself waiting for the kingdom of God, went boldly to Pilate and asked for Jesus' body. ⁴⁴ Pilate was surprised to hear that he was already dead. Summoning the centurion, he asked him if Jesus had already died. ⁴⁵ When he learned from the centurion that it was so, he gave the body to Joseph. ⁴⁶ So Joseph bought some linen cloth, took down the body, wrapped it in the linen, and placed it in a tomb cut out of rock. Then he rolled a stone against the entrance of the tomb. ⁴⁷ Mary Magdalene and Mary the mother of Joseph saw where he was laid.

Jesus has risen

16 When the Sabbath was over, Mary Magdalene, Mary the mother of James, and Salome bought spices so that they might go to anoint Jesus' body. ² Very early on the first day of the week, just after sunrise, they were on their way to the tomb ³ and they asked each other, 'Who will roll the stone away from the entrance of the tomb?'

⁴ But when they looked up, they saw that the stone, which was very large, had been rolled away. ⁵ As they entered the tomb, they saw a young man dressed in a white robe sitting on the right side, and they were alarmed.

⁶ 'Don't be alarmed,' he said. 'You are looking for Jesus the Nazarene, who was crucified. He has risen! He is not here. See the place where they laid him. ⁷ But go, tell his disciples and Peter, "He is going ahead of you into Galilee. There you will see him, just as he told you." '

⁸ Trembling and bewildered, the women went out and fled from the tomb. They said nothing to anyone, because they were afraid.

 **Mark
15:42–16:8**

Most people thought that the crucifixion ended any possibility of Jesus' being the Messiah. No one was expecting what would happen next.

Discuss in Study H // Page 213

[The earliest manuscripts and some other ancient witnesses do not have verses 9 – 20.]

⁹ When Jesus rose early on the first day of the week, he appeared first to Mary Magdalene, out of whom he had driven seven demons. ¹⁰ She went and told those who had been with him and who were mourning and weeping. ¹¹ When they heard that Jesus was alive and that she had seen him, they did not believe it.

¹² Afterwards Jesus appeared in a different form to two of them while they were walking in the country. ¹³ These returned and reported it to the rest; but they did not believe them either.

¹⁴ Later Jesus appeared to the Eleven as they were eating; he rebuked them for their lack of faith and their stubborn refusal to believe those who had seen him after he had risen.

¹⁵ He said to them, 'Go into all the world and preach the gospel to all creation. ¹⁶ Whoever believes and is baptised will be saved, but whoever does not believe will be condemned. ¹⁷ And these signs will accompany those who believe: in my name they will drive out demons; they will speak in new tongues; ¹⁸ they will pick up snakes with their hands; and when they drink deadly poison, it will not hurt them at all; they will place their hands on people who are ill, and they will get well.'

¹⁹ After the Lord Jesus had spoken to them, he was taken up into heaven and he sat at the right hand of God. ²⁰ Then the disciples went out and preached everywhere, and the Lord worked with them and confirmed his word by the signs that accompanied it.

Questions about the end of Mark?
Go to uncover.org.uk/mark16

Notes

Read.

The entirety of Mark's Gospel, one
of the accounts of the life of Jesus.

Start here.

There was nothing quite like Mark's Gospel before he wrote it. It was a new form of writing he invented for the sake of his message; a message he describes as 'good news'.

At its heart, his message was an announcement – a proclamation – about the arrival of someone who, Mark believes, would change everything. Mark's excitement about his message is infectious. His style is fresh, vivid and breathless. The episodes come in rapid succession like snapshots that together begin to build a picture. From the very beginning he draws us in, telling his story as you would tell a secret.

And as he draws us in to this story, full of mystery and puzzles, many have found – to their surprise – that they become, somehow, a part of it. They see Jesus challenge traditions and expectations, and find their own beliefs and priorities quietly shaken. They see Jesus meet people in the midst of their despair and glimpse new hope for themselves and the world. And as Mark gradually uncovers the story of Jesus, they find their own hearts being uncovered and laid bare.

Mark's story is, in many ways, deeply unsettling. It shows us new depths of darkness and blindness, new capacities for failure, new needs we are reluctant to admit to. But through it all Mark shows that Jesus is for people just like us. He shows us one who, like no one else, can open our eyes, dispel our darkness and bring forgiveness, healing and life.

Mark thinks it's good news. Read his account and decide for yourself.

***Anybody home?* - a short video**
Watch at uncover.org.uk/anybodyhome

Discuss what you've been reading ⟶

Discuss.

Questions and ideas to help you think about Mark's Gospel. See for yourself.

The world we all want is nearly here

A

Many of us are motivated by
the hope of a better future –
for ourselves, our loved ones
and our world.

Where do people you know
look for motivation and
hope?

**How hopeful do you feel
about the future?**

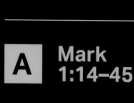
**Mark
1:14–45**

Historical context

Mark was writing from the great city of Rome in the second half of the first century.

He was part of a small, persecuted Jewish sect known dismissively at the time as 'the Galileans'. People saw them as followers of a nobody religious teacher from nowhere of any significance.

Yet Mark starts his short biography of this religious teacher with a remarkably bold claim. In words carefully chosen to strike both his Jewish and his pagan readers, he opens:

'The beginning of the good news about Jesus the Messiah, the Son of God'
Mark 1:1

To the Romans, the term 'gospel' (literally 'good news') was familiar political jargon. It was used when announcing great historic moments such as when emperors came to power. For the Jews, the word was even more loaded.

It recalled ancient hopes of a future time when God himself would come as king to bring healing, justice and liberation to a broken world.

Mark wants his readers to be in no doubt about the world-changing significance of what he is claiming about Jesus. According to Mark, the world rulers are nothing in comparison to this Jewish Galilean teacher. In Jesus, God himself has come into the world to make things right.

It seemed then, as it seems now, utterly outrageous. What compelled Mark and the other Galileans to make this remarkable claim? Why were they even willing to die at the hands of the Romans because of it? What could they have seen that led them to believe that Jesus was the Son of God?

This is what Mark will help us uncover as we consider his Gospel.

Mark's first chapter is fast-paced. It reads almost like a notebook. He describes events as snapshots that together begin to build a picture.

We'll read a section and then pause for breath.

Read Mark 1:14–34

[14] After John was put in prison, Jesus went into Galilee, proclaiming the good news of God. [15] 'The time has come,' he said. 'The kingdom of God has come near. Repent and believe the good news!'

[16] As Jesus walked beside the Sea of Galilee, he saw Simon and his brother Andrew casting a net into the lake, for they were fishermen. [17] 'Come, follow me,' Jesus said, 'and I will send you out to fish for people.' [18] At once they left their nets and followed him.

[19] When he had gone a little farther, he saw James son of Zebedee and his brother John in a boat, preparing their nets. [20] Without delay he called them, and they left their father Zebedee in the boat with the hired men and followed him.

[21] They went to Capernaum, and when the Sabbath came, Jesus went into the synagogue and began to teach. [22] The people were amazed at his teaching, because he taught them as one who had authority, not as the teachers of the law. [23] Just then a man in their synagogue who was possessed by an impure spirit cried out, [24] 'What do you want with us, Jesus of Nazareth? Have you come to destroy us? I know who you are – the Holy One of God!'

[25] 'Be quiet!' said Jesus sternly. 'Come out of him!' [26] The impure spirit shook the man violently and came out of him with a shriek. [27] The people were all so amazed that they asked each other, 'What is this? A new teaching – and with authority! He even gives orders to impure spirits and they obey him.' [28] News about him spread quickly over the whole region of Galilee.

29 As soon as they left the synagogue, they went with James and John to the home of Simon and Andrew. 30 Simon's mother-in-law was in bed with a fever, and they immediately told Jesus about her. 31 So he went to her, took her hand and helped her up. The fever left her and she began to wait on them.

32 That evening after sunset the people brought to Jesus all who were ill and demon-possessed. 33 The whole town gathered at the door, 34 and Jesus healed many who had various diseases. He also drove out many demons, but he would not let the demons speak because they knew who he was.

1 What are your immediate impressions of what you've just read? What confuses, interests or disturbs you?

Jesus enters the public stage with an announcement about something he calls the 'kingdom of God' (verse 15).

2 What do you think Jesus could have meant by his phrase 'the kingdom of God'? What might he mean by saying it is 'near'?

Why might it be such good news?

'The people were amazed at his teaching, because he taught them as one who had authority, not as the teachers of the law.'

Mark 1:22

Mark will continue to explore this theme but, whatever he means, Jesus says that the appropriate response is to repent and believe. To 'repent' is to do a U-turn in your mind. Jesus' announcement is of such significance that it requires a radical change of priorities from those who hear it. The next snapshot (verses 16–20) shows us just such a response.

3   How easy do you find it to make sense of the actions of these four fishermen? They left their families, professions and homes to follow Jesus. What could have caused them to take this step, which seemed so reckless?

4   What does it suggest about Jesus that he is able to command such a response?

Jesus next visits the small town of Capernaum on the Sea of Galilee (verses 21–34).

5   The word translated 'amazed' includes fear and alarm. What provoked this reaction to Jesus?

6   In that day, 'authority' came from being royal or divine. What do you think caused people to describe Jesus as one who taught with authority (verse 22)?

7   That evening the 'whole town' came to where Jesus was staying (verses 32–34). Can you understand what attracted people to Jesus?

Do you think you would have been drawn to him?

Throughout the early chapters of his Gospel, Mark presents us with a person around whom extraordinary things seem to happen. With a word from Jesus, sickness left people and those in spiritual bondage were set free.

Yet intriguingly, in this next snapshot, we begin to see that Jesus is not comfortable with his growing reputation for miracles.

Read Mark 1:35–45

35 Very early in the morning, while it was still dark, Jesus got up, left the house and went off to a solitary place, where he prayed. 36 Simon and his companions went to look for him, 37 and when they found him, they exclaimed: 'Everyone is looking for you!' 38 Jesus replied, 'Let us go somewhere else – to the nearby villages – so that I can preach there also. That is why I have come.' 39 So he travelled throughout Galilee, preaching in their synagogues and driving out demons.

40 A man with leprosy came to him and begged him on his knees, 'If you are willing, you can make me clean.'

⁴¹ Jesus was indignant. He reached out his hand and touched the man. 'I am willing,' he said. 'Be clean!' ⁴² Immediately the leprosy left him and he was cleansed. ⁴³ Jesus sent him away at once with a strong warning: ⁴⁴ 'See that you don't tell this to anyone. But go, show yourself to the priest and offer the sacrifices that Moses commanded for your cleansing, as a testimony to them.' ⁴⁵ Instead he went out and began to talk freely, spreading the news. As a result, Jesus could no longer enter a town openly but stayed outside in lonely places. Yet the people still came to him from everywhere.

8 Simon and friends are clearly very excited about Jesus' sudden popularity (verse 37). How does Jesus' attitude contrast with theirs?

When Jesus heals the man with leprosy, he gives him a strong warning not to tell anyone (verses 43–44). Earlier when Jesus cast out demons he silenced them 'because they knew who he was' (verses 25 and 34).

9 Do you find this surprising? Why do you think Jesus is being so secretive about who he is and what he can do?

What does this mean for us?

Jesus' announcement of the coming 'kingdom of God' is followed by an outbreak of miraculous healings. These aren't simply impressive demonstrations of power; in fact, Jesus was reluctant to draw attention to them. They are rather to be seen as signs of a damaged world being restored; foretastes of how things will be when God is king. One writer puts it like this:

> *'Jesus' healings are not supernatural miracles in a natural world. They are the only truly "natural" thing in a world that is unnatural, demonized and wounded.'* [1]

10   How do you view the claim that our world is not as it should be?

11   What do you imagine 'the world we all want' would look like?

12   What questions does Mark's opening chapter leave you with?

Glossary

- **Capernaum** – *fishing village on the northern shore of Lake Galilee*
- **Demon-possessed** – *controlled by evil spirits*
- **Galilee** – *region in northern Israel*
- **Leprosy** – *contagious skin infection*
- **Synagogue** – *Jewish place of worship*

Bursting bubbles

secure in our bubbles that we accept only information, whether true or not, that fits our opinions, instead of basing our opinions on the evidence that's out there.
Barack Obama during his farewell address [2]

Obama uses the word 'bubble' to refer to a situation that is isolated from reality, in which you only experience opinions you agree with, or people who are similar to you.

Do you see any evidence of this in people today?

To what extent do you feel you live in a 'bubble'?

B **Mark**
2:1–22, 3:1–6

Historical context

Jesus was not the only one talking about the kingdom of God.

The Jews of Jesus' day were fed up with life under Roman occupation and were looking for change. 'No king but God!' was the religious and politically charged slogan on the streets. Someday soon, they believed, the promised Messiah – the saviour king – would come to bring justice and deliverance for Israel.

But everyone agreed that before that time came there would need to be spiritual reform. Religious laws, holy days and fasts must be strictly observed. Before they could hope for God's rescue they must prove to God, by their religious observances, that they were worthy of it.

In Mark's next set of quick-fire snapshots, we meet the Pharisees – a highly respected religious group. Of all the Jewish groups, they are the most committed to keeping the laws and the most earnest in their desire to see God's kingdom come. How will they respond to Jesus? He claims to be the very one they are waiting for, but, as will become clear, he doesn't exactly fit their profile.

Will they be open to having their ideas challenged, or will they react in defence of their traditions?

Read Mark 2:1–12

A few days later, when Jesus again entered Capernaum, the people heard that he had come home. ²They gathered in such large numbers that there was no room left, not even outside the door, and he preached the word to them. ³Some men came, bringing to him a paralysed man, carried by four of them. ⁴Since they could not get him to Jesus because of the crowd, they made an opening in the roof above Jesus by digging through it and then lowered the mat the man was lying on. ⁵When Jesus saw their faith, he said to the paralysed man, 'Son, your sins are forgiven.'

⁶Now some teachers of the law were sitting there, thinking to themselves, ⁷'Why does this fellow talk like that? He's blaspheming! Who can forgive sins but God alone?'

⁸Immediately Jesus knew in his spirit that this was what they were thinking in their hearts, and he said to them, 'Why are you thinking these things? ⁹Which is easier: to say to this paralysed man, "Your sins are forgiven," or to say, "Get up, take your mat and walk"? ¹⁰But I want you to know that the Son of Man has authority on earth to forgive sins.' So he said to the man, ¹¹'I tell you, get up, take your mat and go home.' ¹²He got up, took his mat and walked out in full view of them all. This amazed everyone and they praised God, saying, 'We have never seen anything like this!'

1   The friends of the paralysed man took extreme measures to get him in front of Jesus! What does this say about their expectations of what Jesus would do?

2 Jesus' first response wasn't what they were expecting (verse 5). How might the paralysed man and his friends have reacted to what Jesus said?

How might Jesus' words have challenged their understanding of what was most important?

Mark doesn't record the response of the paralysed man. Instead, he focuses on the reaction of the religious scholars who were present in the crowd.

3 Blasphemy means making a mockery of God, and religious people see it as one of the worst sins. Why were the teachers of the law so offended by Jesus' words?

4 Consider Jesus' question to the Pharisees (verse 9). How did Jesus demonstrate his authority to do what only God can do? What do you make of this claim?

The next controversy is over Jesus' social circle. Tax officials worked for the Roman occupiers in taxing their fellow Jews. As a result they were hated as traitors to their people and to God. Furthermore, they were well known for their corruption and greed.

Read Mark 2:13–17

13 Once again Jesus went out beside the lake. A large crowd came to him, and he began to teach them. 14 As he walked along, he saw Levi son of Alphaeus sitting at the tax collector's booth. 'Follow me,' Jesus told him, and Levi got up and followed him.

15 While Jesus was having dinner at Levi's house, many tax collectors and sinners were eating with him and his disciples, for there were many who followed him. 16 When the teachers of the law who were Pharisees saw him eating with the sinners and tax collectors, they asked his disciples: 'Why does he eat with tax collectors and sinners?'

17 On hearing this, Jesus said to them, 'It is not the healthy who need a doctor, but those who are ill. I have not come to call the righteous, but sinners.'

5   In that society, sharing a meal was of deep social significance. Every religious Jew knew who they were allowed to eat with and who they weren't. What point was Jesus making by eating with Levi and his friends (verse 17)?

6   Why do you think it mattered to the Pharisees who Jesus was friends with?

'No one pours
new wine into old
wineskins. Otherwise,
the wine will burst the
skins...No, they pour
new wine into new
wineskins'

7 Jesus' reply had a strong hint of sarcasm. How was he challenging the Pharisees' attitudes?

The next dispute arises because Jesus and his friends are not fasting like other groups. People fasted to show they were sorry for their sin, in the hope that God would forgive them and restore his favour. Jesus' response is at first puzzling and then shocking in its implications...

Read Mark 2:18–22

[18] Now John's disciples and the Pharisees were fasting. Some people came and asked Jesus, 'How is it that John's disciples and the disciples of the Pharisees are fasting, but yours are not?'

[19] Jesus answered, 'How can the guests of the bridegroom fast while he is with them? They cannot, so long as they have him with them. [20] But the time will come when the bridegroom will be taken from them, and on that day they will fast.

[21] 'No one sews a patch of unshrunk cloth on an old garment. Otherwise, the new piece will pull away from the old, making the tear worse. [22] And no one pours new wine into old wineskins. Otherwise, the wine will burst the skins, and both the wine and the wineskins will be ruined. No, they pour new wine into new wineskins.'

One of the most daring images used in the Jewish Bible to describe God's relationship with his people was that of a loving husband separated from an unfaithful wife. Despite their repeated betrayals, God had promised to one day forgive his people and restore the relationship forever:

> "'In that day,'" declares the LORD, "you will call me 'my husband'…I will betroth you to me for ever'"
> (Hosea 2:16 and 19).

8   Considering this background, what might Jesus be claiming about himself in verse 19?

9   Jesus follows this with two images highlighting the mistake of trying to make new things fit in with old worn-out structures (verses 21–22). What point could Jesus be making to his religious critics?

The next issue is the Sabbath. This was a Jewish holy day, which involved complete rest from work. This day of rest each week was meant to be a foretaste of a future time when hardship, suffering and sadness would end and the world would experience true rest forever.

For the Pharisees, however, the Sabbath had become, like fasting, yet another way of proving themselves to God. In the story before this (Mark 2:23–28) Jesus had boldly claimed to be 'Lord of the Sabbath'. Was he the one who would at last bring true rest to a hurting world?

Read Mark 3:1–6

Another time Jesus went into the synagogue, and a man with a shrivelled hand was there. ² Some of them were looking for a reason to accuse Jesus, so they watched him closely to see if he would heal him on the Sabbath. ³ Jesus said to the man with the shrivelled hand, 'Stand up in front of everyone.'

⁴ Then Jesus asked them, 'Which is lawful on the Sabbath: to do good or to do evil, to save life or to kill?' But they remained silent.

⁵ He looked around at them in anger and, deeply distressed at their stubborn hearts, said to the man, 'Stretch out your hand.' He stretched it out, and his hand was completely restored. ⁶ Then the Pharisees went out and began to plot with the Herodians how they might kill Jesus.

10   Jesus is reluctant to be known as a miracle worker (see study A), yet this healing is both very public and deliberately controversial. What reasons might Jesus have had for healing on the Sabbath?

11   The Pharisees refuse to answer Jesus' question (verse 4). How does Jesus respond to their silence?

Jesus' challenge to the Pharisees results in their making plans with the political authorities (the Herodians) to see Jesus destroyed. Jesus was saving a life; they were plotting to kill.

12 How would you summarise what Jesus is claiming about himself through these snapshots? Why do you think it was so hard for the Pharisees to accept?

What does this mean for us?

Jesus was exploding the categories and expectations of his day. By forgiving sins and welcoming those seen as unholy, Jesus was doing what only God had the right to do. By replacing fasts with feasting and using the Sabbath for healing, Jesus was refocusing humanity's hopes for a better world upon himself. The Pharisees could see what was at stake. It just couldn't be true. Jesus had to be silenced.

13 What do you think is the difference between honest doubt about new ideas and a stubborn reluctance to change one's beliefs?

14 How would Jesus challenge your own beliefs and priorities, if what he claimed were true?

? Questions about sin?
Go to uncover.org.uk/sin

Glossary

- **Betroth** – *formally engaged to be married*
- **Fast** – *to eat no food for a period of time*
- **Pharisees** – *a strict religious group of Jews who emphasised the importance of the Old Testament law as well as many traditions*
- **Sabbath** – *a holy day of rest, free from work*

No one is beyond hope

*Your life is in your hands ...
There is no such thing as a
hopeless situation. Every
single circumstance of your
life can change!*
Rhonda Byrne[3]

Positive thinking is a
central belief in the self-help
movement. How reasonable
do you think it is to 'believe in
yourself' no matter what?

Can you think of any
circumstances that can't be
changed by the power of
positive thinking?

C **Mark
5:21–43**

Historical context

Jesus' reputation is attracting large crowds.

People were travelling from far around to see for themselves what they had heard about the man, his message and (most of all) his miracles. Jesus was clearly reluctant to become famous as a miracle worker and yet he continued to heal people.

As we will see again in this study, when confronted with the suffering and fears of those who came to him, Jesus healed. It may not have been what he had come to do, but it was what he did.

So far our selections from Mark's account have built up a picture of Jesus through fast-paced sequences of short stories. In this chapter, the pace slows and Mark focuses our attention on two rather contrasting characters who both come to Jesus in desperate need.

The vivid detail of these incidents suggests that Mark relies heavily on eyewitness accounts of the events.

Read Mark 5:21–24

²¹ When Jesus had again crossed over by boat to the other side of the lake, a large crowd gathered around him while he was by the lake. ²² Then one of the synagogue leaders, named Jairus, came, and when he saw Jesus, he fell at his feet. ²³ He pleaded earnestly with him, "My little daughter is dying. Please come and put your hands on her so that she will be healed and live." ²⁴ So Jesus went with him. A large crowd followed and pressed around him.

Despite Jesus' growing reputation, the sight of a respected synagogue ruler falling at the feet of this self-appointed rural rabbi may well have seemed odd and inappropriate to the people watching – especially because of the increasing disapproval expressed by the religious authorities.

1   What does Jairus' behaviour and request suggest about his situation?

2   Laying hands on the sick was a common religious practice that Jairus would have done for others. What's striking about how Jairus makes this request of Jesus?

Following Jairus' request Mark simply tells us that Jesus went with him.

3 Considering his reluctance to be known as a miracle worker, why do you think Jesus continues to agree to these requests?

Read Mark 5:25–34

[25] And a woman was there who had been subject to bleeding for twelve years. [26] She had suffered a great deal under the care of many doctors and had spent all she had, yet instead of getting better she grew worse. [27] When she heard about Jesus, she came up behind him in the crowd and touched his cloak, [28] because she thought, "If I just touch his clothes, I will be healed." [29] Immediately her bleeding stopped and she felt in her body that she was freed from her suffering.

[30] At once Jesus realized that power had gone out from him. He turned around in the crowd and asked, "Who touched my clothes?"

[31] "You see the people crowding against you," his disciples answered, "and yet you can ask, 'Who touched me?' "

[32] But Jesus kept looking around to see who had done it. [33] Then the woman, knowing what had happened to her, came and fell at his feet and, trembling with fear, told him the whole truth. [34] He said to her, "Daughter, your faith has healed you. Go in peace and be freed from your suffering."

4   What do we learn in verses 25–28 about the woman in the crowd who touched Jesus? How would this woman have felt?

In what ways does her situation seem desperate and beyond hope?

> **As well as chronic illness, the woman's condition meant social isolation owing to the cultural stigma attached to her bleeding. Desperate, having spent all her money on doctors' cures, she took the risky step of entering the crowd to get near Jesus. A touch, she thought, might be enough to heal her.**

5   When the woman was brought to Jesus, why do you think she was fearful rather than being overjoyed about her healing?

6   How do these verses demonstrate Jesus' tenderness towards this desperate woman?

7   Jesus could have let her be healed quietly, but instead he draws attention to her. Why do you think Jesus made the woman talk with him about her healing so publicly? What did he want her to understand?

'Jesus told him,
"Don't be afraid;
just believe."'

8   How is this woman different from Jairus? Yet what do they have in common? What does it show about Jesus that he delayed helping Jairus to meet the needs of this unnamed woman?

Read Mark 5:35–40

35 While Jesus was still speaking, some people came from the house of Jairus, the synagogue leader. "Your daughter is dead," they said. "Why bother the teacher anymore?" 36 Overhearing what they said, Jesus told him, "Don't be afraid; just believe."

37 He did not let anyone follow him except Peter, James and John the brother of James. 38 When they came to the home of the synagogue leader, Jesus saw a commotion, with people crying and wailing loudly. 39 He went in and said to them, "Why all this commotion and wailing? The child is not dead but asleep." 40 But they laughed at him.

After he put them all out, he took the child's father and mother and the disciples who were with him, and went in where the child was.

You can imagine Jairus' and the disciples' frustration. From their perspective, Jesus had delayed helping a critically ill child from an important family in order to speak with an unnamed woman about a twelve-year chronic condition. We now discover that during the delay the child had died.

9 Why, despite Jesus' being known as a healer, might everyone at the home of Jairus have lacked any hope for the little girl?

10 Consider Jesus' reaction. How does it contrast with their lack of hope? What do you think would be the effect of Jesus' words if he turned out to be wrong?

Read Mark 5:41–43

[41] He took her by the hand and said to her, "*Talitha koum!*" (which means "Little girl, I say to you, get up!"). [42] Immediately the girl stood up and began to walk around (she was twelve years old). At this they were completely astonished. [43] He gave strict orders not to let anyone know about this, and told them to give her something to eat.

11 How does Jesus respond to the fact of death? How does he speak to the girl?

What does this mean for us?

Twice in this account Jesus has emphasised the importance of faith in him.

12 Try to imagine that this account was all you had to help you understand the meaning of the word 'faith'. What is faith? What does it feel like? What does it involve?

Faith in Jesus is an important theme in Mark that is easily misunderstood. Put simply, it involves giving up confidence or trust in ourselves and our own resources and instead placing our confidence in Jesus as the one who alone can meet our deepest needs.

As with the woman and Jairus, faith is displayed most strongly by those who find themselves otherwise powerless and beyond hope.

13 What things do you hope will provide peace or fulfilment in your own life? Have you ever questioned your faith in the ability of these things to provide what you're looking for?

14   Can you understand why people put their faith in Jesus?

What have you seen in Jesus that might encourage you
to put faith in him?

Questions about Jesus' view of women?
Go to uncover.org.uk/women

Glossary

- **Rabbi** – *Jewish teacher*

Who - a short video

Watch at uncover.org.uk/who

Partially sighted

D

It was 7:51 a.m. on Friday [in] the middle of the morning rush hour. ... No one knew it, but the fiddler standing outside the Metro was one of the finest classical musicians in the world, playing some of the most elegant music ever written on one of the most valuable violins ever made.[4]

Of the 1,097 people who passed by Joshua Bell that morning, only seven paused, even briefly, to listen. How often do you think we miss the significance of what is in front of us?

What can prevent us from seeing things the way they really are?

D **Mark 8:22–33, 9:30–37**

Historical context

Jesus has repeatedly bewildered people by doing the unexpected.

In response to his miracles, his teaching and his claims, the question the people are left asking is 'Who is this?' Seeing him as simply a rabbi or a revolutionary didn't seem to fit. Some suggested he was a prophet like those they'd read about from their history. Others remembered predictions that a great prophet, like Moses or Elijah, would one day return to get people ready for God's kingdom. Everyone was wondering what to make of him.

The disciples, despite their privileged access to Jesus, seemed no more certain than anyone else. In the story immediately before our passage today, Jesus had challenged their failure to understand him with a barrage of questions: 'Can you not see?', 'Can you not hear?', 'Don't you remember?', 'Do you still not understand?' (Mark 8:18–21).

But now there is a breakthrough. At this important turning point in Mark's account the disciples at last acknowledge what Mark has announced to his readers from the beginning (Mark 1:1).

Perhaps things are starting to become clear.

Read Mark 8:22–26

22 They came to Bethsaida, and some people brought a blind man and begged Jesus to touch him. 23 He took the blind man by the hand and led him outside the village. When he had spat on the man's eyes and put his hands on him, Jesus asked, 'Do you see anything?'

24 He looked up and said, 'I see people; they look like trees walking around.'

25 Once more Jesus put his hands on the man's eyes. Then his eyes were opened, his sight was restored, and he saw everything clearly. 26 Jesus sent him home, saying, 'Don't even go into the village.'

1   What features in the story of this blind man's healing have we seen before? What is unusual?

With Jesus' first touch the man was able to see things, but his brain seemed unable to make sense of what he saw. He needed a second touch from Jesus to see things clearly.

2   This is an unusual healing. Why might Jesus have chosen to heal this man in this way? What might he be showing us?

3   Consider what you've seen of Jesus so far. Why do you think Jesus' identity is the subject of so much speculation?

Read Mark 8:27–30

27 Jesus and his disciples went on to the villages around Caesarea Philippi. On the way he asked them, 'Who do people say I am?'

28 They replied, 'Some say John the Baptist; others say Elijah; and still others, one of the prophets.' 29 'But what about you?' he asked. 'Who do you say I am?' Peter answered, 'You are the Messiah.' 30 Jesus warned them not to tell anyone about him.

4 Jesus' question to his disciples is direct and urgent. What do you make of the fact that Jesus' teaching is so often about himself (rather than about, say, morality or spiritual practice)?

Peter's answer, 'You are the Messiah', is of massive significance. Messiah meant 'anointed one', referring to the Jewish practice of anointing kings with oil. But the Messiah was to be no ordinary king.

The Messiah, they believed, would end all evil, heal all diseases and enable the world to become all that it could and should be. If Peter is right, then the world we all want is nearly here.

5 Mark has already let us, his readers, know that Peter is on the right track (Mark 1:1), but Jesus immediately warns them to keep it secret (verse 30). What possible reasons could Jesus have for this?

At last the disciples have recognised what Mark stated at the very beginning of his Gospel. But, at this very moment of insight, Jesus begins to say some very confusing and disturbing things.

Read Mark 8:31–33

[31] He then began to teach them that the Son of Man must suffer many things and be rejected by the elders, the chief priests and the teachers of the law, and that he must be killed and after three days rise again. [32] He spoke plainly about this, and Peter took him aside and began to rebuke him.

[33] But when Jesus turned and looked at his disciples, he rebuked Peter. 'Get behind me, Satan!' he said. 'You do not have in mind the concerns of God, but merely human concerns.'

6 How does Peter respond to Jesus' words? To what extent can you understand this reaction?

'Anyone who wants to be first must be the very last, and the servant of all.'

Mark 9:35

7 Jesus responds equally strongly. What does Jesus' response suggest about how Peter's words may have affected him?

8 Jesus twice uses the word 'must' in his description of what will happen to him. What does this imply?

We now jump ahead to where Jesus brings up this uncomfortable topic with his disciples for a second time.

Read Mark 9:30–37

30 They left that place and passed through Galilee. Jesus did not want anyone to know where they were, 31 because he was teaching his disciples. He said to them, 'The Son of Man is going to be delivered into the hands of men. They will kill him, and after three days he will rise.' 32 But they did not understand what he meant and were afraid to ask him about it.

33 They came to Capernaum. When he was in the house, he asked them, 'What were you arguing about on the road?' 34 But they kept quiet because on the way they had argued about who was the greatest.

35 Sitting down, Jesus called the Twelve and said, 'Anyone who wants to be first must be the very last, and the servant of all.' 36 He took a little child whom he placed among them. Taking the child in his arms, he said to them, 37 'Whoever welcomes one of these little children in my name welcomes me; and whoever welcomes me does not welcome me but the one who sent me.'

9   Jesus is clearly keen for his disciples to understand what is going to happen to him (Mark 8:32). Why do you think they struggle to grasp what he means? Why might they be afraid to ask him about it?

10   Consider the disciples' rather embarrassing argument. What do they seem to think the benefits will be for themselves if Jesus is the Messiah?

The Messiah that everyone was waiting for was going to be the one through whom God would rescue Israel and establish his kingdom. As the Messiah's closest friends, therefore, the disciples were sure they were on a fast track to greatness.

11   Children and servants (the same word is used for both in Aramaic, the language Jesus spoke) had the lowest status in society. How is Jesus challenging the disciples' understanding of what kind of king he will be?

What does this mean for us?

12   What, if anything, is becoming clearer for you about Jesus? What remains obscure?

Like those commuters rushing past the great violinist, or the disciples in their pursuit of greatness, our personal priorities can sometimes prevent us from seeing things clearly.

13 What priorities motivate you personally? To what extent do you think these things may help or hinder you as you seek to understand Jesus and his significance?

? Questions about about why Jesus had to suffer?
Go to uncover.org.uk/jesus-suffers

Glossary

- **Caesarea Philippi** – *Roman city in the north of Galilee*
- **Messiah/Christ** – *anointed one/saviour king*
- **Moses or Elijah** – *Old Testament prophets*
- **Prophet** – *someone chosen by God to communicate truth, sometimes about the future*
- **Priests** – *the men responsible for taking care of the temple and burning animals as sacrifices for the people's sin*

Slave master

Freedom for the wolves has often meant death to the sheep. Isaiah Berlin[5]

Many people wish for greater freedom; however, the British philosopher Isaiah Berlin argued that being free to do as we want can often mean that others, less powerful or talented, end up hurt or oppressed. Have you seen evidence of this?

Why do you think our freedoms sometimes conflict?

In what ways do you wish you were more free?

E **Mark 10:32-52**

Historical context

The disciples had no category for a Messiah who was to be rejected and killed. It made no sense to them.

If Jesus really was the Messiah, it might well mean death for his enemies and those of Israel, but surely not his own death! Maybe they thought he was speaking symbolically? They certainly hoped he would stop talking about it and move on to something more upbeat.

But Jesus didn't stop. And, as they got closer to Jerusalem, where opposition to Jesus was strongest, his persistent warnings became even more specific and even more worrying.

Read Mark 10:32–34

³² They were on their way up to Jerusalem, with Jesus leading the way, and the disciples were astonished, while those who followed were afraid. Again he took the Twelve aside and told them what was going to happen to him. ³³ 'We are going up to Jerusalem,' he said, 'and the Son of Man will be delivered over to the chief priests and the teachers of the law. They will condemn him to death and will hand him over to the Gentiles, ³⁴ who will mock him and spit on him, flog him and kill him. Three days later he will rise.'

1   For a third time (Mark 8:31 and 9:31), Jesus takes the disciples aside to tell them what is going to happen to him. What does he repeat? What's new?

Each time Jesus teaches about his death he calls himself the 'Son of Man'. Jesus will later make it clear that the title points to a visionary figure described by the Jewish prophet Daniel:

'There before me was one like a son of man, coming with the clouds of heaven ... He was given authority, glory and sovereign power; all nations and peoples of every language worshipped him. His dominion is an everlasting dominion that will not pass away, and his kingdom is one that will never be destroyed' **(Daniel 7:13–14).**

2 What kind of figure is Daniel describing? What do you think Jesus is claiming by using this title?

> **No wonder the disciples were confused. Jesus seems to be claiming for himself extraordinary majesty and power, yet in the same breath says that he is to be mocked, spat at, beaten and killed.**

Read Mark 10:35–45

[35] Then James and John, the sons of Zebedee, came to him. 'Teacher,' they said, 'we want you to do for us whatever we ask.'

[36] 'What do you want me to do for you?' he asked. [37] They replied, 'Let one of us sit at your right and the other at your left in your glory.' [38] 'You don't know what you are asking,' Jesus said. 'Can you drink the cup I drink or be baptised with the baptism I am baptised with?' [39] 'We can,' they answered.

Jesus said to them, 'You will drink the cup I drink and be baptised with the baptism I am baptised with, [40] but to sit at my right or left is not for me to grant. These places belong to those for whom they have been prepared.'

[41] When the ten heard about this, they became indignant with James and John. [42] Jesus called them together and said, 'You know that those who are regarded as rulers of the Gentiles lord it over them, and their high officials exercise authority over them. [43] Not so with you. Instead, whoever wants to become great among you must be your servant, [44] and whoever wants to be first must be slave of all. [45] For even the Son of Man did not come to be served, but to serve, and to give his life as a ransom for many.'

James and John were, along with Peter, among Jesus' closest friends.

3   The two brothers ask Jesus to give them what they ask for even before telling him what it is! Why do you think they do this?

4   James and John were asking for positions of honour and power. What does this reveal about their understanding of Jesus?

When Jesus talks of his 'cup' and 'baptism' (literally 'immersion'), he is once again referring to his death. Cup and baptism were frequently used metaphors in the Hebrew Bible for bitter and overwhelming suffering. Strikingly, the cup metaphor was especially related to God's judgement against sin:

> *'You ... have drunk from the hand of the LORD the cup of his wrath'* (Isaiah 51:17).

5   Why do you think Jesus says to James and John, 'You don't know what you're asking'? What don't they understand?

'For even the Son of Man did not come to be served, but to serve, and to give his life as a ransom for many.'

6   For what reason might the others have been annoyed
       when they found out about James and John's request?

**Jesus' teaching in response to their argument about greatness is the
key to unlocking Mark's entire Gospel.**

7   What new insights does Jesus give us about how he
       sees his own significance and purpose?

**The word 'ransom' in verse 45 refers to the sum needed to pay for the
freedom of those who are prisoners of war or slaves because of debt.**

8   What does Jesus imply about humankind by saying
       that he has come to give his life as a ransom for us?

**There is, again, a background to Jesus' language in this verse. The
prophet Isaiah describes a 'servant' who 'poured out his life unto
death' and 'bore the sins of many'. He says, 'We all, like sheep, have
gone astray, each of us has turned to his own way, and the Lord has
laid on him the iniquity of us all' (Isaiah 53:6, 11 and 12).**

9   What does this background suggest about why we need
       to be set free? How will Jesus' death accomplish this?

Many people with power or influence use it to get their own way and end up oppressing others (verse 42). Jesus has immense power, yet he didn't come so that we could serve him. Amazingly, he came to serve us by giving his life in our place to free us from our sin and self-centredness.

Read Mark 10:46–52

46 Then they came to Jericho. As Jesus and his disciples, together with a large crowd, were leaving the city, a blind man, Bartimaeus (which means 'son of Timaeus'), was sitting by the roadside begging. 47 When he heard that it was Jesus of Nazareth, he began to shout, 'Jesus, Son of David, have mercy on me!'

48 Many rebuked him and told him to be quiet, but he shouted all the more, 'Son of David, have mercy on me!' 49 Jesus stopped and said, 'Call him.' So they called to the blind man, 'Cheer up! On your feet! He's calling you.' 50 Throwing his cloak aside, he jumped to his feet and came to Jesus. 51 'What do you want me to do for you?' Jesus asked him. The blind man said, 'Rabbi, I want to see.'

52 'Go,' said Jesus, 'your faith has healed you.' Immediately he received his sight and followed Jesus along the road.

The story of blind Bartimaeus is the last healing Mark writes about in his Gospel. As Jesus and his disciples pass by, Bartimaeus is at the roadside, begging. The title 'Son of David' is another way of referring to Jesus as the Messiah. Blind and marginalised, Bartimaeus could see what others could not.

10 In verse 51 we see Jesus ask, for the second time in this section (verse 36), 'What do you want me to do for you?' What does this question reveal about Jesus? How is the outcome different this time?

What does this mean for us?

Whereas we tend to see 'going our own way' (as in the Isaiah quote above) as an expression of our freedom, Jesus teaches that self-centredness ultimately enslaves and oppresses, not only others, but ourselves. The journalist Malcolm Muggeridge once described vividly his experience of this slavery to self:

> *'I am confined in the tiny dark dungeon of my ego; manacled with the appetites of the flesh, shackled with the inordinate demands of the will – a prisoner serving a life sentence with no hope of deliverance.'* [6]

11 To what extent do you recognise the experience of slavery to self that Muggeridge describes?

12 What have you seen in Jesus that could offer hope for a deeper kind of freedom?

? Questions about forgiveness?
Go to uncover.org.uk/forgiveness

Glossary

- **Baptism** – *the immersion of someone in water; baptism represented the death of an old life and the start of a new life as well as cleansing from sin*
- **Jericho** – *a city 25km from Jerusalem*
- **Nazareth** – *the capital and largest city in the north of Israel*
- **Ransom** – *the sum needed to pay for the freedom of slaves and prisoners of war*
- **Son of Man** – *a title for Jesus, first used in the Old Testament prophecy of Daniel*

Only human after all

We commonly excuse
our moral weaknesses
or failures by saying
'We're only human'.

What do we mean
by this? Why do you
think people so often
fall short of their own
standards and ideals?

Mark
14:27–72

Historical context

When Jesus arrived in Jerusalem he went straight to the temple.

The temple was the heart of Jewish religion and the pride of Israel. Yet Jesus entered this glorious building as if it belonged to him, as if he'd come back home and found his house in a mess.

He started clearing people out and condemned the commercialism he found there. Many were amazed and many were appalled. 'What gives you the right to do this?' was the obvious question. Even some of his followers began to think he was taking things too far.

The authorities who had been determined to kill Jesus for a long time were delighted when Judas, one of the twelve, came to them with his offer of betrayal.

From that point, the events Jesus had predicted were quick to unfold.

Read Mark 14:27–31

27 'You will all fall away,' Jesus told them, 'for it is written:

' "I will strike the shepherd,
and the sheep will be scattered."

28 But after I have risen, I will go ahead of you into Galilee.' 29 Peter declared, 'Even if all fall away, I will not.' 30 'Truly I tell you,' Jesus answered, 'today – yes, tonight – before the cock crows twice you yourself will disown me three times.' 31 But Peter insisted emphatically, 'Even if I have to die with you, I will never disown you.' And all the others said the same.

Jesus warns his friends yet again of coming events. He quotes a prophecy telling of a time when God will strike down his appointed king in judgement, scattering his people like sheep without a shepherd.

1   Why, of all Jesus' predictions, will this one be especially hard for his friends to accept?

2   How does Peter react to Jesus' warning? Describe your impressions of Peter from here and from what we saw of him in study D.

Read Mark 14:32–42

[32] They went to a place called Gethsemane, and Jesus said to his disciples, 'Sit here while I pray.' [33] He took Peter, James and John along with him, and he began to be deeply distressed and troubled. [34] 'My soul is overwhelmed with sorrow to the point of death,' he said to them.
'Stay here and keep watch.'

[35] Going a little farther, he fell to the ground and prayed that if possible the hour might pass from him. [36] '*Abba*, Father,' he said, 'everything is possible for you. Take this cup from me. Yet not what I will, but what you will.'

[37] Then he returned to his disciples and found them sleeping. 'Simon,' he said to Peter, 'are you asleep? Couldn't you keep watch for one hour? [38] Watch and pray so that you will not fall into temptation. The spirit is willing, but the flesh is weak.'

[39] Once more he went away and prayed the same thing. [40] When he came back, he again found them sleeping, because their eyes were heavy. They did not know what to say to him.

[41] Returning the third time, he said to them, 'Are you still sleeping and resting? Enough! The hour has come. Look, the Son of Man is delivered into the hands of sinners. [42] Rise! Let us go! Here comes my betrayer!'

Jesus goes with his friends to a quiet olive grove called Gethsemane, a short walk from Jerusalem. While praying, Jesus again speaks of a cup he has to drink.

As we've seen (study E), this image is strongly associated with the experience of suffering under God's judgement. Yet in the same prayer Jesus addresses God with remarkable intimacy as 'Abba' (the informal term for 'Father' in Aramaic).

3   Many people throughout history have faced death heroically, with great composure, yet Jesus is 'overwhelmed with sorrow'. What might Jesus be about to experience that so completely overwhelms him?

4   Despite his sorrow, how does Jesus nevertheless demonstrate courage in this moment of trial?

5   How does Jesus' internal struggle compare with his friends' struggle to support him in prayer in his hour of need?

Read Mark 14:43–52

⁴³ Just as he was speaking, Judas, one of the Twelve, appeared. With him was a crowd armed with swords and clubs, sent from the chief priests, the teachers of the law, and the elders.

⁴⁴ Now the betrayer had arranged a signal with them: 'The one I kiss is the man; arrest him and lead him away under guard.' ⁴⁵ Going at once to Jesus, Judas said, 'Rabbi!' and kissed him. ⁴⁶ The men seized Jesus and arrested him. ⁴⁷ Then one of those standing near drew his sword and struck the servant of the high priest, cutting off his ear.

⁴⁸ 'Am I leading a rebellion,' said Jesus, 'that you have come out with swords and clubs to capture me? ⁴⁹ Every day I was with you, teaching in the temple courts, and you did not arrest me. But the Scriptures must be fulfilled.' ⁵⁰ Then everyone deserted him and fled.

⁵¹ A young man, wearing nothing but a linen garment, was following Jesus. When they seized him, ⁵² he fled naked, leaving his garment behind.

6   Jesus knows full well of Judas' betrayal and of the arrest that will follow, yet he doesn't resist the guards or even Judas' kiss. Why do you think Jesus allows himself to be treated this way?

Read Mark 14:53–65

53 They took Jesus to the high priest, and all the chief priests, the elders and the teachers of the law came together. 54 Peter followed him at a distance, right into the courtyard of the high priest. There he sat with the guards and warmed himself at the fire.

55 The chief priests and the whole Sanhedrin were looking for evidence against Jesus so that they could put him to death, but they did not find any. 56 Many testified falsely against him, but their statements did not agree.

57 Then some stood up and gave this false testimony against him: 58 'We heard him say, "I will destroy this temple made with human hands and in three days will build another, not made with hands." ' 59 Yet even then their testimony did not agree.

60 Then the high priest stood up before them and asked Jesus, 'Are you not going to answer? What is this testimony that these men are bringing against you?' 61 But Jesus remained silent and gave no answer.

Again the high priest asked him, 'Are you the Messiah, the Son of the Blessed One?' 62 'I am,' said Jesus. 'And you will see the Son of Man sitting at the right hand of the Mighty One and coming on the clouds of heaven.'

63 The high priest tore his clothes. 'Why do we need any more witnesses?' he asked. 64 'You have heard the blasphemy. What do you think?'

They all condemned him as worthy of death. [65] Then some began to spit at him; they blindfolded him, struck him with their fists, and said, 'Prophesy!' And the guards took him and beat him.

7 How does Mark describe the trial? Is it fair?

The trial turns on the one question that Jesus breaks his silence to answer. The high priest, obviously frustrated by the lack of progress, rises to his feet and presses Jesus directly: 'Are you the Messiah, the Son of God?' It is this question of his identity that has been at the very heart of Mark's account since the beginning.

For the first and only time in the Gospel, Jesus gives an undeniably clear answer.

8 Jesus stands on trial before his enemies, betrayed and abandoned by his friends. Why do you think he chooses this, of all moments, to be open about the truth of his identity?

9 Blasphemy means mocking or misrepresenting God. Anyone who claimed to be divine was automatically judged to be guilty of it. Is Jesus guilty of the charge? What is the irony here if Jesus is telling the truth?

'I don't know this man you're talking about.'

Mark now focuses again on the story of Peter, having left him earlier (verse 54) outside the trial, warming himself by a courtyard fire.

Read Mark 14:66–72

66 While Peter was below in the courtyard, one of the servant-girls of the high priest came by. 67 When she saw Peter warming himself, she looked closely at him. 'You also were with that Nazarene, Jesus,' she said. 68 But he denied it. 'I don't know or understand what you're talking about,' he said, and went out into the entrance.

69 When the servant-girl saw him there, she said again to those standing round them, 'This fellow is one of them.' 70 Again he denied it.

After a little while, those standing near said to Peter, 'Surely you are one of them, for you are a Galilean.' 71 He began to call down curses, and he swore to them, 'I don't know this man you're talking about.'

72 Immediately the cock crowed the second time. Then Peter remembered the word Jesus had spoken to him: 'Before the cock crows twice you will disown me three times.' And he broke down and wept.

10   What similarities are there between Jesus' and Peter's experiences? How do their experiences and responses under trial contrast?

11 Mark tells us that, when he remembered Jesus' words, Peter broke down and wept. Does it surprise you that Peter was so unaware of his weakness before this moment (verses 29 and 31)? How easy/difficult do you find it to sympathise with Peter?

What does this mean for us?

On the face of it, Jesus is the one who stands condemned. According to Jesus, however, it is everyone else who is on trial. Peter and the disciples thought that they could protect and defend Jesus, but when put to the test they ran away and denied him.

The Sanhedrin thought that they had the right to judge Jesus, but Jesus tells them that he is, in fact, their judge. Though the priests accused Jesus of blasphemy, it was they who mocked and spat at the one who sits at the right hand of God.

12 Mark paints an ugly picture of human arrogance and moral weakness in these episodes. How realistic a picture of human nature do you find this to be?

13   What impressions of Jesus do these episodes leave you with?

> **?**   **Questions about human nature?**
> **Go to uncover.org.uk/human**

Glossary

- **Abba Father** – *an intimate name for God as Father*
- **Gethsemane** – *a garden at the bottom of the Mount of Olives*
- **Sanhedrin** – *the name of the Jewish religious court and the members of it*
- **Scriptures** – *another way of referring to the Bible*

God forsaken

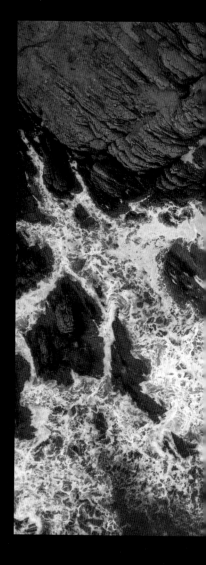

We stand on the shore of an ocean, crying to the night and the emptiness; sometimes a voice answers out of the darkness. But it is a voice of one drowning; and in a moment the silence returns. Bertrand Russell[7]

What do you think Russell is trying to say about human experience? Have there been times in your life when the universe has seemed to you especially dark, empty and silent?

 Mark 15:16–41

Historical context

After the verdict of blasphemy was agreed, Jesus was beaten, bound and handed over to the Romans.

The Roman governor found no reason to condemn Jesus and tried to release him as part of an annual custom, but the crowds, stirred up by the priests, instead chose a murderer named Barabbas. Jesus was condemned to be crucified and Barabbas went free.

Crucifixion was a slow, degrading and agonising method of execution, involving what would today be described as extreme physical, sexual and mental humiliation and abuse. Mark records what happened with brutal simplicity letting the events speak for themselves.

Yet, although Mark doesn't comment on what happened, it is clear that he has carefully selected and ordered the details he records.

As we take note of these details, we see that behind the awful violence of the crucifixion there is a deeper, and even darker, significance to what is going on.

Read Mark 15:16–32

¹⁶ The soldiers led Jesus away into the palace (that is, the Praetorium) and called together the whole company of soldiers. ¹⁷ They put a purple robe on him, then twisted together a crown of thorns and set it on him. ¹⁸ And they began to call out to him, 'Hail, king of the Jews!' ¹⁹ Again and again they struck him on the head with a staff and spat on him. Falling on their knees, they paid homage to him. ²⁰ And when they had mocked him, they took off the purple robe and put his own clothes on him. Then they led him out to crucify him.

²¹ A certain man from Cyrene, Simon, the father of Alexander and Rufus, was passing by on his way in from the country, and they forced him to carry the cross. ²² They brought Jesus to the place called Golgotha (which means 'the place of the skull'). ²³ Then they offered him wine mixed with myrrh, but he did not take it. ²⁴ And they crucified him. Dividing up his clothes, they cast lots to see what each would get.

²⁵ It was nine in the morning when they crucified him. ²⁶ The written notice of the charge against him read: THE KING OF THE JEWS.

²⁷ They crucified two rebels with him, one on his right and one on his left. ²⁹ Those who passed by hurled insults at him, shaking their heads and saying, 'So! You who are going to destroy the temple and build it in three days, ³⁰ come down from the cross and save yourself!' ³¹ In the same way the chief priests and the teachers of the law mocked him among themselves. 'He saved others,' they said, 'but he can't save himself! ³² Let this Messiah, this king of Israel, come down now from the cross, that we may see and believe.' Those crucified with him also heaped insults on him.

1   Jesus was constantly taunted and mocked as he was crucified. Who was involved? What was the content of their mockery?

2   Why do you think Mark chooses to record the mockery in such detail? What is the irony in much of what is said, considering what we've learned about who Jesus is and why he came?

Jesus will later cry out words taken from the beginning of an ancient poem from the Hebrew Bible (verse 34). In Psalm 22, the writer speaks of his complete defeat and powerlessness:

> *'I am a worm and not a man, scorned by everyone, despised by the people. All who see me mock me; they hurl insults, shaking their heads...I am poured out like water, and all my bones are out of joint; my heart has turned to wax; it has melted within me. My mouth is dried up...my tongue sticks to the roof of my mouth; you lay me in the dust of death. Dogs surround me; a pack of villains encircles me; they pierce my hands and feet. All my bones are on display; people stare and gloat over me. They divide my clothes among them and cast lots for my garment.'*

3   What similarities are there between these words and what is happening to Jesus? What insights into his experience does Jesus offer us by quoting from this poem?

Read Mark 15:33–36

³³ At noon, darkness came over the whole land until three in the afternoon. ³⁴ And at three in the afternoon Jesus cried out in a loud voice, '*Eloi, Eloi, lema sabachthani?*' (which means 'My God, my God, why have you forsaken me?').

³⁵ When some of those standing near heard this, they said, 'Listen, he's calling Elijah.' ³⁶ Someone ran, filled a sponge with wine vinegar, put it on a staff, and offered it to Jesus to drink. 'Now leave him alone. Let's see if Elijah comes to take him down,' he said.

Between midday and 3pm darkness fell over the land. The Jewish prophets understood darkness during daytime as a potent symbol of God's judgement.

4   Consider the darkness and Jesus' cry. What insight might they give us into Jesus' experience of God as he hangs on the cross?

Some people watching misinterpreted *'Eloi'* as referring to Elijah the prophet and thought Jesus was praying for rescue (verse 35). Many considered that, if Jesus really was innocent, God would save him. To extend the experiment they gave him a drink, but no help came.

5 Throughout Mark's account Jesus has demonstrated his power to save others from sickness, evil and even death. Why then didn't he save himself? Was it just the nails that kept him there?

Read Mark 15:37–41

37 With a loud cry, Jesus breathed his last. 38 The curtain of the temple was torn in two from top to bottom. 39 And when the centurion, who stood there in front of Jesus, saw how he died, he said, 'Surely this man was the Son of God!'

40 Some women were watching from a distance. Among them were Mary Magdalene, Mary the mother of James the younger and of Joseph, and Salome. 41 In Galilee these women had followed him and cared for his needs. Many other women who had come up with him to Jerusalem were also there.

The temple was sub-divided by massive curtains up to 30 metres high. One great curtain separated the main part of the temple from the inner sanctum, the most holy place, which only the high priest could enter one day a year. Another curtain introduced separate sections for women and Gentiles (non-Jews). These curtains were powerful reminders of God's separateness and hiddenness.

'Surely this
man was the
Son of God!'

6   As Jesus dies, crying out in his isolation from God, the curtain of the temple rips from top to bottom. What might this signify?

7   Contrast the centurion with everyone else around the cross. What does he somehow see that others can not? What might cause him to come to this conclusion?

The priests had challenged Jesus to come down from the cross so that they might 'see and believe' (Mark 15:32). Yet remarkably, at the very moment of Jesus' death, a hardened Roman centurion sees and believes what no one else in the entire Gospel has been able to. This man, whose body now hung lifeless and disfigured, was the Son of God.

8   Mark twice pauses in his account of events to record the names of those who witness the events (see also 15:21). Why do you think he does this?

9   At the end, it is a Gentile and a group of women who stand as witnesses of Jesus' death. In your view, why might Mark pay particular attention to this fact?

STUDY G

What does this mean for us?

Writing just after the horrors of the First World War, Edward Shillito composed a famous poem named *Jesus of the Scars*. The final verse reads:

'The other gods were strong; but Thou wast weak;
They rode, but Thou didst stumble to a throne;
But to our wounds only God's wounds can speak,
And not a god has wounds, but Thou alone.'

The Gospels consistently present the cross as an unveiling of who God really is.

10 If Jesus really is God as the centurion came to believe, what does the cross reveal to us about what God is like?

11 How might knowing that 'God has wounds', speak to our own experiences of pain and aloneness?

On the cross, Jesus was not only identifying with us in our experiences of pain and loneliness, he was substituting himself for us. As he had said (10:45), he came to 'give his life as a ransom for many' – Jesus was putting himself where we should be so that we could be forgiven. Dying in agony, alone in the dark, Jesus was forsaken by his Father so that we would never have to be. Though he had lived entirely for others, instead of us, he was facing the terrible isolation that will ultimately come from living for ourselves.

12 How do you feel about the possibility that Jesus suffered what he did in your place?

? **Questions about the cross?**
Go to uncover.org.uk/cross

Glossary

- **Cast lots** – *a way of making decisions using a game of chance*
- **Centurion** – *an officer in the army of ancient Rome who was responsible for 100 soldiers*

The opening

Thomas Kuhn famously described the struggle involved in accepting a new view of the world:

'In science ... novelty emerges only with difficulty, manifested by resistance, against a background provided by expectation.'[8]

Why is changing our mind so hard? How open to the unexpected do you feel you are?

 Mark 15:42–16:8

Historical context

Most people thought that the crucifixion ended any possibility of Jesus' being the Messiah.

For the Romans, crucifixion was the ultimate demonstration of weakness and failure. For the Jews, it was the final proof that he was a blasphemer and a fraud. To die in such a way could only mean that he had been rejected by God himself. A crucified Messiah was no Messiah at all. Case closed; end of story.

Except, of course, that Jesus had said this was exactly how things would happen. He'd told his disciples on several occasions how he would be betrayed and abandoned by his friends, rejected by his people and handed over to suffer and die at the hands of the Romans. And he'd also said something else. Repeatedly, after explaining how the Son of Man would have to die, he went on to say, 'and three days later he will rise.'

These warnings were so unthinkable at the time, and the events so terrible when they finally took place, that Jesus' words had apparently been ignored and were now forgotten. They had made no sense to his followers and therefore offered them no comfort or hope.

No one was expecting what would happen next.

Read Mark 15:42–47

⁴²It was Preparation Day (that is, the day before the Sabbath). So as evening approached, ⁴³Joseph of Arimathea, a prominent member of the Council, who was himself waiting for the kingdom of God, went boldly to Pilate and asked for Jesus' body. ⁴⁴Pilate was surprised to hear that he was already dead. Summoning the centurion, he asked him if Jesus had already died. ⁴⁵When he learned from the centurion that it was so, he gave the body to Joseph.

⁴⁶So Joseph bought some linen cloth, took down the body, wrapped it in the linen, and placed it in a tomb cut out of rock. Then he rolled a stone against the entrance of the tomb. ⁴⁷Mary Magdalene and Mary the mother of Joseph saw where he was laid.

1   What particular details does Mark focus on here? Why might these details be of significance?

Romans usually left executed prisoners hanging on the cross to be eaten by scavengers. Special permission was needed to take a body for burial. Jews, however, required everyone, even criminals, to be buried on the day of death – especially with the Sabbath the next day. Since none of Jesus' followers stepped forward, a devout Pharisee named Joseph made the request to bury Jesus himself.

2   Why did Joseph's action take courage? What does this imply about the absent disciples?

Read Mark 16:1–3

When the Sabbath was over, Mary Magdalene, Mary the mother of James, and Salome bought spices so that they might go to anoint Jesus' body. [2] Very early on the first day of the week, just after sunrise, they were on their way to the tomb [3] and they asked each other, 'Who will roll the stone away from the entrance of the tomb?'

3   The women went to visit the tomb at the earliest opportunity. Why were they in such a rush? What were they expecting that morning?

Despite Jesus' repeated promises, no one seemed to be anticipating anything unusual happening on that third day. The women went expecting to find a rapidly decomposing body shut inside a sealed tomb. Peter and the other male disciples didn't even show up.

4   Considering what you've seen and learned of Jesus, might you have gone to check whether anything had happened? Why/why not?

5   Why, considering what Jesus had promised, do you think the disciples were so closed to the possibility of his rising from the dead?

Read Mark 16:4–8

[4] But when they looked up, they saw that the stone, which was very large, had been rolled away. [5] As they entered the tomb, they saw a young man dressed in a white robe sitting on the right side, and they were alarmed.

[6] 'Don't be alarmed,' he said. 'You are looking for Jesus the Nazarene, who was crucified. He has risen! He is not here. See the place where they laid him. [7] But go, tell his disciples and Peter, "He is going ahead of you into Galilee. There you will see him, just as he told you." '

[8] Trembling and bewildered, the women went out and fled from the tomb. They said nothing to anyone, because they were afraid.

6   The tomb was open! What thoughts might have gone through the women's minds when they saw the stone rolled back? How might they have tried to make sense of it?

The tombs had a low entrance tunnel leading to a burial chamber where bodies were laid on shelves cut into the wall. The women would have had to stoop or crawl to enter the chamber.

'He has risen! He is not here. See the place where they laid him.'

Mark 16:6

7 The word translated 'alarmed' describes a mixture of fear, wonder, astonishment and distress. What was it about the young man's appearance that may have caused this reaction?

8 Consider the stranger's remarkable words. What insights into the situation does he display?

Mark has carefully named Salome and the two Marys as witnesses to Jesus' death (Mark 15:40), the two Marys as witnesses of the burial (Mark 15:47) and now all three women as witnesses of the empty tomb.

9 Why do you think Mark emphasises the eyewitness evidence for these three events in particular? What alternative explanations are being ruled out?

This heavy reliance on women as eyewitnesses is significant, since, at the time, women were seen (by men, at least) as unreliable and their testimony was not accepted in court.

10 Considering this background, why would Mark take such care to name these women as eyewitnesses? What implications might this have for the reliability of Mark's account?

The most reliable manuscripts end suddenly at Mark 16:8. Some suggest that the original ending has been lost, but, if this is indeed how Mark ends, he finishes with a punchline. Again and again, Jesus has been telling people not to say who he is or what he can do, yet no one could keep quiet. Now, at last, the women hear 'Go, tell!', but instead 'they say nothing to anyone because they are afraid'!

11   We would expect the women to be thrilled at the thought that they might see Jesus alive. Why do you think they were so afraid that they kept silent?

12   Why might Mark have chosen to end his Gospel in this dramatic way?

The message that the women did, eventually, tell others recalls Jesus' final words to the disciples: 'You will all fall away ... but after I have risen, I will go ahead of you into Galilee' (Mark 14:27–28).

13   The message was for 'the disciples and Peter'. Why do you think Peter was mentioned specifically? How would you feel, if you were Peter, on hearing that this message was also intended for you?

As other accounts make clear, the women, the disciples and Peter soon saw Jesus face to face. Over the next five or six weeks Jesus appeared to them and many others. He walked with them, ate with them, comforted them and taught them. These meetings were so obvious and tangible that not one of these once disbelieving and fearful disciples ever again denied what they had witnessed. Their testimony was uniform: Jesus, the one who was crucified, is alive.

What does this mean for us?

This was a wild, unorthodox claim then and it remains so today. It left the women confused and afraid, unable to make sense of what they'd seen.

14 How hard do you find it to make sense of what you've heard about Jesus in Mark's Gospel?

Many, like Peter, struggle to see how Mark's good news could possibly be meant for someone like them.

15 Is there anything still holding you back from accepting the good news of Jesus for yourself?

Glossary

- **Anoint** – *a Jewish burial ritual involving oils and aromatic herbs which are applied to help fight the effects of rapid decomposition*
- **Nazarene** – *a person from the city of Nazareth*

Roll away your stone - a short video
Watch at uncover.org.uk/rollaway

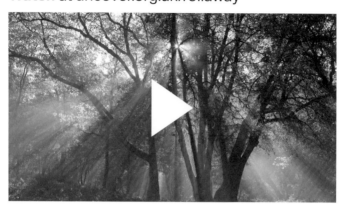

Postscript.

The empty tomb changes everything. If Jesus has risen from the dead then what he claimed was true: his death was not a meaningless tragedy, it was the price he willingly paid to set us free and to heal his broken world.

At the very beginning, Jesus invited those who heard him to rethink their beliefs and priorities and to accept for themselves this good news that changes everything. The invitation still stands.

It may be that you feel you would like to accept Jesus' invitation now. A prayer like this may help you begin speaking to Jesus about what you have come to believe and wish to accept for yourself:

Jesus, I think you may be alive and so able to set me free. If you are, please help me to believe as you helped the disciples. I am sorry that I have lived for myself for so long. Thank you that you lived for me and died for me so that I could be forgiven. I'm willing to trust and follow you. Amen.

If you have decided to follow Jesus, tell a Christian you know and find a local church – a family of others who have uncovered who Jesus is and want to follow him together.

There may still be many things you are unsure of. If you haven't already done so, work through the eight studies in this book with a friend and continue uncovering Jesus online.

Read. Watch. Discuss. Ask. Share.

uncover.org.uk/mark

References

[1] Moltmann, J, *The Way of Jesus Christ: Christology in Messianic Dimensions* (Augsburg, MN: Fortress Press, 1993).

[2] Obama, B, 'Farewell address'. (Reprinted in *The New York Times*, January 2017).

[3] Byrne, R, *The Secret* (London: Simon and Schuster, 2008).

[4] Weingarten, G, 'Pearls before breakfast: Can one of the nation's great musicians cut through the fog of a DC rush hour? Let's find out' (*Washington Post*, 8 April 2007).

[5] Berlin, I, *Four Essays on Liberty* (Oxford: Oxford University Press, 1969).

[6] Muggeridge, M, 'Living through an apocalypse' (*Christianity Today*, 16 August 1974).

[7] Russell, B, *The Autobiography of Bertrand Russell, Vol. II 1914–1944* (London, Allen and Unwin; 1968).

[8] Kuhn, TS, *The Structure of Scientific Revolutions* (Chicago, IL: University of Chicago Press, 1962).

bethinking

Questions about _____?

If you've still got questions about Jesus then check out Bethinking. Brought to you by the makers of Uncover, Bethinking is full of resources to help you dig deeper and find answers.

Start here: bethinking.org/uncover

Notes

uccf:thechristianunions

This resource is produced by UCCF: The Christian Unions.
UCCF is made up of hundreds of university Christian Unions across Britain. We exist to give every student on campus an opportunity to hear about Jesus. This resource has been developed to help you engage with the narrative of Mark's Gospel.

To find out more about Christian Unions, visit uccf.org.uk

Contact

UCCF: The Christian Unions
Blue Boar House
5 Blue Boar Street
Oxford
OX1 4EE

T: 01865 253678
E: email@uccf.org.uk
W: uccf.org.uk

Registered Charity No: 306137

Design by Sam Lucas
Photography by Kieran Dodds (www.kierandodds.com)

Exam Ref 70-483
Programming in C#
Second Edition

Rob Miles

Exam Ref 70-483 Programming in C#, Second Edition

Published with the authorization of Microsoft Corporation by:
Pearson Education, Inc.

Copyright © 2019 by Pearson Education

ISBN-978-1-5093-0698-5
ISBN-1-5093-0698-6

Library of Congress Control Number: 2018952507
1 18

Trademarks

Warning and Disclaimer

Special Sales

For information about buying this title in bulk quantities, or for special sales opportunities (which may include electronic versions; custom cover designs; and content particular to your business, training goals, marketing focus, or branding interests), please contact our corporate sales department at corpsales@pearsoned.com or (800) 382-3419.

For government sales inquiries, please contact governmentsales@pearsoned.com.

For questions about sales outside the U.S., please contact intlcs@pearson.com.

Editor-in-Chief	Greg Wiegand
Senior Editor	Loretta Yates
Development Editor	Troy Mott
Managing Editor	Sandra Schroeder
Senior Project Editor	Tracey Croom
Editorial Production	Backstop Media
Copy Editor	Liv Bainbridge
Indexer	MAP Systems
Proofreader	Jana Gardner
Technical Editors	Hendrik Bulens
Cover Designer	Twist Creative, Seattle

I would like to dedicate this book to Immy, a proper ray of sunshine.

—ROB MILES

Contents at a glance

Contents

Introduction

This book is not an introductory programming text, instead it is aimed at developers who have been using C# for a while and want to improve their understanding of the language and the .NET libraries. The text builds on existing knowledge of C# to give a deeper understanding of the language and provide preparation for the examination.

To work with the programming examples supplied with the book, you will need a copy of Visual Studio Community 2017 running on Windows 10. The bulk of the examples are WIN 32 console applications, along with some Universal Applications and ASP.NET Core Web Applications.

The Microsoft 70-483 certification exam tests your skills as a programmer. It tests your knowledge of the C# language and how you use .NET libraries in a variety of different situations. The exam is as much a test of "doing" as it is a test of "knowing." To that end, you should make good use of the example programs that illustrate the text. You should also work through all of the Thought Experiments, because these are a great way to reinforce your understanding of key concepts.

This book covers every major topic area found on the exam, but it does not cover every exam question. Only the Microsoft exam team has access to the exam questions, and Microsoft regularly adds new questions to the exam, making it impossible to cover specific questions. You should consider this book a supplement to your relevant real-world experience and other study materials. If you encounter a topic in this book that you do not feel completely comfortable with, use the "Need more review?" links you'll find in the text to find more information and take the time to research and study the topic. Great information is available on MSDN, TechNet, and in blogs and forums.

Organization of this book

This book is organized by the "Skills measured" list published for the exam. The "Skills measured" list is available for each exam on the Microsoft Learning website: *http://aka.ms/examlist*. Each chapter in this book corresponds to a major topic area in the list, and the technical tasks in each topic area determine a chapter's organization. If an exam covers six major topic areas, for example, the book will contain six chapters.

Microsoft certifications

Microsoft certifications distinguish you by proving your command of a broad set of skills and experience with current Microsoft products and technologies. The exams and corresponding certifications are developed to validate your mastery of critical competencies as you design and develop, or implement and support, solutions with Microsoft products and technologies both on-premises and in the cloud. Certification brings a variety of benefits to the individual and to employers and organizations.

> **MORE INFO   ALL MICROSOFT CERTIFICATIONS**
>
> For information about Microsoft certifications, including a full list of available certifications, go to *http://www.microsoft.com/learning*.

Check back often to see what is new!

Quick access to online references

Throughout this book are addresses to webpages that the author has recommended you visit for more information. Some of these addresses (also known as URLs) can be painstaking to type into a web browser, so we've compiled all of them into a single list that readers of the print edition can refer to while they read.

The list is included in the companion content, which you can download here: *https://aka.ms/examref483ed2/downloads* or *https://github.com/ExamRef70-483/Sample-Code*

The URLs are organized by chapter and heading. Every time you come across a URL in the book, find the hyperlink in the list to go directly to the webpage.

Errata, updates, & book support

We've made every effort to ensure the accuracy of this book and its companion content. You can access updates to this book—in the form of a list of submitted errata and their related corrections—at:

https://aka.ms/examref483ed2/errata

If you discover an error that is not already listed, please submit it to us at the same page.

If you need additional support, email Microsoft Press Book Support at *mspinput@microsoft.com*.

Please note that product support for Microsoft software and hardware is not offered through the previous addresses. For help with Microsoft software or hardware, go to *http://support.microsoft.com*.

Stay in touch

Let's keep the conversation going! We're on Twitter: *http://twitter.com/MicrosoftPress*.

Preparing for the exam

Microsoft certification exams are a great way to build your resume and let the world know about your level of expertise. Certification exams validate your on-the-job experience and product knowledge. Although there is no substitute for on-the-job experience, preparation through study and hands-on practice can help you prepare for the exam. We recommend that you augment your exam preparation plan by using a combination of available study materials and courses. For example, you might use the Exam ref and another study guide for your "at home" preparation, and take a Microsoft Official Curriculum course for the classroom experience. Choose the combination that you think works best for you.

Note that this Exam Ref is based on publicly available information about the exam and the author's experience. To safeguard the integrity of the exam, authors do not have access to the live exam.

Acknowledgments

I'd like to thank Trina Fletcher Macdonald for giving me the chance to write this, Troy Mott for keeping me on the straight and narrow, Liv Bainbridge for putting in the missing words, and Hendrik Bulens for stopping me from writing silly things. Oh, and of course Mary, for the endless cups of tea.

About the Author

 ROB MILES spent over 30 years teaching programming to a succession of students at the University of Hull in the UK. He's a Microsoft MVP with a passion for programming, C# and creating new things. If he had any spare time he'd spend it writing even more code. He reckons that programming is the most creative thing you can learn how to do. He loves making programs and then running them to see what happens. He claims to know a lot of really good jokes, but nobody has ever heard him tell one. If you want an insight into the Wacky World(tm) of Rob Miles you can read his blog at www.robmiles.com and follow him on Twitter via @RobMiles.

Manage program flow

This chapter is focused on the way that programs run inside your computer. In the early days of computing this was a very simple process, with a single program executing on a single *Central Processing Unit* (CPU). Modern applications, however, are not implemented by an individual program following a single sequence of instructions. Today's applications typically contain large numbers of cooperating processes. There are two reasons why this is the case.

> **IMPORTANT**
> **Have you read page xix?**
> It contains valuable information regarding the skills you need to pass the exam.

First, adding additional CPU elements increases the amount of data that can be processed in a given time. In the same way that two cars can carry twice as many passengers as one, adding a second CPU will increase the amount of data that a computer can work with at any given time. Note, however, that adding extra CPU resources doesn't increase the speed at which data can be processed; any more than two cars can go twice as fast as one.

The second reason for breaking an application into multiple processes is that it makes it much easier for a developer to organize the elements of their solution. Consider a word processing application. At any given instant the word processor may be accepting text from the user, performing a spell check of the document, auto-saving the text into a file and sending pages to the printer. It is much easier to create each of these operations as an individual process rather than trying to write a single application that tries to perform all these actions at the same time.

The first personal computers were powered by a single CPU and gave the appearance of the ability to run multiple programs at the same time by rapidly switching between them. The advent of multi-CPU computers has now made it possible for systems to use genuine multi-tasking, where elements of a solution can run in parallel on the hardware.

Of course, with the great power provided by the ability to execute multiple processes comes an extra layer of responsibility. A developer must ensure that all the elements in a multi-process powered solution work together correctly and that any errors are propagated through the system in a meaningful way.

This chapter explains the fundamentals of multi-process programming and describes the C# features and libraries that you can use to work with processes, how processes are created, managed and communicate with each other. You will also explore the C# language features that allow the management of error conditions in multi-process systems and discover the fundamental C# elements that control program flow.

Skills in this chapter:

- Skill 1.1: Implement multithreading and asynchronous processing
- Skill 1.2: Manage multithreading
- Skill 1.3: Implement program flow
- Skill 1.4: Create and implement events and callbacks
- Skill 1.5: Implement exception handling

Skill 1.1: Implement multithreading and asynchronous processing

Consider a busy kitchen that needs to serve a large number of diners at the same time. If that kitchen has only one chef, that chef must rapidly switch between cooking each meal. While one dish is in the oven baking, the chef must prepare the ingredients for another dish. At any given instant the chef can work on only one meal. This is an example of how a single processor (the chef) is *multi-tasking* between the preparation of several meals. When two things are happening at exactly the same time we say that they are concurrent. Nothing is happening *concurrently* in this situation, because we only have a single chef. In this case the chef is the CPU and the task is the preparation of a particular meal.

You can improve the performance of your kitchen by adding extra chefs, each of which will be working on a particular meal at any one time. This is analogous to adding extra CPUs to a multi-tasking system. In a kitchen you might decide to allocate particular tasks to a particular chef, so all of the desserts can be prepared by the pastry chef. In a multi-threaded computer system this would not happen, because tasks are allocated to the next processor that becomes available. If one task is delayed for some reason, perhaps because it is waiting for some data to arrive from a mass storage device, then the processor running that task can move onto a different task.

This ability of a computer system to execute multiple processes at the same time (concurrency) is not provided by the C# language itself. It is the underlying operating system that controls which programs are active at any instant. The .NET framework provides classes to represent items of work to be performed, and in this section you learn how to use these classes.

It is not possible for a developer to make any assumptions concerning which processes are active at any one time, how much processing time a given process has, or when a given operation will be completed.

In this section you will also discover the abstractions used by C# to manage the simultaneous execution of program elements, how to add parallel elements to sequential programs, and how to manage access to data in applications that use concurrency.

The Task Parallel library

You can think of a task as an abstraction of a unit of work to be performed. The work itself will be described by some C# program code, perhaps by a method or a lambda expression. A task may be performed concurrently with other tasks.

The Task Parallel Library (TPL) provides a range of resources that allow you to use tasks in an application. The Task.Parallel class in the library provides three methods that can be used to create applications that contain tasks that execute in parallel.

Parallel.Invoke

The Task.Parallel class can be found in the System.Threading.Tasks namespace. The Parallel. Invoke method accepts a number of Action delegates and creates a Task for each of them.

An Action delegate is an encapsulation of a method that accepts no parameters and does not return a result. It can be replaced with a lamba expression, as shown in Listing 1-1, in which two tasks are created.

LISTING 1-1 Parallel.Invoke in use

```
using System;
using System.Threading.Tasks;
using System.Threading;

namespace Listing_1._1Parallel_Invoke
{
    class Program
    {
        static void Task1()
        {
            Console.WriteLine("Task 1 starting");
            Thread.Sleep(2000);
            Console.WriteLine("Task 1 ending");
        }

        static void Task2()
        {
            Console.WriteLine("Task 2 starting");
            Thread.Sleep(1000);
```

```
        Console.WriteLine("Task 2 ending");
    }

    static void Main(string[] args)
    {
        Parallel.Invoke(()=>Task1(), ()=>Task2());
        Console.WriteLine("Finished processing. Press a key to end.");
        Console.ReadKey();
    }
  }
}
```

The `Parallel.Invoke` method can start a large number of tasks at once. You have no control over the order in which the tasks are started or which processor they are assigned to. The `Parallel.Invoke` method returns when all of the tasks have completed. You can see the output from the program here.

```
Task 1 starting
Task 2 starting
Task 2 ending
Task 1 ending
Finished processing. Press a key to end.
```

Parallel.ForEach

The `Task.Parallel` class also provides a `ForEeach` method that performs a parallel implementation of the foreach loop construction, as shown in Listing 1-2, in which the `WorkOnItem` method is called to process each of the items in a list.

LISTING 1-2 ParallelForEach in use

```
static void WorkOnItem(object item)
{
    Console.WriteLine("Started working on: " + item);
    Thread.Sleep(100);
    Console.WriteLine("Finished working on: " + item);
}

static void Main(string[] args)
{
    var items = Enumerable.Range(0, 500);
    Parallel.ForEach(items, item =>
    {
        WorkOnItem(item);
    });

    Console.WriteLine("Finished processing. Press a key to end.");
    Console.ReadKey();
}
```

The `Parallel.ForEach` method accepts two parameters. The first parameter is an `IEnumerable` collection (in this case the list `items`). The second parameter provides the action to be performed on each item in the list. You can see some of the output from this program below. Note that the tasks are not completed in the same order that they were started.

```
Finished working on: 472
Started working on: 473
Finished working on: 488
Started working on: 489
Finished working on: 457
Finished working on: 473
Finished working on: 489
Finished processing. Press a key to end.
```

Parallel.For

The Parallel.For method can be used to parallelize the execution of a for loop, which is governed by a control variable (see Listing 1-3).

LISTING 1-3 ParallelFor in use

```
static void Main(string[] args)
{
    var items = Enumerable.Range(0, 500).ToArray();

    Parallel.For(0, items.Length, i =>
    {
        WorkOnItem(items[i]);
    });
    Console.WriteLine("Finished processing. Press a key to end.");
    Console.ReadKey();
}
```

This implements a counter starting at 0 (the first parameter of the Parallel.For method), for the length of the items array (the second parameter of the Parallel.For method). The third parameter of the method is a lambda expression, which is passed a variable that provides the counter value for each iteration. You can find out more about delegate and lambda expressions in the section, "Create and Implement Callbacks," later in this chapter. The example produces the same output as Listing 1-2.

Managing Parallel.For and Parallel.Foreach

The lambda expression that executes each iteration of the loop can be provided with an additional parameter of type ParallelLoopState that allows the code being iterated to control the iteration process. The For and ForEach methods also return a value of type ParallelLoopResult that can be used to determine whether or not a parallel loop has successfully completed.

Listing 1-4 shows how these features are used. The code in the lambda expression checks the number of the work item (in the range 0 to 500). If the work item is number 200 the code calls the Stop method on the loopState value which is controlling this loop to request that the iterator stop running any more iterations. Note that this doesn't mean that the iterator will instantly stop any executing iterations. Note also that this doesn't mean that work items with a number greater than 200 will never run, because there is no guarantee that the work item with number 200 (which triggers the stop) will run before work items with higher numbers.

LISTING 1-4 Managing a parallel For loop

```
static void Main(string[] args)
{
    var items = Enumerable.Range(0, 500).ToArray();

    ParallelLoopResult result = Parallel.For(0, items.Count(), (int i, ParallelLoopState
loopState) =>
    {
        if (i == 200)
            loopState.Stop();

        WorkOnItem(items[i]);
    });

    Console.WriteLine("Completed: " + result.IsCompleted);
    Console.WriteLine("Items: " + result.LowestBreakIteration);

    Console.WriteLine("Finished processing. Press a key to end.");
    Console.ReadKey();
}
```

The iterations can be ended by calling the Stop or Break methods on the ParallelLoopState variable. Calling Stop will prevent any new iterations with an index value greater than the current index. If Stop is used to stop the loop during the 200th iteration it might be that iterations with an index lower than 200 will not be performed. If Break is used to end the loop iteration, all the iterations with an index lower than 200 are guaranteed to be completed before the loop is ended.

Parallel LINQ

Language-Integrated Query, or LINQ, is used to perform queries on items of data in C# programs. *Parallel Language-Integrated Query* (PLINQ) can be used to allow elements of a query to execute in parallel. The code in Listing 1-5 creates a tiny dataset and then performs a parallel query on the data in it.

LISTING 1-5 A parallel LINQ query

```
using System;
using System.Linq;

namespace LISTING_1_5_A_parallel_LINQ_query
{
    class Program
    {
        class Person
        {
            public string Name { get; set; }
            public string City { get; set; }
```

```
        }

    static void Main(string[] args)
    {
        Person [] people = new Person [] {
            new Person { Name = "Alan", City = "Hull" },
            new Person { Name = "Beryl", City = "Seattle" },
            new Person { Name = "Charles", City = "London" },
            new Person { Name = "David", City = "Seattle" },
            new Person { Name = "Eddy", City = "Paris" },
            new Person { Name = "Fred", City = "Berlin" },
            new Person { Name = "Gordon", City = "Hull" },
            new Person { Name = "Henry", City = "Seattle" },
            new Person { Name = "Isaac", City = "Seattle" },
            new Person { Name = "James", City = "London" }};

        var result = from person in people.AsParallel()
                    where person.City == "Seattle"
                    select person;

        foreach (var person in result)
            Console.WriteLine(person.Name);

        Console.WriteLine("Finished processing. Press a key to end.");
        Console.ReadKey();
    }
}
}
```

The AsParallel method examines the query to determine if using a parallel version would speed it up. If it is decided that executing elements of the query in parallel would improve performance, the query is broken down into a number of processes and each is run concurrently. If the AsParallel method can't decide whether parallelization would improve performance the query is not executed in parallel. If you really want to use AsParallel you should design the behavior with this in mind, otherwise performance may not be improved and it is possible that you might get the wrong outputs.

Informing parallelization

Programs can use other method calls to further inform the parallelization process, as shown in Listing 1-6.

LISTING 1-6 Informing parallelization

```
var result = from person in people.AsParallel().
                WithDegreeOfParallelism(4).
                WithExecutionMode(ParallelExecutionMode.ForceParallelism)
                where person.City == "Seattle"
                select person;
```

This call of AsParallel requests that the query be parallelized whether performance is improved or not, with the request that the query be executed on a maximum of four processors.

A non-parallel query produces output data that has the same order as the input data. A parallel query, however, may process data in a different order from the input data. In other words, the query in Listing 1-5 produces the following output.

```
Henry
Beryl
David
Issac
```

The name Henry is printed first, even though it is not the first item in the source data. If it is important that the order of the original data be preserved, the AsOrdered method can be used to request this from the query (see Listing 1-7).

LISTING 1-7 Using AsOrdered to preserve data ordering

```
var result = from person in
    people.AsParallel().AsOrdered()
                where person.City == "Seattle"
                select person;
```

The AsOrdered method doesn't prevent the parallelization of the query, instead it organizes the output so that it is in the same order as the original data. This can slow down the query.

Another issue that can arise is that the parallel nature of a query may remove ordering of a complex query. The AsSequential method can be used to identify parts of a query that must be sequentially executed (see Listing 1-8) . AsSequential executes the query in order whereas AsOrdered returns a sorted result but does not necessarily run the query in order.

LISTING 1-8 Identifying elements of a parallel query as sequential

```
var result = (from person in people.AsParallel()
                where person.City == "Seattle"
                orderby (person.Name)
                select new
                {
                    Name = person.Name
                }).AsSequential().Take(4) ;
```

The query in Listing 1-8 retrieves the names of the first four people who live in Seattle. The query requests that the result be ordered by person name, and this ordering is preserved by the use of AsSequential before the Take, which removes the four people. If the Take is executed in parallel it can disrupt the ordering of the result.

Iterating query elements using ForAll

The ForAll method can be used to iterate through all of the elements in a query. It differs from the foreach C# construction in that the iteration takes place in parallel and will start before the query is complete (see Listing 1-9).

LISTING 1-9 Using the ForAll method

```
var result = from person in
    people.AsParallel()
```

```
            where person.City == "Seattle"
            select person;
result.ForAll(person => Console.WriteLine(person.Name));
```

The parallel nature of the execution of ForAll means that the order of the printed output above will not reflect the ordering of the input data.

Exceptions in queries

It is possible that elements of a query may throw exceptions:

```
public static bool CheckCity(string name)
{
    if (name == "")
        throw new ArgumentException(name);
    return name == "Seattle";
}
```

This CheckCity method throws an exception when the city name is empty. Using this method in a PLINQ query (Listing 1-10) will cause exceptions to be thrown when empty city names are encountered in the data.

LISTING 1-10 Exceptions in PLINQ queries

```
try
{
    var result = from person in
        people.AsParallel()
                    where CheckCity(person.City)
                    select person;
    result.ForAll(person => Console.WriteLine(person.Name));
}
catch (AggregateException e)
{
    Console.WriteLine(e.InnerExceptions.Count + " exceptions.");
}
```

The code in Listing 1-10 uses the CheckCity method in a query. This will cause exceptions to be thrown when empty city names are encountered during the query. If any queries generate exceptions an AgregateException will be thrown when the query is complete. This contains a list, InnnerExceptions, of the exceptions that were thrown during the query.

Note that the outer catch of AggregateException does catch any exceptions thrown by the CheckCity method. If elements of a query can generate exceptions it is considered good programming practice to catch and deal with them as close to the source as possible.

Tasks

The parallelization tools covered in this chapter so far have operated at a very high level of abstraction. Tasks have been created, but the code hasn't interacted with them directly. Now let's consider how to create and manage tasks.

Create a task

The code in Listing 1-11 creates a task, starts it running, and then waits for the task to complete.

LISTING 1-11 Create a task

```
using System;
using System.Threading;
using System.Threading.Tasks;

namespace LISTING_1_11_Create_a_task
{
    class Program
    {
        public static void DoWork()
        {
            Console.WriteLine("Work starting");
            Thread.Sleep(2000);
            Console.WriteLine("Work finished");
        }

        static void Main(string[] args)
        {
            Task newTask = new Task(() => DoWork());
            newTask.Start();
            newTask.Wait();
        }
    }
}
```

A task can also be created and started using a single method, called Run, as shown in Listing 1-12.

LISTING 1-12 Run a task

```
static void Main(string[] args)
{
    Task newTask = Task.Run(() => DoWork());
    newTask.Wait();
}
```

Your application can use tasks in this way if you just want to start the tasks and have them run to completion.

Return a value from a task

A task can be created that will return a value, as shown in Listing 1-13, where the task returns an integer. Note that a program will wait for the task to deliver the result when the Result property of the Task instance is read.

LISTING 1-13 Task returning a value

```
using System;
using System.Threading;
using System.Threading.Tasks;
```

```
namespace LISTING_1_13_Task_returning_a_value
{
    class Program
    {
        public static int CalculateResult()
        {
            Console.WriteLine("Work starting");
            Thread.Sleep(2000);
            Console.WriteLine("Work finished");
            return 99;
        }
        static void Main(string[] args)
        {
            Task<int> task = Task.Run(() =>
            {
                return CalculateResult();
            });

            Console.WriteLine(task.Result);

            Console.WriteLine("Finished processing. Press a key to end.");
            Console.ReadKey();
        }
    }
}
```

The Task.Run method uses the TaskFactory.StartNew method to create and start the task, using the default task scheduler that uses the .NET framework thread pool. The Task class exposes a Factory property that refers to the default task scheduler.

You can create your own task scheduler or run a task scheduler in the synchronization context of another processor. You can also create your own TaskFactory if you want to create a number of tasks with the same configuration. The Run method, however, is the preferred way to create a simple task, particularly if you want to use the task with *async* and *await* (covered later in this chapter).

Wait for tasks to complete

The Task.Waitall method can be used to pause a program until a number of tasks have completed, as shown in Listing 1-14. This listing also illustrates an additional issue with the use of loop control variables when they are passed into lambda expressions. The loop counter is copied into a local variable called taskNum in the loop that creates each task. If the variable i was used directly in the lambda expression, all of the tasks would have number 10, which is the value of the limit of the loop.

LISTING 1-14 Task waitall

```
using System;
using System.Threading;
using System.Threading.Tasks;
```

```
namespace LISTING_1_14_Task_waitall
{
    class Program
    {
        public static void DoWork(int i)
        {
            Console.WriteLine("Task {0} starting",i );
            Thread.Sleep(2000);
            Console.WriteLine("Task {0} finished", i);
        }

        static void Main(string[] args)
        {
            Task [] Tasks = new Task[10];

            for (int i = 0; i < 10; i++)
            {
                int taskNum = i;  // make a local copy of the loop counter so that the
                                  // correct task number is passed into the
                                  //       lambda expression
                Tasks[i] = Task.Run( () => DoWork(taskNum) ) ;
            }
            Task.WaitAll(Tasks);

            Console.WriteLine("Finished processing. Press a key to end.");
            Console.ReadKey();
        }
    }
}
```

Another use for Task.Waitall is to provide a place where a program can catch any exceptions that may be thrown by tasks. Note that, as with exceptions generated by PLINQ queries, the exceptions are aggregated.

You can use Task.WaitAny to make a program pause until any one of a number of concurrent tasks completes. If you think of each task as a horse in a race; WaitAll will pause until all the horses have finished running, whereas WaitAny will pause until the first horse has finished running. In the same way that horses still run after the winner has finished, some tasks will continue to run after a WaitAny call has returned.

Continuation Tasks

A continuation task can be nominated to start when an existing task (the *antecedent* task) finishes. If the antecedent task produces a result, it can be supplied as an input to the continuation task. Continuation tasks can be used to create a "pipeline" of operations, with each successive stage starting when the preceding one ends.

Create a continuation task

Listing 1-15 shows how a continuation task can be created from a task. A Task object exposes a ContinueWith method that can be used to specify a continuation task.

The lambda expression that executes the continuation task is provided with a reference to the antecedent task, which it can use to determine if the antecedent completed successfully. You can add continuation tasks to tasks that deliver a result, in which case the continuation task can use the Result property of the antecedent task to obtain its input data.

LISTING 1-15 Continuation tasks

```
using System;
using System.Threading;
using System.Threading.Tasks;

namespace LISTING_1_15_Continuation_tasks
{
    class Program
    {
        public static void HelloTask()
        {
            Thread.Sleep(1000);
            Console.WriteLine("Hello");
        }

        public static void WorldTask()
        {
            Thread.Sleep(1000);
            Console.WriteLine("World");
        }

        static void Main(string[] args)
        {
            Task task = Task.Run(() => HelloTask());
            task.ContinueWith( (prevTask) => WorldTask());

            Console.WriteLine("Finished processing. Press a key to end.");
            Console.ReadKey();
        }
    }
}
```

The ContinueWith method has an overload that you can use to specify when a given continuation task can run. This version accepts a parameter of type TaskContinuationOptions. Listing 1-16 shows how these can be used.

LISTING 1-16 Continuation options

```
Task task = Task.Run(() => HelloTask());

task.ContinueWith((prevTask) => WorldTask(), TaskContinuationOptions.
                                OnlyOnRanToCompletion);
task.ContinueWith((prevTask) => ExceptionTask(), TaskContinuationOptions.OnlyOnFaulted);
```

The method WorldTask (the method to be performed by the continuation task) is now only called if the method HelloTask (the method run by the first task) completes successfully. If HelloTask throws an exception, a task will be started that runs the method ExceptionTask.

Child tasks

Code running inside a *parent* Task can create other tasks, but these "child" tasks will execute independently of the parent in which they were created. Such tasks are called *detached child tasks* or *detached nested tasks*. A parent task can create child tasks with a task creation option that specifies that the child task is attached to the parent. The parent class will *not* complete until all of the *attached child tasks* have completed.

Listing 1-17 shows a parent Task creating 10 attached child tasks. The tasks are created by calling the StartNew method on the default Task Factory provided by the Task class. This overload of the StartNew method accepts three parameters: the lambda expression giving the behavior of the task, a state object that is passed into the task when it is started, and a TaskCreationOption value that requests that the new task should be a child task.

LISTING 1-17 Attached child tasks

```
using System;
using System.Threading;
using System.Threading.Tasks;

namespace LISTING_1_17_Attached_child_tasks
{
    class Program
    {
        public static void DoChild(object state)
        {
            Console.WriteLine("Child {0} starting", state);
            Thread.Sleep(2000);
            Console.WriteLine("Child {0} finished", state);
        }

        static void Main(string[] args)
        {
            var parent = Task.Factory.StartNew(() => {
                Console.WriteLine("Parent starts");
                for (int i = 0; i < 10; i++)
                {
                    int taskNo = i;
                    Task.Factory.StartNew(
                        (x) => DoChild(x), // lambda expression
                            taskNo, // state object
                            TaskCreationOptions.AttachedToParent);
                }
            });

            parent.Wait(); // will wait for all the attached children to complete

            Console.WriteLine("Parent finished. Press a key to end.");
            Console.ReadKey();
        }
    }
}
```

You can create a task without any attached child tasks by specifying the `TaskCreationOptions.DenyChildAttach` option when you create the task. Children of such a task will always be created as detached child tasks. Note that tasks created using the `Task.Run` method have the `TaskCreationOptions.DenyChildAttach` option set, and therefore can't have attached child tasks.

Threads and ThreadPool

Threads are a lower level of abstraction than tasks. A `Task` object represents an item of work to be performed, whereas a `Thread` object represents a process running within the operating system.

Threads and Tasks

When creating your first threads you will notice that the code looks rather similar to that used to create your first tasks, There are, however, some important differences between the two that you need to be aware of:

- Threads are created as *foreground* processes (although they can be set to run in the background). The operating system will run a foreground process to completion, which means that an application will not terminate while it contains an active foreground thread. A foreground process that contains an infinite loop will execute forever, or until it throws an uncaught exception or the operating system terminates it. Tasks are created as *background* processes. This means that tasks can be terminated before they complete if all the foreground threads in an application complete.

- Threads have a *priority* property that can be changed during the lifetime of the thread. It is not possible to set the priority of a task. This gives a thread a higher priority request so a greater portion of available processor time is allocated.

- A thread cannot deliver a result to another thread. Threads must communicate by using shared variables, which can introduce synchronization issues.

- It is not possible to create a continuation on a thread. Instead, threads provide a method called a join, which allows one thread to pause until another completes.

- It is not possible to aggregate exceptions over a number of threads. An exception thrown inside a thread must be caught and dealt with by the code in that thread. Tasks provide exception aggregation, but threads don't.

Create a thread

The `Thread` class is located in the `System.Threading` namespace. When you create a `Thread` you can pass the constructor the name of the method the thread will run. Once the thread has been created, you can call the `Start` method on the thread to start it running. Listing 1-18 shows how this is done.

LISTING 1-18 Creating threads

```
using System;
using System.Threading;

namespace LISTING_1_18_Creating_threads
{
    class Program
    {
        static void ThreadHello()
        {
            Console.WriteLine("Hello from the thread");
            Thread.Sleep(2000);
        }

        static void Main(string[] args)
        {
            Thread thread = new Thread(ThreadHello);
            thread.Start();
        }
    }
}
```

Threads and ThreadStart

Note that earlier versions of .NET required the creation of a `ThreadStart` delegate to specify the method to be executed by the thread. Listing 1-19 shows how this is done. It's not currently necessary, but you may see it used in older programs.

LISTING 1-19 Using ThreadStart

```
static void Main(string[] args)
{
    ThreadStart ts = new ThreadStart(ThreadHello);
    Thread thread = new Thread(ts);
    thread.Start();
}
```

The `ThreadStart` delegate is no longer required.

Threads and lambda expressions

It is possible to start a thread using a lambda expression to specify the action of the thread, as shown in Listing 1-20.

LISTING 1-20 Threads and lambda expressions

```
static void Main(string[] args)
{
    Thread thread = new Thread(() =>
    {
        Console.WriteLine("Hello from the thread");
        Thread.Sleep(1000);
    });
```

```
        thread.Start();
        Console.WriteLine("Press a key to end.");
        Console.ReadKey();
    }
```

When this program runs you might be surprised to see the output below:

```
Press a key to end.
Hello from the thread
```

It looks like the program is printing things in the wrong order. However, if you think about it, the ordering makes sense. The thread running inside the Main method calls Start to start the new thread. However, before the new thread has started running, the thread running inside the Main method then reaches the WriteLine method and displays "Press any key to end." Then the background thread gets control and prints, "Hello from the thread."

Passing data into a thread

A program can pass data into a thread when it is created by using the ParameterizedThread-Start delegate. This specifies the thread method as one that accepts a single object parameter. The object to be passed into the thread is then placed in the Start method, as shown in Listing 1-21.

LISTING 1-21 ParameterizedThreadStart

```
using System;
using System.Threading;

namespace LISTING_1_21_ParameterizedThreadStart
{
    class Program
    {
        static void WorkOnData(object data)
        {
            Console.WriteLine("Working on: {0}", data);
            Thread.Sleep(1000);
        }
        static void Main(string[] args)
        {
            ParameterizedThreadStart ps = new ParameterizedThreadStart(WorkOnData);
            Thread thread = new Thread(ps);
            thread.Start(99);
        }
    }
}
```

Another way to pass data into a thread is to specify the behavior of the thread as a lambda expression that accepts a parameter. The parameter to the lambda expression is the data to be passed into the thread. Listing 1-22 shows how this is done; the parameter is given the name data in the lamba expression and the value 99 is passed into the lambda expression via the Start method.

LISTING 1-22 thread lambda parameters

```
static void Main(string[] args)
{
    Thread thread = new Thread((data) =>
    {
        WorkOnData(data);
    });
    thread.Start(99);
}
```

Note that the data to be passed into the thread is always passed as an object reference. This means that there is no way to be sure at compile time that thread initialization is being performed with a particular type of data.

Abort a thread

A Thread object exposes an Abort method, which can be called on the thread to abort it. The thread is terminated instantly. Listing 1-23 shows how one thread can abort another.

LISTING 1-23 Aborting a thread

```
using System;
using System.Threading;

namespace LISTING_1_23_aborting_a_thread
{
    class Program
    {
        static void Main(string[] args)
        {
            Thread tickThread = new Thread(() =>
            {
                while (true)
                {
                    Console.WriteLine("Tick");
                    Thread.Sleep(1000);
                }
            });

            tickThread.Start();

            Console.WriteLine("Press a key to stop the clock");
            Console.ReadKey();
            tickThread.Abort();
            Console.WriteLine("Press a key to exit");
            Console.ReadKey();
        }
    }
}
```

When a thread is aborted it is instantly stopped. This might mean that it leaves the program in an ambiguous state, with files open and resources assigned. A better way to abort a thread is to use a shared flag variable. Listing 1-24 shows how to do this. The variable tickRunning is used to control the loop in tickThread. When tickRunning is set to false the thread ends.

LISTING 1-24 A shared flag variable

```
using System;
using System.Threading;

namespace LISTING_1_24_shared_flag_variable
{
    class Program
    {
        static bool tickRunning;  // flag variable

        static void Main(string[] args)
        {
            tickRunning = true;

            Thread tickThread = new Thread(() =>
            {
                while (tickRunning)
                {
                    Console.WriteLine("Tick");
                    Thread.Sleep(1000);
                }
            });

            tickThread.Start();

            Console.WriteLine("Press a key to stop the clock");
            Console.ReadKey();
            tickRunning = false;
            Console.WriteLine("Press a key to exit");
            Console.ReadKey();
        }
    }
}
```

Thread Synchronization using join

The join method allows two threads to synchronize. When a thread calls the join method on another thread, the caller of join is held until the other thread completes. Listing 1-25 shows how this works.

LISTING 1-25 Using join

```
Thread threadToWaitFor = new Thread(() =>
{
    Console.WriteLine("Thread starting");
    Thread.Sleep(2000);
    Console.WriteLine("Thread done");
});

threadToWaitFor.Start();
Console.WriteLine("Joining thread");
threadToWaitFor.Join();
Console.WriteLine("Press a key to exit");
Console.ReadKey();
```

Thread data storage and ThreadLocal

Listing 1-24 earlier, shows how threads can "share" variables, which are declared in the program that the thread is running within. In this program two threads made use of the same variable, threadRunning. One thread read from the variable, and another thread wrote into it.

If you want each thread to have its own copy of a particular variable, you can use the ThreadStatic attribute to specify that the given variable should be created for each thread. The best way to understand this is to consider that if the threadRunning variable in Listing 1-24 was made ThreadStatic it would not stop a thread if threadRunning was made false, because there would be a copy of threadRunning for each thread. Changes to the variable in one thread would not affect the value in another.

If your program needs to initialize the local data for each thread you can use the ThreadLocal<t> class. When an instance of ThreadLocal is created it is given a delegate to the code that will initialize attributes of threads. Listing 1-26 shows how you can use it. The RandomGenerator member of the class returns a random number generator that is to be used by a thread to produce random behaviors. You want each thread to have the same "random" behavior, so the RandomGenerator produces a new Random number generator with the same seed each time it is called.

LISTING 1-26 ThreadLocal

```
using System;
using System.Threading;

namespace LISTING_1_27_ThreadLocal
{
    class Program
    {
        public static ThreadLocal<Random> RandomGenerator =
            new ThreadLocal<Random>(() =>
            {
                return new Random(2);
            });

        static void Main(string[] args)
        {
            Thread t1 = new Thread(() =>
            {
                for (int i = 0; i < 5; i++)
                {
                    Console.WriteLine("t1: {0}", RandomGenerator.Value.Next(10));
                    Thread.Sleep(500);
                }
            });

            Thread t2 = new Thread(() =>
            {
                for (int i = 0; i < 5; i++)
                {
                    Console.WriteLine("t2: {0}", RandomGenerator.Value.Next(10));
```

```
                Thread.Sleep(500);
            }
        });
        t1.Start();
        t2.Start();
        Console.ReadKey();
    }
  }
}
```

When different threads use the value of their `RandomGenerator` they will all produce the same sequence of random numbers. This is the output from the program:

```
t2: 7
t1: 7
t2: 4
t1: 4
t1: 1
t2: 1
t2: 9
t1: 9
t1: 1
t2: 1
```

Thread execution context

A `Thread` instance exposes a range of context information, and some items can be read and others read and set. The information available includes the name of the thread (if any) priority of the thread, whether it is foreground or background, the threads *culture* (this contains culture specific information in a value of type *CultureInfo*) and the security context of the thread. The Thread.CurentThread property can be used by a thread to discover this information about itself. Listing 1-27 shows how the information can be displayed.

LISTING 1-27 Thread context

```
using System;
using System.Threading;

namespace LISTING_1_27_Thread_context
{
    class Program
    {
        static void DisplayThread(Thread t)
        {
            Console.WriteLine("Name: {0}", t.Name);
            Console.WriteLine("Culture: {0}", t.CurrentCulture);
            Console.WriteLine("Priority: {0}", t.Priority);
            Console.WriteLine("Context: {0}", t.ExecutionContext);
            Console.WriteLine("IsBackground?: {0}", t.IsBackground);
            Console.WriteLine("IsPool?: {0}", t.IsThreadPoolThread);

        }
        static void Main(string[] args)
```

```
        {
            Thread.CurrentThread.Name = "Main method";
            DisplayThread(Thread.CurrentThread);

        }
    }
}
```

Thread pools

Threads, like everything else in C#, are managed as objects. If an application creates a large number of threads, each of these will require an object to be created and then destroyed when the thread completes. A *thread pool* stores a collection of reusable thread objects. Rather than creating a new Thread instance, an application can instead request that a process execute on a thread from the thread pool. When the thread completes, the thread is returned to the pool for use by another process. Listing 1-28 shows how this works. The ThreadPool provides a method QueueUserWorkItem, which allocates a thread to run the supplied item of work.

The item of work is supplied as a WaitCallback delegate. There are two versions of this delegate. The version used in Listing 1-28 accepts a state object that can be used to provide state information to the thread to be started. The other version of WaitCallback does not accept state information.

LISTING 1-28 Thread pool

```
using System;
using System.Threading;

namespace LISTING_1_28_Thread_pool
{
    class Program
    {
        static void DoWork(object state)
        {
            Console.WriteLine("Doing work: {0}", state);
            Thread.Sleep(500);
            Console.WriteLine("Work finished: {0}", state);
        }

        static void Main(string[] args)
        {
            for (int i = 0; i < 50; i++)
            {
                int stateNumber = i;
                ThreadPool.QueueUserWorkItem(state => DoWork(stateNumber));
            }
            Console.ReadKey();
        }
    }
}
```

If you run the sample program in Listing 1-28 you discover that not all of the threads are started at the same time. The ThreadPool restricts the number of active threads and maintains a queue of threads waiting to execute. A program that creates a large number of individual threads can easily overwhelm a device. However, this does not happen if a `ThreadPool` is used. The extra threads are placed in the queue. Note that there are some situations when using the `ThreadPool` is not a good idea:

- If you create a large number of threads that may be idle for a very long time, this may block the `ThreadPool`, because the `ThreadPool` only contains a finite number of threads.

- You cannot manage the priority of threads in the `ThreadPool`.

- Threads in the `ThreadPool` have background priority. You cannot obtain a thread with foreground priority from the `ThreadPool`.

- Local state variables are not cleared when a ThreadPool thread is reused. They therefore should not be used.

Tasks and the User Interface

A Universal Application (Windows Store) Windows Presentation Foundation (WPF) application or a WinForms application can be regarded as having a single thread of execution that is dealing with the user interface. At any given instant this thread will be performing a particular action. In other words, when code in an event handler is running in response to a particular event, such as a button press, it is not possible for code in any other part of the user interface to execute. You sometimes see this behavior in badly written applications, where the user interface of the application becomes unresponsive while an action is carried out.

Figure 1-1 shows a simple Universal Windows application that calculates the average of a very large number of values.

FIGURE 1-1 The Random Averages application

The user can investigate the behavior of the C# random number generator over a very large number of operations. The number of averages to be generated is entered and when the Start button is pressed the program generates that number of random values and then prints out their average. Listing 1-29 shows the code for this application.

LISTING 1-29 **LISTING 1-29** Blocking the user interface

```
private double computeAverages(long noOfValues)
{
    double total = 0;
    Random rand = new Random();

    for (long values = 0; values < noOfValues; values++)
    {
        total = total + rand.NextDouble();
    }

    return total / noOfValues;
}

private void StartButton_Click(object sender, RoutedEventArgs e)
{
    long noOfValues = long.Parse(NumberOfValuesTextBox.Text);
    ResultTextBlock.Text = "Result: " + computeAverages(noOfValues);
}
```

Entering a very large number of averages causes the entire user interface to lock up while the program runs the event handler behind the "Start" button. The button appears to be "stuck down" for the time it takes the event handler to run and interactions with the user interface, for exampling resizing the application screen, are not possible until the button "pops back up" and the answer is displayed.

Tasks provide a means to solve this problem. Rather than performing an action directly, the event handler can instead start a task to perform the action in the background. The event handler then returns and the user interface can respond to other events. Listing 1-30 shows how a task can be used to perform the calculation in the background.

The idea behind this code is that the action of the button press starts a task running that completes in the background. This means that the button does not appear to "stick down" and lock up the user interface.

LISTING 1-30 Using a task

```
private void StartButton_Click(object sender, RoutedEventArgs e)
{
    long noOfValues = long.Parse(NumberOfValuesTextBox.Text);
    Task.Run( () =>
    {
        ResultTextBlock.Text = "Result: " + computeAverages(noOfValues);
    }
    );
}
```

This code is correct from a task management point of view, but it will fail when it runs. This is because interaction with display components is strictly managed by the process that generates the display. A background task cannot simply set the properties of a display element; instead it must follow a particular protocol to achieve the required update. Figure 1-2 shows what happens when the task attempts to display the result of the calculation.

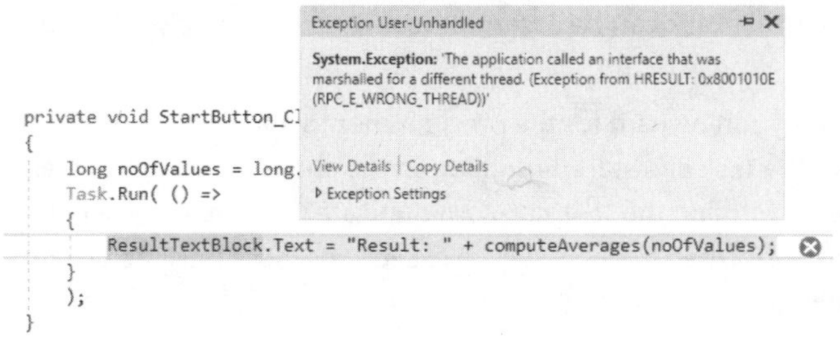

```
private void StartButton_Cl
{
    long noOfValues = long.
    Task.Run( () =>
    {
        ResultTextBlock.Text = "Result: " + computeAverages(noOfValues);  ⊗
    }
    );
}
```

Exception User-Unhandled

System.Exception: 'The application called an interface that was marshalled for a different thread. (Exception from HRESULT: 0x8001010E (RPC_E_WRONG_THREAD))'

View Details | Copy Details
▷ Exception Settings

FIGURE 1-2 Exception thrown by a display thread error

Listing 1-31 shows how the UI can be updated from a background task.

LISTING 1-31 Updating the UI

```
private void StartButton_Click(object sender, RoutedEventArgs e)
{
    long noOfValues = long.Parse(NumberOfValuesTextBox.Text);
    Task.Run(() =>
    {
        double result = computeAverages(noOfValues);

        ResultTextBlock.Dispatcher.RunAsync(CoreDispatcherPriority.Normal, () =>
        {
            ResultTextBlock.Text = "Result: " + result.ToString();
        });
    });
}
```

Each component on a display has a `Dispatcher` property that can be used to run tasks in the context of the display. The `RunAsync` method is given a priority level for the task, followed by the action that is to be performed on the thread. In the case of the code in Listing 1-31, the action to be performed is displaying the result.

Note that the code in Listing 1-31 does not show good programming practice. The `RunAsync` method is designed to be called asynchronously (you will discover what this means in the next section). The code in Listing 1-31 does not do this, which will result in compiler warnings being produced when you build the example. The best way to display a result from a task is to make use of async and `await`, as you will see in the next section.

Using async and await

A `Task` is a very useful way to get things done. It provides a means by which a program can partition and dispatch items of work. Tasks are particularly useful if a program has something else it can do while a given task is being performed. For example, a user interface can continue to respond to actions from the user while a long-running background task completes, or a web server can create tasks to assemble responses to web page requests. Tasks are particularly useful when performing actions that may take some time to complete, for example with input/output or network requests. If one task is waiting for a file to be loaded from a disk, another task can be assembling a message to be sent via the network.

A difficulty with tasks is that they can be hard for the programmer to manage. The application must contain code to create the Task and start it running, so the application must contain some means by which the code performing the Task can communicate that it has finished. If any of the actions that are being performed might generate exceptions these must be caught and passed back to the application.

The async and await keywords allow programmers to write code elements that execute asynchronously. The async keyword is used to flag a method as "asynchronous." An asynchronous method must contain one or more actions that are "awaited."

An action can be awaited if it returns either a Task (I just want do something asynchronously) or a Task<t> (I want to do something asynchronously that returns a result of a particular type).

The asyncComputeAverages method next returns a Task rather than a result. The task returns a double value, which is the computed average. You can regard the method as a "wrapper" around the original method, which creates a task that runs the method and delivers the result.

```
private Task<double> asyncComputeAverages(long noOfValues)
{
    return Task<double>.Run(() =>
    {
        return computeAverages(noOfValues);
    });
}
```

The StartButton_Click method in Listing 1-32 below uses the asyncComputeAverages method to calculate the average value and then display the result in the ResultTextBlock. When the user presses the button, the event handler instantly returns. Then, after a short interval, the ResultTextBlock displays the average value.

LISTING 1-32 Using async

```
private async void StartButton_Click(object sender, RoutedEventArgs e)
{
    long noOfValues = long.Parse(NumberOfValuesTextBox.Text);

    ResultTextBlock.Text = "Calculating";

    double result = await (asyncComputeAverages(noOfValues));

    ResultTextBlock.Text = "Result: " + result.ToString();
}
```

So, how does this work? The StartButton_Click event handler method is marked as async. This tells the compiler to treat this method as special. It means that the method will contain one or more uses of the await keyword. The await keyword represents "a statement of intent" to perform an action. The keyword precedes a call of a method that will return the task to be performed. The compiler will generate code that will cause the `async` method to return to the caller at the point the `await` is reached. It will then go on to generate code that will perform the awaited action asynchronously and then continue with the body of the `async` method.

In the case of the `Button_Click` method in Listing 1-32, this means that the result is displayed upon completion of the task returned by `asyncComputeAverages`. The code does not block the user interface when it runs, the display is updated on the correct thread (the original event handler), and it is very simple to use.

Exceptions and await/async

Figure 1-3 shows a simple Universal Windows application that can be used to view the text in a web page.

FIGURE 1-3 The Webpage Viewer application

The application uses an asynchronous method from the .NET library to fetch a web page from a given URL:

```
private async Task<string> FetchWebPage(string url)
{
    HttpClient httpClient = new HttpClient();
    return await httpClient.GetStringAsync(url);
}
```

The act of loading a web page may fail because the server is offline or the URL is incorrect. The `FetchWebPage` method will throw an exception in this situation. Listing 1-33 shows how this is used. The `await` is now enclosed in a try – catch construction. If an exception is thrown during the await, it can be caught and dealt with. In the case of the code in Listing 1-33, the StatusTextBlock is used to display the message from the exception.

LISTING 1-33 Exceptions and async

```
private async void Button_Click(object sender, RoutedEventArgs e)
{
    try
    {
        ResultTextBlock.Text = await FetchWebPage(URLTextBox.Text);
        StatusTextBlock.Text = "Page Loaded";
    }
    catch (Exception ex)
    {
        StatusTextBlock.Text = ex.Message;
    }
}
```

It is very important to note that exceptions can only be caught in this way because the FetchWebPage method returns a result; the text of the web page. It is possible to create an async method of type void that does not return a value. These are, however, to be avoided as there is no way of catching any exceptions that they generate. The only async void methods that a program should contain are the event handlers themselves, such as the Button_Click method in Listing 1-33. Even a method that just performs an action should return a status value so that exceptions can be caught and dealt with.

Awaiting parallel tasks

An async method can contain a number of awaited actions. These will be completed in sequence. In other words, if you want to create an "awaitable" task that returns when a number of parallel tasks have completed you can use the Task.WhenAll method to create a task that completes when a given lists of tasks have been completed. Listing 1-34 shows how this works. The task FetchWebPages returns uses the FetchWebPage method from Listing 1-32 to generate a list of strings containing the text from a given list of urls. The Task.WhenAll method is given a list of tasks and returns a collection which contains their results when they have completed.

LISTING 1-34 Awaiting parallel tasks

```
static async Task<IEnumerable<string>> FetchWebPages(string [] urls)
{
    var tasks = new List<Task<String>>();

    foreach (string url in urls)
    {
        tasks.Add(FetchWebPage(url));
    }

    return await Task.WhenAll(tasks);
}
```

Note that Listing 1-34 shows how `WhenAll` is used, but it doesn't necessarily show good programming practice. The order of the items in the returned collection may not match the order of the submitted site names and there is no aggregation of any exceptions thrown by the calls to `FetchWebPage`. There is also a `WhenAny` method that will return when any one of the given tasks completes. This works in the same way as the WaitAny method that you saw earlier.

Using concurrent collections

The phrase *thread safe* describes code elements that work correctly when used from multiple processes (tasks) at the same time. The standard .NET collections (including `List`, `Queue` and `Dictionary`) are not thread safe. The .NET libraries provide thread safe (concurrent) collection classes that you can use when creating multi-tasking applications:

```
BlockingCollection<T>
ConcurrentQueue<T>
ConcurrentStack<T>
ConcurrentBag<T>
ConcurrentDictionary<TKey, TValue>
```

BlockingCollection<T>

From a design perspective, it is best to view a task in a multi-threaded application as either a *producer* or a *consumer* of data. A task that both produces and consumes data is vulnerable to "deadly embrace" situations. If task A is waiting for something produced by task B, and task B is waiting for something produced by Task A, and neither task can run.

The `BlockingCollection<T>` class is designed to be used in situations where you have some tasks producing data and other tasks consuming data. It provides a thread safe means of adding and removing items to a data store. It is called a *blocking* collection because a `Take` action will block a task if there are no items to be taken. A developer can set an upper limit for the size of the collection. Attempts to `Add` items to a full collection are also blocked.

Listing 1-35 shows how a `BlockingCollection` is used. The program creates a thread that attempts to add 10 items to a `BlockingCollection`, which has been created to hold five items. After adding the 5th item this thread is blocked. The program also creates a thread that takes items out of the collection. As soon as the read thread starts running, and takes some items out of the collection, the writing thread can continue.

LISTING 1-35 Using BlockingCollection

```
using System;
using System.Collections.Concurrent;
using System.Threading.Tasks;

namespace LISTING_1_35_Using_BlockingCollection
{
    class Program
    {
        static void Main(string[] args)
```

```
    {
        // Blocking collection that can hold 5 items
        BlockingCollection<int> data = new BlockingCollection<int>(5);

        Task.Run(() =>
        {
            // attempt to add 10 items to the collection - blocks after 5th
            for(int i=0;i<11;i++)
            {
                data.Add(i);
                Console.WriteLine("Data {0} added sucessfully.", i);
            }
            // indicate we have no more to add
            data.CompleteAdding();
        });

        Console.ReadKey();
        Console.WriteLine("Reading collection");

        Task.Run(() =>
        {
            while (!data.IsCompleted)
            {
                try
                {
                    int v = data.Take();
                    Console.WriteLine("Data {0} taken sucessfully.", v);
                }
                catch (InvalidOperationException) { }
            }
        });

        Console.ReadKey();
    }
  }
}
```

The output from this program looks like this:

```
Data 0 added successfully.
Data 1 added successfully.
Data 2 added successfully.
Data 3 added successfully.
Data 4 added successfully.
 Reading collection
Data 0 taken successfully.
Data 1 taken successfully.
Data 2 taken successfully.
Data 3 taken successfully.
Data 4 taken successfully.
Data 5 taken successfully.
Data 5 added successfully.
Data 6 added successfully.
Data 7 added successfully.
Data 8 added successfully.
```

```
Data 9 added successfully.
Data 6 taken successfully.
Data 7 taken successfully.
Data 8 taken successfully.
Data 9 taken successfully.
```

The adding task calls the CompleteAdding on the collection when it has added the last item. This prevents any more items from being added to the collection. The task taking from the collection uses the IsCompleted property of the collection to determine when to stop taking items from it. The IsCompleted property returns true when the collection is empty and CompleteAdding has been called. Note that the Take operation is performed inside try-catch construction. The Take method can throw an exception if the following sequence occurs:

1. The taking task checks the IsCompleted flag and finds that it is false.

2. The adding task (which is running at the same time as the taking task) then calls the CompleteAdding method on the collection.

3. The taking task then tries to perform a Take from a collection which has been marked as complete.

Note that this does not indicate a problem with the way that the BlockingCollection works; it instead shows how you need to be careful when using any kind of data store from multiple tasks. The BlockingCollection class provides the methods TryAdd and TryTake that can be used to attempt an action. Each returns true if the action succeeded. They can be used with timeout values and cancellation tokens.

The BlockingCollection class can act as a wrapper around other concurrent collection classes, including ConcurrentQueue, ConcurrentStack, and ConcurrentBag. Listing 1-36 shows how this is done. The collection class to be used is given as the first parameter of the BlockingCollection constructor.

LISTING 1-36 Block ConcurrentStack

```
BlockingCollection<int> data = new BlockingCollection<int>(new ConcurrentStack<int>(), 5);
```

If you execute this example you will see that items are added and taken from the stack on a "last in–first out" basis. If you don't provide a collection class the BlockingCollection class uses a ConcurrentQueue, which operates on a "first in-first out" basis. The ConcurrentBag class stores items in an unordered collection.

Concurrent Queue

The ConcurrentQueue class provides support for concurrent queues. The Enqueue method adds items into the queue and the TryDequeue method removes them. Note that while the Enqueue method is guaranteed to work (queues can be of infinite length) the TryDequeue method will return false if the dequeue fails. A third method, TryPeek, allows a program to inspect the element at the start of the queue without removing it. Note that even if the TryPeek method returns an item, a subsequent call of the TryDequeue method in the same task removing that item from the queue would fail if the item is removed by another task. Listing 1-37 shows how a concurrent queue is used. It places two strings on the queue, peeks the top of the queue, and then removes one item from it.

It's possible for a task to enumerate a concurrent queue (a program can use the foreach construction to work through each item in the queue). At the start of the enumeration a concurrent queue will provide a snapshot of the queue contents.

LISTING 1-37 Concurrent queue

```
ConcurrentQueue<string> queue = new ConcurrentQueue<string>();
queue.Enqueue("Rob");
queue.Enqueue("Miles");
string str;
if (queue.TryPeek(out str))
    Console.WriteLine("Peek: {0}", str);
if (queue.TryDequeue(out str))
    Console.WriteLine("Dequeue: {0}", str);
```

When this program runs it prints out "Rob," because that is the item at the start of the queue; and a queue is a first in–first out data store.

Concurrent Stack

The ConcurrentStack class provides support for concurrent stacks. The Push method adds items onto the stack and the TryPop method removes them. There are also methods, PushRange and TryPopRange, which can be used to push or pop a number of items. Listing 1-38 shows how a ConcurrentStack is used.

LISTING 1-38 A concurrent stack

```
ConcurrentStack<string> stack = new ConcurrentStack<string>();
stack.Push("Rob");
stack.Push("Miles");
string str;
if (stack.TryPeek(out str))
    Console.WriteLine("Peek: {0}", str);
if (stack.TryPop(out str))
    Console.WriteLine("Pop: {0}", str);
Console.ReadKey();
```

When this program runs it prints out "Miles," because it is at the top of the stack, and the stack is a last in–first out data store.

ConcurrentBag

You can use a ConcurrentBag to store items when the order in which they are added or removed isn't important. The Add items puts things into the bag, and the TryTake method removes them. There is also a TryPeek method, but this is less useful in a ConcurrentBag because it is possible that a following TryTake method returns a different item from the bag. Listing 1-39 shows how a ConcurrentBag is used.

LISTING 1-39 A concurrent bag

```
ConcurrentBag<string> bag = new ConcurrentBag<string>();
bag.Add("Rob");
bag.Add("Miles");
bag.Add("Hull");
string str;
if (bag.TryPeek(out str))
    Console.WriteLine("Peek: {0}", str);
if (bag.TryTake(out str))
    Console.WriteLine("Take: {0}", str);
```

When I ran this program in Listing 1-39 it printed the word "Hull," but there is no guarantee that it will do this when you run it, especially if multiple tasks are using the ConcurrentBag.

ConcurrentDictionary

A dictionary provides a data store indexed by a key. A ConcurrentDictionary can be used by multiple concurrent tasks. Actions on the dictionary are performed in an *atomic* manner. In other words, an update action on an item in the dictionary cannot be interrupted by an action from another task. A ConcurrentDictionary provides some additional methods that are required when a dictionary is shared between multiple tasks. Listing 1-40 shows how these are used.

LISTING 1-40 Concurrent dictionary

```
ConcurrentDictionary<string, int> ages = new ConcurrentDictionary<string, int>();
if (ages.TryAdd("Rob", 21))
    Console.WriteLine("Rob added successfully.");
Console.WriteLine("Rob's age: {0}", ages["Rob"]);
// Set Rob's age to 22 if it is 21
if (ages.TryUpdate("Rob", 22, 21))
    Console.WriteLine("Age updated successfully");
Console.WriteLine("Rob's new age: {0}", ages["Rob"]);
// Increment Rob's age atomically using factory method
Console.WriteLine("Rob's age updated to: {0}",
    ages.AddOrUpdate("Rob", 1, (name,age) => age = age+1));
Console.WriteLine("Rob's new age: {0}", ages["Rob"]);
```

The TryAdd method tries to add a new item. If the item already exists, the TryAdd method returns false. The TryUpdate method is supplied with the key that identifies the item to be updated and two values. The first value provides a new value to be stored in the item, and the second value provides the value that is to be overwritten. In the example above, the age of the item indexed by "Rob" will only be updated to 22 if the existing value is 21. This allows a program to only update an item if it is at an expected value.

You might wonder when this is useful. Consider a situation where two processes decide that the age value of a person in the dictionary needs to be increased from 21 to 22. If both processes went ahead and increased the age value that would mean that the age would end up being 23, which is wrong. Instead, each process could use the TryUpdate method to try and increase the age. One process will succeed and change the age value to 22. The other process will fail, because it is not updating an age which is 21.

The AddOrUpdate method allows you to provide a behavior that will perform the update of a given item or add a new item if it does not already exist. In the case of the example above, the age of item "Rob" will not be set to 1 by the call of AddOrUpdate, because the item already exists. Instead, the action is performed, which increases the age of item "Rob" by 1. This action can be regarded as atomic, in that no other actions will be performed on this item until the update behavior has completed.

Skill 1.2: Manage multithreading

You have seen how we can create threads and tasks and use concurrent collections to safely share data between them. Now it is time to dig a little deeper into tasks and processes and discover how to manage them.

When running some of the applications in the previous section we noticed that their behavior was not predictable. The order in which actions were performed was different each time a program ran. For example, the output from Listing 1-2 "ParallelForEach in use" is different each time you run it. This is because the operating system decides when a thread runs and the decisions are made based on the workload on the computer. If the machine suddenly gets very busy—perhaps performing an update—this will affect when threads get to run.

We call this way of working *asynchronous* because the operations are not synchronized. When you design asynchronous solutions that use multi-threading you must be very careful to ensure that uncertainty about the timings of thread activity does not affect the working of the application or the results that are produced. In this section you'll discover how to synchronize access to resources that your application uses. You will see that if access to resources is not synchronized correctly it can result in programs calculating the wrong result. A badly written multi-threaded application might even get stuck because two processes are waiting for each other to complete. You'll discover how to stop tasks that may have got stuck and how to ensure that threads work together irrespective of the order in which they are performed.

> **This section covers how to:**
> - Synchronize resources
> - Implement locking
> - Cancel a long-running task
> - Implement thread-safe methods to handle race conditions

Resource synchronization

When an application is spread over several asynchronous tasks, it becomes impossible to predict the sequencing and timing of individual actions. You need to create applications with the understanding that any action may be interrupted in a way that has the potential to damage your application.

Let's start with a simple application that adds up the numbers in an array. Listing 1-41 creates an array containing the values 0 to 500,000,000. It then uses a for loop to calculate the total of the array.

LISTING 1-41 Single task summing

```
using System;
using System.Linq;

namespace LISTING_1_41_Single_task_summing
{
    class Program
    {
        // make an array that holds the values 0 to 50000000
        static int[] items = Enumerable.Range(0, 50000001).ToArray();

        static void Main(string[] args)
        {
            long total = 0;

            for (int i = 0; i < items.Length; i++)
                total = total + items[i];

            Console.WriteLine("The total is: {0}", total);
            Console.ReadKey();
        }
    }
}
```

When you run this program, it prints out the sum of the array:

```
The total is: 1250000025000000
```

This is a single tasking solution that has to work through the entire array. You may decide to make use of the multiple processors in your computer and create a solution that creates a number of tasks, each of which will add up a particular area of the array.

Listing 1-42 serves as a refresher showing how tasks are created, and also illustrates how resource synchronization can cause problems in an application. It creates a number of tasks, each of which runs the method addRangeOfValues, which adds the contents of a particular range of values in the array to a total value. The idea is that the first task will add the values in the elements from 0 to 999, the second task will add the values in the elements 1000 to 1999, and so on up the array. The main method creates all of the tasks and then uses the Task.WaitAll method to cause the program to wait for the completion all of the tasks.

LISTING 1-42 Bad task interaction

```
using System;
using System.Collections.Generic;
using System.Linq;
using System.Threading.Tasks;

namespace LISTING_1_42_Bad_task_interaction
```

```
{
    class Program
    {
        static long sharedTotal;

        // make an array that holds the values 0 to 5000000
        static int[] items = Enumerable.Range(0, 500001).ToArray();

        static void addRangeOfValues(int start, int end)
        {
            while (start < end)
            {
                sharedTotal = sharedTotal + items[start];
                start++;
            }
        }

        static void Main(string[] args)
        {
            List<Task> tasks = new List<Task>();

            int rangeSize = 1000;
            int rangeStart = 0;

            while (rangeStart < items.Length)
            {
                int rangeEnd = rangeStart + rangeSize;

                if (rangeEnd > items.Length)
                    rangeEnd = items.Length;

                // create local copies of the parameters
                int rs = rangeStart;
                int re = rangeEnd;

                tasks.Add(Task.Run(() => addRangeOfValues(rs, re)));
                rangeStart = rangeEnd;
            }

            Task.WaitAll(tasks.ToArray());

            Console.WriteLine("The total is: {0}", sharedTotal);
            Console.ReadKey();
        }
    }
}
```

You may expect that the program in Listing 1-42 prints out the same value as our original program. When running it on my machine, however, I received the following:

```
The total is: 98448836618
```

Apparently many updates to the variable sharedTotal didn't take place. What is happening here? The problem is caused by the way in which all of the tasks interact over the same shared value. Consider the following sequence of events:

1. Task number 1 starts performing an update of sharedTotal. It fetches the contents of the sharedTotal variable into the Central Processor Unit (CPU) and adds the contents of an array element to the value of sharedTotal. But, just as the CPU is about to write the result back into memory, the operating system stops task number 1 and switches to task number 2.

2. Task number 2 also wants to update sharedTotal. It fetches the content of sharedTotal, adds the value of an array element to it, and then writes the result back into memory. Now the operating system returns control to task number 1.

3. Task number 1 writes the sharedTotal value it was working on from the CPU back into memory. This means that the update performed by task number 2 has been lost.

This is called a *race condition*. There is a race between two threads, and the behavior of the program is dependent on which threads first get to the sharedTotal variable. It's impossible to predict what a badly written program like this will do. I've seen situations where programs that contain this kind of mistake work perfectly on one kind of computer, and then fail when they run on a machine that has a smaller or larger number of processors. Remember that the nature of an *asynchronous* solution is that as programmers we really don't have any control over the order in which any parts of our system may execute.

Note that this threading issue can arise even if you use C# statements that look like they are atomic. The statement below adds 1 to the variable x. It looks like it is an atomic operation, but it actually involves reading, updating and storing the result, which are all steps that can be interrupted and may not be performed correctly owing to a race condition.

x += 1;

In the previous section you identified a need for *concurrent collections* that can be used by multiple asynchronous tasks. These collections have been implemented in a way that avoids problems like the one shown in Listing 1-42. Now let's investigate how to ensure that your own programs can work correctly in multi-threaded environments.

Implementing locking

When examining the ConcurrentDictionary collection we discovered that the actions on a dictionary that can be used by multiple processes are referred to as *atomic*. This means that an action by one process on a given dictionary entry cannot be interrupted by another process. The data corruption that you saw in Listing 1-41 is caused by the fact that adding one to a variable is not an atomic action. It can be interrupted, leading to tasks "fighting" over a single value.

Locks

A program can use *locking* to ensure that a given action is *atomic*. Atomic actions are performed to completion, so they cannot be interrupted. Access to an atomic action is controlled by a locking object, which you can think of as the keys to a restroom operated by a restaurant. To get access to the restroom you ask the cashier for the key. You can then go and use the restroom and, when finished, hand the key back to the cashier. If the restroom is in use when you request the key, you must wait until the person in front of you returns the key, so you can then go and use it.

Listing 1-43 shows how to create a locking object that works in the same way as the restroom key. The object is called sharedTotalLock, and it controls access to the statement that updates the value of sharedTotal. The lock statement is followed by a statement or block of code that is performed in an atomic manner, so it will not be possible for a task to interrupt the code protected by the lock. If you run the program now you will find that the correct value is printed out.

LISTING 1-43 Using locking

```
static object sharedTotalLock = new object();

static void addRangeOfValues(int start, int end)
{
    while (start < end)
    {
        lock (sharedTotalLock)
        {
            sharedTotal = sharedTotal + items[start];
        }
        start++;
    }
}
```

At this point you may be pleased that you know how to create multi-threaded programs and use locks to prevent them from interacting in dangerous ways, but I have some bad news for you. While you have stopped the tasks from interacting in a dangerous manner, you've also removed any benefit from using multi-tasking. If you run the program in Listing 1-43 you will discover that it takes *longer* to sum the elements in the arrays than the previous versions.

This is because the tasks are not executing in parallel any more. Most of the time tasks are in a queue waiting for access to the shared total value. Adding a lock solved the problem of contention, but it has also stopped the tasks from executing in parallel, because they are waiting for access to a variable that they all need to use.

The solution to this problem is simple. Listing 1-44 shows a version of addRangeOfValues, which calculates a sub-total in the loop and works down the array adding up array elements. The sub-total is then added to the total value once this loop has completed. Rather than updating the shared total every time it adds a new element of the array; this version of the method only updates the shared total once. So there is now a thousandth of the amount of use of the shared variables, and the program now performs a lot better.

LISTING 1-44 Sensible locking

```
static void addRangeOfValues(int start, int end)
{
    long subTotal = 0;

    while (start < end)
```

```
    {
        subTotal = subTotal + items[start];
        start++;
    }
    lock (sharedTotalLock)
    {
        sharedTotal = sharedTotal + subTotal;
    }
}
```

When you create a parallel version of an operation you need to be mindful of potential value corruption when you use shared variables, and you should also carefully consider the impact of any locking that you use to prevent corruption. You also need to remember that when a task is running code protected by a lock, the task is in a position to block other tasks. This is similar to how a person taking a long time in the restroom will cause a long queue of people waiting to use it. Code in a lock should be as short as possible and should not contain any actions that might take a while to complete. As an example, your program should never perform input/output during a locked block of code.

Monitors

A Monitor provides a similar set of actions to a lock, but the code is arranged slightly differently. They allow a program to ensure that only one thread at a time can access a particular object. Rather than controlling a statement or block of code, as the lock keyword does, the atomic code is enclosed in calls of Monitor.Enter and Monitor.Exit. The Enter and Exit methods are passed a reference to an object that is used as the lock. In Listing 1-45 the lock object is sharedTotalLock. If you run the program you will find it behaves in exactly the same way as the one shown in Listing 1-43.

LISTING 1-45 Using monitors

```
static object sharedTotalLock = new object();

static void addRangeOfValues(int start, int end)
{
    long subTotal = 0;

    while (start < end)
    {
        subTotal = subTotal + items[start];
        start++;
    }

    Monitor.Enter(sharedTotalLock);
    sharedTotal = sharedTotal + subTotal;
    Monitor.Exit(sharedTotalLock);
}
```

If atomic code throws an exception, you need to be sure that any locks that have been claimed to enter the code are released. In statements managed by the lock keyword this happens automatically, if you use a Monitor, make sure that the lock is released.

In the case of the `Monitor` used in the `addRangeOfValues` method in Listing 1-45, there is no chance of the atomic code (the statement that updates the value of `sharedTotal`) throwing an exception. However, if an exception is thrown, it is important to ensure that `Monitor.Exit` is performed, otherwise this stops any other task from accessing the code.

Make sure that the `Monitor.Exit` method is always performed by enclosing the atomic code in a try block, and that you call `Monitor.Exit` in the final clause, which will always run:

```
Monitor.Enter(lockObject);
try
{
    // code that might throw an exception
}
finally
{
    Monitor.Exit(lockObject);
}
```

Note that if an atomic action throws an exception it indicates that something has gone wrong with your application. In such a situation, consider designing things so that the application reports the error and then terminates in the tidiest manner possible. It is possible that the atomic action that threw an exception will throw another one, with the potential of even more data corruption as the application limps along.

At this point you may be wondering why you might want to use monitors rather than locks. A program that uses the `lock` keyword has no way to check whether or not it will be blocked when it tries to enter the locked segment of code. If, however, a monitor is used, the program can do the following:

```
if (Monitor.TryEnter(lockObject))
{
    // code controlled by the lock
}
else
{
    // do something else because the lock object is in use
}
```

The `TryEnter` method attempts to enter the code controlled by the lock. If this is not possible because the lock object is in use, the `TryEnter` method returns false. There are also versions of `TryEnter` that can atomically set a flag variable to indicate whether or not the lock was obtained, along with variable that will wait for the lock for a given number of milliseconds before giving up. These features add extra flexibility to task design.

Deadlocks in multi-threaded code

When looking at the use of the `BlockingCollection` in "Implement multithreading" we considered the problem posed by a *deadly embrace,* where two different tasks are waiting for each other to perform an action on a shared collection, which blocks from adding items when the collection is full and removing items when the collection is empty. This situation is also called *a deadlock.* The application in Listing 1-46 contains two methods and two lock objects. The methods use the lock objects in different order so that each task gets a lock object each, and then waits for the other lock object to become free. When the program runs, the two methods are called one after another.

LISTING 1-46 Sequential locking

```csharp
using System;

namespace LISTING_1_46_Sequential_locking
{

    class Program
    {
        static object lock1 = new object();
        static object lock2 = new object();

        static void Method1()
        {
            lock (lock1)
            {
                Console.WriteLine("Method 1 got lock 1");
                Console.WriteLine("Method 1 waiting for lock 2");
                lock (lock2)
                {
                    Console.WriteLine("Method 1 got lock 2");
                }
                Console.WriteLine("Method 1 released lock 2");
            }
            Console.WriteLine("Method 1 released lock 1");
        }

        static void Method2()
        {
            lock (lock2)
            {
                Console.WriteLine("Method 2 got lock 2");
                Console.WriteLine("Method 2 waiting for lock 1");
                lock (lock1)
                {
                    Console.WriteLine("Method 2 got lock 1");
                }
                Console.WriteLine("Method 2 released lock 1");
            }
            Console.WriteLine("Method 2 released lock 2");
        }

        static void Main(string[] args)
        {
            Method1();
            Method2();
            Console.WriteLine("Methods complete. Press any key to exit.");
            Console.ReadKey();
        }
    }
}
```

Running this program creates the following output:

```
Method 1 got lock 1
Method 1 waiting for lock 2
Method 1 got lock 2
Method 1 released lock 2
Method 1 released lock 1
Method 2 got lock 2
Method 2 waiting for lock 1
Method 2 got lock 1
Method 2 released lock 1
Method 2 released lock 2
Methods complete. Press any key to exit.
```

The program runs to completion. Each method gets the lock objects in turn because they are running sequentially. You can change the program so that the methods are performed by tasks. Listing 1-47 shows a main method that creates two tasks that will run the methods concurrently.

LISTING 1-47 Deadlocked tasks

```
static void Main(string[] args)
{
    Task t1 = Task.Run(() => Method1());
    Task t2 = Task.Run(() => Method2());
    Console.WriteLine("waiting for Task 2");
    t2.Wait();
    Console.WriteLine("Tasks complete. Press any key to exit.");
    Console.ReadKey();
}
```

Running this program generates the following output:

```
waiting for Task 2
Method 1 got lock 1
Method 1 waiting for lock 2
Method 2 got lock 2
Method 2 waiting for lock 1
```

The tasks in this case never complete. Each task is waiting for the other's lock object, and neither can continue. Note that this is not the same as creating an *infinite loop,* in which a program repeats a sequence of statements forever. You will not find that the program error in Listing 1-47 will use up the entire CPU in the same way as an infinitely repeated loop will do. Instead, these two tasks will sit in memory unable to do anything.

Writing the example in Listing 1-47 was difficult for me to do. When using synchronization objects, I make sure to never "nest" one use of a lock inside another.

The lock object

An incorrect use of the `lock` statement can introduce deadlocks into your applications. Any object managed by reference can be used as a locking object, which represents "the key to our restroom." The scope of the object should be restricted to the part of your application containing the cooperating tasks; remember that access to a lock object provides a means by which other code can lock out your tasks.

It is important to carefully consider the object that is to be used as a lock. It may be tempting to use a data object, or the reference to "this" in a method as the lock, but this is confusing. I recommend a policy of explicitly creating an object to be used as a lock.

It is not a good idea to use a string as a locking object, because the .NET string implementation uses a pool of strings during compilation. Every time a program assigns text to a string, the pool is checked to see if a string contains that text already. If the text is already in the string pool, the program uses a reference to it. In other words, the string "the" would only be stored once when an application is running. If two tasks use the same word as their locking object, they are sharing that lock, which leads to problems.

Interlocked operations

You saw that when we using multiple tasks to sum the contents of an array, you must protect access to the shared total by means of a lock. There's a better way of achieving thread safe access to the contents of a variable, which is to use the Interlocked class. This provides a set of thread-safe operations that can be performed on a variable. These include increment, decrement, exchange (swap a variable with another), and add.

Listing 1-48 shows how a program can use an interlocked version of Add to update the shared total with a value calculated by the addRangeOfValues in the array summing program.

LISTING 1-48 Interlock total

```
static void addRangeOfValues(int start, int end)
{
    long subTotal = 0;

    while (start < end)
    {
        subTotal = subTotal + items[start];
        start++;
    }

    Interlocked.Add(ref sharedTotal, subTotal);
}
```

There is also a compare and exchange method that can be used to create a multi-tasking program to search through an array and find the largest value in that array.

Volatile variables

The source of a C# program goes through a number of stages before it is actually executed. The compilation process includes the examination of the sequence of statements to discover ways that a program can be made to run more quickly. This might result in statements being executed in a different order to the order they were written. Consider the following sequence of statements.

```
int x;
int y=0;
x = 99;
y = y + 1;
Console.WriteLine("The answer is: {0}", x);
```

The first statement assigns a value to variable x, the second does some work on the variable y, and the third statement prints the value in variable x. After compilation we may find that the order of the first two statements has been swapped, so that the value in x can be held inside the computer processor rather than having to be re-loaded from memory for the write statement.

In a single threaded situation this is perfectly acceptable, but if multiple threads are working on the code, this may result in unexpected behaviors. Furthermore, if another task changes the value of x while statements are running, and if the C# compiler caches the value of x between statements, this results in an out of date value being printed. C# provides the keyword volatile, which can be used to indicate that operations involving a particular variable are not optimized in this way.

```
volatile int x;
```

Operations involving the variable x will now not be optimized, and the value of x will be fetched from the copy in memory, rather than being cached in the processor. This can make operations involving the variable x a lot less efficient.

Cancelling a long-running task

When covering threads in the previous section we noted that it was possible for a thread to be aborted using the Abort method that can be called on an active Thread instance. In this section we'll investigate how an application can stop an executing Task.

The Cancellation Token

There is an important difference between threads and tasks, in that a Thread can be aborted at any time, whereas a Task must monitor a *cancellation token* so that it will end when told to.

Listing 1-49 shows how a task is cancelled. The Clock method is run as a task and displays a "tick" message every half second. The loop inside the Clock method is controlled by an instance of the CancellationTokenSource class. This instance is shared between the Task running the clock and the foreground program. The CancellationTokenSource instance exposes a property called IsCancellationRequested. When this property becomes true the loop in the Clock method completes and the task ends. This means that a Task has the opportunity to tidy up and release resources when it is told that it is being cancelled.

LISTING 1-49 Cancel a task

```
using System;
using System.Threading;
using System.Threading.Tasks;
```

```
namespace LISTING_1_49_cancel_a_task
{
    class Program
    {
        static CancellationTokenSource cancellationTokenSource =
        new CancellationTokenSource();

        static void Clock()
        {
            while (!cancellationTokenSource.IsCancellationRequested)
            {
                Console.WriteLine("Tick");
                Thread.Sleep(500);
            }
        }

        static void Main(string[] args)
        {
            Task.Run(() => Clock());
            Console.WriteLine("Press any key to stop the clock");
            Console.ReadKey();
            cancellationTokenSource.Cancel();
            Console.WriteLine("Clock stopped");
            Console.ReadKey();
        }
    }
}
```

If you run the program in Listing 1-49 you will find that the clock will continue ticking until you press a key and trigger the call of the Cancel method on the cancellationTokenSource object.

Raising an exception when a task is cancelled

A Task can indicate that it has been cancelled by raising an exception. This can be useful if a task is started in one place and monitored in another. The Clock method below ticks 20 times and then exits. It is supplied with a CancellationToken reference as a parameter, which is tested each time around the tick loop. If the task is cancelled, it throws an exception.

```
static void Clock(CancellationToken cancellationToken)
{
    int tickCount = 0;

    while (!cancellationToken.IsCancellationRequested && tickCount<20)
    {
        tickCount++;
        Console.WriteLine("Tick");
        Thread.Sleep(500);
    }

    cancellationToken.ThrowIfCancellationRequested();
}
```

Listing 1-50 shows how this method is used in a task. A CancellationTokenSource instance is created and the token from this instance is passed into the task running the Clock method. The clock method uses the variable tickCount to count the number of times it has gone around the tick loop. When tickCount reaches 20, the Clock method completes. A task instance exposes an IsCompleted property that indicates whether or not a task completes correctly. This property is tested when the user presses a key during a run of the program. If a key is pressed before the clock task is complete, the clock task is cancelled. The ThrowIfCancellationRequested method is called in the Clock method to throw an exception if the task has been cancelled. This exception is captured and displayed in the main method.

LISTING 1-50 Cancel with exception

```
static void Main(string[] args)
{
    CancellationTokenSource cancellationTokenSource =
    new CancellationTokenSource();

    Task clock = Task.Run(() => Clock(cancellationTokenSource.Token));

    Console.WriteLine("Press any key to stop the clock");

    Console.ReadKey();

    if (clock.IsCompleted)
    {
        Console.WriteLine("Clock task completed");
    }
    else
    {
        try
        {
            cancellationTokenSource.Cancel();
            clock.Wait();
        }
        catch (AggregateException ex)
        {
            Console.WriteLine("Clock stopped: {0}",
                ex.InnerExceptions[0].ToString());
        }
    }
    Console.ReadKey();
}
```

This code requires careful study. Note that if you run the program in Visual Studio and press a key to interrupt the clock, Visual Studio will report an unhandled exception in the Clock method. If you let the program continue you will find that it will then reach the exception handler in the Main method. This happens because Visual Studio is detecting the cancellation exception and telling you about it. If the program was running outside Visual Studio, as it would be when a customer is using the program, the cancellation exception would not be detected and only the exception handler for the AggregateException would run.

Implementing thread-safe methods

An object can provide services to other objects by exposing methods for them to use. If an object is going to be used in a multi-threaded application it is important that the method behaves in a *thread safe* manner. Thread safe means that the method can be called from multiple tasks simultaneously without producing incorrect results, and without placing the object that it is a member of into an invalid state.

Thread safety and member variables

You have seen the difficulties that can be caused by race conditions appearing when two tasks use a shared variable. Without locking, the program that attempts to use multiple tasks to sum the contents of an array fails because there is unmanaged access to the shared total value. You can see the same issues arising when a method uses the value of a member of an object.

Consider the class Counter in Listing 1-51. It is intended to be used to collect values and add them to a total value that can then be read by users of the object. It works well in a single threaded application. In an application that uses multiple tasks, however, it fails in the same way as the program shown in Listing 1-42. If several tasks make use of the IncreaseCounter method at the same time, race conditions cause updates to totalValue to be overwritten.

LISTING 1-51 Unsafe thread method

```
class Counter
{
    private int totalValue = 0;

    public void IncreaseCounter(int amount)
    {
        totalValue = totalValue + amount;
    }

    public int Total
    {
        get { return totalValue; }
    }
}
```

You can get the program to calculate the correct result by using an interlocking operation to update the totalValue member as shown in Listing 1-42. The problem is that you need to know that you have to do this. You've seen how easy it is to add multi-tasking to an existing application but be sure that all of the objects used in the application contain thread safe code. Otherwise, the application may be prone to the worst kind of errors; those that appear sporadically and inconsistently across different platforms.

Any use of a member of a class must be thread safe, and this must be done in a way that does not compromise multi-threaded performance. You've seen how adding locks can make things thread safe, but you also saw how doing this incorrectly can actually make performance worse. This may mean that creating a multi-tasked implementation of a system involves a complete re-write, with processes refactored as either producers or consumers of data.

Thread safety and method parameters

Parameters passed into a method by value are delivered as copies of the data that was given in the arguments to the method call. They are unique to that method call and cannot be changed by code running in any other task. Objects on the end of reference parameters, however, are susceptible to change by code running in other tasks. As an illustration of what can go wrong, consider a factory method called `CreateCustomerFromRawData`:

```
Customer CreateCustomerFromRawData( RawData inputInfo)
{
    // validates the information in inputInfo and creates a Customer object
    // if the information is valid
}
```

The `CreateCustomerFromRawData` method validates the input information held in a `RawData` instance and, if the information is correct, it creates a new `Customer` built from this data and returns it. If, however, `RawData` is a reference to an object, there is nothing to stop another task from changing the contents of this object at the same time as the `CreateCustomer` method is running. This can lead to a `Customer` instance being created that contains invalid or inconsistent data and generates errors that are hard to trace.

There are two ways that this issue can be addressed. The first is to make the `RawData` object a struct type, which will be passed by value into the method call. The second method is to create an atomic action that copies the incoming data into local variables that are specific to that call of the method. Either way, it is important to consider the ramifications of parallel execution when creating methods that accept reference parameters.

Skill 1.3 Implement program flow

Now that you have spent some time considering how to create and manage threads we can take a look at what a program actually does. A program is a sequence of instructions that is followed that works on some input and produces an output. You can think of the execution process as flowing through the C# statements in the same way that water might flow down a riverbed. In this section we will consider the elements of C# that are associated with program flow.

Programs frequently have to work with large collections of data, and C# provides a range of collection types. From a program flow point of view, a program frequently has to work through such collections and you will explore the C# constructions that you can use to do this.

You will also discover the C# constructions that allow a program to react to the values in the data that it is working with and change its behavior appropriately. You will explore the `if` constructions that allows a program to make a decision. You will also take a look at the logical expressions that are evaluated to control and if condition and the switch construction that makes it easier to create decisions

And finally, a program must perform the actual data processing element by evaluating the results of expressions and using the values to update the contents of variables. You'll take a look at how expressions are evaluated in C# programs.

Iterating across collections

C# provides a number of constructions that can implement looping behaviors: the *while* loop, the *do* loop, and the *for* loop. Let's examine each of these in turn.

The while loop construction

A `while` loop construction will perform a given statement or block, while a given logical expression has a true value. The code in Listing 1-52 is an example of an *infinite loop* that will never terminate.

LISTING 1-52 While loops

```
while(true)
{
    Console.WriteLine("Hello");
}
```

This is completely legal C# code that will write Hello a great many times. In contrast, the code here will never write Hello:

```
while(false)
{
    Console.WriteLine("Hello");
}
```

This illustrates an important aspect of the `while` loop. The condition that controls the looping behavior is tested before the statements controlled by the loop are obeyed. The `while(false)` loop will produce a compiler warning because the compiler will detect that the loop contains statements that are unreachable. A `while` construction can be used with a counter to repeat an action a number of times, as shown here:

```
int count = 0;
while(count < 10)
{
    Console.WriteLine("Hello {0}", count);
    count = count + 1;
}
```

This will print the Hello message 10 times. If you wish to use a counter in this manner you should instead make use of a `for` loop, which is described next. A `while` loop is very effective when creating a consumer of data. The construction next consumes data while it is available.

```
while(dataAvailable())
{
    processData();
}
```

The do–while loop construction

The do–while loop construction also uses a logical expression to control the execution of a given statement or block. In the case of this loop, however, the condition is tested after the block has been performed once. The code in Listing 1-53 shows a do–while construction.

LISTING 1-53 Do–while loops

```
do
{
    Console.WriteLine("Hello");
} while (false);
```

The important thing to note about this code is that although the logical expression controlling it is false, which means that the loop will never repeat, the message Hello will be printed once, since the printing takes place *before* the logical expression is tested.

A do–while construction is useful when you want to create code that continuously fetches data until a valid value is entered:

```
do
{
    requestData();
while (!dataValid());
```

The for loop construction

A loop that is not infinite (one that should terminate at some point) can be made up of three things:

1. Initialization that is performed to set the loop up

2. A test that will determine if the loop should continue

3. An update to be performed each time the action of the loop has been performed

The for loop provides a way of creating these three elements in a single construction. Listing 1-54 shows how this works. Each of the actions made into a method that is called by the loop construction.

LISTING 1-54 For loops

```
using System;

namespace LISTING_1_54_for_loops
{
    class Program
    {
        static int counter;
```

```csharp
        static void Initalize()
        {
            Console.WriteLine("Initialize called");
            counter = 0;
        }

        static void Update()
        {
            Console.WriteLine("Update called");
            counter = counter + 1;
        }

        static bool Test()
        {
            Console.WriteLine("Test called");
            return counter < 5;
        }
        static void Main(string[] args)
        {
            for(Initalize(); Test();  Update() )
            {
                Console.WriteLine("Hello {0}", counter);
            }
            Console.ReadKey();
        }
    }
}
```

When you run this program, the following output is displayed:

```
Initialize called
Test called
Hello 0
Update called
Test called
Hello 1
Update called
Test called
Hello 2
Update called
Test called
Hello 3
Update called
Test called
Hello 4
Update called
Test called
```

This output shows that a test is performed immediately after initialization, so it is possible that the statement controlled by the loop may never be performed. This illustrates a very important aspect of the for loop construction, in that the initialize, test, and update behaviors can be anything that you wish.

A more conventional use of the for loop construction to repeat an action five times is shown below. A variable local to the code to be repeated is created within the for loop. This variable, called counter, is then printed by the code in the loop.

```
for(int counter = 0; counter < 5; counter++)
{
    Console.WriteLine("Hello {0}", counter);
}
```

You can leave out any of the elements of a for loop. You can also perform multiple statements for the initialize, update, and test elements. The statements are separated by a comma. Note that while it is possible to do exotic things like this, I advise that you don't do this in your programs.

Programming is not a place to show how clever you are, because it is more important that it is a place where you create code that is easy to understand. It is very unlikely that your "clever" construction will be more efficient than a much simpler one. And even if your clever construction is a bit faster, person time (the time spent by someone trying to understand your "clever" code) is much more expensive than computer time.

The foreach construction

It is perfectly possible to use a for loop to iterate through a collection of items. Listing 1-55 shows how a for loop can create an index variable used to obtain successive elements in an array of names.

LISTING 1-55 Iterate with for

```
using System;

namespace LISTING_1_55_iterate_with_for
{
    class Program
    {
        static void Main(string[] args)
        {
            string[] names = { "Rob", "Mary", "David", "Jenny", "Chris", "Imogen" };

            for (int index = 0; index < names.Length; index++)
            {
                Console.WriteLine(names[index]);
            }
            Console.ReadKey();
        }
    }
}
```

The foreach construction makes iterating through a collection much easier. Listing 1-56 shows how a foreach construction is used. Each time around the loop, the value of name is loaded with the next name in the collection.

LISTING 1-56 Iterate with foreach

```
foreach(string name in names)
{
    Console.WriteLine(name);
}
```

Note how the type of the iterating value must match the type of the items in the collection. In other words, the following code generates a compilation error, because the names array holds a collection of strings, not integers.

```
foreach(int name in names)
{
    Console.WriteLine(name);
}
```

It isn't possible for code in a foreach construction to modify the iterating value. The following code, which attempts to convert the list of names to upper case, does not compile.

```
foreach(string name in names)
{
    name = name.ToUpper();
}
```

If the foreach loop is working on a list of references to objects, the objects on the ends of those references can be changed. The code in Listing 1-57 works through a list of Person objects, changing the Name property of each person in the list to upper case. This compiles and runs correctly.

LISTING 1-57 Uppercase Person

```
foreach(Person person in people)
{
    person.Name = person.Name.ToUpper();
}
```

The foreach construction can iterate through any object which implements the IEnumerable interface. These objects expose a method called GetIterator(). This method must return an object that implements the System.Collections.IEnumerator interface. This interface exposes methods that the foreach construction can use to get the next item from the enumerator and determine if there any more items in the collection. Many collection classes, including lists and dictionaries, implement the IEnumerable interface. In chapter 2, "Create and implement a class hierarchy," you will discover how to make a class that implements the IEnumerable interface.

Note that the iteration can be implemented in a "lazy" way; the next item to be iterated only needs to be fetched when requested. The results of database queries can be returned as objects that implement the IEnumerable interface and then only fetch the actual data items when needed. It is important that the item being iterated is not changed during iteration, if the iterating code tried to remove items from the list it was iterating through this would cause the program to throw an exception when it ran.

The break statement

Any of the above loop constructions can be ended early by the use of a break statement. When the break statement is reached, the program immediately exits the loop. Listing 1-58 shows how break works. The loop is ended when it reaches the name "David."

LISTING 1-58 Using break

```
for (int index = 0; index < names.Length; index++)
{
    Console.WriteLine(names[index]);
    if (names[index] == "David")
        break;
}
```

A loop can many break statements, but from a design point of view this is to be discouraged because it can make it much harder to discern the flow through the program.

The continue statement

The continue statement does not cause a loop to end. Instead, it ends the current pass through the code controlled by the loop. The terminating condition is then tested to determine if the loop should continue. Listing 1-59 shows how continue is used. The program will not print out the name "David" because the conditional statement will trigger, causing the continue statement to be performed, and abandoning that pass through the loop.

LISTING 1-59 Using continue

```
for (int index = 0; index < names.Length; index++)
{
    if (names[index] == "David")
        continue;

    Console.WriteLine(names[index]);
}
```

Program decisions

As a program runs, it can make decisions. There are two program constructions that can be used to conditionally execute code: the if construction and the switch construction.

The if construction

An if construction allows the use of a *logical expression* to control the execution of a statement or block of code. A logical expression is one that evaluates to the Boolean value true or the Boolean value false. When the logical expression is true the statement is obeyed. An if construction can have an else element that contains code that is to be executed when the Boolean expression evaluates to false. The code in Listing 1-60 shows how this works.

LISTING 1-60 If construction

```
if(true)
{
    Console.WriteLine("This statement is always performed");
}
else
{
    Console.WriteLine("This statement is never performed");
}
```

The else element of an if construction is optional. It is possible to "nest" if constructions inside one another.

```
if (true)
{
    Console.WriteLine("This statement is always performed");
    if (true)
    {
        Console.WriteLine("This statement is always performed");
    }
    else
    {
        Console.WriteLine("This statement is never performed");
    }
}
```

Not all if constructions are required to have else elements. There is never any confusion about which if condition a given else binds to, since it is always the "nearest" one. If you want to modify this binding you can use braces to force different bindings, as you can see here. Note that the indenting also helps to show the reader the code statements that are controlled by each part of the if construction.

```
if(true)
{
    Console.WriteLine("This statement is always performed");
    if (true)
    {
        Console.WriteLine("This statement is always performed");
    }
}
else
{
    Console.WriteLine("This statement is never performed");
}
```

Logical expressions

A logical expression evaluates to a logical value, which is either true or false. We've seen that true and false are Boolean literal values and can be used in conditions, although this is not terribly useful. A logical expression can contain operators used to compare values. Relational operators are used to compare two values (see Table 1-1).

TABLE 1-1 Relational operators

Name	Operator	Behavior
Less than	<	True if the left-hand operand is less than the right-hand operand
Greater than	>	True if the left-hand operand is greater than the right-hand operand
Less than or equals	<=	True if the left-hand operand is less than or equal to the right-hand operand
Greater than or equals	<=	True if the left-hand operand is greater than or equal to the right-hand operand

Relational operators can be used between numeric variables and strings. In the context of a string, less than and greater than are evaluated alphabetically, as in "Abbie" is less than "Allen." A program can use equality operators to compare for equality (see Table 1-2).

TABLE 1-2 Equality operators

Name	Operator	Behavior
Equal to	==	True if the left-hand operand is equal to the right-hand operand
Not equal to	!=	True if the left-hand operand is not equal to the right-hand operand

These can be used between numeric variables and strings, but they should not be used when testing floating point (float and double) values as the nature of number storage on a computer means that values of these types are not held exactly. A program should not test to see if two floating point values are equal, instead it should subtract one from the other and determine if the absolute value of the result is less than a given tolerance value.

Logical values can be combined using logical operators (see Table 1-3).

TABLE 1-3 Logical operators

Name	Operator	Behavior
And	&	True if the left-hand operand and the right-hand operand are true
Or	|	True if the left-hand operand or the right-hand operand (or both) is/are true
Exclusive Or	^	True if the left-hand operand is not the same as the right-hand operandcc

The & and | operators have *conditional* versions: && and ||. These are only evaluated until it can be determined whether the result of the expression is true or false. In the case of &&, if the first operand is false, the program will not evaluate the second operand since it is already established that the result of the expression is false. In the case of ||, if the first operand is true the second operand will not be evaluated as it is already established that the result of the expression is true. This is also referred to as *short circuiting* the evaluation of the expression. Listing 1-61 shows how this works. It contains instrumented methods that are called during the evaluation of the expression.

LISTING 1-61 Logical expressions

```
using System;

namespace LISTING_1_61_logical_expressions
{
    class Program
    {
        static int mOne()
        {
            Console.WriteLine("mOne called");
            return 1;
        }

        static int mTwo()
        {
            Console.WriteLine("mTwo called");
            return 2;
        }

        static void Main(string[] args)
        {
            if (mOne() == 2 && mTwo() == 1)
                Console.WriteLine("Hello world");

            Console.ReadKey();
        }
    }
}
```

When the program runs, it only outputs a message from the method mOne. The method mTwo is never called, even though it is in the expression. This is because the condition involving the value returned by mOne evaluates to false, which means there is no need to call mTwo. It is standard practice to use the conditional versions of the logical operators because it can improve program performance. If methods called in the logical expressions have side effects (which is bad programming practice) it may cause data-dependent faults to occur.

The switch construction

The switch construction let's a program use a value to select one of a number of different options. It replaces a long sequence of if–then–else constructions that would otherwise be required. The switch keyword is followed by an expression that controls the switch. At run time the program will look for a matching value on a particular case clause, which identifies the code to be executed for that value. The code controlled by the case continues until a break statement, which marks the end of that clause. A switch can contain a default clause, identifying a clause to be performed if the control value doesn't match any case.

Listing 1-62 shows how the switch construction is used. The user specifies which of three commands they want to invoke by entering a number. If there is no matching command for the value that the user enters, the program prints out a message.

LISTING 1-62 The switch construction

```csharp
using System;

namespace LISTING_1_62_The_switch_construction
{
    class Program
    {
        static void Main(string[] args)
        {
            Console.Write("Enter command: ");
            int command = int.Parse(Console.ReadLine());

            switch(command)
            {
                case 1:
                    Console.WriteLine("Command 1 chosen");
                    break;
                case 2:
                    Console.WriteLine("Command 2 chosen");
                    break;
                case 3:
                    Console.WriteLine("Command 3 chosen");
                    break;
                default:
                    Console.WriteLine("Please enter a command in the range 1-3");
                    break;
            }
            Console.ReadKey();
        }
    }
}
```

The switch construction will switch on character, string and enumerated values, and it is possible to group cases, as shown in Listing 1-63, which allows a user to select a command by entering a string. Note that the string that is entered is converted into lower case, and that both a long form (save) and a short form of the command (s) can be used.

LISTING 1-63 Switching on strings

```csharp
Console.Write("Enter command: ");
string commandName = Console.ReadLine().ToLower() ;

switch (commandName)
{
    case "save":
    case "s":
        Console.WriteLine("Save command");
        break;
    case "load":
    case "l":
        Console.WriteLine("Load command");
        break;
    case "exit":
    case "e":
```

```
        Console.WriteLine("Exit command");
        break;
    default:
        Console.WriteLine("Please enter save, load or exit");
        break;
}
```

In C# it is not permissible for a program to "fall through" from the end of one case clause into another. Each clause must be explicitly ended with a break, a return, or by the program throwing an exception.

Switches are a nice example of a "luxury" C# feature in that they don't actually make something possible that you can't do any other way. You can create C# programs without using any switch statements, but they make it easier to create code that selects one behavior based on the value in a control variable.

Evaluating expressions

C# expressions are comprised of *operators* and *operands*. Operators specify the action to be performed, and are either literal values (for example the number 99) or variables. You have seen examples of operators and operands in use in the logical expressions that control the if constructions in previous sections. An operator can work on one operand, and such operands are called *unary* or *monadic*.

Monadic operators are either *prefix* (given before the operand) or postfix (given after the operand). Alternatively, an operand can work on two (*binary*), or in the case of the conditional operator ?: three (ternary) operands.

The *context* of the use of an operator determines the actual behavior that the operator will exhibit. For example, the addition operator can be used to add two numeric operands together, or concatenate two strings together. The use of an incorrect context (for example adding a number to a string) will be detected by the compiler and cause a compilation error.

Each operator has a *priority* or *precedence* that determines when it is performed during expression evaluation. This precedence can be overridden by the use of parenthesis; elements enclosed in parenthesis are evaluated first. Operators also have an *associability*, which gives the order (left to right or right to left) in which they are evaluated if a number of them appear together. Listing 1-64 shows expression evaluation in action.

LISTING 1-64 Expression evaluation

```
int i = 0; // create i and set to 0

// Monadic operators - one operand
i++; // monadic ++ operator increment - i now 1
i--; // monadic -- operator decrement - i now 0

// Postfix monadic operator - perform after value given
Console.WriteLine(i++); // writes 0 and sets i to 1
// Prefix monadic operator - perform before value given
Console.WriteLine(++i); // writes 2 and sets i to 2
```

```
// Binary operators - two operands
i = 1 + 1; // sets i to 2
i = 1 + 2 * 3; // sets i to 7 because * performed first
i = (1 + 2) * 3; // sets i to 9 because + performed first

string str = "";

str = str + "Hello"; // + performs string addition

// ternary operators - three operands
i = true ? 0 : 1; // sets i to 0 because condition is true;
```

Full details of precedence and associability for C# operators can be found on the web page: *https://docs.microsoft.com/en-us/dotnet/csharp/programming-guide/statements-expressions-operators/operators*.

Skill 1.4: Create and implement events and callbacks

You have seen that a program flows from statement to statement, processing data according to the statements that are performed. In early computers a program would flow from beginning to end, starting with the input data and producing some output before stopping. However, modern applications are not structured in this way. A large application will be made up of a large number of cooperating components which pass messages from one to another.

For example, one component of an application could be tasked with getting commands from the user. When the input component receives a valid user request, it passes this request into another component for processing. Each component can be created and tested individually before being integrated into the solution.

In order to create solutions that work in this way we need a mechanism by which one component can send a message to another. C# provides *events* to achieve this. In this section we discover the C# language features that provide event management, and then explore how these are used in modern application design.

> **This section covers how to:**
> - Create event handlers
> - subscribe to and unsubscribe from events
> - use built-in delegate types to create events
> - create delegates
> - use lambda expressions and anonymous methods

Event handlers

In the days before `async` and `await` were added to the C# language, a program would be forced to use events to manage asynchronous operations. Before initiating an asynchronous task, such as fetching a web page from a server, a program would need to bind a method to an event that would be generated when the action was complete. Today, events are more frequently used for inter-process communication.

We have seen that an object can provide a service for other objects by exposing a public method that can be called to perform that service. For example, in a console application, a program can use the `WriteLine` method exposed by the `Console` to display messages to the user of the program.

Events are used in the reverse of this situation, when you want an object to notify another object that something has happened. An object can be made to *publish* events to which other objects can *subscribe*. Components of a solution that communicate using events in this way are described as *loosely coupled*. The only thing one component has to know about the other is the design of the publish and subscribe mechanism.

Delegates and events

To understand how events are implemented you have to understand the concept of a C# *delegate*. This is a piece of data that contains a reference to a particular method in a class. When you take your car for a service you give the garage attendant your phone number so they can call you when your car is ready to be picked up. You can think of a delegate as the "phone number" of a method in a class. An event publisher is given a delegate that describes the method in the subscriber. The publisher can then call that delegate when the given event occurs and the method will run in the subscriber.

Action delegate

The .NET libraries provide a number of pre-defined delegate types. In the section, "Create Delegates," you will discover how to create your own delegate types.

There are a number of pre-defined `Action` delegate types. The simplest `Action` delegate represents a reference to a method that does not return a result (the method is of type `void`) and doesn't accept any parameters. You can use an `Action` to create a binding point for subscribers.

Listing 1-64 shows how an `Action` delegate can be used to create an event publisher. It contains an `Alarm` class that publishes to subscribers when an alarm is raised. The event `Action` delegate is called `OnAlarmRaised`. A process interested in alarms can bind subscribers to this event. The `RaiseAlarm` method is called in the alarm to raise the alarm. When `RaiseAlarm` runs it first checks to see if any subscriber methods have been bound to the `OnAlarmRaised` delegate. If they have, the delegate is called.

LISTING 1-65 Publish and subscribe

```
using System;

namespace LISTING_1_64_Publish_and_subscribe
{
    class Alarm
```

```
{
    // Delegate for the alarm event
    public Action OnAlarmRaised { get; set; }

    // Called to raise an alarm
    public void RaiseAlarm()
    {
        // Only raise the alarm if someone has
        // subscribed.
        if (OnAlarmRaised != null)
        {
            OnAlarmRaised();
        }
    }
}

class Program
{
    // Method that must run when the alarm is raised
    static void AlarmListener1()
    {
        Console.WriteLine("Alarm listener 1 called");
    }

    // Method that must run when the alarm is raised
    static void AlarmListener2()
    {
        Console.WriteLine("Alarm listener 2 called");
    }

    static void Main(string[] args)
    {
        // Create a new alarm
        Alarm alarm = new Alarm();

        // Connect the two listener methods
        alarm.OnAlarmRaised += AlarmListener1;
        alarm.OnAlarmRaised += AlarmListener2;

        // raise the alarm
        alarm.RaiseAlarm();
        Console.WriteLine("Alarm raised");

        Console.ReadKey();
    }
}
}
```

This program outputs the following:

```
Alarm listener 1 called
Alarm listener 2 called
Alarm raised
```

Event subscribers

Subscribers bind to a publisher by using the += operator. The += operator is *overloaded* to apply between a delegate and a behavior. It means "add this behavior to the ones for this delegate." The methods in a delegate are not guaranteed to be called in the order that they were added to the delegate. You can find out more about overloading in the "Create Types" section.

Delegates added to a published event are called on the same thread as the thread publishing the event. If a delegate blocks this thread, the entire publication mechanism is blocked. This means that a malicious or badly written subscriber has the ability to block the publication of events. This is addressed by the publisher starting an individual task to run each of the event subscribers. The Delegate object in a publisher exposes a method called GetInvokcationList, which can be used to get a list of all the subscribers. You can see this method in use later in the "Exceptions in event subscribers" section.

You can simplify the calling of the delegate by using the *null conditional* operator. This only performs an action if the given item is not null.

```
OnAlarmRaised?.Invoke();
```

The null conditional operator ".?" means, "only access this member of the class if the reference is not null." A delegate exposes an Invoke method to invoke the methods bound to the delegate. The behavior of the code is the same as that in Listing 1-64, but the code is shorter and clearer.

Unsubscribing from a delegate

You've seen that the += operator has been overloaded to allow methods to bind to events. The -= method is used to unsubscribe from events. The program in Listing 1-66 binds two methods to the alarm, raises the alarm, unbinds one of the methods, and raises the alarm again.

LISTING 1-66 Unsubscribing

```
static void Main(string[] args)
{
    // Create a new alarm
    Alarm alarm = new Alarm();

    // Connect the two listener methods
    alarm.OnAlarmRaised += AlarmListener1;
    alarm.OnAlarmRaised += AlarmListener2;

    alarm.RaiseAlarm();
    Console.WriteLine("Alarm raised");

    alarm.OnAlarmRaised -= AlarmListener1;
    alarm.RaiseAlarm();
    Console.WriteLine("Alarm raised");

    Console.ReadKey();
}
```

This program outputs the following:

```
Alarm listener 1 called
Alarm listener 2 called
Alarm raised
Alarm listener 2 called
```

If the same subscriber is added more than once to the same publisher, it will be called a corresponding number of times when the event occurs.

Using events

The `Alarm` object that we've created is not particularly secure. The `OnAlarmRaised` delegate has been made `public` so that subscribers can connect to it. However, this means that code external to the `Alarm` object can raise the alarm by directly calling the `OnAlarmRaised` delegate. External code can overwrite the value of `OnAlarmRaised`, potentially removing subscribers.

C# provides an event construction that allows a delegate to be specified as an *event*. This is shown in Listing 1-67. The keyword event is added before the definition of the delegate. The member `OnAlarmRaised` is now created as a data *field* in the `Alarm` class, rather than a *property*. `OnAlarmRaised` no longer has `get` or `set` behaviors. However, it is now not possible for code external to the `Alarm` class to assign values to `OnAlarmRaised`, and the `OnAlarmRaised` delegate can only be called from within the class where it is declared. In other words, adding the event keyword turns a delegate into a properly useful event.

LISTING 1-67 Event based alarm

```
class Alarm
{
    // Delegate for the alarm event
    public event Action OnAlarmRaised = delegate {};

    // Called to raise an alarm
    public void RaiseAlarm()
    {
            OnAlarmRaised();
    }
}
```

The code in Listing 1-67 above has one other improvement over previous versions. It creates a delegate instance and assigns it when `OnAlarmRaised` is created, so there is now no need to check whether or not the delegate has a value before calling it. This simplifies the `RaiseAlarm` method.

Create events with built-in delegate types

The event delegates created so far have used the `Action` class as the type of each event. This will work, but programs that use events should use the `EventHandler` class instead of `Action`. This is because the `EventHandler` class is the part of .NET designed to allow subscribers to be given data about an event. `EventHandler` is used throughout the .NET framework to manage events. An `EventHandler` can deliver data, or it can just signal that an event has taken place. Listing 1-68 shows how the `Alarm` class can use an `EventHandler` to indicate that an alarm has been raised.

LISTING 1-68 EventHandler alarm

```
class Alarm
{
    // Delegate for the alarm event
    public event EventHandler OnAlarmRaised = delegate { };

    // Called to raise an alarm
    // Does not provide any event arguments
    public void RaiseAlarm()
    {
        // Raises the alarm
        // The event handler receivers a reference to the alarm that is
        // raising this event
        OnAlarmRaised(this, EventArgs.Empty);
    }
}
```

The `EventHandler` delegate refers to a subscriber method that will accept two arguments. The first argument is a reference to the object raising the event. The second argument is a reference to an object of type `EventArgs` that provides information about the event. In the Listing 1-68 the second argument is set to `EventArgs.Empty`, to indicate that this event does not produce any data, it is simply a notification that an event has taken place.

The signature of the methods to be added to this delegate must reflect this. The `AlarmListener1` method accepts two parameters and can be used with this delegate.

```
private static void AlarmListener1(object sender, EventArgs e)
{
    // Only the sender is valid as this event doesn't have arguments
    Console.WriteLine("Alarm listener 1 called");
}
```

Use EventArgs to deliver event information

The `Alarm` class created in Listing 1-68 allows a subscriber to receive a notification that an alarm has been raised, but it doesn't provide the subscriber with any description of the alarm. It is useful if subscribers can be given information about the alarm. Perhaps a string describing the location of the alarm would be useful.

You can do this by creating a class that can deliver this information and then use an `EventHandler` to deliver it. Listing 1-69 shows the `AlarmEventArgs` class, which is a sub class of the `EventArgs` class, and adds a `Location` property to it. If more event information is required, perhaps the date and time of the alarm, these can be added into the `AlarmEventArgs` class.

LISTING 1-69 EventHandler data

```
class AlarmEventArgs : EventArgs
{
    public string Location { get; set; }

    public AlarmEventArgs(string location)
    {
        Location = location;
    }
}
```

You now have your own type that can be used to describe an event which has occurred. The event is the alarm being raised, and the type you have created is called `AlarmEventAgs`. When the alarm is raised we want the handler for the alarm event to accept `AlarmEventArgs` objects so that the handler can be given details of the event.

The `EventHandler` delegate for the `OnAlarmRaised` event is declared to deliver arguments of type `AlarmEventArgs`. When the alarm is raised by the `RaiseAlarm` method the event is given a reference to the alarm and a newly created instance of `AlarmEventArgs` which describes the alarm event.

```
class Alarm
{
    // Delegate for the alarm event
    public event EventHandler<AlarmEventArgs> OnAlarmRaised = delegate { };

    // Called to raise an alarm
    public void RaiseAlarm(string location)
    {
        OnAlarmRaised(this, new AlarmEventArgs(location));
    }
}
```

Subscribers to the event accept the `AlarmEventArgs` and can use the data in it. The method `AlarmListener1` below displays the location of the alarm that it obtains from its argument.

```
static void AlarmListener1(object source, AlarmEventArgs args)
{
    Console.WriteLine("Alarm listener 1 called");
    Console.WriteLine("Alarm in {0}", args.Location);
}
```

Note that a reference to the same `AlarmEventArgs` object is passed to each of the subscribers to the `OnAlarmRaised` event. This means that if one of the subscribers modifies the contents of the event description, subsequent subscribers will see the modified event. This can be useful if subscribers need to signal that a given event has been dealt with, but it can also be a source of unwanted side effects.

Exceptions in event subscribers

You now know how events work. A number of programs can *subscribe* to an event. They do this by binding a delegate to the event. The delegate serves as a reference to a piece of C# code which the subscriber wants to run when the event occurs. This piece of code is called an event handler.

In our example programs the event is an alarm being triggered. When the alarm is triggered the event will call all the event handlers that have subscribed to the alarm event. But what happens if one of the event handlers fails by throwing an exception? If code in one of the subscribers throws an uncaught exception the exception handling process ends at that point and no further subscribers will be notified. This would mean that some subscribers would not be informed of the event.

To resolve this issue each event handler can be called individually and then a single aggregate exception created which contains all the details of any exceptions that were thrown by event handlers. Listing 1-70 shows how this is done. The GetInvocationList method is used on the delegate to obtain a list of subscribers to the event. This list is then iterated and the DynamicInvoke method called for each subscriber. Any exceptions thrown by subscribers are caught and added to a list of exceptions. Note that the exception thrown by the subscriber is delivered by a TypeInvocationException, and it is the inner exception from this that must be saved.

LISTING 1-70 Aggregating exceptions

```
public void RaiseAlarm(string location)
{
    List<Exception> exceptionList = new List<Exception>();

    foreach (Delegate handler in OnAlarmRaised.GetInvocationList())
    {
        try
        {
            handler.DynamicInvoke(this, new AlarmEventArgs(location));
        }
        catch (TargetInvocationException e)
        {
            exceptionList.Add(e.InnerException);
        }
    }
    if (exceptionList.Count > 0)
        throw new AggregateException(exceptionList);
}
```

The subscribers in Listing 1-70 both throw exceptions.

```
static void AlarmListener1(object source, AlarmEventArgs args)
{
    Console.WriteLine("Alarm listener 1 called");
    Console.WriteLine("Alarm in {0}", args.Location);
    throw new Exception("Bang");
}

static void AlarmListener2(object source, AlarmEventArgs args)
{
    Console.WriteLine("Alarm listener 2 called");
    Console.WriteLine("Alarm in {0}", args.Location);
    throw new Exception("Boom");
}
```

These can be caught and dealt with when the event is raised. The code below raises the alarm in the kitchen location, catches any exceptions that are thrown by subscribers to the alarm event, and then prints out the exception description.

```
try
{
    alarm.RaiseAlarm("Kitchen");
}
catch(AggregateException agg)
{
    foreach(Exception ex in agg.InnerExceptions)
        Console.WriteLine(ex.Message);
}
```

When this sample program runs it outputs the following. Note that the exceptions are listed after the subscriber methods have completed.

```
Alarm listener 1 called
Alarm in Kitchen
Alarm listener 2 called
Alarm in Kitchen
Bang
Boom
Alarm raised
```

Create delegates

Up until now we have used the `Action` and `EventHandler` types, which provide pre-defined delegates. We can, however, create our own delegates. Up until now the delegates that we have seen have maintained a collection of method references. Our applications have used the `+=` and `-=` operators to add method references to a given delegate. You can also create a delegate that refers to a single method in an object.

A delegate type is declared using the `delegate` keyword. The statement here creates a delegate type called `IntOperation` that can refer to a method of type integer that accepts two integer parameters.

```
delegate int IntOperation(int a, int b);
```

A program can now create delegate variables of type `IntOperation`. When a delegate variable is declared it can be set to refer a given method. In Listing 1-71 below the op variable is made to refer first to a method called `Add`, and then to a method called `Subtract`. Each time that op is called it will execute the method that it has been made to refer to.

LISTING 1-71 Create delegates

```
using System;

namespace LISTING_1_71_Create_delegates
{
    class Program
    {
        delegate int IntOperation(int a, int b);
```

```
static int Add(int a, int b)
{
    Console.WriteLine("Add called");
    return a + b;
}

static int Subtract(int a, int b)
{
    Console.WriteLine("Subtract called");
    return a - b;
}

static void Main(string[] args)
{
    // Explicitly create the delegate
    op = new IntOperation(Add);
    Console.WriteLine(op(2, 2));

    // Delegate is created automatically
    // from method
    op = Subtract;
    Console.WriteLine(op(2, 2));
    Console.ReadKey();
}
```

Note that the code in Listing 1-71 also shows that a program can explicitly create an instance of the delegate class. The C# compiler will automatically generate the code to create a delegate instance when a method is assigned to the delegate variable.

Delegates can be used in exactly the same way as any other variable. You can have lists and dictionaries that contain delegates and you can also use them as parameters to methods.

Delegate vs delegate

It is important to understand the difference between delegate (with a lower-case d) and Delegate (with an upper-case D). The word delegate with a lower-case d is the keyword used in a C# program that tells the compiler to create a delegate type. It is used in Listing 1-71 to create the delegate type IntOperation.

```
delegate int IntOperation(int a, int b);
```

The word Delegate with an upper-case D is the abstract class that defines the behavior of delegate instances. Once the delegate keyword has been used to create a delegate type, objects of that delegate type will be realized as Delegate instances.

```
IntOperation op;
```

This statement creates an IntOperation value called op. The variable op is an instance of the System.MultiCastDelegate type, which is a child of the Delegate class. A program can use the variable op to either hold a collection of subscribers or to refer to a single method.

Use lambda expressions (anonymous methods)

Delegates allow a program to treat behaviors (methods in objects) as items of data. A delegate is an item of data that serves as a reference to a method in an object. This adds a tremendous amount of flexibility for programmers. However, delegates are hard work to use. The actual delegate type must first be declared and then made to refer to a particular method containing the code that describes the action to be performed.

Lambda expressions are a pure way of expressing the "something goes in, something happens and something comes out" part of behaviors. The types of the elements and the result to be returned are inferred from the context in which the lambda expression is used. Consider the following statement.

```
delegate int IntOperation(int a, int b);
```

This statement declares the IntOperation delegate that was used in Listing 1-71. The IntOperation delegate can refer to any operation that takes in two integer parameters and returns an integer result. Now consider this statement, which creates an IntOperation delegate called add and assigns it to a lambda expression that accepts two input parameters and returns their sum.

```
IntOperation add = (a, b) => a + b;
```

The operator => is called the *lambda operator*. The items a and b on the left of the lambda expression are mapped onto method parameters defined by the delegate. The statement on the right of the lambda expression gives the behavior of the expression, and in this case adds the two parameters together.

When describing the behavior of the lambda expression you can use the phrase "goes into" to describe what is happening. In this case you could say "a and b go into a plus b." The name lambda comes from *lambda calculus*, a branch of mathematics that concerns "functional abstraction."

This lambda expression accepts two integer parameters and returns an integer. Lambda expressions can accept multiple parameters and contain multiple statements, in which case the statements are enclosed in a block. Listing 1-72 shows how to create a lambda expression that prints out a message as well as performing a calculation.

LISTING 1-72 Lambda expressions

```
add = (a,b) =>
{
    Console.WriteLine("Add called");
    return a + b;
};
```

Closures

The code in a lambda expression can access variables in the code around it. These variables must be available when the lambda expression runs, so the compiler will extend the lifetime of variables used in lambda expressions.

Listing 1-73 shows how this works. The method SetLocal declares a local variable called localInt and sets its value to 99. Under normal circumstances the variable localInt would be destroyed upon completion of the SetLocal method. However, the localInt variable is used in a lambda expression, which is assigned to the delegate getLocal. The compiler makes sure that the localInt variable is available for use in the lambda expression when it is subsequently called from the Main method. This extension of variable life is called a *closure*.

LISTING 1-73 Closures

```
using System;

namespace LISTING_1_73_Closures
{
    class Program
    {
        delegate int GetValue();

        static GetValue getLocalInt;

        static void SetLocalInt()
        {
            // Local variable set to 99
            int localInt = 99;

            // Set delegate getLocalInt to a lambda expression that
            // returns the value of localInt
            getLocalInt = () => localInt;
        }

        static void Main(string[] args)
        {
            SetLocalInt ();
            Console.WriteLine("Value of localInt {0}", getLocalInt ());
            Console.ReadKey();
        }
    }
}
```

Built in types for use with lambda expressions

Consider the following three statements:

```
delegate int IntOperation(int a, int b);
IntOperation add = (a, b) => a + b;
Console.WriteLIne(add(2,2);
```

The first statement creates a delegate called IntOperation that accepts two integer values and returns an integer result. The second statement creates an IntOperation called add which uses a lambda expression to describe what it does, which is to add the two parameters together and return the result. The third statement actually uses the add operation to calculate and print 2+2.

This works, but we had to create the IntOperation delegate type to specify a behavior that accepts two integers and returns their sum before we could create something that referred to a lambda expression of that type. There are a number of "built-in" delegate types that we can use to provide a context for a lambda expression.

The Func types provide a range of delegates for methods that accept values and return results. Listing 1-74 shows how the Func type is used to create an add behavior that has the same return type and parameters as the IntOperation delegate in Listing 1-71. There are versions of the Func type that accept up to 16 input items. The add method here accepts two integers and returns an integer as the result.

LISTING 1-74 Built in delegates

```
Func<int,int,int> add = (a, b) => a + b;
```

If the lambda expression doesn't return a result, you can use the Action type that you saw earlier when we created our first delegates. The statement below creates a delegate called logMessage that refers to a lambda expression that accepts a string and then prints it to the console. For different forms of loging the logMessage delegate can be attached to other methods that save the log data to a file.

```
static Action<string> logMessage = (message) => Console.WriteLine(message);
```

The Predicate built in delegate type lets you create code that takes a value of a particular type and returns true or false. The dividesByThree predicate below returns true if the value is divisible by 3.

```
Predicate<int> dividesByThree = (i) => i % 3 == 0;
```

Anonymous methods

Up until now we have been using lambda expressions that are attached to delegates. The delegate provides a name by which the code in the lambda expression can be accessed. However, a lambda expression can also be used directly in a context where you just want to express a particular behavior. The program in Listing 1-75 uses Task.Run to start a new task. The code performed by the task is expressed directly as a lambda expression, which is given as an argument to the Task.Run method. At no point does this code ever have a name.

LISTING 1-75 Lambda expression task

```
using System;
using System.Threading;
using System.Threading.Tasks;

namespace LISTING_1_75_lambda_expression_task
{
    class Program
    {
        static void Main(string[] args)
        {
            Task.Run( () =>
            {
                for (int i = 0; i < 5 ; i++)
```

```
                {
                    Console.WriteLine(i);
                    Thread.Sleep(500);
                }
            });

            Console.WriteLine("Task running..");
            Console.ReadKey();
        }
    }
}
```

A lambda expression used in this way can be described as an *anonymous method*; because it is a piece of functional code that doesn't have a name.

Skill 1.5 Implement exception handling

The need to handle errors is a natural consequence of writing useful programs. Exceptions are, as their name implies, errors that occur in exceptional circumstances. I don't consider something like an invalid user input as a situation that should be managed by the use of exceptions. User error is to be expected and dealt with in the normal running of a solution.

A program should use an exception to manage an error if it is not meaningful for the program to continue execution at the point the error occurs. For example if a network connection fails or a storage device becomes full. In this section you will learn how to deal with exceptions and how to create and manage exception events of your own.

This section covers how to:

- Handle exception types, including SQL exceptions, network exceptions, communication exceptions, network timeout exceptions
- Use catch statements
- Use base class of an exception
- Implement try-catch-finally blocks
- Throw exceptions
- Rethrow an exception
- Create custom exceptions
- Handle inner exceptions
- Handle aggregate exceptions

Exception types

A program can indicate an error condition by *throwing* an exception object that may be *caught* by an *exception handler*. The purpose of the exception handler is to mitigate the effect of the exception. Handing an exception may involve such actions as alerting the user (if any), creating a log entry, releasing resources, and perhaps even shutting down the application in a well-managed way.

If an exception is not caught by an exception handler within the program it will be caught by the .NET environment and will cause the thread or task to terminate. Uncaught exceptions may cause threads and tasks to fail silently with no message to the user. An uncaught exception thrown in the foreground thread of an application will cause the application to terminate. Exceptions can be nested. When an exception is thrown, the .NET runtime searches up the call stack to find the "closest" exception handler to deal with the exception. This is a comparatively time-consuming process, which means that exceptions should not be used for "run of the mill" errors, but only invoked in exceptional circumstances.

A particular exception is described by an object, which is passed to the exception handler element of a program. The parent type of all exception objects is the Exception class. There are many exception types that describe particular error conditions. Start by considering exceptions that are thrown when a program uses elements of the .NET libraries.

- Input/output exceptions (IOException) are thrown during input/output operations.

- SQL (Structured Query Language) exceptions (SqlException) are thrown in response to an invalid SQL query. The SQL exception object contains a list of SqlError items that describe the error that occurred. In the case of an SQL exception generated by a LINQ query, the actual exception will not be thrown during the execution of the statement containing the query expression. It will be produced within the code that is iterating through the result returned by the expression. LINQ only begins evaluating the query when the results are requested.

- Communications exceptions (CommunicationsException) are thrown during Windows Communication Framework (WCF) operations and network timeout exceptions (TimeOutExceptions) are thrown when a network operation takes too long to compete.

As we shall see in the next section, it is possible to specifically handle a particular exception type by adding a matching catch clause. The signature of a given method does not indicate whether or not the method will generate any exceptions, so when using methods a programmer should carefully check the method documentation to determine whether or not exception handling is required.

The try-catch construction

Exception handling is performed by placing code to be protected in a block following the try keyword. This block of code can be followed by exception handler code, which is preceded by a catch keyword. The exception handler runs in the event of an exception being thrown. Listing 1-76 shows how this works. It contains a program that reads a string of text from the user and uses the Parse method from the int class to convert the text into an integer. This method will throw an exception if it can't convert the string into a valid integer.

LISTING 1-76 Try catch

```
using System;

namespace LISTING_1_76_try_catch
{
    class Program
    {
        static void Main(string[] args)
        {
            try
            {
                Console.Write("Enter an integer: ");
                string numberText = Console.ReadLine();
                int result;
                result = int.Parse(numberText);
                Console.WriteLine("You entered {0}", result);
            }
            catch
            {
                Console.WriteLine("Invalid number entered");
            }
            Console.ReadKey();
        }
    }
}
```

The program in Listing 1-76 does not use the exception object that is produced when the exception is thrown. The program in Listing 1-77 catches the exception and uses the Message and StackTrace properties of the exception to generate an error message.

LISTING 1-77 Exception object

```
try
{
    Console.Write("Enter an integer: ");
    string numberText = Console.ReadLine();
    int result;
    result = int.Parse(numberText);
    Console.WriteLine("You entered {0}", result);
}
catch(Exception ex)
{
    Console.WriteLine("Message: " + ex.Message);
    Console.WriteLine("Stacktrace: " + ex.StackTrace);
    Console.WriteLine("HelpLink: " + ex.HelpLink);
    Console.WriteLine("TargetSite: " + ex.TargetSite);
    Console.WriteLine("Source:" + ex.Source);
}
```

The catch keyword is followed by the type of the exception to be caught and the name to be used to refer to the exception object during the exception handler. In Listing 1-77 the value of ex is set to refer to the exception that is generated by the Parse method if it fails. If the user enters an invalid number, the output of the program will be listed as shown next. The first line of the output gives the error message and the `StackTrace` gives the position in the program at which the error occurred. The `HelpLink` property can be set to give further information about the exception. The `TargetSite` property gives the name of the method that causes the exception, and the `Source` property gives the name of the application that caused the error, or the name of the assembly if the application name has not been set. The output here shows the result of the exception.

```
Enter an integer: fred
Message: Input string was not in a correct format.
Stacktrace: at System.Number.StringToNumber(String str, NumberStyles options,
NumberBuffer& number, NumberFormatInfo info, Boolean parseDecimal)
   at System.Number.ParseInt32(String s, NumberStyles style, NumberFormatInfo info)
   at System.Int32.Parse(String s)
   at LISTING_1_77_Exception_object.Program.Main(String[] args) in C:\Users\Rob\
Documents\GitHub\Sample-Code\LISTING 1-77 Exception object\LISTING 1-77 Exception
object\Program.cs:line 14
HelpLink:
TargetSite: Void StringToNumber(System.String, System.Globalization.NumberStyles,
NumberBuffer ByRef, System.Globalization.NumberFormatInfo, Boolean)
Source:mscorlib
```

Using the base class of an exception

The example in Listing 1-77 catches all exceptions because the `Exception` class is the base class of all exception types. The program in Listing 1-78 reads an integer and then performs an integer division, dividing 1 by the entered number. This action can generate two exceptions; the user might not enter a valid number or the user might enter the value 0, which will cause a divide by zero exception. The program also contains a third catch element, which will catch any other exceptions that might be thrown by this code. The order of the catch elements is important. If the first catch element caught the `Exception` type the compiler would produce the error "A previous catch clause already catches all exceptions of this or of a super type ('Exception')". You must put the most abstract exception type last in the sequence.

LISTING 1-78 Exception types

```csharp
using System;

namespace LISTING_1_78_Exception_types
{
    class Program
    {
        static void Main(string[] args)
        {
            try
            {
                Console.Write("Enter an integer: ");
                string numberText = Console.ReadLine();
                int result;
                result = int.Parse(numberText);
                Console.WriteLine("You entered {0}", result);
                int sum = 1 / result;
```

```
            Console.WriteLine("Sum is {0}", sum);
        }
        catch (NotFiniteNumberException nx)
        {
            Console.WriteLine("Invalid number");
        }
        catch (DivideByZeroException zx)
        {
            Console.WriteLine("Divide by zero");
        }
        catch (Exception ex)
        {
            Console.WriteLine("Unexpected exception");
        }

        Console.ReadKey();
    }
  }
}
```

Note that not all arithmetic errors will throw an exception at this point in the code; if the same division is performed using the floating point or double precision type, the result will be evaluated as "infinity."

Implement try-catch-finally blocks

The try construction can contain a finally element that identifies code that will be executed irrespective of whatever happens in the try construction. The program in Listing 1-79 displays the thank you message, whether or not any exceptions are thrown when the program runs.

LISTING 1-79 The finally block

```
using System;

namespace LISTING_1_79_The_finally_block
{
    class Program
    {
        static void Main(string[] args)
        {
            try
            {
                Console.Write("Enter an integer: ");
                string numberText = Console.ReadLine();
                int result;
                result = int.Parse(numberText);
                Console.WriteLine("You entered {0}", result);
                int sum = 1 / result;
                Console.WriteLine("Sum is {0}", sum);
            }
            catch (NotFiniteNumberException nx)
            {
                Console.WriteLine("Invalid number");
```

```
        }
        catch (DivideByZeroException zx)
        {
            Console.WriteLine("Divide by zero");
        }
        catch (Exception ex)
        {
            Console.WriteLine("Unexpected exception");
        }
        finally
        {
            Console.WriteLine("Thanks for using my program.");
        }

        Console.ReadKey();
        }
    }
}
```

Note that code in this block is guaranteed to run irrespective of what happens during the try construction. This includes situations where the code in the construction returns to a calling method or code in the exception handlers cause other exceptions to be thrown. The finally block is where a program can release any resources that it may be using.

The only situation in which a finally block will *not* be executed are:

- If preceding code (in either the try block or an exception handler) enters an infinite loop.
- If the programmer uses the Environment.FailFast method in the code protected by the try construction to explicitly request that any finally elements are ignored.

Throwing exceptions

A program can create and throw its own exceptions by using the throw statement to throw an exception instance. The Exception object constructor accepts a string that is used to deliver a descriptive message to the exception handler. The program in Listing 1-80 throws an exception and catches it, displaying the message.

LISTING 1-80 Throwing an exception

```
using System;

namespace LISTING_1_80_Throwing_an_exception
{
    class Program
    {
        static void Main(string[] args)
        {
            try
            {
                throw new Exception (
                        "I think you should know that I'm feeling very depressed.");
            }
            catch(Exception ex)
```

```
        {
            Console.WriteLine(ex.Message);
        }
        Console.ReadKey();
    }
  }
}
```

Rethrowing an exception

One of the fundamental principles of exception design is that catching an exception should not lead to errors being hidden from other parts of an application. Sometimes an exception will be caught that needs to be "passed up" to an enclosing exception handler. This might be because the low-level handler doesn't recognize the exception, or it might be because a handler at a higher level must also be alerted to the occurring exception. An exception can be re-thrown by using the keyword throw with no parameter:

```
throw;
```

You might think that when re-throwing an exception, you should give the exception object to be re-thrown, as shown here:

```
catch(Exception ex)
{
    Console.WriteLine(ex.Message);
    throw ex; // this will not preserve the original stack trace
}
```

This is bad practice because it will remove the stack trace information that is part of the original exception and replace it with stack trace information that describes the position reached in the exception handler code. This will make it harder to work out what is going on when the error occurs, because the location of the error will be reported as being in your handler, rather than at the point at which the original exception was generated.

Inner exceptions

Another way to manage the propagation of error conditions in an application is to pass the original exception object as an *inner exception* for a higher-level exception handler to deal with. The Exception class contains an InnerException property that can be set when the exception is constructed. The constructor for the newly created exception is given a reference to the original exception.

```
catch(Exception ex)
{
    Console.WriteLine(ex.Message);
    throw new Exception("Something bad happened", ex);
}
```

Handler inner exceptions are covered in the "Handling Inner Exceptions" section.

Creating custom exceptions

When designing an application, you should also decide (and design) how the application will respond to any error conditions. This can include the creation of custom exception types for your program. The name of the exception class should end with "Exception." The CalcException class in Listing 1-81 contains an error code value that is set when the exception is constructed. This error code can then be used in the exception handler.

LISTING 1-81 Custom exceptions

```
using System;

namespace LISTING_1_81_Custom_exceptions
{
    class CalcException : Exception
    {
        public enum CalcErrorCodes
        {
            InvalidNumberText,
            DivideByZero
        }

        public CalcErrorCodes Error { get; set; }

        public CalcException(string message, CalcErrorCodes error) : base(message)
        {
            Error = error;
        }
    }

    class Program
    {

        static void Main(string[] args)
        {
            try
            {
                throw new CalcException("Calc failed",
                CalcException.CalcErrorCodes.InvalidNumberText);
            }
            catch (CalcException ce)
            {
                Console.WriteLine("Error: {0}", ce.Error);
            }
            Console.ReadKey();
        }
    }
}
```

Conditional clauses in catch blocks

An exception handler can re-throw an exception if it is not in a position to deal with the exception. You saw this in the "Throwing exceptions" section earlier in this chapter. An alternative to re-throwing an exception is to create a handler that only catches exceptions that contain particular data values.

The code in Listing 1-82 shows how this is achieved. The when keyword is followed by a conditional clause that performs a test on the exception object. The exception handler will only trigger in the event of an exception being thrown that has an Error property set to DivideByZero. An exception with any other error code is ignored, and in the case of the example program, will cause the program to terminate immediately as an unhandled exception has been thrown.

LISTING 1-82 Conditional clauses

```
try
{
    throw new CalcException("Calc failed", CalcException.CalcErrorCodes.DivideByZero);
}
catch (CalcException ce) when (ce.Error == CalcException.CalcErrorCodes.DivideByZero)
{
    Console.WriteLine("Divide by zero error");
}
```

If the program in Listing 1-82 is executed it will display the message: "Divide by zero error." If the error value in the throw statement is changed from DivideByZero to InvalidNumberText, the program will instead fail with an unhandled exception.

This mechanism is more efficient than re-throwing an exception, because the .NET runtime doesn't have to rebuild the exception object prior to re-throwing it.

Handling inner exceptions

An exception can contain an inner exception property that is set when it is constructed. An exception handler can extract this and use it as part of the exception management process. The program in Listing 1-83 contains an exception handler that throws a new exception containing an inner exception that describes the error. If the user enters text that cannot be parsed into an integer, an exception is thrown that is caught, and then a new exception is raised with the error, "Calculator Failure." The new exception contains the original exception as an inner exception. The new exception is then caught and displayed.

LISTING 1-83 Inner exceptions

```
using System;

namespace LISTING_1_83_Inner_exceptions
{
    class Program
    {
        static void Main(string[] args)
        {
            try
            {
                try
```

```
            {
                Console.Write("Enter an integer: ");
                string numberText = Console.ReadLine();
                int result;
                result = int.Parse(numberText);
            }
            catch (Exception ex)
            {
                throw new Exception("Calculator failure", ex);
            }
        }
        catch (Exception ex)
        {
            Console.WriteLine(ex.Message);
            Console.WriteLine(ex.InnerException.Message);
            Console.WriteLine(ex.InnerException.StackTrace);
        }

        Console.ReadKey();
        }
    }
}
```

Note that the use of inner exceptions must be planned, because handlers must be expecting the inner exception to refer to meaningful information about the error that has occurred.

Handling aggregate exceptions

Some .NET exception types contain lists of inner exceptions. These are called "aggregate exceptions." They occur when more than one thing can fail as an operation is performed, or when the results of a series of actions need to be brought together.

The program in Listing1-84 shows a situation in which aggregate exceptions are used to deliver results from a method that is called to read the text from a web page. The AgregateException is caught and the message from each exception is displayed.

LISTING 1-84 Aggregate exceptions

```
using System;
using System.Net.Http;
using System.Threading.Tasks;

namespace LISTING_1_84_Aggregate_exceptions
{
    class Program
    {
        async static Task<string> FetchWebPage(string uri)
        {
            var httpClient = new HttpClient();
            var response = await httpClient.GetAsync(uri);
            return await response.Content.ReadAsStringAsync();
        }

        static void Main(string[] args)
```

```
        {
            try
            {
                Task<string> getpage = FetchWebPage("invalid uri");
                getpage.Wait();
                Console.WriteLine(getpage.Result);
            }
            catch ( AggregateException ag)
            {
                foreach(Exception e in ag.InnerExceptions)
                {
                    Console.WriteLine(e.Message);
                }
            }
            Console.ReadKey();
        }
    }
}
```

You have also seen the use of aggregate exceptions when considering how to deal with exceptions thrown by parallel LINQ enquiries (LISTING_1_10_Exceptions_in_PLINQ) and when aggregating exceptions raised during event handers (LISTING_1_70_Aggregating_exceptions).

Exceptions as part of managed error handing

You should make sure that your code deals with any exceptions that may be thrown by methods, propagating the exception onward if necessary to ensure that exception events are not hidden from different parts of your application.

Your methods should also throw exceptions in situations where it is not meaningful to continue with an action. If a method throws an exception the caller must deal with that exception if the program is to continue running. However, if a method returns an error code when something goes wrong, this error code could be ignored by the caller.

It is important that you consider how to manage error conditions during the design of an application. It is very hard to add error management to an application once it has been created.

Thought experiments

In these thought experiments, demonstrate your skills and knowledge of the topics covered in this chapter. You can find the answers to these thought experiments in the next section.

1 Using multiple tasks

At the design stage of an application you will have to decide whether/how to use tasks and threads. Here are some questions that you might like to consider:

1. Given the difficulties in synchronization and management, is it worth the effort to implement applications using multiple tasks?

2. Is it still worth the effort to use multiple-tasks if you only have one processor in your computer?

3. What kind of applications benefit the most from the use of multi-tasking applications?

4. Are there situations when you really should not use multi-tasking?

5. I need a background process that is going to compress a large number of data files. Should I use a task or a thread?

6. What is the difference between the `WaitAll` and `WaitAny` method when waiting for a large number of tasks to complete?

7. What is the difference between a continuation task and a child task?

8. What is the difference between the `WaitAll` and `WhenAll` methods?

9. What happens when a method call is awaited?

10. What is special about a concurrent collection?

2 Managing multithreading

Multithreaded applications will need to give special consideration to the way that data is processed and the ordering of operations. They will also have to contain provision for process management.

Here are some questions that you might like to consider:

1. Will program errors caused by a poor multithreading implementation always manifest themselves as faults in an application?

2. Does the fact that the processor is suddenly at 100% loading indicate that two processes are stuck in a deadly embrace?

3. Could you make an object thread safe by enclosing the body code of all the methods in lock statements to make all the method actions atomic?

4. If you're not sure about potential race conditions, is it best to add lock statements around critical sections of your code "just in case?"

5. Should a task always generate an exception if it is cancelled?

6. Could you make an application that automatically cancelled deadlocked processes?

3 Program flow

The C# language provides constructions that the programmer can use to manage the flow of program execution. Statements can be repeated a given number of times, until a specific state has been reached, or over a collection of items. Statements can be executed conditionally using the `if` construction, or selected on the basis of a particular control variable in the case of a switch.

Here are some questions which you might like to consider:

1. Is it necessary to have both the while and the do-while looping construction?

2. Is a break statement the only way of exiting a loop before it completes?

3. Can you identify a situation where you would use a for loop to iterate through a collection rather than a foreach loop?

4. The and (&) logical operator and the or (|) logical operator have "short circuit" versions (&& and ||), which only evaluate elements until it can be determined whether or not a given expression is true or false. Why does the exclusive-or (^) operator not have a short circuit version?

5. Is it true that each C# operator has a behavior that is the same for every context in which it is used?

6. Can you always be certain of the precise sequence of operations when an expression is evaluated?

4 Events and callbacks

Programmers can use delegates to create applications from "loosely coupled" objects that communicate by message events. An object can subscribe to events published by another object which exposes a delegate.

A lambda expression can be used to create "anonymous functions" that exists as pure behaviors. Delegates can be made to refer to anonymous functions.

Here are some questions that you might like to consider:

1. How does a delegate actually work?

2. What happens if a delegate is assigned to a delegate?

3. What happens if a delegate is assigned to itself?

4. Is there an upper limit for the number of subscribers that a publisher delegate can have?

5. What does the lambda operator (=>) actually do?

6. Can code in a lambda expression access data from the enclosing code?

5 Exceptions

Exceptions are an important part of application development. At the very least an application will have to handle exceptions that may be produced by .NET methods that it uses. For a large application you may have to design custom exception types and create an error handling strategy that manages how exceptions are propagated and managed. It is important to put exceptions in the correct perspective; any error that you would expect the system to deal with in the normal course of events should not be handled by the use of an exception, they should be reserved for situations where it is not meaningful for the application to continue.

Here are some questions that you might like to consider:

1. Is a method receiving a date of "31ˢᵗ of February" something that should cause an exception?

2. Should I make sure that all exceptions are always caught by my program?

3. Can you return to the code after an exception has been caught?

4. Why do we need the finally clause? Can't code to be run after the code in a try clause just be put straight after the end of the catch?

5. Should my application always use custom exceptions?

Though experiment answers

This section provides the solutions for the tasks included in the thought experiments.

1 Using multiple tasks

1. Breaking an application into separate tasks is not just something that you would do to make use of the performance advantages. Tasks provide a very useful level of abstraction. Once the communication between the tasks has been designed, each one can be worked on independently. Partitioning an application into tasks can be seen as a natural extension of component-based design.

2. Consider a program that is performing a numeric analysis of a particular data set. Once the data has been loaded into memory the time it takes to be processed is determined by the speed of the CPU. We would say that this program was *cpu bound*. If a system only has one processor, converting the program to use a multi-threaded implementation would not improve the rate at which the data is processed. However, consider a program that is continuously interacting with the file system. We would say this application was *IO (input/output) bound*, in that the rate at which it can work is determined by performance of the file system. When an IO bound program is active it will frequently be unable to do any work as it waits file transactions to complete. A multi-threaded solution would be able to perform processing at the times when one task was waiting for an input/output operation to complete.

3. A CPU bound application will benefit from a multi-tasking approach if the host system has more than one CPU. Note that the programmer may have to spend some effort re-working the application to allow it to work over multiple tasks. An application that contains a mix of CPU bound and IO bound tasks can benefit most from a multi-threading approach as there will always be something for the processor to do.

4. The asynchronous nature of a multi-threaded application makes it very hard to guarantee that a given operation will be completed within a specified time. Threads can be given priority levels, but these are not hard and fast. Applications with critical timing requirements should not be implemented using multiple threads.

5. When choosing between tasks and threads you need to consider what you want to achieve. Tasks are good for background processes. Threads can be used for background processes but can also run as foreground processes. Tasks are easier to create. In this situation a Task would make the most sense, because it would be easier to create and will never need to operate in the foreground.

6. The WaitAll method will return when all the tasks that are running have completed. The WaitAny method will return when the first of the running tasks completes.

7. A continuation task is a task that is started when an existing task completes. A child task is created by a parent task and executes independently of the parent.

8. The WaitAll method accepts a list of Task references as an argument and returns when all the tasks have completed. The WaitAll method does not return a result. The WhenAll method accepts a list of Task references as an argument and returns a Task that delivers the results returned by those tasks. The WhenAll method is can be awaited, which allows it to be used in asynchronous code.

9. Methods that can be awaited return a reference to a Task. When a program performs an await in an asynchronous method, the asynchronous method returns immediately. When the task returned by the awaited method completes the remainder of the asynchronous method will complete. A good example of a situation where this can be used to good effect is in user interfaces. A user interface method, for example the code that implements a behavior when a button is clicked in the user interface, must return as quickly as possible. Otherwise the user interface will become unresponsive. By using await the button click handler can complete and return, while the action initiated by the button click runs in parallel.

10. A concurrent collection is one which has behaviors that can be used by multiple processes at the same time. Some concurrent collections, for example Concurrent-Dictionary, have additional behaviors that allow processes to only perform updates to data stored in the collection when it is valid to do so.

2 Managing multithreading

1. There is no guarantee that the conditions that might cause a race condition to cause a problem will arise. Natural delays in a system might mean that events occur in an order that means race conditions do not cause a problem. For example, if one task is writing a file to a disk, there is a good chance that this task will take longer to complete than another which is updating the display. However, problems might suddenly appear when the user buys a faster disk-drive or installs more memory. This might speed up the write action and cause the application to become unstable. In fact, these symptoms are the best way of diagnosing problems like this. The first question you should ask a user whose program has suddenly become unreliable is "Have you made any changes to the underlying system?"

2. The simplest form of deadlock occurs when two tasks are waiting for locks to be released by each other. More complex deadlocks can be spread over a larger number of tasks. However, when a deadlock occurs a program is not executing very rapidly, in fact nothing is happening at all, all the tasks are waiting for each other, and the application is taking no processor time at all.

3. Making all method calls in an object atomic is a very heavy handed and dangerous approach to achieving thread safety. It may well make an application vulnerable to deadlocks and could also remove any performance advantage that would be gained by using multiple processors. Furthermore, it does not protect against issues caused by the use of reference parameters to a method.

4. Adding lock statements around critical pieces of code without thinking about what the code actually does is very dangerous. It may well lead to performance bottlenecks and deadlocks. It is very difficult to add thread safety to a program once it has been written. The only sure-fire way I've found of writing thread safe code is to design it that way from the start.

5. A task can be cancelled "silently", in which case it will just end. Alternatively, it can be made to generate an exception when cancelled. From a design perspective I tend to regard cancelling a task as an exceptional action and would therefore expect there to be some way of propagating this event through the system so that it can be registered in some way.

6. If you use the Monitor construction to manage entry into atomic actions it is possible for a task to retain control when it fails to get a lock and enter an atomic action. You can even establish a time-out by adding a timeout value to a call of the TryEnter method to try and enter an atomic action. It would therefore be possible for a program to recognize that a given lock had been unavailable for a more than a certain length of time. It could then use a cancellation token to try and stop a task that might have obtained the synchronization object. Of course, this would only work correctly if the task that is causing the deadlock is checking its cancellation token while it is waiting for its lock. In other words, yes it would be possible to do this, but it would entail a lot of extra work. The best way to avoid deadlocks is to make sure that they are not present in the design of your system.

3 Program flow

1. The while and do-while loop constructions differ in only one respect. The while construction will not execute any code if the control condition is false, whereas the do-while construction tests the control condition at the completion of the loop, so the code controlled by it is always executed once, even if the control condition is false at the start. At the expense of a slightly more complicated program, it is possible to only use one form of the loop construction, both are provided to make the programmers life slightly easier.

2. If a break is used in a loop the program will exit the loop at that point. It is also possible to exit a loop by returning from the method in which the loop is declared. Finally a program will exit a loop if it throws an exception within the loop.

3. A `foreach` construction provides a very convenient way to express a need to enumerate each of the items in a collection. However, each enumerated item is provided on a "read-only" basis. If the program wants to change the value of an enumerated item it is necessary to use a `for` loop to access each item. Note that if the `foreach` construction is iterating through a collection of reference types it is perfectly permissible to change properties of each iterated item.

4. There is no short-circuit version of the exclusive-or operator because it is not possible to determine whether an exclusive-or is true by just examining one of the operands. Remember that an exclusive-or operation returns true if the two operands are different. It is not possible to make this determination by just examining one of the operands.

5. No. C# operators have different behaviors depending on the *context* in which they are used. The integer and floating-point types are held in quite different ways in the memory of the computer. When arithmetic operators are used between these types the compiler will select the correct operator to be used depending on the type of the operands in the expression.

6. The C# compiler guarantees that expressions will be evaluated according to the rules of *precedence* and *associability* for the operators in the expression. However, the precise sequence in which the operations are performed is not something that a programmer can make any assumptions about.

4 Events and callbacks

1. A delegate is a type that can refer to a method in an object with a particular signature. A delegate can also contain lists of method references. A delegate is called in exactly the same way as the method it can refer to. If the delegate contains a list of method references, each method is called in no particular order. The base type of all delegate objects is the Delegate class.

2. Delegates can be assigned to other delegates, as long as they have the same signature. Delegates can also be added to the subscribers of a multi-cast delegate.

3. A delegate can be assigned to itself, but this is not a sensible thing to do. If the delegate is ever called the program will enter an infinite loop.

4. There is no upper limit, over and above the capacity of the data structure in the `Delegate` class which holds references to subscribers.

5. The lambda operator (=>) separates the items that go into the expression (the input parameters) from the statement or statement block that implements the behavior of the lambda expression.

6. Code in a lambda expression can access variables declared in code enclosing the lambda expression. Note that code in a lambda expression is not executed when the lambda expression is declared, a reference to the lambda expression may be followed at a much later time. The C# compiler will generate code that maintains variables used by the code in the lambda expression even if they would normally be out of scope at the time the code in the lambda expression is performed.

5 Exceptions

1. It all depends on the context of the action. If the date is being entered by the user, it is reasonable for the program to display an error message and request that the date be re-entered. In this case no exception will be thrown. However, if the date is being supplied to a method that is expected to create a transaction with this date, it is reasonable for that method to throw an exception if given an invalid date value, as it would not be meaningful for the method to generate anything. Throwing an exception, rather than returning an error code or a null value, is a way of ensuring that the program will fail in a properly noticeable way and maximizes the chances of the mistake being detected. From a design perspective, the need for exceptions in this situation would be completely removed if the method creating the transaction was passed a DateTime structure. This can only contain a valid date.

2. No. There is only one thing worse than a program that fails, and that is a program that fails silently. You might think it is a good idea to wrap your entire program in a try construction. This would mean that the program would never fail due to an uncaught exception. However, it would also make the program impossible to debug and prone to failing silently. You should take care to catch all the exceptions that you know how to deal with, and let the remaining ones pass through so that they are either caught by layers above (in a managed and designed way) or propagate as errors which can be caught and dealt with.

3. There is no way to return to the statements after an exception has been thrown. If a program wants to re-try code that may throw exceptions, this code must be placed in a loop.

4. We need a finally clause because code in the catch clause may return from a method or throw other exceptions, in which case the program will not reach the statements following the catch. The finally clause is guaranteed to be executed in all circumstances.

5. The standard Exception type provides a great deal of flexibility; it contains a Dictionary which can be filled with name-value pairs that describe an error. Custom exception types can be useful if none of the existing exception types are suitable for the exception context. Because different catch clauses can be allocated to different exception types, they also make exceptions easier to manage.

Chapter summary

- Multi-threading allows an application to be made up of a number of cooperating processes.

- When you create a multi-threaded application, its behaviors are spread amongst a number of co-operating tasks. The tasks may be performed in parallel if the host computer has multiple central processor units (CPUs). A single CPU will execute each active task in turn on a round-robin basis.

- Creating a multi-threaded application can be as simple as taking an existing set of actions and using the Task.Parallel library or Parallel LINQ to execute the actions as multiple tasks.

- The .NET Task class provides a high-level abstraction of a running task. Tasks can return values and continuation tasks can run automatically when one or more tasks complete. Tasks can also start child tasks, with the *parent* task being held until all the child tasks have completed.

- The .NET Thread class provides a lower level abstraction of a running task. Threads cannot return results, nor can you create continuation threads. However, threads can run as foreground or background processes. Tasks can only run as background processes. A foreground process will run until complete, whereas a background process will be terminated upon the completion of the foreground process that created it. It is also possible to set the priority of a thread (although this is purely advisory, it doesn't guarantee that a given thread will be allowed a particular level of access to the processor).

- Async and await make it very easy to create multi-threaded applications. The await keyword precedes a call to a method that has been identified as asynchronous by the async keyword. An asynchronous method can return a Task (if the asynchronous method returns void) or a Task<type> (if the method wishes to return a value). The compiler will generate code that allows an asynchronous method to return to the caller when the await keyword is reached. The statements following the await will be performed concurrently. This way of working is of particular value when building the user interface to a program. An asynchronous action bound to a button press will unblock the user interface at the first await, rather than stopping the user interface until the action performed by the button has completed. An application can catch exceptions thrown during asynchronous calls by enclosing the awaited action in an exception handler, but this only works if the awaited action returns a value. For this reason, void asynchronous calls should be avoided as there is no way of determining whether they succeeded or not.

- The standard .NET collection classes are not *thread safe*. This means that if multiple tasks attempt to share data using a List, the contents of the list will be corrupted. The .NET framework provides a set of concurrent collections that can be shared by multiple active tasks. The BlockingCollection class provides a wrapper around ConcurrentStack, ConcurrentQueue and ConcurrentBag concurrent collections. Tasks using a BlockingCollection will be blocked (paused) if there is no room for additional items, or if they try to take items from an empty collection. The concurrent collections provide "try" versions of methods to extract items which return whether an action succeeded or not. This is because in the time between determining that there are items available and reading them it is possible that another task could have removed the items. The ConcurrentDictionary class provides additional methods for the conditional update of items in the dictionary.

- Multi-threaded applications are vulnerable to *race conditions* where actions by a task on a shared data item are not run to completion before that task is replaced by another.

- Race conditions can be addressed by making actions *atomic,* in that they will always complete before another task is allowed to perform the action. This is achieved by the use of lock objects. A task claims the lock and while it has the lock, other tasks trying to claim that lock and enter the atomic code will be blocked. This may result in a queue of blocked tasks waiting for a particular lock to be released.

- Two tasks waiting for locks from each other are said to be *deadlocked* or in a *deadly embrace.* Deadlocks can arise as a result of code which waits for access to a lock object while inside an atomic action. This should be addressed by good design.

- The Monitor mechanism for locking can be used in preference to the lock keyword if an application would benefit from tasks being able to determine whether or not they can have access to an atomic action, rather than being blocked as soon as they try to acquire the lock.

- Simple actions, such as updating a particular variable, can be achieved by using the interlocked operations, rather than creating atomic blocks of code.

- Variables that may be used by multiple processes can be marked as "volatile." This tells the compiler not to perform optimization such as caching the value of the variable in a processor register, or changing the order of instructions.

- Tasks can be cancelled by the use of cancellation tokens. As a task runs it must check state of the token to determine if a cancellation has been requested. This is an important difference between a Task and a Thread. Threads can be aborted by another process at any time. One task can request that another task be cancelled, but this will only actually result in that thread ending if the code in the task is checking the cancellation token. Note that this does not mean that an active task can never be removed from memory however, because tasks run in the background they are automatically terminated upon completion of the foreground process that created them.

- Methods in an object must be made *thread safe* if they are to be used in applications that contain multiple tasks. Access to data members of the class containing the thread safe method must be managed in an atomic manner. Parameters passed into the method by reference are vulnerable to changes to elements in the parameter that may occur while the method is running.

- A while construction is useful in situations where you want to repeat something as long as a condition is true. A do-while construction is useful in situations where you want to do something and then repeat it if the action failed.

- A for construction is an easy way to perform initialization, test and update actions on a loop. A for construction frequently involves the management of a counter value, but this is not the only way in which this construction can be used.

- A foreach construction can be used to enumerate the items in a collection. The collection provides a method that will provide an enumerator which is then iterated by the foreach construction. The items in the collection are provided as read-only.

- The break statement allows a program to exit a loop immediately. A large number of breaks in a loop can make it hard to discern the circumstances in which the loop exited. A loop can also be exited upon return from the method in which the loop is running and when code in the loop throws an exception that is not caught in the loop.

- The continue statement allows a program to return to the "top" of a loop and repeat the loop without going any further through the loop code. Note that any update and test behaviors will be performed when a continue statement runs.

- An if construction allows the conditional execution of a statement or block of statements. If constructions are controlled by a logical expression and can be followed by an else clause that identifies the statement to be performed if the condition is false. If conditions can be nested, an else portion of an if construction always binds to the "closest" if.

- Logical expressions evaluate to true or false. Variables can be compared using relational and equality operators. Logical values can be combined using and, or and exclusive or operators. The and operator and the or operator have "short circuit" versions that are only evaluated to the point where the value of the expression result can be determined.

- The switch construction allows the selective of a given behavior from the value of a control value which can be an integer, string or character. A default behavior can be specified if the control value does not match any of the selections.

- An expression contains operands and operators. The operands are literal values or variables. Operators have priority and associability that determine the point that the operator is applied during the evaluation of the expression.

- C# programs can use delegates to create variables that can serve as references to methods in objects. An object wishing to receive notifications from a publisher can use a delegate to specify a method to be called by the event publisher. A single publisher delegate makes calls to its subscribers, each of which has provided a delegate.

- The event keyword allows a delegate to be used in a secure way and the EventArgs classes describe a pattern that is used throughout .NET to allow events to deliver data into a subscriber.

- Delegates can also be used as references to individual methods. A delegate referring to a method can be regarded as a piece of data which describes an action.

- A lambda expression allows an action to be expressed directly and provides a convenient shorthand when writing code. The type of parameters and value returned by a lambda expression are inferred from the context of the call.

- An exception is thrown by a program to indicate a situation in which the program cannot continue normal operation. Execution is transferred from the statements being executed in a try block of code to an exception handler in a catch block, which was written to deal with the exception. An exception that is thrown in code that is not within a try construction will cause the executing thread to terminate.

- A `finally` element can be used in a try construction to specify code that will be always be executed.

- A program throws an exception by creating a new exception instance and then using the `throw` keyword to throw it. All exception objects are derived from the Exception class. There are a large number of exception types that are used in the .NET libraries to describe error conditions; a programmer can also create their own exception types that contain their own error-specific information.

- An exception object contains information that describes the error, including a "stack trace" that indicates the point in the program source where the exception is thrown. An exception can also contain an inner exception reference so that a new exception can be wrapped round one that has been caught, before passing the exception to another layer of exception management.

CHAPTER 2

Create and use types

The first thing you have to learn when you start programming is how to create the instructions that tell the computer what to do with incoming data. In Chapter 1, "Manage program flow," the focus was on how to control the flow of execution through code in terms of single programs, but also when to use threads, tasks, and events.

In this chapter the focus is on how to use object-oriented techniques to make it easier to create large scale solutions that contain many different elements that can be worked on by a large number of developers.

You will learn how to create custom data types to hold information that matches the problem requirements. These types may also have behaviors, allowing them to operate as software components that have integrity and provide services for other objects.

You will also learn how to programmatically generate object behaviors, and how to manage the life-cycle of objects in a solution. Finally, you'll discover the powerful features behind the string type provided as part of the C# language.

Skills in this chapter:

- Skill 2.1: Creating types
- Skill 2.2: Consuming types
- Skill 2.3: Enforcing encapsulation
- Skill 2.4: Create and implement a class hierarchy
- Skill 2.5: Find, execute and create types at runtime
- Skill 2.6: Manage the object lifecycle
- Skill 2.7: Manipulate strings

Skill 2.1: Create types

C# provides a range of "built-in" types. You have already encountered such types as `int` and `float` and have seen how to use these types to process data when your program runs. From a software point of view, there is no technical reason why every program in the world can't be written using the "built-in" types provided by C#. The ability to create our own data types in the programs that we write makes software development much easier and less prone to error.

Value and reference types

The first question to be addressed when creating a type in a program is whether the data you are representing should be stored using a *value* type or a *reference* type. A proper understanding of the difference between these types is crucial. The key to understanding the difference between value and reference types is appreciating what happens during the assignment process.

Consider the following two assignment statements. The first statement sets the variable x to equal the variable y. The second statement sets the Data property of the variable x to have the value 100.

```
x = y;
x.Data = 100;
```

If the variables x and y are value types, the result of the first assignment is that the value of y is copied into the variable x. The result of the second assignment is that the Data property of the variable x is then set to the value 100. The Data property in the variable y is not affected by the second assignment.

If the variables x and y are reference types, the result of the first assignment is that the variable x is made to refer to the same object as that referred to by variable y. The result of the second assignment is that the Data property of this single object is set to 100.

The program in Listing 2-1 below shows these behaviors in action. The two assignment statements are performed on structure and class variables. One of these types is managed by reference, and the other is managed by value.

LISTING 2-1 Value and reference types

```
using System;

namespace LISTING_2_1_Value_and_reference_types
{
    class Program
    {
        struct StructStore
        {
            public int Data { get; set; }
        }
```

```
class ClassStore
{
    public int Data { get; set; }
}

static void Main(string[] args)
{
    StructStore xs, ys;
    ys = new StructStore();
    ys.Data = 99;
    xs = ys;
    xs.Data = 100;
    Console.WriteLine("xStruct: {0}", xs.Data);
    Console.WriteLine("yStruct: {0}", ys.Data);

    ClassStore xc, yc;
    yc = new ClassStore();
    yc.Data = 99;
    xc = yc;
    xc.Data = 100;
    Console.WriteLine("xClass: {0}", xc.Data);
    Console.WriteLine("yClass: {0}", yc.Data);

    Console.ReadKey();
}
}
```

When you run this program, you will see the following output:

xStruct: 100

yStruct: 99

xClass: 100

yClass: 100

This shows that structure variables are managed by value (because changes to the variable xStruct do not affect the value of yStruct) and class variables are managed by reference (because xClass and yClass both refer to the same object, so changes via the xClass reference will affect the value referred to by yClass). You should study this code until you understand exactly why it behaves the way that it does, and why the action of the assignment operation is so different for each of the two types.

Value and reference types in .NET

You can learn more about the use of these types by considering some .NET types. The .NET libraries contain a range of types for programmers to use. Some are value types, and others are reference types.

A good example of a value type is the DateTime structure provided by the .NET library. This holds a value that represents a particular date and time. You can represent date values in the form of a collection of individual values, with one for the year, another for the month and so on, but assigning one date to another will be time-consuming because the program has to transfer each value in turn. Having a `DateTime` type that represents a date means that you can move a date value from one variable to another by performing a single assignment. When an assignment to a `DateTime` variable is performed, all of the values that represent the date are copied into the destination variable.

A good example of a reference type is the `Bitmap` class from the `System.Drawing` library in .NET. The `Bitmap` class is used to create objects that hold all of the pixels that make up an image on the screen. Images can contain millions of pixels. If a `Bitmap` is held as a value type, when one `Bitmap` image is assigned to another, all of the pixels in the source `Bitmap` must be copied from the source image into the destination. Because bitmaps are managed by reference, an assignment simply makes the destination reference refer to the same object as the source reference.

Type design

You can build an understanding of value and reference types by considering some data items to store in your program and deciding whether or not they should be held in value or reference types. Perhaps you've been employed to write a "space shooter" game in which the player must shoot missiles at invading aliens.

The first item to consider is the location on the screen of an alien invader. Each alien is to be drawn at a particular X and Y coordinate on the screen. Should this coordinate be stored in a value type, or a reference type?

The answer is value type. This is because the program will want to treat the position of an alien as a single value, and you don't want to share coordinates between different aliens.

The next item to consider is the sound effect that is played when an alien is shot by the player. The sound effect will be held in the program as a large array of integers that represent the particular sound sample. This should be stored as a reference type. You may want to have several aliens share the same sound effect. This is very easy to achieve using references because each alien just has to contain a reference to the one sound effect object held in memory.

It turns out that value types are great for working with objects that you want to think of in terms of values, and reference types are great for working with objects that you want to manage by reference. In other words, the clue is in the name. In a C# program, value types are enumerated types and structures. Reference types are classes.

Immutability in types

When talking about value and reference types we need to mention *immutability*. An immutable type is one whose instances cannot be changed. The `DateTime` structure in the .NET libraries is an example of an immutable type. Once you have created a `DateTime` instance you cannot change any of the elements of that instance. You can read the year, month, and day elements of the instance, but you can't edit them. The only way to edit a `DateTime` value is by creating a new `DateTime` value that contains the updated values.

Listing 2-2 shows how a date can be advanced to the next day. The `DateTime` structure provides a method called `AddDays` to add days to a date, but this does not change the contents of a `DateTime` instance, and instead it returns a new date with the updated value.

LISTING 2-2 Immutable DateTime

```
// Create a DateTime for today
DateTime date = DateTime.Now;

// Move the date on to tomorrow
date = date.AddDays(1);
```

The modification of an immutable value will require the creation of a new object each time, which is less efficient than just changing a value inside an object. However, using an immutable type for a type removes any possibility of elements in a variable changing once it has been created.

Immutable types bring advantages when writing concurrent programs. In Skill 1-2, "Manage multithreading," you saw how race conditions can cause data corruption. An immutable object can never be corrupted because it cannot be changed. The string type in C# is immutable—it is not possible to change the content of a string once it has been created. We will discuss this in more detail when we consider strings later in this section.

Creating value types

There are two kinds of value types that can be created in a C# program. There are structures and enumerated types. Let's take a look at structures first.

Structures

We have already created a simple structure in the program in Listing 2-1. Structures can contain methods, data values, properties and can have constructors. When comparing a structure with a class (which can also contain methods, data values, properties, and constructors) there are some differences between the classes and structures:

- The constructor for a structure must initialize all the data members in the structure. Data members cannot be initialized in the structure.

- It is not possible for a structure to have a parameterless constructor. However, as you shall see, it is possible for a structure to be created by calling a parameterless constructor on the structure type, in which case all the elements of the structure are set to the default values for that type (numeric elements are set to zero and strings are set to null).

- It is not possible to create a structure by extending a parent structure object.

- Structure instances are generally created on the program stack unless they are used in closures (see "Closures" in Skill 1-4, "Create and Implement Event Handlers"). An array of structure instances will be created as a block of contiguous memory, which holds all of the required items. See "Memory allocation" later in this section for more detail on this.

The program in Listing 2-3 creates a structure called Alien, which could be used to keep track of an Alien in the computer game mentioned earlier. An Alien has an X and Y position on the screen, which is set when the alien is created, along with a number of lives set to 3 by the Alien constructor. Note that the program in the listing creates two Alien instances. The first one, called a, is declared and then has its X, Y, and Lives data members set up. The second Alien, called x, is created at the position 100,100 on the screen. The sample program then creates an array of Aliens called swarm. Each element in the array is initialized with the default values for each data member type (in other words the values of X, Y and Lives will be 0).

LISTING 2-3 Creating a structure

```
using System;

namespace LISTING_2_3_Creating_a_structure
{
    struct Alien
    {
        public int X;
        public int Y;
        public int Lives;

        public Alien(int x, int y)
        {
            X = x;
            Y = y;
            Lives = 3;
        }

        public override string ToString()
        {
            return string.Format("X: {0} Y: {1} Lives: {2}", X, Y, Lives);
        }
    }

    class Program
    {
        static void Main(string[] args)
        {
            Alien a;
            a.X = 50;
            a.Y = 50;
            a.Lives = 3;
            Console.WriteLine("a {0}", a.ToString());

            Alien x = new Alien(100, 100);
            Console.WriteLine("x {0}", x.ToString());

            Alien[] swarm = new Alien[100];
            Console.WriteLine("swarm [0] {0}", swarm[0].ToString());

            Console.ReadKey();
        }
    }
}
```

Note that the structure definition contains an override for the ToString method. This is perfectly acceptable; although a structure cannot be used in a class hierarchy, because it is possible to override methods from the parent type of struct. For a more detailed description of overriding, consult "Create overload and overridden methods" later in this section.

Enumerated types

Enumerated types are used in situations where the programmer wants to specify a range of values that a given type can have. For example, in the computer game you may want to represent three states of an alien: sleeping, attacking, or destroyed. You can use an integer variable to do this and adopt the convention that: the value 0 means sleeping, 1 means attacking, and 2 means destroyed. This works, but it raises the possibility that code in the program can set the state of an alien to the value of 4, which would be meaningless.

Listing 2-4 shows a program that creates an enum type to represent the state of an alien and then creates a variable of this type and sets its state to attacking.

LISTING 2-4 Creating an enum

```
using System;

namespace LISTING_2_4_Creating_an_enum
{
    enum AlienState
    {
        Sleeping,
        Attacking,
        Destroyed
    };

    class Program
    {
        static void Main(string[] args)
        {
            AlienState x = AlienState.Attacking;
            Console.WriteLine(x);

            Console.ReadKey();
        }
    }
}
```

This program prints the ToString result returned by the AlienState variable, which will output the string "Attacking" in this case.

Unless specified otherwise, an enumerated type is based on the int type and the enumerated values are numbered starting at 0. You can modify this by adding extra information to the declaration of the enum.

You would do this if you want to set particular values to be used in JSON and XML files when enumerated variables are stored. The code here creates an AlienState enum that is stored in a byte type, and has the given values for sleeping, attacking, and destroyed.

```
enum AlienState :
byte {
    Sleeping=1,
    Attacking=2,
    Destroyed=4
};
```

A program can use casting (see the Cast Types section) to obtain the numeric value that is held in an enum variable.

Creating reference types

The basis of C# reference types is the C# class. A class is declared in a very similar manner to a structure, but the way that classes are manipulated in a program is significantly different. You can declare the Alien type as a class by changing one word in the declaration of the Alien type. Listing 2-5 declares an Alien class and then creates a single Alien reference called x, which is made to refer to a new Alien object. This is followed by the creation of an array called swarm, which contains 100 Alien references. Each reference in the array is then made to refer to a new Alien object. The use of the new keyword to create a new object is said to create a new *instance* of a class.

LISTING 2-5 Creating a reference

```
using System;

namespace LISTING_2_5_Creating_a_reference
{
    class Alien
    {
        public int X;
        public int Y;
        public int Lives;

        public Alien(int x, int y)
        {
            X = x;
            Y = y;
            Lives = 3;
        }

        public override string ToString()
        {
            return string.Format("X: {0} Y: {1} Lives: {2}", X, Y, Lives);
        }
    }

    class Program
    {
        static void Main(string[] args)
        {
            Alien x = new Alien(100, 100);
```

```
            Console.WriteLine("x {0}", x);

            Alien[] swarm = new Alien[100];

            for (int i = 0; i < swarm.Length; i++)
                swarm[i] = new Alien(0, 0);

            Console.WriteLine("swarm [0] {0}", swarm[0]);

            Console.ReadKey();
        }
    }
}
```

Note that when a variable of type Alien is declared, the variable is now a reference to an Alien, and initially the reference does not refer to anything. When we created the alien swarm we had to explicitly set each element in the array to refer to an Alien instance.

Memory allocation

Memory to be used to store variables of value type is allocated on the *stack*. The stack is an area of memory that is allocated and removed as programs enter and leave blocks. Any value type variables created during the execution of a block are stored on a local *stack frame* and then the entire frame is discarded when the block completes. This is an extremely efficient way to manage memory.

Memory to be used to store variables of reference type is allocated on a different structure, called the *heap*. The heap is managed for an entire application. The heap is required because, as references may be passed between method calls as parameters, it is not the case that objects managed by reference can be discarded when a method exits. Objects can only be removed from the heap when the garbage collection process determines that there are no references to them.

Generic types

Generic types are used extensively in C# collections, such as with the List and Dictionary classes. They allow you to create a List of any type of data, or a Dictionary of any type, indexed on any type.

Without generic types you either have to reduce the type safety in your programs by using collections that manage only objects, or you have to waste a lot of time creating different collection classes for each different type of data that you want to store.

The program in Listing 2-6 shows how generics can be used to create a stack type (called MyStack) that can be used to hold a stack of any type of object. The generic type to be used is specified in the declaration of MyStack (in the example below it is given the name T). The name T is then used within the MyStack declaration to represent the type that will be supplied when a variable of type MyStack is declared. The Push and Pop methods in the MyStack class also work with objects of type T. The program creates a MyStack that can hold strings.

LISTING 2-6 Using generic types

```
using System;

namespace LISTING_2_6_Using_generic_types
{
    class Program
    {
        class MyStack<T>
        {
            int stackTop = 0;
            T[] items = new T[100];

            public void Push(T item)
            {
                if (stackTop == items.Length)
                    throw new Exception("Stack full");
                items[stackTop] = item;
                stackTop++;
            }

            public T Pop()
            {
                if (stackTop == 0)
                    throw new Exception("Stack empty");
                stackTop--;
                return items[stackTop];
            }
        }

        static void Main(string[] args)
        {
            MyStack<string> nameStack = new MyStack<string>();
            nameStack.Push("Rob");
            nameStack.Push("Mary");
            Console.WriteLine(nameStack.Pop());
            Console.WriteLine(nameStack.Pop());
            Console.ReadKey();
        }
    }
}
```

Generic Constraints

The MyStack class in Listing 2-6 can hold any type of data. If you want to restrict it to only store reference types you can add a constraint on the possible types that T can represent. The MyStack declaration restricts the stack to holding reference types, so it isn't now possible to store integers (which are value types) in the stack.

```
class MyStack<T> where T:class
```

There are other constraints that you can use, as shown in Table 2-1.

TABLE 2-1 Generic constraints

Constraint	Behavior
where T : class	The type T must be a reference type.
where T : struct	The type T must be a value type.
where T : new()	The type T must have a public, parameterless, constructor. Specify this constraint last if you are specifying a list of constraints
where T : <base class>	The type T must be of type base class or derive from base class.
where T : <interface name>	The type T must be or implement the specified interface. You can specify multiple interfaces.
where T : unmanaged	The type T must not be a reference type or contain any members which are reference types.

Investigating how the generic collection classes work is a great way to build your understanding of how the generic features in C# are used.

Constructors

A constructor allows a programmer to control the process by which objects are created. Constructors can be used with value types (structures) and reference types (classes). A constructor has the same name as the object it is part of but does not have a return type.

Constructors can perform validation of their parameters to ensure that any objects that are created contain valid information. If the validation fails, the constructor must throw an exception to prevent the creation of an invalid object. The code in Listing 2-7 shows a constructor for the Alien class that throws an exception if an attempt is made to create an Alien with negative coordinate values.

LISTING 2-7 Constructors

```
using System;

namespace LISTING_2_7_Constructors
{
    class Alien
    {
        public int X;
        public int Y;
        public int Lives;

        public Alien(int x, int y)
        {
            if (x < 0 || y < 0)
                throw new ArgumentOutOfRangeException ("Invalid position");

            X = x;
            Y = y;
            Lives = 3;
        }
    }
```

```
        public override string ToString()
        {
            return string.Format("X: {0} Y: {1} Lives: {2}", X, Y, Lives);
        }
    }

    class Program
    {
        static void Main(string[] args)
        {
            Alien x = new Alien(100, 100);
            Console.WriteLine("x {0}", x);
            Console.ReadKey();
        }
    }
}
```

Constructors can be given access to modifiers (see "Enforce encapsulation" later in this section). If an object only has a private constructor it cannot be instantiated unless the object contains a public *factory method* that can be called to create instances of the class.

Constructors can be overloaded, so an object can contain multiple versions of a constructor with different signatures. Listing 2-8 shows an Alien class that allows an alien to be constructed with a particular number of lives, or a value of three lives, depending on which constructor is called.

LISTING 2-8 Overloaded constructors

```
class Alien
{
    public int X;
    public int Y;
    public int Lives;

    public Alien(int x, int y, int lives)
    {
        if (x < 0 || y < 0)
            throw new ArgumentOutOfRangeException ("Invalid position");

        X = x;
        Y = y;
        Lives = lives;
    }

    public Alien(int x, int y)
    {
        X = x;
        Y = y;
        Lives = 3;
    }
}
```

A program can avoid code repetition by making one constructor call another constructor by use of the keyword this. The this keyword is used in the constructor method signature as shown in Listing 2-9. It forms a call of another constructor in the object. In the program below the parameters to the call of one constructor are passed into a call of another, along with an additional lives value. Note that this means the actual body of the constructor is empty, because all of the work is performed by the call to the other constructor. Another way to provide default values to a constructor is to make use of optional parameters. These are described in "Optional and named parameters" in the section below.

LISTING 2-9 Calling constructors

```
class Alien
{
    public int X;
    public int Y;
    public int Lives;

    public Alien(int x, int y, int lives)
    {
        if (x < 0 || y < 0)
            throw new ArgumentOutOfRangeException ("Invalid position");

        X = x;
        Y = y;
        Lives = lives;
    }

    public Alien(int x, int y) : this(x, y, 3)
    {
    }

    public override string ToString()
    {
        return string.Format("X: {0} Y: {1} Lives: {2}", X, Y, Lives);
    }
}
```

When creating objects that are part of a class hierarchy, a programmer must ensure that information required by the constructor of a parent object is passed into a parent constructor. This will be discussed in more detail in Skill 2.4, Create and implement a class hierarchy."

Static constructors

A class can contain a *static constructor* method. This is called once before the creation of the very first instance of the class. The Alien class in Listing 2-10 contains a static constructor that prints a message when it is called. When the program runs, the message is printed once, before the first alien is created. The static constructor is not called when the second alien is created.

LISTING 2-10 Static constructors

```
class Alien
{
    // Alien code here
    static Alien()
    {
        Console.WriteLine("Static Alien constructor running");
    }
}
```

A static constructor is a good place to load resources and initialize values that will be used by instances of the class. This can include the values of static members of the class, as described in the next section.

Static variables

A static variable is a member of a type, but it is not created for each instance of a type. A variable in a class is made static by using the keyword `static` in the declaration of that variable.

As an example of a situation where static is useful, you may decide that you want to set a maximum for the number of lives that an `Alien` is allowed to have in our video game. This is a value that should be stored once for all aliens. A static variable is a great place to store such a value, since it will be created once for all class instances. Listing 2-11 shows how a static variable (Max_Lives) can be added to the `Alien` class and used in the `Alien` constructor to reject any attempts to create aliens with too many lives.

LISTING 2-11 Static variables

```
class Alien
{
    public static int Max_Lives = 99;

    public int X;
    public int Y;
    public int Lives;

    public Alien(int x, int y, int lives)
    {
        if (x < 0 || y < 0)
            throw new Exception("Invalid position");

        if(lives > Max_Lives)
            throw new Exception("Invalid lives");

        X = x;
        Y = y;
        Lives = lives;
    }
}
```

Code outside of the `Alien` class must refer to the `Max_Lives` static variable via the class name, rather than the name of any particular instance of the class. The statement next changes the value of `Max_Lives` to 150:

```
Alien.Max_Lives = 150;
```

Making a variable `static` does not stop it from being changed when the program runs (to achieve this use the `const` keyword or make the variable `readonly`). Rather, the word static in this context means that the variable is "always present." A program can use a static variable from a type without needing to have created any instances of that type. Types can also contain static methods. These can be called without the need for an instance of the object containing the method. Libraries of useful functions are often provided as static members of a library class.

Static variables are very useful for validation values for a type, such as the maximum number of lives, and also for default values. They can be made private to a class so that their values can be managed by the class.

Methods

You have seen methods used in several of the types that you have worked with in this section. A method is a member of a class. It has a *signature* and a *body*. The signature defines the type and number of parameters that the method will accept. The body is a block of code that is performed when the method is called. If the method has a type other than void, all code paths through the body of the code must end with a return statement that returns a value of the type of the method.

Listing 2-12 shows a method called RemoveLives, which is called to remove lives from an Alien. The method is provided with a parameter that gives the number of lives to remove. If the number of lives that are left is less than zero, the lives value is set to zero and the Alien is moved off the display screen so that it is not visible any more. The RemoveLives method is of type Boolean and returns true if the alien is still alive and false if it is not.

LISTING 2-12 Simple method

```
class Alien
{
    public int X;
    public int Y;
    public int Lives;

    public bool RemoveLives(int livesToRemove)
    {
        Lives = Lives - livesToRemove;

        if (Lives <= 0)
        {
            Lives = 0;
            X = -1000;
            Y = -1000;
            return false;
        }
        else
        {
            return true;
        }
    }
}
```

This method can be called on an Alien instance to remove lives and determine if the given alien is still alive.

```
Alien x = new Alien(100, 100);
Console.WriteLine("x {0}", x);
if (x.RemoveLives(2))
{
    Console.WriteLine("Still alive");
}
else
{
    Console.WriteLine("Alien destroyed");
}

Console.WriteLine("x {0}", x);
```

You might like to consider a design approach where an alien fires an event when it is destroyed, using delegates as described in Skill 1-4, "Create and implement events and callbacks."

The name of a method is best expressed in a "verb-noun" manner, with an action followed by the thing that the action is acting on. Names such as "DisplayMenu," "SaveCustomer," and "DeleteFile" are very descriptive of what the method does. When talking about the method signature and the code body of a method we will talk in terms of the *parameters* used in the method. In the case of the call of a method we will talk in terms of the *arguments* supplied to the call. In other words, in the example shown in Listing 2-12 the parameter to the method is called livesToRemove and the argument to the method call is the value 2.

Classes

You can think of a class as providing the template or plans that are required to create an instance of that class. Note that declaring a class does not create any instances of that class. An instance of a class is created when the new keyword is used. When the new keyword is used to create an instance of a class the following sequence is performed:

1. The program code that implements the class is loaded into memory, if it is not already present.

2. If this is the first time that the class has been referenced, any static members of the class are initialized and the static constructor is called.

3. The constructor in the class is called.

A class can contain members that are methods, data variables, or properties. A class method allows a class to provide behaviors that can be used by code running in other classes. Data variables allow a class to maintain state and manage the storage of information and properties provide a means for managing access to data within a class.

Extension methods

A class can provide methods for other classes to call. In Skill 2-4, "Create and implement a class hierarchy," you will see how a class can be extended by a child class that can add members to the base class, including new methods that can implement additional behaviors. However, extension methods provide a way in which behaviors can be added to a class without needing to extend the class itself. You can think of the extension methods as being "bolted on" to an existing class.

Listing 2-13 shows how to create an extension method for the String class. The first parameter to the method specifies the type that the extension method should be added to, by using the keyword this followed by the name of the type. The extension method created, called NoLines, counts the number of lines in a string, and then returns this result as an integer. The method works by splitting the string on the linefeed character and then counting the number of elements in the resulting array. The extension method is declared in a static class (in this case called MyExtensions).

LISTING 2-13 Extension method

```
using System;

namespace ExtensionMethods
{
    public static class MyExtensions
    {
        public static int LineCount(this String str)
        {
            return str.Split(new char[] { '\n' },
                            StringSplitOptions.RemoveEmptyEntries).Length;
        }
    }
}
```

Once the extension method has been created it can be used from the namespace in which the class containing the method is declared. When the program calls an extension method the compiler searches the included namespaces for a matching method for that type, and then generates a call of that method. When the program below runs, it prints out the number of lines in the string text.

```
namespace LISTING_2_13_Extension_method
{
    using ExtensionMethods;

    class Program
    {
        static void Main(string[] args)
        {
            string text = @"A rocket explorer called Wright,
Once travelled much faster than light,
He set out one day,
In a relative way,
And returned on the previous night";

            Console.WriteLine(text.LineCount());

            Console.ReadKey();
        }
    }
}
```

Note that extension methods are never part of the object they are attached to, since they don't have any access to private members of the method class. An extension method can never be used to replace an existing method in a class. In other words, if the String type already contained a method called LineCount, the extension method created in Listing 2-13 is not called. Instead, the LineCount method inside String is used.

Extension methods allow you to add behaviors to existing classes and use them as if they were part of that class. They are very powerful. LINQ query operations are added to types in C# programs by the use of extension methods.

Optional and named parameters

When you create a method with parameters, the signature of the method gives the name and type of each parameter in turn (see Listing 2-14)

LISTING 2-14 Named parameters

```
static int ReadValue (
    int low,      // lowest allowed value
    int high,     // highest allowed value
    string prompt // prompt for the user
    )
{
    // method body...
}
```

The ReadValue method has been defined as having three parameters. A call of the method must have three argument values: a prompt, a low value, and a high value. This means that the following call of readValue is rejected by the compiler:

```
x = ReadValue("Enter your age: ", 1, 100);
```

This is because the prompt string is defined as the last parameter to the method call, not the first. If you want to make method calls without worrying about the order of the arguments, you can name each one when you call the method:

```
x = ReadValue(low:1, high:100, prompt: "Enter your age: ");
```

Now the compiler is using the name of each argument, rather than its position in the list. Another programmer reading your code can now see the meaning of each argument value. Using this format also removes the possibility of any confusion of the ordering of the values in the method call. You should use named parameters whenever you call a method that has more than one parameter.

Sometimes the value of an argument might have a sensible default value. For example, if you only want the readValue to fetch a value from the user and not display a prompt, you can do this by providing an empty string:

```
x = readValue(low:25, high:100, prompt: "");
```

This, however, is a bit messy. Instead, you can change the definition of the method to give a default value for the prompt parameter as shown in Listing -2-15.

LISTING 2-15 Optional parameters

```
static int readValue (
    double low,            // lowest allowed value
    double high,           // highest allowed value
    string prompt = "",    // optional prompt for the user
    )
{
    // method body...
}
```

You can now call the method and leave the prompt out:

```
x = readValue(25, 100);
```

When the method runs, the prompt will be set to an empty string if the user doesn't provide a value. Optional parameters must be provided after all of the required ones.

Indexed properties

A program can access a particular array element by using an index value that identifies the element. The code here shows how this works:

```
int [] array = new int[20];
array[0] = 99;
```

A class can use the same indexing mechanism to provide indexed property values. The code in Listing 2-16 shows how this works. The IntArrayWrapper class is a wrapper around an integer array. The indexer property accepts an integer value (called i in Listing 2-16), which is used to index the array that stores the value.

LISTING 2-16 Indexed properties

```
using System;

namespace LISTING_2_16_Indexed_properties
{
    class IntArrayWrapper
    {
        // Create an array to store the values
        private int[] array = new int[100];

        // Declare an indexer property
        public int this[int i]
        {
            get { return array[i]; }
            set { array[i] = value; }
        }
    }

    class Program
    {
        static void Main(string[] args)
        {
            IntArrayWrapper x = new IntArrayWrapper();
```

```
        x[0] = 99;
        Console.WriteLine(x[0]);
        Console.ReadKey();
    }
  }
}
```

Note that there is nothing stopping the use of other types in indexed properties. This is how the Dictionary collection is used to index on a particular type of key value. Listing 2-17 shows an indexer property that is extended to allow all of the elements in the integer array to be accessed by name. The first couple of values only have been implemented for reasons of space.

LISTING 2-17 Indexing on strings

```
class NamedIntArray
{
    // Create an array to store the values
    private int[] array = new int[100];

    // Declare an indexer property
    public int this[string name]
    {
        get
        {
            switch (name)
            {
                case "zero":
                    return array[0];
                case "one":
                    return array[1];
                default:
                    return -1;
            }
        }
        set
        {
            switch (name)
            {
                case "zero":
                    array[0] = value;
                    break;
                case "one":
                    array[1] = value;
                    break;
            }
        }
    }
}
```

A program can now access elements in the array by specifying a text indexer for the location. This program stores the value 99 in location "zero:"

```
NamedIntArray x = new NamedIntArray();
x["zero"] = 99;
Console.WriteLine(x["zero"]);
```

Create overload and overridden methods

It's very important to understand the difference between *overloading* and *overriding* when applied to methods in a class. Overloading means, "providing a method with the same name, but a different signature in a given type." It is useful when you want to provide several ways of performing a particular behavior, depending on the circumstances in which the behavior is being used. We've seen overloading in the context of constructor methods earlier, in order to construct an Alien with a specified number of lives or construct an Alien with a default number of lives.

The DateTime structure provided by .NET has a large number of overloaded constructors, because there are many different ways a programmer might want to initialize a DateTime value. You might have the number of ticks since January 1, 0001 at 00:00:00.000 in the Gregorian calendar. Alternatively, and perhaps more likely, you might have year, month, and day values. Listing 2-18 shows how these values are used to create DateTime values. Both of the DateTime values are set to the same date and time by this code.

LISTING 2-18 Overloaded DateTime constructor

```csharp
using System;

namespace LISTING_2_18_Overloaded_DateTime_constructor
{
    class Program
    {
        static void Main(string[] args)
        {
            DateTime d0 = new DateTime(ticks:636679008000000000);
            DateTime d1 = new DateTime(year:2018, month:7, day:23);
            Console.WriteLine(d0);
            Console.WriteLine(d1);
            Console.ReadKey();
        }
    }
}
```

The overriding of methods takes place when class hierarchies are used. In a class hierarchy a child class is derived from a parent or base class. A method in a base class is *overridden* by a method in a child when the child class contains a method with exactly the same name and signature as a method in the parent class. Only methods that have been marked as *virtual* in the parent class can be overridden.

The key to understanding overriding is to discover why you need to use it. The underlying principle of a class hierarchy is that classes at the top of the hierarchy are more abstract, and classes toward the bottom of the hierarchy are more specific. So, a base class might be called Document and child class might be called Invoice.

The Document class will hold all of the behaviors that are common to all documents, for example, all documents must provide a method that gets the date when the document was created. However, the print behavior of an Invoice will have to be different from the print behavior of the more abstract Document type. Overriding allows us to create a print method in the Invoice that overrides that in the Document.

Listing 2-19 shows how method overriding works. The GetDate method is declared in Document. The method DoPrint is declared in Document and overridden in Invoice. The program creates an instance of Invoice and then calls the GetDate and DoPrint methods on the instance. When GetDate is called, the GetDate from Document is called. When DoPrint is called on the Invoice, the DoPrint from Invoice is called, because this overrides the DoPrint in the parent class.

LISTING 2-19 Method overriding

```
using System;

namespace LISTING_2_19_Method_overriding
{
    class Document
    {
        // All documents have the same GetDate behavior so
        // this method will not be overridden
        public void GetDate()
        {
            Console.WriteLine("Hello from GetDate in Document");
        }

        // A document may have its own DoPrint behavior so
        // this method is virtual so it can be overriden
        public virtual void DoPrint()
        {
            Console.WriteLine("Hello from DoPrint in Document");
        }
    }

    // The Invoice class derives from the Document class
    class Invoice:Document
    {
        // Override the DoPrint method in the base class
        // to provide custom printing behaviour for an Invoice
        public override void DoPrint()
        {
            Console.WriteLine("Hello from DoPrint in Invoice");
        }
    }

    class Program
    {
        static void Main(string[] args)
        {
            // Create an Invoice
            Invoice c = new Invoice();
            // This will run the SetDate method from Document
            c.GetDate();
            // This will run the DoPrint method from Invoice
            c.DoPrint();

            Console.ReadKey();
        }
    }
}
```

The output from the program is shown here:

```
Hello from GetDate in Document
Hello from DoPrint in Invoice
```

If you create a `PrePaidInvoice` to represent pre-paid invoices, you can extend the `Invoice` class and provide an override of the `DoPrint` method in the `PrePaidInvoice` class. The `DoPrint` method in `PrePaidInvoice` can use the `DoPrint` method in the parent class by using the `base` keyword, as shown in Listing 2-20 below.

LISTING 2-20 Using base

```
class PrePaidInvoice: Invoice
{
    public override void DoPrint()
    {
        base.DoPrint();
        Console.WriteLine("Hello from DoPrint in PrePaidInvoice");
    }
}
```

When the `DoPrint` method is called on an instance of the `PrePaidInvoice` class, it first makes a call of the `DoPrint` method in the parent object. The listing below shows how these calls are made.

```
PrePaidInvoice p = new PrePaidInvoice();
p.GetDate();
p.DoPrint();
```

The output from the calls to the methods is shown here:

```
Hello from GetDate in Document
Hello from DoPrint in Invoice
Hello from DoPrint in PrePaidInvoice
```

The use of method overriding allows the behavior of different items to be customized for each particular item, and you can also re-use code in parent objects by using the base keyword. You can find more discussion of class hierarchies in Skill 2.4, "Create and Implement a Class Hierarchy."

Skill 2.2: Consume types

Everything in C# is an object of a particular type and the compiler ensures that interactions between types are always meaningful. In the previous section you discovered value and reference types and considered how to create types that hold data and provide behaviors.

In this section we're going to build on this knowledge and learn how to use differently typed objects in our programs. We're going to find out about the process performed in C# when a value type is converted into a reference type, and how to use casting to inform the compiler of our intentions when working with types. Finally, we are going to discover how the programs from the statically typed world of C# can be made to interact with environments that have a dynamically typed way of working; notably Component Object Model (COM) interfaces.

Boxing and unboxing

From Skill 2.1, "Creating types," we know that C# programs can use value types and reference types. We know that value types are managed directly in terms of their value, whereas reference types are managed in terms of a reference that refers to an object that holds the data. The built-in types int, float, and double are value types, as are structures that we create. Classes are used to define reference types.

From a computational point of view, value types such as int and float have the advantage that the computer processor can manipulate value types directly. Adding two int values together can be achieved by fetching the values into the processor, performing the addition operation, and then storing the result.

It can be useful to treat value types as reference types, and the C# runtime system provides a mechanism called *boxing* that will perform this conversion when required. Listing 2-21 shows boxing and unboxing being performed in a program. The first statement takes the value 99 and casts this into an object called o (you can find out more about casting in the next section). The second statement takes the object o and casts it back into an integer. The process of converting from a reference type (reference o) into a value type (the integer oVal) is called *unboxing*.

LISTING 2-21 Boxing and unboxing

```
namespace LISTING_2_21_Boxing_and_unboxing
{
    class Program
    {
        static void Main(string[] args)
        {
            // the value 99 is boxed into an object
            object o = 99;

            // the boxed object is unboxed back into an int
            int oVal = (int)o;
            Console.WriteLine(oVal);

            Console.ReadKey();
        }
    }
}
```

Boxing and unboxing at this point might seem a bit confusing and magical. The program code in Listing 2-21, which works correctly and prints the value 99, implies that an object is magically able to store an integer value. In fact, this code would work correctly irrespective of the particular value type that the object was assigned to. In other words, you can assign the object o to a floating-point number, or a double precision number.

You can get a better understanding of just what is happening by inspecting the actual code that is produced by the C# compiler when the program in Listing 2-21 is compiled. Listing 2-22 shows the output from a program called ildasm, which is supplied as part of the .NET Software Development Kit. The ildasm program (the name is short for "Intermediate Language Disassembler") will take a compiler output file and show the actual instructions that will be obeyed when the program runs.

A .NET program processes data by moving values onto a stack (called the evaluation stack), performing actions on them, and then storing the results. The instruction at IL_0001 in Listing 2-22 takes the value 99 and places it on the evaluation stack. The instruction at IL_0003 is the box instruction that creates an object of type Int32 on the heap, sets the value of this object to 99 and then places a reference to this object on the evaluation stack. This reference is then stored in storage location 0, which is where the variable o is stored. The instruction at IL_000a performs the reverse of this action, unboxing a reference to an Int32 object and placing the value that results from the unboxing on the evaluation stack.

LISTING 2-22 Compiled and unboxing

```
method private hidebysig static void  Main(string[] args) cil managed
{
  .entrypoint
  // Code size       30 (0x1e)
  .maxstack  1
  .locals init ([0] object o,
           [1] int32 oVal)
  IL_0000:  nop
  IL_0001:  ldc.i4.s    99
  IL_0003:  box         [mscorlib]System.Int32
  IL_0008:  stloc.0
  IL_0009:  ldloc.0
  IL_000a:  unbox.any   [mscorlib]System.Int32
  IL_000f:  stloc.1
  IL_0010:  ldloc.1
  IL_0011:  call        void [mscorlib]System.Console::WriteLine(int32)
  IL_0016:  nop
  IL_0017:  call        valuetype [mscorlib]System.ConsoleKeyInfo [mscorlib]System.
Console::ReadKey()
  IL_001c:  pop
  IL_001d:  ret
} // end of method Program::Main
```

It's worth spending some time examining this code to see how .NET programs are executed. Note that the box instruction (convert a value type to a reference type) and unbox instruction (convert a reference type to a value type) are always given a destination (box) or source (unbox) type to use. Each built-in C# value type (int, float etc) has a matching C# type called its *interface type* to which it is converted when boxing is performed. The interface type for int is int32.

The good news for programmers is that boxing and unboxing process happens automatically when variables are converted between types. The bad news is that if a program spends a lot of time boxing and unboxing values it slows the program down. The need to box and unbox values in a solution is a symptom of poor design, you should be clear in your design which data items are value types and which references, and work with them correctly.

Cast types

The C# language has been designed to reduce the ways in which a programmer can make mistakes, which will cause a program to produce invalid results. One aspect of this design is the way that a C# program will not allow a programmer to perform a conversion between types that result in the loss of data.

The two statements below show a situation in which data is lost when an assignment is made. It is an example of *narrowing*, when a value is transferred into a type which offers a narrower range of values. The integer type does not handle the fractional part of a value, and so the .9 part of the value x is discarded when the assignment takes place. These statements will not compile successfully.

```
float x = 9.9f;
int i = x;
```

C# is perfectly capable of performing the conversion from floating point to integer, but it requires confirmation from the programmer that it is meaningful for this conversion to be performed. This is called *explicit conversion*, in that the programmer is making an explicit request that the conversion be performed. In C# the explicit conversion is requested by the use of a *cast*, which identifies the desired type of value being assigned. The type is given, enclosed in brackets, before the value to be converted. The statements here show how a cast is added to allow a floating-point value to be assigned to an integer.

```
float x = 9.9f;
int i = (int) x;
```

A conversion that performs *widening*, in which the destination type has a wider range of values than the source, does not require a cast, because there is no prospect of data loss.

Note that casting cannot be used to convert between different types, for example with an integer and string. In other words, the following statement will fail to compile:

```
int i = (int) "99";
```

Casting is also used when converting references to objects that may be part of class hierarchies or expose interfaces. You can find out more about this form of casting in Skill 2.4, "Create and implement a class hierarchy."

Convert types

The .NET runtime provides a set of conversion methods that are used to perform casting. You can also write your own type conversion operators for your data classes so that programs can perform implicit and explicit conversions between types. Listing 2-23 shows how to do this.

The type Miles contains a double precision distance value in the property Distance. The Miles class also contains an implicit operator called Kilometers, which returns a value of type Kilometers, representing the same distance. A program can then assign a variable of type Miles value into a variable of type Kilometer. During the assignment the implicit conversion operator is called automatically. The type Miles also contains an explicit conversion that returns the distance value as an integer. This conversion is explicit because it is a narrowing operation that will result in a loss of data, as the fractional part of the double precision distance value is truncated. To use an explicit conversion the programmer must use a cast, as shown in Listing 2-23.

LISTING 2-23 Type conversion

```
using System;

namespace LISTING_2_23_Type_conversion
{
    class Miles
    {
        public double Distance { get; }

        // Conversion operator for implicit converstion to Kilometers
        public static implicit operator Kilometers(Miles t)
        {
            Console.WriteLine("Implicit conversion from miles to kilometers");
            return new Kilometers( t.Distance * 1.6);
        }

        public static explicit operator int(Miles t)
        {
            Console.WriteLine("Explicit conversion from miles to int");
            return (int)(t.Distance + 0.5);
        }

        public Miles(double miles)
        {
            Distance = miles;
        }
    }

    class Kilometers
    {
        public double Distance { get; }

        public Kilometers(double kilometers)
        {
            Distance = kilometers;
```

```
        }
    }

    class Program
    {
        static void Main(string[] args)
        {
            Miles m = new Miles(100);

            Kilometers k = m; // implicity convert miles to km
            Console.WriteLine("Kilometers: {0}", k.Distance);

            int intMiles = (int)m;   // explicitly convert miles to int
            Console.WriteLine("Int miles: {0}", intMiles);
            Console.ReadKey();
        }
    }
}
```

When you run the program, you will see that it writes messages indicating that the implicit and explicit conversions are being performed.

```
Implicit conversion from miles to kilometers
Kilometers: 160
Explicit conversion from miles to int
Int miles: 100
```

Convert types with System.Convert

The System.Convert class provides a set of static methods that can be used to perform type conversion between .NET types. As an example, the code next converts a string into an integer:

```
int myAge = Convert.ToInt32("21");
```

The convert method will throw an exception if the string provided cannot be converted into an integer.

Handle dynamic types

C# is a strongly typed language. This means that when the program is compiled the compiler ensures that all actions that are performed are valid in the context of the types that have been defined in the program. As an example, if a class does not contain a method with a particular name, the C# compiler will refuse to generate a call to that method. As a way of making sure that C# programs are valid at the time that they are executed, strong typing works very well. Such a strong typing regime, however, can cause problems when a C# program is required to interact with systems that do not have their origins in C# code. Such situations arise when using Common Object Model (COM) interop, the Document Object Model (DOM), working with objects generated by C# reflection, or when interworking with dynamic languages such as JavaScript.

In these situations, you need a way to force the compiler to interact with objects for which the strong typing information that is generated from compiled C# is not available. The keyword dynamic is used to identify items for which the C# compiler should suspend static type checking. The compiler will then generate code that works with the items as described, without doing static checking to make sure that they are valid. Note that this doesn't mean that a program using dynamic objects will always work; if the description is incorrect the program will fail at run time.

Listing 2-24 shows how the dynamic keyword is used in this situation. The class MessageDisplay contains a single method, called DisplayMessage. The variable m is set to refer to an instance of this class, and the program calls the DisplayMessage method on this reference. The compiler is very happy with this code, as it can see that the MessageDisplay class contains the required method. The variable d is declared as dynamic and set to refer to a MessageDisplay instance. The program then contains a call of a method called Banana on the variable d. Normally this would not compile, because the compiler can see that this method is not present in the class. Because the variable d has been declared as dynamic, however, the program will compile with no errors.

LISTING 2-24 Bad dynamic code

```
using System;

namespace LISTING_2_24_Bad_dynamic_code
{
    class MessageDisplay
    {
        public void DisplayMessage(string message)
        {
            Console.WriteLine(message);
        }
    }

    class Program
    {
        static void Main(string[] args)
        {
            MessageDisplay m = new MessageDisplay();
            m.DisplayMessage("Hello world");

            dynamic d = new MessageDisplay();
            d.Banana("hello world");
        }
    }
}
```

This program will compile, but when the program is executed an exception will be generated when the Banana method is called. Figure 2-1 shows the result of running the program in the Visual Studio 2017 debugger.

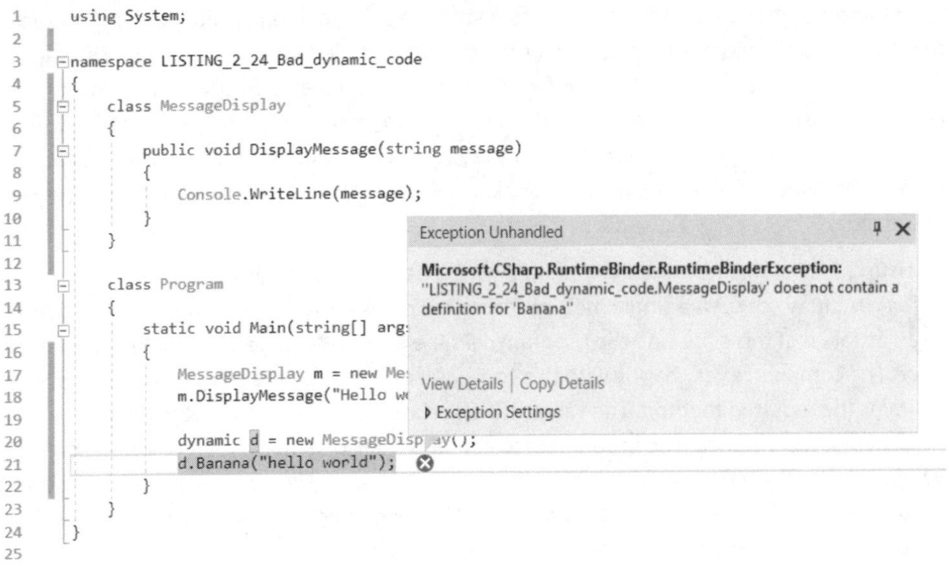

```
1      using System;
2
3    namespace LISTING_2_24_Bad_dynamic_code
4    {
5        class MessageDisplay
6        {
7            public void DisplayMessage(string message)
8            {
9                Console.WriteLine(message);
10           }
11       }
12
13       class Program
14       {
15           static void Main(string[] arg:
16           {
17               MessageDisplay m = new Me:
18               m.DisplayMessage("Hello wo
19
20               dynamic d = new MessageDisplay();
21               d.Banana("hello world");  ⊗
22           }
23       }
24   }
25
```

Exception Unhandled   ⇩ ✕

Microsoft.CSharp.RuntimeBinder.RuntimeBinderException:
"LISTING_2_24_Bad_dynamic_code.MessageDisplay' does not contain a
definition for 'Banana'"

View Details | Copy Details

▸ Exception Settings

FIGURE 2-1 The Bad Dynamic code application

This aspect of the dynamic keyword makes it possible to interact with objects that have behaviors, but not the C# type information that the C# compiler would normally use to ensure that any interaction is valid. There is, however, more to the dynamic type than this.

A variable declared as dynamic is allocated a type that is inferred from the context in which it is used. This is a very similar behavior to that of variables in languages such as Python or JavaScript. The code in Listing 2-25 shows how this works. The variable d is declared as dynamic and used first as an integer and secondly as a string. This program will compile and execute with no errors, printing out the results that you would expect. The type of the variable d will change according to what is stored in it, and the addition operator works as expected, adding an integer to an integer and a string to a string. If the program behaves incorrectly (for example by trying to add "Rob" to the integer incarnation of d) an exception is thrown when the program runs.

LISTING 2-25 Using dynamic variables

```
dynamic d = 99;
d = d + 1;
Console.WriteLine(d);

d = "Hello";
d = d + " Rob";
Console.WriteLine(d);
```

Note, that just because you can do this doesn't mean that you should. The flexibility of the dynamic type was not created so that C# programmers can stop worrying about having to de- cide on the type of variables that they use in their programs. Instead, the flexibility was added to make it easy to interact with other languages and libraries written using the Component Object Model (COM).

Use ExpandoObject

The ExpandoObject class allows a program to dynamically add properties to an object. The code next, which is also in Listing 2-25, shows how this is done. The dynamic variable person is assigned to a new ExpandoObject instance. The program then adds Name and Age properties to the person and then prints out these values.

```
dynamic person = new ExpandoObject();

person.Name = "Rob Miles";
person.Age = 21;

Console.WriteLine("Name: {0} Age: {1}", person.Name, person.Age);
```

A program can add ExpandoObject properties to an ExpandoObject to create nested data structures. An ExpandoObject can also be queried using LINQ and can exposes the IDictionary interface to allow its contents to be queried and items to be removed. ExpandoObject is especially useful when creating data structures from markup languages, for example when reading a JSON or XML document.

Interoperability with unmanaged code that accesses COM APIs

The Component Object Model (COM) is a mechanism that allows software components to interact. The model describes how to express an interface to which other objects can connect. COM is interesting to programmers because a great many resources you would like to use are exposed via COM interfaces.

The code inside a COM object runs as *unmanaged code,* having direct access to the underlying system. While it is possible to run .NET applications in an *unmanaged* mode, .NET applications usually run inside a *managed* environment, limiting the level of access that the applications have to the underlying system.

When a .NET application wants to interact with a COM object it has to perform the following:

1. Convert any parameters for the COM object into an appropriate format
2. Switch to unmanaged execution for the COM behavior
3. Invoke the COM behavior
4. Switch back to managed execution upon completion of the COM behavior
5. Convert any results of the COM request into the correct types of .NET objects

This is performed by a component called the Primary Interop Assembly (PIA) that is supplied along with the COM object. The results returned by the PIA can be managed as dynamic objects, so that the type of the values can be inferred rather than having to be specified directly. As long as your program uses the returned values in the correct way, the program will work correctly. You add a Primary Interop Assembly to an application as you would any other assembly. Figure 2.2 shows the interop assembly added to a Visual Studio solution.

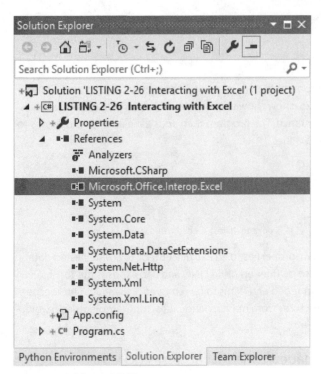

FIGURE 2-2 Adding a COM interop

The C# code uses dynamic types to make the interaction with the Office application very easy. There is no need to cast the various elements that the program is interacting with, as they are exposed by the interop as dynamic types, so conversion is performed automatically based on the inferred type of an assignment destination. Listing 2-26 shows code that opens Excel, creates a new spreadsheet, and adds text into two cells. The program is self-explanatory and very simple to use. You can see the use of the interop object when the excelApp object is created.

LISTING 2-26 Interacting with Excel

```
namespace LISTING_2_26_Interacting_with_Excel
{
    class Program
    {
        static void Main(string[] args)
        {
            // Create the interop
            var excelApp = new Microsoft.Office.Interop.Excel.Application();

            // make the app visible
            excelApp.Visible = true;

            // Add a new workbook
            excelApp.Workbooks.Add();
```

```
            // Obtain the active sheet from the app
            // There is no need to cast this dynamic type
            Microsoft.Office.Interop.Excel.Worksheet workSheet = excelApp.ActiveSheet;

            // Write into two cells
            workSheet.Cells[1, "A"] = "Hello";
            workSheet.Cells[1, "B"] = "from C#";
        }
    }
}
```

You might be wondering about the use of dynamic in the code in Listing 2-26. Figure 2-3 shows the Intellisense for the `Activesheet` component of the application. This is shown as a dynamic type, which is then assigned to a variable of Worksheet type without the need for any casting.

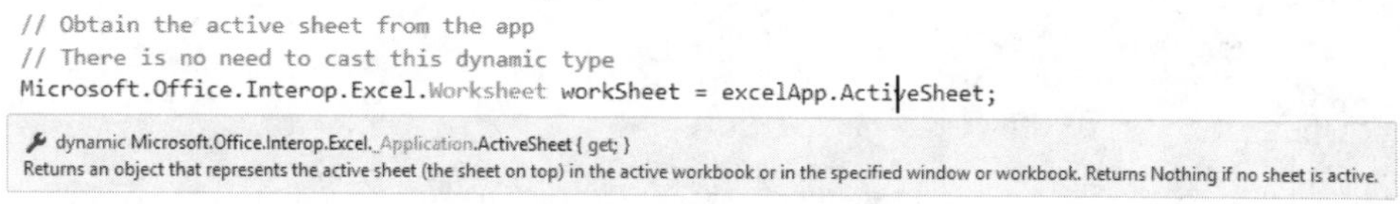

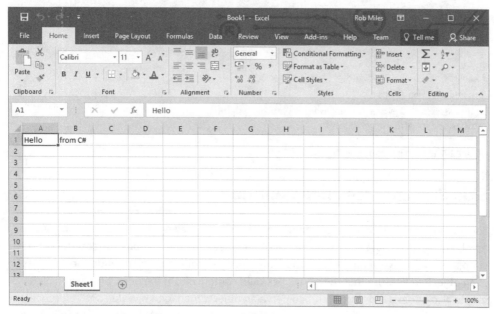

FIGURE 2-3 Using dynamic types

When this program runs it starts Excel running and then sets the values of the top two cells in the spreadsheet as shown in Figure 2-4.

FIGURE 2-4 Interacting with Excel

Embedding Type Information from assemblies

You can create applications that interact with different versions of Microsoft Office by embedding the Primary Interop Assembly in the application. This is achieved by setting the Embed Interop Types option of the assembly reference to True. This removes the need for any interop assemblies on the machine running the application.

FIGURE 2-5 Embed interop assemblies

Skill 2.3: Enforce encapsulation

You are now building up an understanding of how to create and use objects in applications. An object can hold data values by the use of member variables and provide services for other objects by the use of member methods. You can use constructors to set up the contents of an object and ensure that the object has valid contents from the point of creation. You should also understand the difference between objects managed by value and reference, and how dynamic types allow C# programs to interact with external languages and libraries.

One definition of the word encapsulate is to "enclose in a capsule." In this skill you are going to build on this knowledge to discover how to use encapsulation to improve the safety of programs that you write. You will discover how to enclose your software objects in capsules.

When discussing safety, a car designer will talk about *active* and *passive* safety systems. An active safety system is one that stops the car from crashing. Active safety systems include things like stability controls and anti-lock brakes. Passive safety is provided by systems in the car that are activated in the event of a crash. Passive safety systems include things like air-bags and crumple zones designed to absorb impacts.

In Skill 1-5, "Implement Exception Handling," you saw how exception handlers can be added to a program that will allow the program to respond in a managed way when errors occur as the program is running. You can think of this as "passive" program safety, in that exceptions allow you to create handlers that take control in the event of errors occurring.

You can think of encapsulation as a technique that provides *active* program safety. Use encapsulation to reduce the possibility of program errors occurring. Encapsulation lets you hide the elements that actually implement the behaviors of an object, so that the object only exposes the behaviors that it provides by a well-defined interface.

Encapsulation provides protection against accidental damage, where a programmer directly changes an internal element of an object without having a proper understanding of the effect of the change. Encapsulation also provides protection against malicious attacks on an application, where code is written with the intent to corrupt or damage the contents of an object. In this section you will discover the C# features that allow you to implement encapsulation in created objects.

This section covers how to:

- Enforce encapsulation by using properties
- Enforce encapsulation by using accessors, including public, private, protected, and internal
- Enforce encapsulation by using explicit interface implementation

---

Access modifiers

C# allows objects to encapsulate data and methods by providing programmers with the ability to mark members of a type with *access modifiers* that control access to them.

Public and private access

There are a number of different access modifiers, and you can start by considering *public* and *private*. A member of a type given the public access modifier can be accessed by code that is outside that type, whereas a private member of a type can only be accessed by code running inside the type.

Enforce encapsulation by using properties

A property in an object provides a way that a programmer can encapsulate data. Let's start by considering how public data is accessed in a class. Listing 2-27 shows a program that uses a class called Customer, which you might use to store customer records. At the moment the Customer class contains a single data member called Name, which is a string containing the name of the customer. The Name member has been made public, so that it can be set to the name of the customer.

LISTING 2-27 Public data members

```
using System;

namespace LISTING_2_27_Public_data_members
{
    class Customer
    {
        public string Name;
    }

    class Program
    {
        static void Main(string[] args)
        {
            Customer c = new Customer();
            c.Name = "Rob";
            Console.WriteLine("Customer name: {0}", c.Name);

            Console.ReadKey();
        }
    }
}
```

This program works well, but it doesn't provide any control over the contents of the customer name. The name of a customer can be set to any string, including an empty string. You should stop users of the Customer object from setting a customer name to an empty string. We call this "enforcing business rules" on our applications. You may have other rules to enforce, which restrict the characters that can be used in a name and set limits for the minimum and maximum length of a customer name. But for now, we will just focus on how to manage access to the name of a customer and stop invalid customer names from being created.

The program in Listing 2-28 shows how to create a Name property in the Customer class that performs validation of the name. A property is declared as having a get behavior and a set behavior. The set behavior is used when a program sets a value in the property and the get behavior is used when a program gets a value from the property. The get behavior for the Name property returns the value of a private class member variable called _nameValue, which holds the value of the name of the customer. Within the set behavior for the Name property keyword value represents the value being assigned to the property. If this value is an empty string the set behavior throws an exception to prevent an empty string begin set as a Name. If the value is valid, the set behavior sets _nameValue to the incoming name. Note that there is a C# convention that private members of a class have identifiers that start with an underscore (_) character.

LISTING 2-28 Using a property

```
using System;

namespace LISTING_2_28_Using_a_property
{
    class Customer
    {
        private string _nameValue;

        public string Name
        {
            get
            {
                return _nameValue;
            }
            set
            {
                if (value == "")
                    throw new Exception("Invalid customer name");
                _nameValue = value;
            }
        }
    }
}
```

Adding validation to the Name property does not change how the property is used in a program. The code here sets the name of customer c to Rob and then tries to set the name to an empty string, which causes an exception to be thrown:

```
Customer c = new Customer();
c.Name = "Rob";
Console.WriteLine("Customer name: {0}", c.Name);

Console.ReadKey();
// the following statement will throw an exception
c.Name = "";
```

The Name property can throw an exception when an attempt is made to set an empty string. Do this to ensure that the user of the Customer class is always made aware of any error conditions. You can make the set behavior ignore invalid names. or set the name to a default string when an invalid name is provided.

Properties provide a powerful way to enforce encapsulation, which is very natural in use. The user of a property might not even be aware that code is running when they perform what seems like a simple assignment. You can provide "read only" properties by creating properties that only contain a get behavior. These are useful if you want to expose multiple views of the data in an object, for example a Thermometer class can provide different properties that give the temperature value in Fahrenheit and Centigrade. You can also create "write only properties" by only providing the set behavior, although this ability is less frequently used. It is also possible to set different access modifiers for the get and set behaviors, so that a get behavior can be public for anyone to read, but the set behavior is private so that only code running inside the class can assign values to the property.

In the program in Listing 2-28 the private data member _nameValue holds the value of the name that is being managed by the property. This value is called the *backing value* of the property. If you just want to implement a class member as a property, but don't want to get control when the property is accessed, you can use *auto-implemented* properties. The statement here creates an integer property called Age. The C# compiler automatically creates the backing values. If you want to add get and set behaviors and your own backing value later, you can do this.

```
public int Age {get; set;}
```

Enforce encapsulation by using accessors

As a general rule, data held within a type should be made private and methods (which allow managed access to data inside the type) should be made public. Properties provide a way to manage access to individual values in a class, so you can consider how to use accessor methods to provide access to elements in a class.

The program in Listing 2-29 shows how public and private access modifiers can be used to create a very simple bank account application that uses methods to provide access to the account balance value. The member variable _accountBalance is made private to the BankAccount class. This means that it cannot be accessed by code running outside the BankAccount. The method members PayInFunds, GetBalance, and WithdrawFunds are declared as public, which means that code running outside the BankAccount class can use these methods to interact with the account balance value in a managed way.

LISTING 2-29 Creating accessor methods

```
using System;

namespace LISTING_2_29_Creating_accessor_methods
{
    class BankAccount
    {
        private decimal _accountBalance = 0;

        public void PayInFunds(decimal amountToPayIn)
        {
            _accountBalance = _accountBalance + amountToPayIn;
        }

        public bool WithdrawFunds(decimal amountToWithdraw)
        {
            if (amountToWithdraw > _accountBalance)
                return false;

            _accountBalance = _accountBalance - amountToWithdraw;
            return true;
        }

        public decimal GetBalance()
        {
```

```
                return _accountBalance;
            }
        }
    }

    class Program
    {
        static void Main(string[] args)
        {
            BankAccount a = new BankAccount();
            a.PayInFunds(50);
            Console.WriteLine("Pay in 50");
            a.PayInFunds(50);
            if (a.WithdrawFunds(10))
                Console.WriteLine("Withdrawn 10");
            Console.WriteLine("Account balance is: {0}", a.GetBalance());
            Console.ReadKey();
        }
    }
}
```

Making a data member of a class private will stop direct access to that data member. In other words, the following statements will not compile. The cunning attempt to increase the balance of an account by a million is not permitted by the compiler because the _accountBalance member has been declared as private to the BankAccount class.

```
BankAccount a = new BankAccount();
a._accountBalance = a._accountBalance + 1000000;
```

Of course, there is nothing to stop a wayward bank programmer from adding the following statement to the banking application. This would add a million to the account and is accepted by the C# compiler as completely legal code.

```
a.PayInFunds(1000000);
```

In a real bank a request to pay in funds is accompanied by some details that accredit the transaction, and the PayInFunds behavior logs each transaction for audit. This means that, from a design perspective, making a class member private and only providing public methods that allow access to that member is a good first step to creating secure code, but you also may also have to make sure that you provide a secure workflow that manages access to the data. In this respect the behavior of the BankAccount class in Listing 2-29 is sadly lacking; you might like to consider the effect of withdrawing a negative amount of money from the account. You might also like to consider how to fix this issue.

Default access modifiers

If you don't specify an access modifier for a member of a type, the access to that member will default to private. In other words, if you want to make a member visible outside the type, it must be done explicitly by adding public. This means that you don't actually have to add the access modifier private to your private members, but I strongly advise you to do this.

Protected access

Making a member of a class private will prevent code in any external class from having access to that data member. The protected access modifier makes a class member useable in any classes that extend the parent (base) class in which the member is declared. Listing 2-27 shows an OverdraftAccount that adds an overdraft facility to the BankAccount class. The OverdraftAccount contains an override of the WithdrawFunds method that allows the account holder to draw out more than they have in their account, up to the limit of their overdraft. This works because the accountBalance member of the BankAccount class now has the protected access modifier.

LISTING 2-30 Protected access

```
class OverdraftAccount: BankAccount
{
    decimal overdraftLimit = 100;

    public override bool WithdrawFunds(decimal amountToWithdraw)
    {
        if (amountToWithdraw > _accountBalance + overdraftLimit)
            return false;

        accountBalance = accountBalance - amountToWithdraw;
        return true;
    }
}
```

It isn't recommended that you use the protected access modifier to control access to highly important data members of a class such as a bank balance. Doing this makes it very easy for a malicious programmer to gain access to the protected member by extending the parent class. I tend to use the protected access modifier to limit access to helper methods that have no meaningful use outside of the class hierarchy.

Internal access

The internal access modifier will make a member of a type accessible within the assembly in which it is declared. You can regard an assembly as the output of a C# project in Visual Studio. It can be either an executable program (with the language extension .exe) or a library of classes (with the language extension .dll). Internal access is most useful when you have a large number of cooperating classes that are being used to provide a particular library component. These classes may want to share members which should not be visible to programs that use the library. Using the access modifier internal allows this level of sharing.

Readonly access

The readonly access modifier will make a member of a type read only. The value of the member can only be set at declaration or within the constructor of the class.

Access modifiers and classes

The private, public, protected, and internal access modifiers can also be applied to classes that are declared nested inside other classes. LISTING 2-29 shows how a BankAccount class could contain an Address class that is used to hold address information for account holders. If this Address class is made protected it can only be used in the BankAccount class and in classes that extend that class.

The classes in Listing 2-31 show how this would work. The protected Address class is defined in the BankAccount class. The OverdraftAccount class can contain a variable of type Address because it is a child of BankAccount. The OverDraft account contains a member called GuarantorAddress that that gives the address of the person nominated by the account holder to guarantee the overdraft.

LISTING 2-31 Protected class

```
class BankAccount
{
    protected class Address
    {
        public string FirstLine;
        public string Postcode;
    }

    protected decimal accountBalance = 0;
}
class OverdraftAccount : BankAccount
{
    decimal overdraftLimit = 100;

    Address GuarantorAddress;
}
```

Enforce encapsulation by using explicit interface implementation

Looking at Skill 2.4, "Create and implement a class hierarchy," you will see that a class can be defined as implementing an interface. Check out this section now if you're not clear on interface details.

When a class implements an interface it contains methods with signatures that match the ones specified in the interface. You can use an explicit interface implementation to make methods implementing an interface only visible when the object is accessed via an interface reference.

If this sounds confusing, then the best way to understand what is happening is to consider why you would want to do this. You might make an IPrintable interface that specifies methods used to print any object. This is a good idea, because now a printer can be asked to print any item that is referred to by a reference of IPrintable type. In other words, any object that implements the methods in IPrintable can be printed.

If you think about it, the methods in the IPrintable interface only have meaning when being used by something trying to print an object. It is not sensible to call the printing methods in any other context than via the IPrintable reference. You can achieve this by making the implementation of the printing methods *explicit*, thus adding the interface name to the declaration of the method body.

The code here shows a Report class that implements the IPrintable interface. The Report class contains two methods: GetPrintableText and GetTitle, which are declared in the IPrintable interface. These methods have been made explicit implementations of the interface by preceding the method name with the name of the interface they are implementing.

```
class Report : IPrintable
{
    string IPrintable. GetPrintableText(int pageWidth, int pageHeight)
    {
        return "Report text to be printed";
    }

    string IPrintable.GetTitle()
    {
        return "Report title to be printed";
    }
}
```

Once you have done this, the only way to access these methods in a Report instance is by a reference of IPrintable type. Figure 2-6 below shows the effect in Visual Studio of making the GetPrintableText and GetTitle methods explicit implementations of the IPrintable interface. The Intellisense shows that a reference to Report does not expose either of these methods.

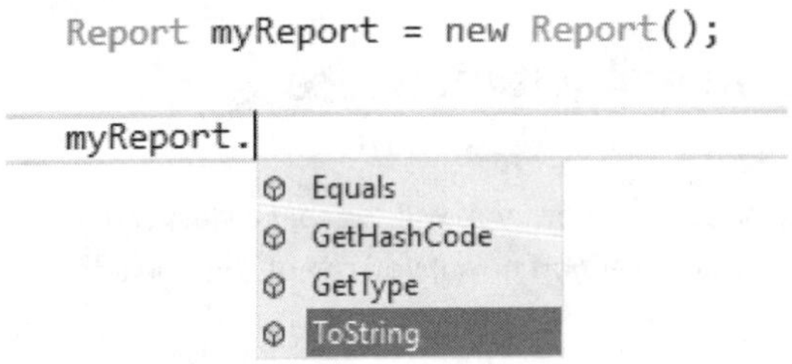

FIGURE 2-6 Explicit method implementation

If, however, you use Intellisense on a reference to an object that implements the IPrintable interface, you will see how the two methods in the interface are now available. Figure 2.7 shows the effect of using a reference to the IPrintable interface. The Intellisense for this reference includes the two interface methods.

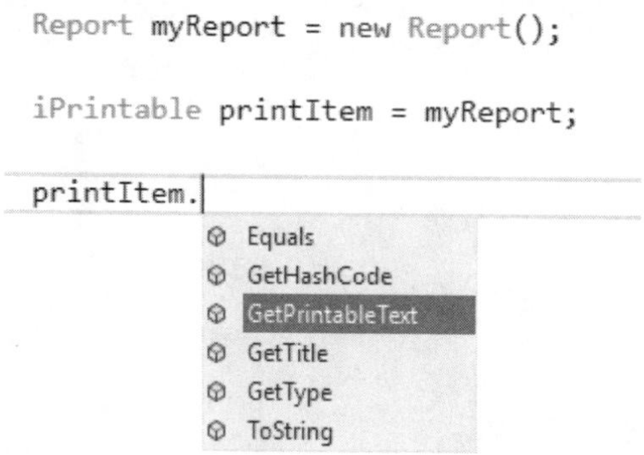

```
Report myReport = new Report();

iPrintable printItem = myReport;
```

```
printItem.|
        ⊕  Equals
        ⊕  GetHashCode
        ⊕  GetPrintableText
        ⊕  GetTitle
        ⊕  GetType
        ⊕  ToString
```

FIGURE 2-7 Using a reference to an interface

When you use an interface in a program you should ensure that all the implementations of any interface methods are explicit. This reduces the chances of the interface methods being used in an incorrect context.

Resolving duplicate method signatures by using explicit implementation

When a class implements an interface it must contain an implementation of all methods that are defined in the interface. Sometimes a class may implement multiple interfaces, in which case it must contain all the methods defined in all the interfaces. This can lead to problems, in that two interfaces might contain a method with the same name. For example the IPrintable and IDisplay interfaces might both specify a method called GetTitle to get the title of a document. The designers of the interfaces will have added these methods to the interface because a printed page and an on-screen menu might both need to have titles that need to be displayed. This can lead to confusion when an object implements both interfaces; either a document or a menu might end up with the incorrect title. Listing 2-32 shows how the Report class can contain explicit implementations of both GetTitle methods.

LISTING 2-32 Printing interface

```
interface IPrintable
{
    string GetPrintableText(int pageWidth, int pageHeight);
    string GetTitle();
}

interface IDisplay
{
    string GetTitle();
}

class Report : IPrintable, IDisplay
{
    string iPrintable.GetPrintableText(int pageWidth, int pageHeight)
    {
        return "Report text to be printed";
```

```
    }

    string IPrintable.GetTitle()
    {
        return "Report title to be printed";
    }

    string IDisplay.GetTitle()
    {
        return "Report title to be displayed";
    }
}
```

Skill 2.4: Create and implement a class hierarchy

You now know how to create your own types, consume them, and encapsulate their data and state to reduce the chances of accidental or malicious damage to objects in your program.

In this section you will discover how to create component objects that can be managed in terms of their abilities. You will also find out how to reduce the amount of code that you need to write for an application by using class hierarchies to reuse code in objects. Finally, we will explore some of the interfaces that are used by the .NET framework to manage objects and consider how these can be usefully implemented by created objects.

> **This section covers how to:**
> - Design and implement an interface
> - Inherit from a base class
> - Create and implement classes based on the IComparable, IEnumerable, IDisposable, and IUnknown interfaces

Design and implement an interface

Many items in the real world are designed as "components" that are interchangeable. You can connect a wide variety of devices to the main power in our house because, as far as the power supply is concerned, each device can be regarded in the same way – as a device that requires a particular voltage to work. You can think of the voltage and power elements of a power specification as an "interface" that defines how an electrical device can be connected to a power supply.

For this to work the people who make main boards and the people who make graphics adapters must agree on an interface between two devices. The interface specification describes exactly how the two components interact, for example which signals are inputs, which signals are outputs, and so on. Any main board which contains a socket built to the interface standard can accept a graphics card built to the same standard.

So, from the point of view of hardware, components are possible because we have created standard interfaces to describe exactly how they fit together. Software components are exactly the same.

At the moment you might not see a need for software components. When creating a system you must work out what each of the parts of it need to do, and then create those parts and fit them together. It may not be obvious why components are required. However, systems designed without components are like a computer with a graphics adapter that is part of the main board. It is not possible to change the main boad or the graphics adapter because they are "hard wired" together.

Software components and interfaces

One point to consider here is that we are not talking about the user interface to our program. The user interface is the way a person using a program makes it work for them. These are usually either text-based (the user types in commands and gets responses) or graphical (the user clicks "buttons" on a screen using the mouse).

An interface in a C# program specifies how a software component could be used by another software component. So, instead of starting to build an application by designing classes. you should instead be thinking about describing their interfaces (what each software component will do). How the component performs its function can be encapsulated inside the component.

A C# interface contains a set of method signatures. If a class contains an implementation of all of the methds described in the interface it can be defined as "implementing" that interface. Interfaces allow a program to regard objects in terms of their abilities (or the interfaces that they implement), rather than what type an object actually is. Humans do this all the time. If you hire someone to paint your house you will be dealing with that person in terms of their ability to paint, not who they really are.

As an example of a situation where interfaces are useful, consider a printing service that will print objects in an application. You can create an interface containing the definition of the methods that can be used to print a document on paper. Listing 2-33 shows the definition of an IPrintable interface that allows a printer to get the text to be printed and the title of a document from an object that wishes to be printed.

LISTING 2-33 IPrintable interface

```
interface IPrintable
{
    string GetPrintableText(int pageWidth, int pageHeight);
    string GetTitle();
}
```

Note that the methods in the interface do not ask a document to print itself, rather they ask the document to provide the text strings that the printer will put onto paper. The Report class shown below implements the IPrintable interface and contains implementations of the GetPrintableText and GetTitle methods.

```
class Report : IPrintable
{
    public string GetPrintableText(int pageWidth, int pageHeight)
    {
        return "Report text";
```

```
    }

    public string GetTitle()
    {
        return "Report title";
    }
}
```

A printer object can now be created that will accept and print reports. along with any other objects that implements the `IPrintable` interface. The `ConsolePrinter` class below provides a method called `PrintItem` that will output printable items onto the console. You can create other printers that print onto paper, web pages, or Adobe PDF documents.

```
class ConsolePrinter
{
    public void PrintItem( iPrintable item)
    {
        Console.WriteLine(item.GetTitle());
        Console.WriteLine(item.GetPrintableText(pageWidth:80, pageHeight:25));
    }
}
```

Note that the interface decouples the printer from the object being printed. If you create new document types that need to be printed, they can be added to the application without modifying the printer class. Conversely, you can add new types of printer and be sure that the new printer type can be used to print any document object.

You can even create test objects that can be used at either end of the interface. A test printer object can be created to make sure that an object implements all the print methods correctly and a test document object can be used to test the behaviors of a printer. The printing ability of a printer (for example add a document to the print queue and check if a document has been printed) can even be exposed as another interface, to make it even easier to switch between printing devices.

Design an interface

You can build your knowledge of interfaces by considering how to create an interface to describe the behavior of a class that will implement a bank account. In Listing 2-29 we looked at some behaviors that can be used to implement a bank account. You can express these behaviors in the form of an interface that sets out the methods that a bank account class should implement.

LISTING 2-34 IAccount interface

```
public interface IAccount
{
    void PayInFunds ( decimal amount );
    bool WithdrawFunds ( decimal amount );
    decimal GetBalance ();
}
```

Listing 2-34 says that the IAccount interface is comprised of three methods: one to pay money in, another to withdraw it, and a third to return the balance on the account. From the balance management point of view this is all you need. Note that at the interface level we are not saying how any of these tasks should be performed, but we are just identifying the tasks.

An interface is placed in a source file just like a class, and compiled in the same way. It sets out a number of methods that relate to a particular task or role, which in this case is what a class must do to be considered a bank account. There is a convention in C# programs that the name of an interface starts with the letter I. It is interesting to note that one of the refactoring tools available in Visual Studio is one that will extract the method signatures from a class and create an interface that contains those methods.

In the case of the bank account, you can now create a class implementing the interface, so that it can be thought of as an account component, irrespective of what it really is.

```
public class BankAccount: IAccount
{
    private decimal _balance = 0;

    bool IAccount .WithdrawFunds ( decimal amount )
    {
        if ( _balance < amount )
        {
            return false ;
        }
        _balance = _balance - amount ;
        return true;
    }

    void IAccount .PayInFunds ( decimal amount )
    {
        _balance = _balance + amount ;
    }

    decimal IAccount.GetBalance ()
    {
        return _balance;
    }
}
```

This code does not look much different from the previous BankAccount class. One difference is on the top line:

```
public class BankAccount: IAccount
{
...
```

This tells the compiler that this class implements the IAccount interface. This means that the class contains implementations of all the methods described in the interface. Note that I have added the inferface name to all the interface methods so that they are *explicitly implemented*. This means that these methods are only exposed when the BankAccount object is referred to by a reference of type IAccount. You can refer to the section "Enforce encapsulation by using explicit interface implementation" in Skill 2.4 for more details of how this works.

References to Interfaces

A program can now work with a BankAccount instance as an object of type BankAccount or an object that implements the IAccount interface. People do this all the time. You can think of me as Rob Miles the individual or Rob Miles the writer.

If you think of me as a writer, you would use an interface that contains methods with names such as WriteBook. And you can use these same methods with any other person who can behave like a writer. From the point of view of a publisher, which has to manage a large number of interchangeable writers, it is much more useful to think of me as a writer, rather than Rob Miles the individual. Should I ever join a golf club, that club will think of me in terms of my "IGolfer" interface.

So, with interfaces you are moving away from considering classes in terms of what they are, and starting to think about them in terms of what they can do. In the case of your bank, this means that you want to deal with objects in terms of IAccount, (the set of account abilities) rather than BankAccount (a particular account class).

In C# terms this means that you need to create reference variables that refer to objects in terms of interfaces they implement, rather than the particular type that they are. It turns out that this is quite easy:

```
IAccount account = new BankAccount ();
account.PayInFunds(50);
Console.WriteLine("Balance: " + account.GetBalance());
```

The account variable is allowed to refer to objects that implement the IAccount interface. The compiler will check to make sure that BankAccount does this, and if it does, the compilation is successful.

Note that there will never be an instance of IAccount interface. It is simply a way that you can refer to something which has that ability (i.e. contains the required methods).

This is the same in real life. There is no such physical thing as a "writer," merely a large number of people who can be referred to as having that particular ability or role.

Inherit from a base class

One of the fundamental principles of software development is to ensure that you create every piece of code in an application precisely once. Rather than copying code from one part of a program to another, you would create a method and then call that method.

The reason to do this is quite simple. If you find a bug in a piece of your program you only want to have to fix the bug once. You don't want to have to search through the program looking for all of the places where you have used a particular lump of code. If you have to do this, you may miss one place and end up with a program that is mostly fixed, but will still fail sometimes. A class hierarchy is a great way to reuse code so that you only have to create a behavior in one place and can then reuse the behavior everywhere it makes sense to do this.

A class hierarchy is used when you have an application that must manipulate items that are part of a particular group. For example, if you want to work with different types of bank account, or stock item, or customer, or space alien, you can make use of inheritance to save you writing a lot of code. For an example of how this might work, consider the BankAccount class that we have been working with. You may need to create another type of account that is exactly the same as an ordinary account but is used by very small children. This type of account, called BabyAcccount works in exactly the same way as a BankAccount, but it doesn't allow withdrawals of more than 10. Listing 2-35 shows how to create a BabyAccount that has the required behaviors.

LISTING 2-35 BabyAccount

```
public class BabyAccount : IAccount
{
    private decimal _balance = 0;

    bool IAccount.WithdrawFunds(decimal amount)
    {
        if (amount > 10)
        {
            return false;
        }
        if (_balance < amount)
        {
            return false;
        }
        _balance = _balance - amount;
        return true;
    }

    void IAccount.PayInFunds(decimal amount)
    {
        _balance = _balance + amount;
    }

    decimal IAccount.GetBalance()
    {
        return _balance;
    }
}
```

The good news is that because the BabyAccount is a component that implements the IAccount interface, it will work with any of the classes that work with accounts. When you create an account you just have to ask if a standard account or a baby account is required. The rest of the system can then pick up this object and use it without caring about what it is.

The bad news is that you have duplicated a lot of code. The BabyAccount class contains GetBalance and PayInFunds methods that are copies of the ones in the BankAccount class. Why write the same code twice?

What you really want to do is pick up all the behaviors in the BankAccount and then just change the one method that needs to behave differently. This can be done in C# using inheritance. When you create the BabyAccount class, you can tell the compiler that it is based on the BankAccount class:

```
public class BabyAccount : BankAccount, IAccount
{
}
```

The key thing here is the word BankAccount after the class name. This is the name of the class that BabyAccount is extending. This means that everything that BankAccount can do, BabyAccount can do. BankAccount is called the *base* or *parent* class of BabyAccount.

You can now write code like:

```
IAccount b = new BabyAccount();
b.PayInFunds(50);
```

This works because, although BabyAccount does not have a PayInFunds method, the base class does. This means that the PayInFunds method from the BankAccount class is used at this point.

Instances of the BabyAccount class have abilities which they pick up from their base class. In fact, at the moment, the BabyAccount class has no behaviors of its own; it gets everything from its base class.

The is and as operators

A program can use the is and as operators when working with class hierarchies and interfaces. The is operator determines if the type of a given object is in a particular class hierarchy or implements a specified interface. You apply the is operator between a reference variable and a type or interface and the operator returns true if the reference can be made to refer to objects of that type.

The code below prints out a message if the variable x refers to an object that implements the IAccount interface.

```
if (x is IAccount)
    Console.WriteLine("this object can be used as an account");
```

The as operator takes a reference and a type and returns a reference of the given type, or null if the reference cannot be made to refer to the object.

The code below creates an IAccount reference called y that either refers to x (if x implements the IAccount interface) or is null (if x does not implement the IAccount interface).

```
IAccount y = x as IAccount;
```

You might be wondering why we have the as operator, when we can already use casting to convert between reference types (see the "Cast types" section earlier for details on casting). The difference is that if a cast cannot be performed, a program will throw an exception, whereas if the as operator fails it returns a null reference and the program continues running.

Overriding methods

You saw how to override methods in Skill 2.1 in the "Overloading and overriding methods" section. Overriding replaces a method in a base class with a version that provides the behavior appropriate to a child class. In the case of the BabyAccount, you want to change the behavior of the one method that you are interested in. You want to replace the WithdrawFunds method with a new one.

Listing 2-36 shows how this is done. The keyword override means "use this version of the method in preference to the one in the base class." This means that when the code here runs the call, PayInFunds will use the method in the parent (since that has not been overridden), but the call of WithdrawFunds will use the method in BabyAccount.

LISTING 2-36 Overridden WithdrawFunds

```
public class BankAccount : IAccount
{
    protected decimal _balance = 0;

    public virtual bool WithdrawFunds(decimal amount)
    {
        if (_balance < amount)
        {
            return false;
        }
        _balance = _balance - amount;
        return true;
    }

    void IAccount.PayInFunds(decimal amount)
    {
        _balance = _balance + amount;
    }

    decimal IAccount.GetBalance()
    {
        return _balance;
    }
}

public class BabyAccount : BankAccount, IAccount
{
    public override bool WithdrawFunds(decimal amount)
    {
        if (amount > 10)
        {
            return false;
        }

        if (_balance < amount)
        {
            return false;
        }
        _balance = _balance - amount;
```

```
        return true;
    }
}
```

There are some other things to be aware of in Listing 2-36:

- The C# compiler needs to know if a method is going to be overridden. This is because it must call an overridden method in a slightly different way from a "normal" one. The WithDrawFunds method in the BankAccount class has been declared as *virtual* so that the compiler knows it may be overridden. It might be overridden in classes which are children of the parent class.

- The C# language does not allow the overriding of explicit implementations of interface methods. This means that you have to sacrifice a slight measure of encapsulation in order to use class hierarchies in this manner. In Listing 2-36, you can see that the WithDrawFunds method in the BankAccount class is declared as virtual, but it has not been declared as an interface method.

- The WithdrawFunds method in the BabyAccount class makes use of the _balance value that is declared in the parent BankAccount class. To make this possible the _balance value has had its access modifier changed from private to protected so that it can be used in classes that extend the BankAccount class.

The ability to override a method is very powerful. It means that you can make more general classes (for example the BankAccount) and customize it to make them more specific (for example the BabyAccount). Of course, this should be planned and managed at the design stage. This calls for information to be gathered from the customer and used to decide which parts of a behavior need to be changed during the life of the project.

You can make the WithDrawFunds method virtual because you discovered that different accounts might need to withdraw funds in a different way. Note that the PayInFunds and GetBalance methods have not been made virtual because you will always be using the versions of these declared in the BankAccount class.

Using the base method

Remember the importance of only writing any given piece of code once? Well, it looks as if I'm breaking my own rules here, in that the WithDrawFunds method in the BabyAccount class contains all of the code of the method in the parent class.

We have already noted that we don't like this much, in that it means that the balance value has to be made more exposed than we might like. It is now protected (visible to any class in the BankAccount class hierarchy) rather than private to just the BankAccount class. Fortunately, the designers of C# have thought of this and have provided a way that you can call the base method from one which overrides it.

The word base in this context means "a reference to the thing which has been overridden." I can use this to make the WithDrawFunds method in my BabyAccount much simpler.

Listing 2-37 shows how this works. The very last line of the WithDrawFunds method makes a call to the original WithDrawFunds method in the parent class (the one that the method overrides). This attempts to perform a withdrawal and returns true if the withdrawal works.

LISTING 2-37 The base method

```
public override bool WithdrawFunds(decimal amount)
{
    if (amount > 10)
    {
        return false;
    }
    else
    {
        return base.WithdrawFunds(amount);
    }
}
```

It's important to understand what we're doing here, and why we're doing it:

- I don't want to have to write the same code twice
- I don't want to make the _balance value visible outside the BankAccount class.

The use of the word base to call the overridden method solves both of these problems rather beautifully. Because the method call returns a bool result you can just send whatever it delivers. By making this change you can put the _balance back to private in the BankAccount because it is not accessed by the WithdrawFunds method.

Note that there are other useful spin-offs here. If I need to fix a bug in the behavior of the WithDrawFunds method I just fix it once, in the top-level class, and then it is fixed for all the classes which call back to it.

Replacing methods in base classes

C# allows a program to replace a method in a base class by simply creating a new method in the child class. In this situation there is no overriding, you have just supplied a new version of the method. In fact, the C# compiler will give you a warning that indicates how you should provide the keyword new to indicate this):

```
public class BabyAccount : BankAccount,IAccount
{
    public new bool WithdrawFunds (decimal amount)
    {
        if (amount > 10)
        {
            return false ;
        }
        if (_balance < amount)
        {
            return false ;
        }
        _balance = _balance - amount ;
        return true;
    }
}
```

Note that a replacement method is not able to use base to call the method that it has over-ridden, because it has not overridden a method, it has replaced it. I cannot think of a good reason for replacing a method, and I'm mentioning this feature of C# because I feel you need to know about it; and not because you should use it.

Stopping overriding

Overriding is very powerful. It means that a programmer can just change one tiny part of a class and make a new one with all the behaviors of the parent. This goes well with a design process, so as you move down the "family tree" of classes you get more and more specific implementations.

However, overriding/replacing is not always desirable. Consider the GetBalance method in the BankAccount class. This is never going to need a replacement. And yet a malicious pro-grammer can write their own and override or replace the one in the parent:

```
public new decimal GetBalance ()
{
    return 1000000;
}
```

This is the banking equivalent of the bottle of beer that is never empty. No matter how much cash is drawn out of the account, it always has a balance value of a million pounds! A programmer could insert this into a child class and enjoy a nice spending spree. What this means is that you need a way to mark some methods as not being able to be overridden. C# does this by giving us a sealed keyword which means "You can't override this method any more".

You can only seal an overriding method and sealing a method does not prevent a child class from replacing a method in a parent. However, you can also mark a class as sealed. This means that the class cannot be extended, so it cannot be used as the basis for another class. The BabyAccount below cannot be the base of any other classes.

```
public sealed class BabyAccount : CustomerAccount,IAccount
{
    .....
}
```

Constructors and class hierarchies

A constructor is a method which gets control during the process of object creation. It is used to allow initial values to be set into an object. You can add a constructor to the BankAccount class that allows an initial balance to be set when an account is created. Listing 2-38 shows the constructor method in the BankAccount class.

LISTING 2-38 BankAccount constructor

```
public class BankAccount : IAccount
{
    private decimal _balance ;
```

```
    public BankAccount ( decimal initialBalance)
    {
        _balance = initialBalance;
    }
}
```

You can now set the initial balance of an account when one is created. The following statement creates a new bank account with an initial balance of 100.

```
IAccount a = new BankAccount(100);
```

Unfortunately, adding a constructor like this to a base class in a class hierarchy has the effect of breaking all the child classes. The reason for this is that creating a child class instance involves creating an instance of the base class. When the program tries to create a BabyAccount it must first create a BankAccount. Creating a BankAccount involves the use of its constructor to set the initial balance of the BankAccount. The BabyAccount class must contain a constructor that calls the constructor in the parent object to set that up. The code here shows how this would work. The constructor for the BabyAccount makes a call of the constructor for the base class and passes the initial balance into that constructor.

```
public class BabyAccount : BankAccount, IAccount
{
    public BabyAccount(int initialBalance) : base(initialBalance)
    {
    }
}
```

In "Skill 2.1 Creating Types" we discussed the use of the use of the keyword this when writing constructors. You saw that the keyword is used to allow a constructor in a class to call other constructors in that class. The base keyword in this context is analogous to the this keyword, except that the constructor that is called is in the base class.

Note that in this case, the actual constructor body for the BabyAccount does nothing. However, it might be that other information needs to be stored in a BabyAccount (perhaps the name of a parent or guardian of the account holder). This can be set by the BabyAccount constructor in the BabyAccount constructor body.

Abstract methods and classes

At the moment we are using overriding to modify the behavior of an existing parent method. However, it is also possible to use overriding in a slightly different context. You can use it to force a set of behaviors on items in a class hierarchy. If there are some things that an account must do then we can make these abstract and then force the child classes to provide the implementation.

For example, in the context of the bank application you might want to provide a method that creates the text of a warning letter to the customer telling them that their account is overdrawn. This will have to be different for each type of account (you don't want to use the same language to a baby account holder as you do for a normal account). This means that at the time you create the bank account system you know that you need this method, but you don't know what it does in every situation.

You can provide a virtual "default" method in the BankAccount class and then rely on the programmers overriding this with a more specific message, but you then have no way of making sure that they really do perform the override. C# provides a way of flagging a method as *abstract*. This means that the method body is not provided in this class, but will be provided in a child class:

```
public abstract class BankAccount
{
    public abstract string WarningLetterString();
}
```

The fact that the BankAccount class contains an abstract method means that the class itself is abstract (and must be marked as such). It is not possible to make an instance of an abstract class. If you think about it this is sensible. An instance of BankAccount would not know what to do if the WarningLetterString method was ever called.

An abstract class can be thought of as a kind of template. If you want to make an instance of a class based on an abstract parent you must provide implementations of all the abstract methods given in the parent.

Abstract classes and interfaces

You might decide that an abstract class looks a lot like an interface. This is true, in that an interface also provides a "shopping list" of methods which must be provided by a class. However, abstract classes are different in that they can contain fully implemented methods alongside the abstract ones. This can be useful because it means you don't have to repeatedly implement the same methods in each of the components that implement a particular interface.

A class can only inherit from one parent, so it can only pick up the behaviors of one class. Some languages support *multiple inheritance*, where a class can inherit from multiple parents. C# does not allow this.

References in class hierarchies

A reference to a base class in a class hierarchy can refer to an instance of any of the classes that inherits from that base class. In other words, a variable declared as a reference to BankAccount objects can refer to a BabyAccount instance.

However, the reverse is not true. A variable declared as a reference to a BabyAccount object cannot be made to refer to a BankAccount object. This is because the BabyAccount class may have added extra behaviors to the parent class (for example a method called GetParentName). A BankAccount instance will not have that method.

However, I much prefer it if you manage references to objects in terms of the interfaces than the type of the particular object. This is much more flexible, in that you're not restricted to a particular type of object when developing the code.

Create and implement classes based on the IComparable, IEnumerable, IDisposable, and IUnknown interfaces

The .NET framework provides services that make use of particular behaviors that may be provided by a given object. Each of these behaviors is described by an interface. If you want your objects to be manipulated by .NET in terms of these interfaces you need to make your objects implement the interfaces.

In this section we are going to consider some of these interfaces, when they are useful, and how you can use them in our programs.

IComparable

The IComparable interface is used by .NET to determine the ordering of objects when they are sorted. Below is the definition of the method from the C# .NET library. You can see that the interface contains a single method, CompareTo, which compares this object with another. The CompareTo method returns an integer. If the value returned is less than 0 it indicates that this object should be placed before the one it is being compared with. If the value returned is zero, it indicates that this object should be placed at the same position as the one it is being compared with and if the value returned is greater than 0 it means that this object should be placed after the one it is being compared with.

```
public interface IComparable
{
    //
    // Summary:
    //     Compares the current instance with another object of the same type and
    //     returns
    //     an integer that indicates whether the current instance precedes, follows, or
    //     occurs in the same position in the sort order as the other object.
    //
    // Parameters:
    //   obj:
    //     An object to compare with this instance.
    //
    // Returns:
    //     A value that indicates the relative order of the objects being compared. The
    //     return value has these meanings: Value Meaning Less than zero This instance
    //     precedes
    //     obj in the sort order. Zero This instance occurs in the same position in the
    //     sort order as obj. Greater than zero This instance follows obj in the sort
    //     order.
    //
    // Exceptions:
    //   T:System.ArgumentException:
    //     obj is not the same type as this instance.
    int CompareTo(object obj);
}
```

You can allow your bank accounts to be sorted in order of balance by making the BankAccount class implement the IComparable interface and adding a CompareTo method to the BankAccount class.

Listing 2-39 shows how to do this. The CompareTo method is supplied with an object reference, which must be converted into an IAccount reference so that a BankAccount instance can be compared with any other object that implements the IAccount reference. The CompareTo method is simplified by using the CompareTo method of the decimal balance method to create the result.

LISTING 2-39 Comparing bank accounts

```
public class BankAccount : IAccount, IComparable
{
    public int CompareTo(object obj)
    {
        // if we are being compared with a null object we are definitely after it
        if (obj == null) return 1;

        // Convert the object reference into an account reference
        IAccount account = obj as IAccount;

        // as generates null if the conversion fails
        if (account == null)
            throw new ArgumentException("Object is not an account");

        // use the balance value as the basis of the comparison
        return this.balance.CompareTo(account.GetBalance());
    }

}
```

Once the BankAccount has been made to implement the IComparable interface, you can use the Sort behaviors provided by collection types. The code below creates a list of 20 accounts and sorts them using the Sort method provided by the List collection type.

```
// Create 20 accounts with random balances
List<IAccount> accounts = new List<IAccount>();
Random rand = new Random(1);
for(int i=0; i<20; i++)
{
    IAccount account = new BankAccount(rand.Next(0, 10000));
    accounts.Add(account);
}

// Sort the accounts
accounts.Sort();

// Display the sorted accounts
foreach(IAccount account in accounts)
{
    Console.WriteLine(account.GetBalance());
}
```

Typed IComparable

The IComparable interface uses a CompareTo method that accepts an object reference as a parameter. This reference should refer to an object of the same type as the object that is doing the comparing, i.e. the CompareTo method in type x should be supplied with a reference to type x as a parameter.

As you can see in Listing 2-39 above, the CompareTo method for the BankAccount will throw an exception if a program attempts to compare a bank account with something that isn't a bank account. However, this error will be produced when the program runs, not when the program is compiled. The following two statements compile correctly even though they are clearly incorrect because they are trying to compare a bank account to a string.

```
BankAccount b = new BankAccount(100);
b.CompareTo("hello");
```

There is another version of the IComparable interface that accepts a type. This can be used to create a CompareTo that only accepts parameters of a specified type. Listing 2-40 shows how this works. The CompareTo method now accepts a parameter of type BankAccount, does not need to cast this to a BankAccount before performing the comparison and does not have to throw an exception if an invalid type is supplied.

LISTING 2-40 Typed IComparable

```
public interface IAccount : IComparable<IAccount>
{
    void PayInFunds(decimal amount);
    bool WithdrawFunds(decimal amount);
    decimal GetBalance();
}

public class BankAccount : IAccount, IComparable<BankAccount>
{
    private decimal balance;

    public int CompareTo(IAccount account)
    {
        // if we are being compared with a null object we are definitely after it
        if (account == null) return 1;

        // use the balance value as the basis of the comparison
        return this.balance.CompareTo(account.GetBalance());
    }
}
```

Note that for the use of typed IComparable to be made to work with objects managed by the IAccount interface I had to change the definition of the IAccount interface so that it extends the IComparable interface. This ensures that any objects that implement the IAccount interface also implement the IComparable interface. From this you can see that it is possible to create interface hierarchies as well as class hierarchies, but this is not something you will necessarily do a lot of when you write programs.

IEnumerable

Programs spend a lot of time consuming lists and other collections of items. This is called *iterating* or *enumerating*.

You might think of iteration as something that is performed on lists and arrays of values, with a program working through each element in turn. However, iteration is much more than this. Any C# object can implement the IEnumerable interface that allows other programs to get an enumerator from that object. The enumerator object can then be used to enumerate (or iterate) on the object.

The code in Listing 2-41 shows how this works. The string type supports enumeration, and so a program can call the GetEnumerator method on a string instance to get an enumerator. The enumerator exposes the method MoveNext(), which returns the value true if it was able to move onto another item in the enumeration. The enumerator also exposes a property called Current, which is a reference to the currently selected item in the enumerator.

LISTING 2-41 Get an enumerator

```
using System;

namespace LISTING_2_41_Get_an_enumerator
{
    class Program
    {
        static void Main(string[] args)
        {
            // Get an enumerator that can iterate through a string
            var stringEnumerator = "Hello world".GetEnumerator();

            while(stringEnumerator.MoveNext())
            {
                Console.Write(stringEnumerator.Current);
            }

            Console.ReadKey();
        }
    }
}
```

The program in Listing 2-41 prints out the "Hello world" string one character at a time. The while construction in the Listing 2-41 uses the MoveNext and Current members of the enumerator to do this. You can consume all the iterators in this way, but C# makes life easier by providing the foreach construction, which automatically gets the enumerator from the object and the works through it. Listing 2-42 shows how we would iterate through the same string using a foreach construction.

LISTING 2-42 Using foreach

```
using System;

namespace LISTING_2_42_Using_foreach
{
    class Program
    {
        static void Main(string[] args)
        {
            foreach (char ch in "Hello world")
```

```
            Console.Write(ch);

        Console.ReadKey();
    }
  }
}
```

Making an object enumerable

The IEnumerable interface allows you to create objects that can be enumerated within your programs, for example by the foreach loop construction. Collection classes, and results returned by LINQ queries implement this interface.

Listing 2-43 shows how to create an enumerable object. It creates a class called EnumeratorThing that implements both the IEnumerable interface (meaning it can be enumerated) and the IEenumerator<int> interface (meaning that it contains a call of GetEnumerator to get an enumerator from it). An EnumaratorThing instance performs an iteration up to a limit that was set when it was created. Note that the EmulatorThing class contains the Current property and the MoveNext behavior that was used in Listing 2-41 when we wrote code that consumed an enumerator.

LISTING 2-43 Creating an enumerable type

```
class EnumeratorThing : IEnumerator<int>, IEnumerable
{
    int count;
    int limit;

    public int Current
    {
        get
        {
            return count;
        }
    }

    object IEnumerator.Current
    {
        get
        {
            return count;
        }
    }

    public void Dispose()
    {
    }

    public bool MoveNext()
    {
        if (++count == limit)
            return false;
        else
```

```
            return true;
        }

    public void Reset()
    {
        count = 0;
    }

    public IEnumerator GetEnumerator()
    {
        return this;
    }

    public EnumeratorThing(int limit)
    {
        count = 0;
        this.limit = limit;
    }
}
```

You can use an EnumeratorThing instance in a foreach loop:

```
    EnumeratorThing e = new EnumeratorThing(10);
```

```
foreach(int i in e)
    Console.WriteLine(i);
```

Using yield

You can create enumerators as we did in Listing 2-43, but this is quite complicated. To make it easier to create iterators C# includes the yield keyword. You can see it being used in Listing 2-44. The keyword yield is followed by the return keyword and precedes the value to be returned for the current iteration. The C# compiler generates all the Current and MoveNext behaviors that make the iteration work, and also records the state of the iterator method so that the iterator method resumes at the statement following the yield statement when the next iteration is requested. The EnumeratorThing class in Listing 2-44 provides exactly the same behavior as the one created in Listing 2-43, but it is much simpler.

LISTING 2-44 Using yield

```
class EnumeratorThing : IEnumerable<int>
{
    public IEnumerator<int> GetEnumerator()
    {
        for (int i = 1; i < 10; i++)
        yield return i;
    }

    IEnumerator IEnumerable.GetEnumerator()
    {
        return GetEnumerator();
    }
```

```
    private int limit;
    public EnumeratorThing(int limit)
    {
        this.limit = limit;
    }
}
```

The `yield` keyword does two things. It specifies the value to be returned for a given iteration, and it also returns control to the iterating method. You can express an iterator that returns
the values 1, 2, 3, as follows.

```
public IEnumerator<int> GetEnumerator()
{
        yield return 1;
        yield return 2;
        yield return 3;
}
```

When the first `yield` is reached the enumerator returns the value 1. The next time that the
enumerator is called (in other words the next time round the loop) the enumerator resumes at
the statement following the first `yield`. This is another `yield` that returns 2. This continues, with
the value 3 being returned by the third yield. When the enumerator method ends this has the
effect of ending the loop.

IDisposable

C# provides memory management for applications, but it can't control how programs use
other resources such as file handles, database connections and lock objects. While an object
can get control when it is removed by the garbage collector (see Skill 2.6, "Manage the object
lifecycle" for details on this) it is hard for a developer to know precisely when this happens. It
may not even happen until the program ends.

The `IDisposable` interface provides a way that an object can indicate that it contains an
explicit `Dispose` method that can be used to tidy up an object when an application has finished
using it. A disposed object may exist in memory, but any attempts to use it will result in the
`ObjectDisposedException` being thrown.

Below is the definition of the `IDisposable` interface. If an object implements the `IDisposable`
interface it contains a `Dispose` method that can be called to tidy up the object.

```
//
// Summary:
//      Provides a mechanism for releasing unmanaged resources.
public interface IDisposable
{
    //
    // Summary:
    //      Performs application-defined tasks associated with freeing, releasing, or
    //          resetting
    //      unmanaged resources.
    void Dispose();
}
```

Note that the action of the `Dispose` method depends entirely on the needs of the application. Note also that the `Dispose` method is not called automatically when an object is deleted from memory. There are two ways to make sure that `Dispose` is called correctly; you can call the method yourself in your application, or you can make use of the C# `using` construction.

Listing 2-45 shows how we can create a `CrucialConnection` class that allocates resources that must be disposed of. The `CrucialConnection` class implements `IDisposable` and contains a `Dispose` method which, in this case, just prints a message. The `using` construction creates an instance of the `CrucialConnection` class and is then followed by the block of code that uses this instance. When the program exits, the `using` block the `Dispose` method is called on the `CrucialConnection` instance. When the program runs it will print the message "Dispose called."

LISTING 2-45 Using IDisposable

```csharp
using System;

namespace LISTING_2_45_Using_IDisposable
{
    class CrucialConnection : IDisposable
    {
        public void Dispose()
        {
            Console.WriteLine("Dispose called");
        }

    }
    class Program
    {
        static void Main(string[] args)
        {
            using (CrucialConnection c = new CrucialConnection())
            {
                // do something with the crucial connection
            }

            Console.ReadKey();
        }
    }
}
```

The C# `using` construction is a good way to ensure that `Dispose` is called correctly because it incorporates exception handling so that if an exception is thrown by the code using the object the `Dispose` method is automatically called on the object being used. If you have a number of objects that need to be disposed you can nest `using` blocks inside each other.

IUnknown

In Skill 2.1 we discussed dynamic types in the context of interaction with services provided via the Component Object Model (COM). You saw how a program can use the interop services provided by Microsoft Office to allow you to write a C# program that interacts with Excel. You saw that these interop services returned results that were dynamically typed, and that the program can then use these results simply by assigning them to correctly typed variables.

These interop services are implemented as C# libraries that *marshal* the data between the managed code world of C# and the unmanaged world of COM objects. In the COM world the IUnknown interface is the means by which one object describes the interfaces that it makes available for use by others. The IUnknown interface provides a means by which .NET applications can interoperate with COM objects at this level. You use it when connecting C# applications to COM objects. You can find more detail on how to do this here: *https://docs. microsoft.com/en-us/dotnet/framework/interop/*.

Skill 2.5: Find, execute, and create types at runtime by using reflection

In the previous sections in this chapter the focus has been on features of C# that allow a program to be mapped onto an application domain. You have seen how to create types that implement behaviors in a problem domain, how to use these types, how to give the types integrity by using cohesion, how to use C# interfaces to turn objects into components and how to use class hierarchies that allow a collection of related component objects to share common behaviors.

In this section we're going to look at some C# features that are concerned with the management and manipulation of a code base. These features are not all necessarily concerned with creating an application that solves a problem; they are more concerned with easing the management and generation of software components. You will see how to add descriptive information to classes by the use of attribute objects, how to write programs that generate executable code as their output, and how to use the System.Reflection namespace to create programs that can analyze the content of software objects.

> **This section covers how to:**
> - Create and apply attributes
> - Read attributes
> - Generate code at runtime by using CodeDom and lambda Lambda expressions
> - Use types from the System.Reflection namespace, including Assembly, PropertyInfo, MethodInfo and Type

Create and apply attributes

When describing a piece of data you can talk in terms of the attributes of that data. For example, a data file containing music can have attributes that gave the name of the recording artist. In this context the recording artist attribute can be described as a piece of *metadata*. Metadata is "data about data." In the case of the music; the data is the music itself, and the metadata is the name of the artist.

C# allows you to add metadata to an application in the form of *attributes* that are attached to classes and class members. An attribute is an instance of a class that extends the Attribute class.

The Serializable attribute

The first attribute that you encounter as a developer is usually the `Serializable` attribute. This attribute doesn't actually hold any data, it is the fact that a class has a `Serializable` attribute instance attached to it means that the class is may be opened and read by a serializer.

A serializer takes the entire contents of a class and sends it into a stream. There are possible security implications in serializing a class and so C# requires that a class should "opt in" to the serialization process. For more details on serialization, take a look at Skill 4.4, "Serialize and deserialize data."

Listing 2-46 shows a `Person` class that contains name and age information. The `Person` class has the `Serializable` attribute attached to it; this is expressed by giving the name of the attribute enclosed in square brackets, just before the declaration of the class. The `Person` class also contains a `NonSerialized` attribute that is applied to the `screenPosition` member variable. This member of the class is only used to manage the display of a `Person` object and should not be saved when it is serialized. This tells the serializer not to save the value of `screenPosition`.

LISTING 2-46 The serializable attribute

```
[Serializable]
public class Person
{
    public string Name;

    public int Age;

    [NonSerialized]
    // No need to save this
    private int screenPosition;

    public Person(string name, int age)
    {
        Name = name;
        Age = age;
        screenPosition = 0;
    }
}
```

Note that some serializers, notably the `XMLSerializer` and the `JSONSerializer`, don't need classes to be marked as serializable before they can work with them. You can find out more about serialization in Skill 4.4, "Serialize and deserialize data."

Conditional compilation using attributes

You can use the `Conditional` attribute to activate and de-activate the contents of methods. This attribute is declared in the `System.Diagnostics` namespace. Listing 2-47 shows how it is used. The symbols `TERSE` and `VERBOSE` can be used to select the level of logging that is performed by a program. If the `TERSE` symbol is defined the body of the `terseReport` method will be obeyed when the method is called. If the VERBOSE symbol is defined the body of the verboseReport method will be obeyed. The body of the reportHeader method will be obeyed if either the TERSE or the VERBOSE symbols are defined because two attributes are combined before that method definition.

LISTING 2-47 The conditional attribute

```
//#define TERSE
#define VERBOSE

using System;
using System.Diagnostics;

namespace LISTING_2_47_The_conditional_attribute
{
    class Program
    {
        [Conditional("VERBOSE"), Conditional("TERSE")]
        static void reportHeader()
        {
            Console.WriteLine("This is the header for the report");
        }

        [Conditional("VERBOSE")]
        static void verboseReport()
        {
            Console.WriteLine("This is output from the verbose report.");
        }

        [Conditional("TERSE")]
        static void terseReport()
        {
            Console.WriteLine("This is output from the terse report.");
        }

        static void Main(string[] args)
        {
            reportHeader();
            terseReport();
            verboseReport();
            Console.ReadKey();
        }
    }
}
```

Note that the Conditional attribute controls whether or not the body of a given method is obeyed when the method is called, it does not control whether or not the method itself is passed to the compiler. The Conditional attribute does not perform the same function as conditional compilation in languages such as C and C++, it does not prevent code from being passed to the compiler, rather it controls whether code is executed when it runs. You can find out more about the use of pre-processor directives in Skill 3.4, "Debug an application."

Testing for attributes

A program can check that a given class has a particular attribute class attached to it by using the `IsDefined` method, which is a static member of the `Attribute` class. The `IsDefined` method accepts two parameters; the first is the type of the class being tested and the second type of the attribute class that the test is looking for.

Listing 2-48 shows how a program could check whether the `Person` class defined in Listing 2-46 is Serializable. Note that although the attribute is called `Serializable` when it is used in the source code, the name of the class that implements the attribute has the text `Attribute` appended to it, so that the attribute class we are looking for is called `SerializableAttribute`. The convention of adding the "Attribute" to the end of attribute classes is one that should be followed when creating our own attributes.

LISTING 2-48 Testing for an attribute

```
if (Attribute.IsDefined(typeof(Person), typeof(SerializableAttribute)))
    Console.WriteLine("Person can be serialized");
```

Note that this test just tells us that a given class has an attribute of a particular type. Later you will discover how a program can read data which is stored in attribute instances.

Creating attribute classes

You can create your own attribute classes to help manage elements of your application. These classes can serve as markers in the same way as the `Serializable` attribute specifies that a class can be serialized, or you can store data in attribute instances to give information about the items the attributes are attached to. The data values stored in an attribute instances are set from the class metadata when the attribute is loaded. A program can change them as it runs, but these changes will be lost when the program ends.

Listing 2-49 shows an attribute class that can be used to tag items in our program with the name of the programmer that created it. We can add other details to the attribute, for example the name of the tester and the date the code was last updated.

LISTING 2-49 Creating an attribute class

```
class ProgrammerAttribute: Attribute
{
    private string programmerValue;

    public ProgrammerAttribute (string programmer)
    {
        programmerValue = programmer;
    }

    public string Programmer
    {
        get
        {
            return programmerValue;
        }
    }
}
```

Note that in Listing 2-49 the programmer name is stored as a read-only property of the attribute. We could have made the programmer name a writable property (added a `set` behavior to the `Programmer` property), but this is not sensible, because changes to the programmer name are not persisted when the program ends.

You can add the `Programmer` attribute to elements in your program in the same way as when adding the `Serializable` attribute, although in this case the attribute constructor must be called to set the programmer name.

The code here shows how this is done. Note that we've used named arguments in the call of the constructor to make it clear what is being set. When creating attributes, you should make good use of named and optional arguments.

```
[ProgrammerAttribute(programmer:"Fred")]
class Person
{
    public string Name { get; set; }
}
```

Controlling the use of Attributes

The `ProgrammerAttribute` created earlier can be added to any item in my program, including member variables, methods, and properties. It can also be added to any type of object. When you create an attribute class, the proper practice is to add attribute usage information to the declaration of the attribute class, so that the compiler can make sure that the attribute is only used in meaningful situations. Perhaps you don't want to be able to assign `Programmer` attributes to the methods in a class. You only want to assign a Programmer attribute to the class itself.

This is done by adding an attribute to the declaration of the attribute class. The attribute is called `AttributeUseage` and this is set with a number of values that can control how the attribute is used.

The `AttributeUseage` settings in Listing 2-50 only allow the `Programmer` attribute to be applied to class declarations.

LISTING 2-50 Controlling attribute access

```
[AttributeUsage(AttributeTargets.Class)]
class ProgrammerAttribute: Attribute
{
...
}
```

If you try to use the `ProgrammerAttribute` on anything other than a class you will find that the compiler will generate errors. Note that this means that the compiler is performing reflection on our code as it compiles it, and you will find that Visual Studio does the same thing, in that invalid attempts to add attributes will be flagged as errors in the editor.

```
[ProgrammerAttribute(programmer:"Fred")]
class Person
```

```
{
    // This would cause a compilation error as we
    // are only allowed to apply this attribute to classes
    // [ProgrammerAttribute(programmer: "Fred")]
    public string Name { get; set; }
}
```

You can set values of the AttributeUsage class to control whether children of a class can be given the attribute, specify which elements of your program can have the attribute assigned to them, identify specific types to be given the attribute and specify whether the given attribute can be applied multiple times to the same item. You can also use the or operator (|) to set multiple targets for a given attribute. The attribute class FieldOrProp below can be applied to properties or fields in a class.

```
[AttributeUsage(AttributeTargets.Property | AttributeTargets.Field)]
class FieldOrProp: Attribute
{
...
}
```

Read attributes

You know how to add attributes to objects, so now you need to know how the program can read the attributes back. You saw that the Attribute class provides a static method called IsDefined that be used to determine if a class has a particular attribute defined. The Attribute class also provides a method called GetCustomAttribute to get an attribute from a particular type.

Listing 2-51 shows how this attribute is used. It has the same parameters as IsDefined (the type of the class and the type of the attribute class) and returns a reference to the attribute. If the attribute is not defined on the class, GetCustomAttribute returns null. In the code below the Attribute returned is cast to a ProgrammerAttribute and the name of the programmer is printed.

LISTING 2-51 Read an attribute

```
Attribute a = Attribute.GetCustomAttribute( typeof(Person),
typeof(ProgrammerAttribute));

ProgrammerAttribute p = (ProgrammerAttribute)a;

Console.WriteLine("Programmer: {0}", p.Programmer);
```

Using reflection

Searching for and reading attribute values is an example of a program performing *reflection*. You can think of this as the program reflecting on its own contents, rather in the same way as people like to sit and reflect on their place in the universe.

Reflection is sometimes called *introspection*. Testing systems can use reflection to search for objects that need testing and identify the testing that is required by attributes that have been set on these objects.

You can use reflection to allow an application to automatically identify "plug-in" components, so that the application can be made up of discrete elements that are connected together when the program runs. If faults are found in one component, or new components need to be added, this can be performed without changes to the rest of the system.

You should regard elements discovered and loaded by the use of reflection as the natural endpoint of the process of creating code as components that implement interfaces and communicate by means of events which they publish and subscribe to.

Using type information from an object

You can start considering reflection by looking at the GetType method. All objects in a C# program expose this method, which will return a reference to the type that defines the object. Listing 2-52 shows how GetType can be used to get the type of a Person instance.

LISTING 2-52 The GetType method

```
System.Type type;

Person p = new Person();
type = p.GetType();
Console.WriteLine("Person type: {0}", type.ToString());
```

The Type of an object contains all the fields of an object, along with all the metadata describing the object. You can use methods and objects in the System.Reflection namespace to work with Type objects. Listing 2-53 shows how to extract information about all the fields in the Person type. It prints all the members of the Person.

LISTING 2-53 Investigating a type

```
using System;
using System.Reflection;

namespace LISTING_2_53_Investigating_a_type
{
    class Person
    {
        public string Name { get; set; }
    }

    class Program
    {
        static void Main(string[] args)
        {
            System.Type type;

            Person p = new Person();
            type = p.GetType();
```

```
            foreach(MemberInfo member in type.GetMembers() )
            {
                Console.WriteLine(member.ToString());
            }

            Console.ReadKey();
        }
    }
}
```

When you run the program, it prints out the following information about the Person class:

```
System.String get_Name()
Void set_Name(System.String)
System.String ToString()
Boolean Equals(System.Object)
Int32 GetHashCode()
System.Type GetType()
Void .ctor()
System.String Name
```

Note that the `Name` property has been implemented by the compiler as a pair of `get` and `set` methods (`set_Name` and `get_Name`), and the class contains all the methods that are exposed by an object, including `ToString` and, of course, the `GetType` method.

Calling a method on an object by using reflection

You can use the information provided by a type to create a call to a method in that type. The program in Listing 2-54 will set the name of a person by using the `set_Name` behavior of the `Name` property in the `Person` class. It does this by finding the `MethodInfo` for this method and then calling the `Invoke` method on this reference. The Invoke method is supplied with a reference to the `Person` that is the target of the method invocation and an array of object references which will be used as the arguments to that method call.

LISTING 2-54 Reflection method call

```
System.Type type;

Person p = new Person();
type = p.GetType();

MethodInfo setMethod = type.GetMethod("set_Name");
setMethod.Invoke(p, new object [] { "Fred" });

Console.WriteLine(p.Name);
```

This code would, of course, be much slower than just setting the Name property to the value "Fred," but it illustrates the flexibility provided by reflection. A program can now obtain a reference to an object, find out what behaviors that object exposes, and then make use of the behaviors that it needs.

Finding components in assemblies

You have seen how a program can dynamically locate members of a class but to implement plugins you need to be able to search the classes in an assembly and find components that implement particular interfaces. This behavior is the basis of the Managed Extensibility Framework (MEF). You can find out more about MEF here at https://docs.microsoft.com/en-us/dotnet/framework/mef/.

Listing 2-55 shows how we can search an assembly for a particular type of component class. It can be used in a banking application to find all the classes that implement the IAccount interface. It searches the currently executing assembly for types that implement IAccount. The Assembly type provides a method that will get the currently executing assembly. It is then possible to iterate through all the types in this assembly looking for ones that are not interfaces and implement the IAccount interface. The code uses the IsAssignableFrom method to decide whether or not a given type implements the IAccount interface.

LISTING 2-55 Finding components

```
Assembly thisAssembly = Assembly.GetExecutingAssembly();

List<Type> AccountTypes = new List<Type>();

foreach ( Type t in thisAssembly.GetTypes() )
{
    if (t.IsInterface)
        continue;

    if(typeof(IAccount).IsAssignableFrom(t))
    {
        AccountTypes.Add(t);
    }
}
```

If you run the sample program in Listing 2-55 it will print the names of the BabyAccount and BankAccount types, because these are defined in the same assembly as the sample program. You can simplify the identification of the types by using a LINQ query as shown in Listing 2-56.

LISTING 2-56 LINQ components

```
var AccountTypes = from type in thisAssembly.GetTypes()
                   where typeof(IAccount).IsAssignableFrom(type) && !type.IsInterface
                   select type;
```

It is possible to load an assembly from a file by using the Assembly.Load method. The statement below would load all the types in a file called BankTypes.dll. This means that at its start an application could search a particular folder for assembly files, load them and then search for classes that can be used in the application.

```
Assembly bankTypes = Assembly.Load("BankTypes.dll");
```

Generate code at runtime by using CodeDOM and Lambda expressions

Now that you know that an entire application can be represented by objects such as Assembly and Type, the next thing to discover is how to programmatically add your own elements to these objects so that your applications can create code at runtime. You can use this technology to automate the production of code. It is used in situations where you have to create objects that will have to interact with services providing a particular data schema or when you're automatically generating code in a design tool.

In this section we are going to consider two techniques for generating code at runtime. They are the Code Document Object Model (CodeDOM) and Lambda expressions.

CodeDOM

A document object model is a way of representing the structure of a particular type of document. The object contains collections of other objects that represent the contents of the document. There are document object models for XML, JSON and HTML documents, and there is also one that is used to represent the structure of a class. This is called a CodeDOM object.

A CodeDOM object can be parsed to create a source file or an executable assembly. The constructions that are used in a CodeDOM object represent the logical structure of the code to be implemented and are independent of the syntax of the high-level language that is used to create the document. In other words, you can create either Visual Basic .NET or C# source files from a given CodeDOM object and you can create CodeDOM objects using either language.

Listing 2-57 shows how a CodeDOM object is created. The outer level CodeCompileUnit instance is created first. This serves as a container for CodeNamespace objects that can be added to it. A CodeNameSpace can contain a number of CodeTypeDeclarations and a class is a kind of CodeTypeDeclaration. The class can contain a number of fields. In Listing 2-57 a single data field is created, but there are also types to represent methods, statements within methods and expressions that the statements can work with.

LISTING 2-57 CodeDOM object

```
CodeCompileUnit compileUnit = new CodeCompileUnit();

// Create a namespace to hold the types we are going to create
CodeNamespace personnelNameSpace = new CodeNamespace("Personnel");

// Import the system namespace
personnelNameSpace.Imports.Add(new CodeNamespaceImport("System"));
// Create a Person class
CodeTypeDeclaration personClass = new CodeTypeDeclaration("Person");
personClass.IsClass = true;
personClass.TypeAttributes = System.Reflection.TypeAttributes.Public;

// Add the Person class to personnelNamespace
```

```
personnelNameSpace.Types.Add(personClass);

// Create a field to hold the name of a person
CodeMemberField nameField = new CodeMemberField("String", "name");
nameField.Attributes = MemberAttributes.Private;

// Add the name field to the Person class
personClass.Members.Add(nameField);

// Add the namespace to the document
compileUnit.Namespaces.Add(personnelNameSpace);
```

Once the CodeDOM object has been created you can create a CodeDomProvider to parse the code document and produce the program code from it. The code here shows how this works. It sends the program code to a string and then displays the string.

```
// Now we need to send our document somewhere
// Create a provider to parse the document
CodeDomProvider provider = CodeDomProvider.CreateProvider("CSharp");
// Give the provider somewhere to send the parsed output
StringWriter s = new StringWriter();
// Set some options for the parse - we can use the defaults
CodeGeneratorOptions options = new CodeGeneratorOptions();

// Generate the C# source from the CodeDOM
provider.GenerateCodeFromCompileUnit(compileUnit, s, options);
// Close the output stream
s.Close();

// Print the C# output
Console.WriteLine(s.ToString());
```

The output from this program can be seen here:

```
//------------------------------------------------------------------------------
// <auto-generated>
//     This code was generated by a tool.
//     Runtime Version:4.0.30319.42000
//
//     Changes to this file may cause incorrect behavior and will be lost if
//     the code is regenerated.
// </auto-generated>
//------------------------------------------------------------------------------

namespace Personnel {
    using System;


    public class Person {

        private String name;
    }
}
```

There are a range of types that can be created and added to a document to allow you to programmatically create enumerated types expressions, method calls, properties and all the elements of a complete program. Note that you would normally create such a document model on the basis of some data structure that you were parsing.

Lambda expression trees

You saw lambda expressions in the context of event handlers in Skill 1.4, "Create and implement events and callbacks." A lambda expression is a way of expressing a data processing action (a value goes in and a result comes out). You can express a single action in a program by the use of a single lambda expression. More complex actions can be expressed in expression trees. If you think about it, the structure of a CodeDOM object is very like a tree, in that the root object contains elements that branch out from it. The elements in the root object can also contain other elements, leading to a tree like structure that describes the elements in the program that is being created. Expression trees are widely used in C#, particularly in the context of LINQ. The code that generates the result of a LINQ query will be created as an expression tree.

A lambda expression tree has as its base a lamba expression. Listing 2-58 shows how to create an expression tree that describes a lambda expression that evaluates the square of the incoming value. This code makes use of the FUNC delegate seen in Skill 1-4, "Create and implement events and callbacks." There are a number of built-in types for use with delegates, but the FUNC delegates allow us to define a delegate that accepts a number of inputs and returns a single result.

LISTING 2-58 Lambda expression tree

```
using System;
using System.Linq.Expressions;

namespace LISTING_2_58_Lambda_expression_tree
{
    class Program
    {
        static void Main(string[] args)
        {
            // build the expression tree:
            // Expression<Func<int,int>> square = num => num * num;

            // The parameter for the expression is an integer
            ParameterExpression numParam = Expression.Parameter(typeof(int), "num");

            // The opertion to be performed is to square the parameter
            BinaryExpression squareOperation = Expression.Multiply(numParam,numParam);

            // This creates an expression tree that describes the square operation
            Expression<Func<int, int>> square =
                Expression.Lambda<Func<int, int>>(
                    squareOperation,
                    new ParameterExpression[] { numParam });

            // Compile the tree to make an executable method and assign it to a delegate
            Func<int, int> doSquare = square.Compile();
```

```
        // Call the delegate
        Console.WriteLine("Square of 2: {0}", doSquare(2));

        Console.ReadKey();
    }
  }
}
```

The System.Linq.Expressions namespace contains a range of other types that can be used to represent other code elements in lambda expressions, including conditional operation, loops and collections.

Modifying an expression tree

An expression tree is immutable, which means that the elements in the expression cannot be changed once the expression has been created. To modify an expression tree you must make a copy of the tree which contains the modified behaviors.

Listing 2-59 shows how this is done using a class called ExpressionVisitor, which parses and copies each element of the expression tree. By extending the ExpressionVisitor base class and overriding different visit methods that it provides, you can create a class that will perform modification of the particular elements you are interested in. The MultiplyToAdd class will change any multiply operations in an expression to add.

LISTING 2-59 Modifying an expression tree

```
public class MultiplyToAdd : ExpressionVisitor
{
    public Expression Modify(Expression expression)
    {
        return Visit(expression);
    }

    protected override Expression VisitBinary(BinaryExpression b)
    {
        if (b.NodeType == ExpressionType.Multiply)
        {
            Expression left = this.Visit(b.Left);
            Expression right = this.Visit(b.Right);

            // Make this binary expression an Add rather than a multiply operation.
            return Expression.Add(left, right);
        }

        return base.VisitBinary(b);
    }
}
```

You can use this class to modify the expression created in Listing 2-58 and create a new method that doubles any parameter given to it. The code here shows how this is done.

```
MultiplyToAdd m = new MultiplyToAdd();
```

```
Expression<Func<int, int>> addExpression = (Expression<Func<int, int>>)m.Modify(square);
Func<int, int> doAdd = addExpression.Compile();

Console.WriteLine("Double of 4: {0}", doAdd(4));
```

Use types from the System.Reflection namespace,

The System.Reflection namespace contains a lot of useful types. You've seen some of these in this section, but here we're going to explicitly consider the function of some of them.

Assembly

An assembly is the output produced when a .NET project is compiled. The assembly type represents the contents of an assembly, which can be the currently executing assembly or one that is loaded from a file.

The Assembly class provides a way that programs can use reflection on the contents of the assembly that it represents. It provides methods and properties to establish and manage the version of the assembly, any dependencies that the assembly has on other files, and the definition of any types that are declared in the assembly. We used an assembly instance in Listing 2-55 "Finding components" when we loaded the current assembly and then searched through all of the types defined in that assembly to identify the ones that implement the IAccount interface. Listing 2-60 displays information about an assembly including the modules defined the assembly, the types in the modules and the content of each type.

LISTING 2-60 Assembly object

```
using System;
using System.Reflection;

namespace LISTING_2_60_Assembly_object
{
    class Program
    {
        static void Main(string[] args)
        {
            Assembly assembly = Assembly.GetExecutingAssembly();

            Console.WriteLine("Full name: {0}", assembly.FullName);
            AssemblyName name = assembly.GetName();
            Console.WriteLine("Major Version: {0}", name.Version.Major);
            Console.WriteLine("Minor Version: {0}", name.Version.Minor);
            Console.WriteLine("In global assembly cache: {0}",
                assembly.GlobalAssemblyCache);
            foreach (Module assemblyModule in assembly.Modules)
            {
                Console.WriteLine("  Module: {0}", assemblyModule.Name);
                foreach (Type moduleType in assemblyModule.GetTypes())
                {
                    Console.WriteLine("    Type: {0}", moduleType.Name);
                    foreach (MemberInfo member in moduleType.GetMembers())
```

```
                {
                    Console.WriteLine("        Member: {0}", member.Name);
                }
            }
        }

        Console.ReadKey();
    }
}
}
```

PropertyInfo

A C# property provides a quick way of providing get and set behaviors for a data variable in a type. The `PropertyInfo` class provides details of a property, including the `MethodInfo` information for the get and set behaviors if they are present. Listing 2-61 enumerates the properties in a type and prints information about each one.

LISTING 2-61 Property info

```
using System;
using System.Reflection;

namespace LISTING_2_61_Property_info
{
    public class Person
    {
        public String Name { get; set; }

        public String Age { get; }
    }

    class Program
    {
        static void Main(string[] args)
        {
            Type type = typeof(Person);

            foreach (PropertyInfo p in type.GetProperties())
            {
                Console.WriteLine("Property name: {0}", p.Name);
                if(p.CanRead)
                {
                    Console.WriteLine("Can read");
                    Console.WriteLine("Set method: {0}", p.GetMethod);
                }
                if (p.CanWrite)
                {
                    Console.WriteLine("Can write");
                    Console.WriteLine("Set method: {0}", p.SetMethod);
                }
            }
```

```
            Console.ReadKey();
        }
    }
}
```

MethodInfo

The MethodInfo class holds data about a method in a type. This includes the signature of the method, the return type of the method, details of method parameters and even the byte code that forms the body of the method. The program in Listing 2-62 will work through a method and display this information from all the methods in a class. This code also makes use of the Invoke method to invoke a method from its method information and MethodInvoke to invoke a method from a class.

LISTING 2-62 Method reflection

```
using System;
using System.Reflection;

namespace LISTING_2_62_Method_reflection
{
    public class Calculator
    {
        public int AddInt(int v1, int v2)
        {
            return v1 + v2;
        }
    }

    class Program
    {
        static void Main(string[] args)
        {
            Console.WriteLine("Get the type information for the Calculator class");
            Type type = typeof(Calculator);

            Console.WriteLine("Get the method info for the AddInt method");
            MethodInfo AddIntMethodInfo = type.GetMethod("AddInt");

            Console.WriteLine("Get the IL instructions for the AddInt method");
            MethodBody AddIntMethodBody = AddIntMethodInfo.GetMethodBody();

            // Print the IL instructions.
            foreach (byte b in AddIntMethodBody.GetILAsByteArray())
            {
                Console.Write(" {0:X}", b);
            }
            Console.WriteLine();

            Console.WriteLine("Create Calculator instance");
            Calculator calc = new Calculator();

            Console.WriteLine("Create parameter array for the method");
```

```
        object[] inputs = new object[] { 1, 2 };

        Console.WriteLine("Call Invoke on the method info");
        Console.WriteLine("Cast the result to an integer");
        int result = (int) AddIntMethodInfo.Invoke(calc, inputs);
        Console.WriteLine("Result of: {0}", result);

        Console.WriteLine("Call InvokeMember on the type");
        result = (int) type.InvokeMember("AddInt",
                  BindingFlags.InvokeMethod |
                  BindingFlags.Instance | BindingFlags.Public,
                  null,
                  calc,
                  inputs);
        Console.WriteLine("Result of: {0}", result);

        Console.ReadKey();
    }
  }
}
```

Note that to invoke a method you must provide an array of parameters for the method to work on, and the invoke methods return an object reference that must be cast to the actual type of the method.

Type

You've used the Type type (as it were) in many places in your programs that use reflection. A type instance describes the contents of a C# type, including a collection holding all the methods, another containing all the class variables, another containing properties, and so on. It also contains a collection of attribute class instances associated with this type and details of the Base type from which the type is derived. The GetType method can be called on any instance to obtain a reference to the type for that object, and the typeof method can be used on any type to obtain the type object that describes that type. You can see the typeof method used in Listing 2-62, when it is used to obtain the type object for the Calculator type.

Skill 2.6: Manage the object life cycle

In this section you are going to focus on the way that your applications will create and destroy objects as they run. The good news is that the .NET framework that underpins C# programs provides a *managed environment* for our programs that perform memory management in the form of a garbage collection process that will remove unwanted objects without us having to do anything.

When writing programs in unmanaged languages, such as C++, you need to include code to create and dispose of any objects that programs use. If this is not done properly one of two things will happen. A program will try to use a memory object that has been deleted which will cause the program to crash, or a program will fail to dispose of memory correctly, leading to a "memory leak," which will eventually cause the program to run out of available memory.

You might think that the fact that C# is based on the .NET framework, which provides automatic memory management, would make this a very short skill; but it turns out that our programs must also deal with "unmanaged" resources. For example, a program might create an object that contains a handle to a file or a database connection that connect it to a particular resource. The program must make sure that when this object is destroyed, any resources connected to the object must be released in a managed way. C# provides a finalization process that allows code in an object to get control as it is being removed from memory. C# also allows an object to implement an `IDisposable` interface, which you have already seen in Skill 2.4. In this section you will discover how to use these two features together to ensure that resources are always released correctly when objects are removed from memory.

This section covers how to:

- Manage unmanaged resources
- Implement IDisposable, including interaction with finalization
- Manage IDisposable by using the Using statement
- Manage finalization and garbage collection

Garbage collection in .NET

The precise way that memory is managed in a .NET application has a significant bearing on how to create objects that manage resources correctly. A full description of garbage collection technology would take the rest of this text, so this is a summary. Before we talk about garbage collection, let's first consider the situation in which it needs to happen.

Creating garbage

Consider the following two C# statements. The first statement declares a `Person` reference called p and makes the reference refer to a new `Person` instance. The second statement assigns the reference p to a new `Person` instance. These two statements will cause work for the garbage collector. The first `Person` object that was created can play no further part in the program as there is no way of accessing it.

```
Person p = new Person();
p = new Person();
```

You get a similar situation when a reference variable goes out of scope. This block of code that follows also creates work for the garbage collector. When the program exits from the block the `Person` object that was created it is no longer accessible because the reference p no longer exists. However, the person object will still be occupying memory.

```
{
    Person p = new Person();
}
```

A process has a particular amount allocated to it. Garbage collection only occurs when the amount of memory available for new objects falls below a threshold. Listing 2-63 is a program that deliberately creates a large number of inaccessible objects. I've adjusted the speed of the program and the size of memory allocated to produce a rate of memory use that causes the garbage collector to trigger on my machine.

LISTING 2-63 Garbage collection

```
namespace LISTING_2_63_Garbage_collection
{
    class Person
    {
        long[] personArray = new long[1000000];
    }

    class Program
    {
        static void Main(string[] args)
        {
            for ( long i=0;i<100000000000;i++)
            {
                Person p = new Person();
                System.Threading.Thread.Sleep(3);
            }
        }
    }
}
```

The Visual Studio runtime environment provides a display of memory use that will show the garbage collection process in action. Figure 2-8 below shows the display produced when the program runs.

FIGURE 2-8 Memory usage and the garbage collector

If you look at the graph in Figure 2-8 you will see that the memory usage of the program varies dramatically over time. The rate at which the garbage is collected will change, depending on the loading on the host computer.

Value types and garbage collection

The storage graph in Figure 2-8 shows the size of the *heap*. The heap is the area of memory where an application stores objects that are referred to by reference. The contents of value types are stored on the stack. The stack automatically grows and contracts as programs run. Upon entry to a new block the .NET runtime will allocate space on the stack for values that are declared local to that block. When the program leaves the block the .NET runtime will automatically contract the stack space, which removes the memory allocated for those variables. The following block will not make any work for the garbage collector as the value 99 will be stored in the local stack frame.

```
{
    int i=99;
}
```

The garbage collector

When an application runs low on memory the garbage collector will search the heap for any objects that are no longer required and remove them. The .NET runtime contains an index of all the objects that have been created since the program started, the job of the garbage collector is to decide which of them are still in use, remove them from memory, and then compact the remaining objects so that the area of free memory is a single large area, rather than a number of smaller, free areas.

The first phase of garbage collection is marking all of the objects that are in use by the program. The garbage collector starts by clearing a flag on each object in the heap. It then searches through all the variables in use in the program and follows all the references in these variables to the objects they refer to and sets the flag on that object. After this "mark" phase the garbage collector can now move on to the "compact" phase of the collection, where it works through memory removing all the objects that have not had their flag set.

The final phase of the garbage collection is the "compaction" of the heap. The objects still in use must be moved down memory so that the available space on the stack is in one large block, rather than a large number of holes where unused objects have been removed.

All managed threads are suspended while the garbage collector is running. This means that your application will stop responding to inputs while the garbage collection is performed. It is possible to invoke the garbage collector manually if there are points in your application when you know a large number of objects have been released.

The garbage collector attempts to determine which objects are long lived, and which are short lived (ephemeral). It does this by adding a generation counter to each object on the heap. Objects start at generation 0. If they survive a garbage collection the counter is advanced to generation 1. Surviving a second garbage collection promotes an object to generation 2, the highest generation. The garbage collector will collect different generations, depending on circumstances. A "level 2" garbage collection will involve all objects. A "level 0" garbage collection will target newly created objects.

The garbage collector can run in "workstation" or "server" modes, depending on the role of the host system. There is also an option to run garbage collection concurrently on a separate thread. However, this increases the amount of memory used by the garbage collector and the loading on the host processor.

Reducing the need for garbage collection

Modern applications run in systems with large amounts of memory available. The garbage collection process has been optimized over the various generations of .NET and is now highly efficient and responsive. My strong advice on garbage collection is not to worry about it until you have a problem. There is no need to spend your time worrying about the memory usage of your application when your system will almost certainly have enough memory and processor performance. You can use the displays produced by Visual Studio to watch how your application uses memory, there are also profiling tools that allow you to identify the objects that are affected by garbage collection.

If you find that the garbage collection process is becoming intrusive you can force a garbage collection by calling the `Collect` method on the garbage collector as shown below.

```
GC.Collect();
```

The enforced garbage collection can be performed at points in your application where you know large objects have just been released, for example at the end of a transaction or upon exit from a large and complex user interface dialog. However, under normal circumstances I would strongly advise you to let the garbage collector look after itself. It is rather good at doing that.

Manage unmanaged resources

The .NET framework will take care of the creation and destruction of our objects, but we need to manage the resources that our objects use. For example, if an application creates a file handle and stores it in an object, when then object is destroyed the file handle will be lost. If the file connected to the handle is not closed properly before the object is destroyed, the file the handle is connected to will not be usable.

There are two mechanisms that we can use that allow us to get control at the point an object is being destroyed and tidy up any resources that the object may be using. They are finalization and disposable.

Object finalization using a finalizer method

The finalization of an object is triggered by the garbage collection process. An object can contain a finalizer method that is invoked by the garbage collector in advance of that object being removed from memory. This method gets control and can release any resources that are being used by that object. The finalizer method is given as a type less method with the name of the class pre-ceded by a tilde (~) character. Listing 2-64 shows how to give the Person class a finalizer method. The finalizer method just prints a message, but in an application you would use this method to release any resources that the Person object had allocated.

LISTING 2-64 The finalizer

```
public class Person
{
    long[] personArray = new long[1000000];
```

```
~Person()
{
    // This is where the person would be finalized
    Console.WriteLine("Finalizer called");
}
}
```

Problems with finalization

When the garbage collector is about to remove an object, it checks to see if the object contains a finalizer method. If there is a finalizer method present, the garbage collector adds the object to a queue of objects waiting to be finalized. Once all of these objects have been identified, the garbage collector starts a thread to execute all the finalizer methods and waits for the thread to complete. Once the finalization methods are complete the garbage collector performs another garbage collection to remove the finalized objects. There are no guarantees as to when the finalizer thread will run. Objects waiting to be finalized will remain in memory until all of the finalizer methods have completed and the garbage collector has made another garbage collection pass to remove them.

A slow-running finalizer can seriously impair the garbage collection process. The destructor shown here contains a delay that will cause the program in Listing 2-64 to run out of memory.

```
~Person()
{
    // This is where the person would be finalized
    Console.WriteLine("Finalizer called");

    // This will break the garbage collection process
    // as it slows it down so that it can't complete
    // faster than objects are being created
    System.Threading.Thread.Sleep(100);
}
```

Another problem with finalization is that there is no guarantee that the finalizer method will ever be called. If the program never runs short of memory, it might not need to initiate garbage collection. This means that an object waiting for deletion may remain in memory until the program completes.

You may have noticed that I'm not a fan of finalization. If you're a C++ programmer, who is used to writing destructors (the C++ equivalent of finalizers) to release memory when an object is deleted you might think that you should add finalizers to C# classes when you create them. However, I strongly suggest that you use the Dispose mechanism instead, as part of a planned approach to resource management, which is covered next.

Implement IDisposable, including interaction with finalization

We have already discussed the use of IDisposable and Dispose in the section describing IDisposable in Skill 2.4, "Create and implement a class hierarchy." An object can implement the IDisposable interface, which means it must provide a Dispose method that can be called within the application to request that the object to release any resources that it has allocated. Note that the Dispose method does not cause the object to be deleted from memory, nor does it mark the object for deletion by the garbage collector in any way. Only objects that have no references to them are deleted. Once Dispose has been called on an object, that object can no longer be used in an application.

Objects that implement IDisposable can be used in conjunction with the using statement, which will provide an automatic call of the Dispose method when execution leaves the block that follows the using statement.

The Dispose method is called by the application when an object is required to release all the resources that it is using. This is a significant improvement on a finalizer, in that your application can control exactly when this happens.

Using IDisposable and finalization on the same object

If you want to create an object that contains both a finalizer and a Dispose method you need to exercise some care to avoid the object trying to release the same resource more than once, and perhaps failing as a result of this. The SuppressFinalize method can be used to identify an object, which will not be finalized when the object is deleted. This should be used by the Dispose method in a class to prevent instances being disposed more than once. A *dispose pattern* can be used to allow an object to manage its disposal.

Listing 2-65 shows how an object can implement this pattern. It makes use of a helper method, Dispose(bool disposing), which accepts a flag value that indicates whether the method is being called from a call of Dispose or from the finalizer. If the helper method is being called from a call of Dispose it will free off managed resources as well as unmanaged ones when it runs. The pattern also uses a class flag variable, disposed, which is set when dispose has been called and prevents multiple attempts to dispose items.

LISTING 2-65 The dispose pattern

```
using System;

namespace LISTING_2_65_The_dispose_pattern
{
    class ResourceHolder : IDisposable
    {

        // Flag to indicate when the object has been
        // disposed
        bool disposed = false;

        public void Dispose()
        {
            // Call dispose and tell it that
            // it is being called from a Dispose call
            Dispose(true);
            GC.SuppressFinalize(this);
        }
```

```
public virtual void Dispose(bool disposing)
{
    // Give up if already disposed
    if (disposed)
        return;

    if(disposing)
    {
        // free any managed objects here
    }

    // Free any unmanaged objects here
}

~ResourceHolder()
{
    // Dispose only of unmanaged objects
    Dispose(false);
}
}

class Program
{
    static void Main(string[] args)
    {
        ResourceHolder r = new ResourceHolder();

        r.Dispose();
    }
}
}
```

Note that creating finalizers is a non-trivial exercise. You can find out more about it here: *https://docs.microsoft.com/en-us/dotnet/standard/garbage-collection/implementing-dispose*.

Manage IDisposable by using the Using statement

As seen in the IDisposable item in Skill 2-4, "Create and implement a class hierarchy," the using statement allows you to ensure the calling of Dispose on objects that your program uses when they are no longer required. Listing 2-45 provides an example of how this works.

Note that the using statement ensures that Dispose is called on an object in the event of exceptions being thrown. If you don't use the using statement to manage calls of Dispose in your objects, make sure that your application calls Dispose appropriately. The dispose pattern above results in a disposal behavior that is tolerant of multiple calls of Dispose.

Manage finalization and garbage collection

In this section we can bring together some of the items we learned about garbage collection and consider how to manage the finalization and garbage collection process.

Invoking a garbage collection

You have seen that an application can force a garbage collection to take place by calling the Collect method. After the collection has been performed, a program can then be made to wait until all the finalizer methods have completed:

```
GC.Collect();
GC.WaitForPendingFinalizers();
```

Overloads of the Collect method allow you to specify which generation of objects to garbage collect and set other garbage collection options.

Managing finalization

You have seen that the garbage collector can be ordered to ignore the finalizer on an object. The statement below prevents finalization from being called on the object referred to by p.

```
GC.SuppressFinalize(p);
```

To later re-enable finalization you can use the ReRegisterforFinalize method:

```
GC.ReRegisterForFinalize(p);
```

Skill 2.7: Manipulate strings

As programmers we spend a lot of time manipulating text in our programs. The C# string type has a range of powerful features to make string manipulation easier. In this section we are going to explore these features and discover when they are useful.

This section covers how to:

- Manipulate strings by using the StringBuilder, StringWriter, and StringReader classes
- Search strings
- Enumerate string methods
- Format strings
- Use string interpolation

The string type

The C# type string (with a lower-case s) is mapped onto the .NET type String (with an upper-case S). The string type can hold text. In fact, it can hold a very large amount of text. It is perfectly feasible to hold a complete document as a single string. The theoretical limit on the maximum size of a string is around 2GB, but the practical one will be lower than that.

Immutable strings

Strings in C# are managed by reference, but string values are *immutable*, which means that the contents of a string can't be changed once the string has been created. If you want to change the contents of a string you have to make a new string. All string editing functions return a new string with the edited content. The string being edited is never changed. This ensures that strings are thread safe. There is no need to worry about code on another thread changing the contents of a string that a given thread is using.

The downside of this approach is that if you perform a lot of string editing you will end up creating a lot of string objects. However, the `StringBuilder` type, which we will see soon, provides a mutable string object that a program can use to assemble a string.

String interning

When a program is compiled the compiler uses a process called *string interning* to improve the efficiency of string storage. Consider the following C# statements. They set two string variables, s1 and s2, to the text "hello." The compiler will save program memory by making both s1 and s2 refer to the same string object with the content "hello."

LISTING 2-66 String intern

```
string s1 = "hello";
string s2 = "hello";
```

The process of string interning makes string comparison quicker. If two string references are equal it means that they both contain the same string, there is no need to compare the text in the two strings to see if it is the same. Note that if the string references are different; this doesn't mean that the strings are definitely not different. It means that the program must compare each of the characters in the strings to determine if they are the same.

String interning only happens when the program is compiled. The following statements would make a make a new string with the content "hello" when the program runs, however this string would be a different object from the string created for s1 and s2 above.

```
string h1 = "he";
string h2 = "llo";
string s3 = h1 + h2;
```

String interning doesn't happen when a program is running because every time a new string is created the program has to search through the list of interned strings to see if that string was already present. This slows the program down. However, you can force a given string to be interned at run time by using the `Intern` method provided by the string type. The statement here makes the string s3 refer to an interned version of the string.

```
s3 = string.Intern(s3);
```

Note that I have the same opinion of string interning as I have about many other issues relating to performance. You should only do this if you discover a need to speed up the program. Under normal circumstances the performance of string storage in a C# program is extremely good.

Manipulate strings by using the StringBuilder, StringWriter, and StringReader classes

The string type is accompanied in .NET by some other types that work with strings. Three of these types are StringBuilder, StringWriter, and StringReader. Let's consider each of these in turn.

StringBuilder

The StringBuilder type is very useful when we are writing programs that build up strings. It can improve the speed of a program while at the same time making less work for the garbage collector. Consider the C# statements:

```
string firstName = "Rob";
string secondName = "Miles";

string fullName = firstName + " " + secondName;
```

The string addition in the final statement will create the value of fullName by adding the three strings together, but it will create an intermediate string as it builds the result (firstName + " "). In the case of this program this has a negligible effect on performance, but if a program was performing a lot of string addition to build up a string of text this might result in a lot of work for the garbage collector.

The StringBuilder type provides methods that let a program treat a string as a mutable object. A StringBuilder is implemented by a character array. It provides methods that can be used to append strings to the StringBuilder, remove strings from the StringBuilder and a property, Capacity, which can be used to set the maximum number of characters that can be placed in a StringBuilder instance. Listing 2-67 shows how to use a StringBuilder to create a full name string without making any intermediate objects.

LISTING 2-67 Stringbuilder

```
StringBuilder fullNameBuilder = new StringBuilder();
fullNameBuilder.Append(firstName);
fullNameBuilder.Append(" ");
fullNameBuilder.Append(secondName);
Console.WriteLine(fullNameBuilder.ToString());
```

If you want to assemble strings out of other string you can also use format strings and string interpolation instead of string addition.

StringWriter

The StringWriter class is based on the StringBuilder class. It implements the TextWriter interface, so programs can send their output into a string. Listing 2-68 shows how to create a StringWriter, write some text to it, and then print the text out.

LISTING 2-68 StringWriter

```
using System;
using System.IO;
```

```
namespace LISTING_2_68_StringWriter
{
    class Program
    {
        static void Main(string[] args)
        {
            StringWriter writer = new StringWriter();

            writer.WriteLine("Hello World");

            writer.Close();

            Console.Write(writer.ToString());

            Console.ReadKey();
        }
    }
}
```

You have used the StringWriter class in a previous example; the program Listing 2-57 CodeDOM object, which creates some C# from a CodeDOM object, and sends the C# code to a StringWriter instance so that it can be printed on the screen.

StringReader

Instances of the StringReader class implement the TextReader interface. It is a convenient way of getting string input into a program that would like to read its input from a stream. The program in Listing 2-69 shows how StringReader is used. It creates a StringReader and then reads a string and an integer from it.

LISTING 2-69 StringReader

```
using System;
using System.IO;

namespace LISTING_2_69_StringReader
{
    class Program
    {
        static void Main(string[] args)
        {
            string dataString =
@"Rob Miles
21";
            StringReader dataStringReader = new StringReader(dataString);

            string name = dataStringReader.ReadLine();
            int age = int.Parse(dataStringReader.ReadLine());

            dataStringReader.Close();

            Console.WriteLine("Name: {0} Age: {1}", name, age);
```

```
        Console.ReadKey();
    }
  }
}
```

Search strings

The string type provides a range of methods that can be used to find the position of substrings inside a string. Note that, because strings are immutable it is not possible to change elements of the string once you have found the position of a substring (you can't replace the word "Rob" in a string with the word "Fred"), however, you can use the search methods to control the process of copying from one string to another. You can also use these methods to parse strings and search for particular words and character sequences. The sample code in Listing 2-70 contains all the demonstration code in this section.

Contains

The method `Contains` can be used to test of a string contains another string. It returns true if the source string contains the search string. The code here shows how `Contains` would be used. It prints that the string contains Rob.

```
string input = "     Rob Miles";

if(input.Contains("Rob"))
{
    Console.WriteLine("Input contains Rob");
}
```

StartsWith and EndsWith

The methods `StartsWith` and `EndsWith` can be used to test if a string starts or ends with a particular string. Note that if the string starts or ends with one or more *whitespace* characters these methods will not work. A whitespace character is a space, tab, linefeed, carriage-return, formfeed, vertical-tab or newline character. There are methods you can use to trim a string. `TrimStart` creates a new string with whitespace removed from the start, `TrimEnd` removes whitespace from the end of the string and `Trim` removes whitespace from both ends. The code below shows how this works. It will print that the name starts with Rob, because the input string was trimmed before the test.

```
string input = "     Rob Miles";

string trimmedString = input.TrimStart();

if(trimmedString.StartsWith("Rob"))
{
    Console.WriteLine("Starts with Rob");
}
```

IndexOf and SubString

The method `IndexOf` returns an integer which gives the position of the first occurrence of a character or string in a string. There is also a `LastIndexOf` method that will give the position of the last occurrence of a string. There are overloads for these methods that let you specify the start position for the search. You can use these position values with the `SubString` method to extract a particular substring from a string. The code below shows how this works. It extracts the name `Rob` from a string and prints it.

```
string input = "      Rob Miles";
int nameStart = input.IndexOf("Rob");
string name = input.Substring(nameStart, 3);
Console.Write(name);
```

Replace

The `Replace` method can be used to perform string editing, replacing an element of a source string. The code here shows how `Replace` can be used to convert an informal version of my name into a formal one.

```
string informalString = "Rob Miles";
string formalString = informalString.Replace("Rob", "Robert");
Console.WriteLine(formalString);
```

Split

The `Split` method can be used to split a string into a number of substrings. The split action returns an array of strings, it is given one or more separator strings that will be used to split the string. The code here shows how this works.

```
string sentence = "The cat sat on the mat.";
string[] words = sentence.Split(' ');
foreach (string word in words)
{
    Console.WriteLine(word);
}
```

Note that if the source sentence held a number of consecutive spaces, each of these would be resolved into a separate line in the output.

String comparison and cultures

Strings in C# are made up of *Unicode* characters encoded into 16 bit values the using *UTF-16* encoding format. The Unicode standard provides a range of characters that can lead to culture specific behaviors when strings are being compared. For example, the character pair "ae" can be represented by the single character "æ" in a lot of American and European languages. This means that, from a language point of view, there are situations where the words "encyclopaedia" and "encyclopædia" should be regarded as equal.

You can request that the string comparison process takes this situation into account by adding an additional parameter to string comparison operations. You can use a `StringComparision` value to request a range of useful behaviors.

You can request that strings be compared according to the culture of the currently execut-ing thread (which is useful if we are creating a program for use in a particular region), com-pared according to the ordinal values of the character code of the characters (which is efficient but may cause ordering problems if the items contain characters such as "æ"), or compared according to an ordering scheme based on the English language, but not customized for a particular culture. The code here shows how these options are used. All of the conditions that are shown evaluate to true.

```
// Default comparison fails because the strings are different
if (!"encyclopædia".Equals("encyclopaedia"))
    Console.WriteLine("Unicode encyclopaedias are not equal");
// Set the curent culture for this thread to EN-US
Thread.CurrentThread.CurrentCulture = CultureInfo.CreateSpecificCulture("en-US");
// Using the current culture the strings are equal
if ("encyclopædia".Equals("encyclopaedia", StringComparison.CurrentCulture))
    Console.WriteLine("Culture comparison encyclopaedias are equal");
// We can use the IgnoreCase option to perform comparisions that ignore case
if ("encyclopædia".Equals("ENCYCLOPAEDIA", StringComparison.CurrentCultureIgnoreCase))
    Console.WriteLine("Case culture comparison encyclopaedias are equal");
if (!"encyclopædia".Equals("ENCYCLOPAEDIA", StringComparison.OrdinalIgnoreCase))
    Console.WriteLine("Ordinal comparison encyclopaedias are not equal");
```

Enumerate string methods

You can regard a string as an array of characters. A program can iterate through the charac-ters in a string as it would any other collection. A string also provides a Length property that a program can use to determine the number of characters in a string. Listing 2-71 shows how this works.

LISTING 2-71 Enumerate string

```
foreach(char ch in "Hello world")
{
    Console.WriteLine(ch);
}
```

Format strings

You can use format strings to request that output be formatted in a particular way when it is printed. The sample code in Listing 2-72 shows how this works. It prints out an integer and a double precision value. The WriteLine method is given a string that contains placeholders which start and end with braces. Within the placeholder is first the number of the item in the WriteLine parameters to be printed at that placeholder, the number of characters the item should occupy (negative if the item is to be left justified), a colon (:) and then formatting infor-mation for the item. The formatting information for an integer string conversion can comprise the character 'D' meaning decimal string and 'X' meaning hexadecimal string. The formatting information for a floating-point number can comprise the character 'N,' which is followed by the number of decimal places to be printed.

LISTING 2-72 Format strings

```
int i = 99;
double pi = 3.141592654;

Console.WriteLine(" {0,-10:D}{0, -10:X}{1,5:N2}", i, pi);
```

This program prints the following output. Note that the value of pi is truncated to two decimal places, as requested in the format string, and that the value of i is printed twice, once in decimal and the second time in hexadecimal.

```
99          63          3.14
```

This works because the int and double types can accept formatting commands to specify the string they are to return. A program can give formatting commands to many .NET types. The DateTime structure provides a wide range of formatting commands. You can add behaviors to classes that you create to allow them to be given formatting commands in the same way. Any type that implements the IFormattable interface will contain a ToString method that can be used to request formatted conversion of values into a string.

Listing 2-73 shows how this is done. The MusicTrack class contains an implementation of a ToString method that overrides the ToString in the base class. However, the MusicTrack class also contains a ToString method that accepts two parameters. The first of these is a string that specifies a format for the conversion of the MusicTrack information into a string. The second parameter is format provided that the MusicTrack can use to determine the culture for the conversion.

The format string is used in a switch construction in the ToString method that returns a particular part of the music track information; either the Artist (if the format is A), the Title (if the format is T) or the full description if the format is F. Note that there is also a G format option, this represents a common format that may be requested. The G format should also be used if the formatting information is missing. Note that if the format request is not recognized, the ToString method will throw an exception.

LISTING 2-73 Music track formatter

```
class MusicTrack : IFormattable
{
    string Artist { get; set; }
    string Title { get; set; }

    // ToString that implements the formatting behavior
    public string ToString(string format, IFormatProvider formatProvider)
    {
        // Select the default behavior if no format specified
        if (string.IsNullOrWhiteSpace(format))
            format = "G";

        switch (format)
        {
            case "A": return Artist;
            case "T": return Title;
```

```
            case "G": // default format
            case "F": return Artist + " " + Title;
            default:
                throw new FormatException("Format specifier was invalid.");
        }
    }

    // ToString that overrides the behavior in the base class
    public override string ToString()
    {
        return Artist + " " + Title;
    }

    public MusicTrack(string artist, string title)
    {
        Artist = artist;
        Title = title;
    }
}
```

This formatting behavior can now be used when the object is being printed as shown in the code here. The track information is printed three times, with different amounts of detail each time.

```
MusicTrack song = new MusicTrack(artist: "Rob Miles", title: "My Way");

Console.WriteLine("Track: {0:F}", song);
Console.WriteLine("Artist: {0:A}", song);
Console.WriteLine("Title: {0:T}", song);
```

The format provider in ToString

The second parameter to the ToString method in Listing 2-73 is an object that implements the IFormatter interface. This parameter can be used by the ToString method to determine any culture specific behaviors that may be required in the string conversion process. For example, you might add date of recording and price information to a music track, in which case the display of the date and price information could be customized for different regions.

By default (i.e. unless you specify otherwise) the IFormatter reference that is passed into the ToString call is the current culture. You saw the use of cultures earlier in the "String comparison and cultures" section.

You can create a culture description and explicitly pass it into a call of ToString. In the case of the MusicTrack implementation in Listing 2-73 this will have no effect, because the ToString method in MusicTrack class doesn't make use of the format provider, but the floating-point types implement a ToString method that does make use of culture information.

Listing 2-74 shows how this works. The bank balance value is stored in a double precision value and then displayed twice as a currency value using the format command 'C.' The first time it is displayed using the US culture information to control the output and the second time using the UK culture.

LISTING 2-74 Format provider

```
double bankBalance = 123.45;
CultureInfo usProvider = new CultureInfo("en-US");
Console.WriteLine("US balance: {0}", bankBalance.ToString("C", usProvider));
CultureInfo ukProvider = new CultureInfo("en-GB");
Console.WriteLine("UK balance: {0}", bankBalance.ToString("C", ukProvider));
```

This program prints the following output. Note that the currency character is different.

```
US balance: $123.45
UK balance: £123.45
```

Use string interpolation

You have seen how to use format strings that incorporate placeholders in them. Each place-holder is enclosed in braces { and } and a placeholder relates to a particular value which is iden-tified by its position in the arguments that follow the format string. The statements in Listing 2-75 show how this works. The name and age values are given after the format string.

LISTING 2-75 String interpolation

```
string name = "Rob";
int age = 21;
Console.WriteLine("Your name is {0} and your age is {1,-5:D}", name, age);
```

String *interpolation* allows you to put the values to be converted directly into the string text. An interpolated string is identified by a leading dollar ($) sign at the start of the string literal. The statement below shows how this works. The WriteLine method now only has one parameter.

```
Console.WriteLine($"Your name is {name} and your age is {age,-5:D}");
```

Note that when this program is compiled the compiler will convert the interpolated string into a format string, extract the values from the string, and build a call of WriteLine that looks exactly like the first call of WriteLine. If you use ildasm to look at the code produced by the compiler for the two calls of WriteLine, you will find that they are identical.

String interpolation can be used with String.Format method as shown:

```
Console.WriteLine(String.Format($"Your name is {name} and your age is {age,-5:D}"));
```

Using a FormattedString with string interpolation

The act of assigning a string interpolation literal in a program produces a result of type FormattedString. This provides a ToString method that accepts a FormatProvider. This is useful because it allows you to use interpolated strings with culture providers. The code below uses string interpolation to produce a bank balance value, which is formatted using the "en-US" (English United States) culture info.

```
double bankBalance = 123.45;
FormattableString balanceMessage = $"US balance : {bankBalance:C}";
```

```
CultureInfo usProvider = new CultureInfo("en-US");
Console.WriteLine(balanceMessage.ToString(usProvider));
```

Thought experiments

In these thought experiments, demonstrate your skills and knowledge of the topics covered in this chapter. You can find the answers to these thought experiments in the next section.

1 Creating types

There comes a point in application construction where the data storage for the application must be designed. At this point you need to map data items onto C# data types. Each data item will be mapped onto an object that may be managed by value or reference. State information can be mapped onto enumerated types for which you can set a range of allowed values.

Here are some questions to consider:

1. You want to store information about the employees that work in my company. Is this a job for a value type or a reference type?

2. Can an object be referred to by more than one reference?

3. What happens when an object no longer has any references to it?

4. If you use a value type rather than a reference type, will your program still work correctly?

5. How can you make a data type immutable?

6. Are value types more efficient that reference types?

7. What is the difference between the stack and the heap?

8. Do you need to add a constructor method for every object that you create?

9. Is there ever any point in creating objects that cannot be constructed?

10. What does it mean when a member of a type is made static?

11. Should you provide default values for all of the parameters to a method?

12. Does using a lot of overridden methods slow a program down?

2 Consuming types

Once you have established the types that your program will use, you will have to write code to manipulate the types. This frequently means that the program will have to convert values from one type to another, and sometimes a program will have to interact with external services which do not have type information that can be used by the C# compiler to perform static analysis to establish the correctness of an interaction.

Here are some questions to consider:

1. If every variable in a program was managed by reference, would you ever need to box a value?

2. Do you need to use a cast when your program is widening a type?

3. Does casting between values slow a program down?

4. Can an object have multiple type conversion methods?

5. Could you write a program that used entirely dynamic types?

6. Why do you need to interact with Component Object Model (COM) objects?

3 Enforce encapsulation

Encapsulation is a powerful technique. It allows developers to hide the implementation of an object and control precisely how code outside the object will interact with it. It also means that developers can change the internal design of an object without affecting any of the users of that object.

Here are some questions to consider:

1. Is it better to use a property rather than get and set methods for private data members in your classes?

2. Can structures contain private data members and properties?

3. Does using properties slow down the execution of my program?

4. Which provides a greater amount of access to a class member, protected or internal?

5. Are there any reasons not to use explicit implementation of methods in an object?

4 Create and implement a class hierarchy

The starting point for a class hierarchy should not be the design of the base class of the hierarchy, but the creation of an interface that expresses the behaviors of this base class. Using an interface from the start of your design process allows a great deal of flexibility in that objects can be regarded in terms of their abilities, not their particular type. You can still a class hierarchy to reduce the amount of code that you have to write, by creating child classes that inherit methods from their parents and only override the one that need to provide behaviors specific to the child.

Here are some questions to consider:

1. Should you design your interfaces after you have designed your application?

2. Can a C# interface contain anything other than method signatures?

3. Can a C# interface be extended?

4. Are all the methods defined in an interface public?

5. Does a class have to implement all the methods in an interface that it implements?

6. Can a C# interface contain a constructor method?

7. Is it sensible for an object to implement more than one interface?

8. Can only the base class of a hierarchy implement an interface?

9. Does making methods virtual slow a program down?

10. Does making methods virtual reduce the security of a program?

11. What is the difference between a C# interface and an abstract C# class?

12. Should every class that you create be part of a class hierarchy (either as a base class or a child class)?

13. Can a method be both overridden and overloaded?

14. Can you override a method in a structure type?

15. Can a structure implement an interface?

16. What does it mean when a class is sealed?

17. Can any object implement the IEnumerable interface?

18. Does the yield keyword cause my program to stop?

19. Does calling the Dispose method on an object remove it from memory?

20. If you use IDispose do you have to call the Dispose method myself to dispose of objects.

21. If you use the IDispose interface to tidy up your objects, does this mean that they will be deleted more quickly by the garbage collector?

5 Find, execute, and create types at runtime by using reflection

This skill involves the use of code to work with code. You can improve your development process by adding attribute information to objects and behaviors in the program. You can create programs that dynamically configure their components by searching for code elements that have a particular set of behaviors as defined in an interface. You can also use code to create more code, automatically producing complete classes, which can be converted into program source or a compiled assembly. You can also create expression trees that can be converted into executable methods.

Here are some questions to consider:

1. Where are the values of attributes actually stored?

2. What happens if you change the value of a member of an attribute when the program is running?

3. Can an attribute class have attributes?

4. Where is the type information for a class stored?

5. What is the difference between typeof and GetType?

6. Can the GetType method be called on value types?

7. Can you change the contents of a type description returned by GetType?

8. Can you use reflection to obtain details of private items in objects?

9. Does code created by using a CodeDOM run slower than "normally" written code?

10. Is it possible to read code details from an assembly file?

11. Can you use CodeDOM to create a class that implements a particular interface?

12. Can you use reflection on the compiled output of a CodeDOM object?

6 Manage the object life cycle

The automatic garbage collection enjoyed by C# developers is built on carefully written and highly developed foundations. However, the non-deterministic nature of the garbage collection process (you can't always be sure precisely when an object will be removed from memory) means that programmers must exercise care when working with objects that contain references to resources that are to be shared with other objects. The IDisposable interface provides a way that programmers can enforce a more managed approach to resource management.

Here are some questions to consider:

1. If you use value types rather than reference types, will this stop the garbage collector from being called?

2. Does creating and destroying arrays of value types make work for the garbage collector?

3. Does the garbage collector also collect garbage from the stack?

4. Can a finalizer be called before the Dispose method in an object?

5. Can the finalizer method in a class be overloaded?

6. Does a finalizer in a child class have to call the finalizer in a base class when it runs?

7. Is it possible for the Dispose method in an instance to be called more than once?

8. What happens if an object finalizer takes a long time to run?

9. What happens if an object finalizer creates a new reference to the object being finalized?

10. Should you design your applications from the start to use the minimum possible memory?

7 Manipulate strings

Successive versions of C# have added more and string manipulation abilities to the language and its libraries. It is very unlikely that you will find yourself in a situation where you have to write some code to perform string processing. I strongly advise you to check out the abilities of the string type and the libraries that work with it before you start to write custom code to work with strings.

Here are some questions to consider:

1. Can you hold the text of an entire book in a single string instance?

2. A string object is immutable. Does this mean you can't assign a new value to a string variable once you have set it to a value?

3. Are there any disadvantages to interning strings in a C# program?

4. Is the StringBuilder type based on the string type?

5. Will using StringBuilder always make your programs go faster?

6. Can you store binary data in a StringWriter?

7. Does the Trim method change the contents of a string?

8. What does it mean if an object implements the IFormattable interface?

9. What does a CultureInfo object actually contain?

10. Can you use string interpolation with strings of text that are created as the program runs?

Thought experiment answers

This section provides the solutions for the tasks included in the thought experiments.

1 Creating types

1. Essentially this boils down to the question of whether you want to store your employee records in a structure (value type) or a class (reference type). If you want to handle different types of employee such as part time, shift worker, and manager then you might find that a class hierarchy is useful, in which case a reference type is needed, because structures cannot be used as the basis of class hierarchies. Using reference types will make it much easier to index and sort your employee records. For example, you can have two employee lists, one ordered by employee name and another ordered by pay grade. Each list will contain references to employee objects. Structures are best suited to small value types, which you may want to make immutable. You might create a data type that holds the record of when an employee started with the company. This could contain their age at starting, the day they started and other information. This could be held in a structure as it is a small amount of data that you just want to store somewhere. It might also be worth making this item of data immutable, since there is no need to edit the information once it has been created. Using a structure (value type) to hold the data would be a good idea if the number of data items is very large.

2. Yes, a single object can have multiple references referring to it.

3. It might be that as a program runs, and references are assigned different values, then an object in memory no longer has any references to it from the program. At this point the object can be destroyed, since it can never be used again. The C# runtime environment contains a "garbage collection" process that checks for objects that have no references to them. These objects are removed when they are detected. For more details take a look at Skill 2-6, "Manage the object lifecycle."

4. It is possible to create any program entirely using reference types or value types. The behavior of assignments and the effects of changes to objects means that if your

program treats a value type as a reference type (or vice versa), you will discover that it will not behave as you might expect.

5. A data type can be made immutable by providing no means of changing the variables held inside the type. The values of the data type should be set by the constructor and the type should only provide methods and properties that can be used to read these variables. The variables in the type must all be made private to the type.

6. Value types can be regarded as slightly more efficient to access than reference types. To access a reference type a program must follow the reference to the position in the heap where the object is stored. A value type can be accessed directly and an array of value types is stored in a single block of storage that contains all of the values. The performance difference will not be noticeable except in extreme circumstances where huge numbers of objects are being processed.

7. Space on the stack is allocated as a program runs. Each time a block is entered, an area of stack space is reserved for value type variables that are created when the method runs. When the block exits, all of the stack space is recovered and the value type variables deleted. Space on the heap is allocated when reference types are created. A reference type may have a lifetime that is longer than the block in which it is declared. For example, a method that creates a new Employee record that is a reference type will return the reference. If the Employee is created on the stack it will disappear when the method finishes. The heap has no particular structure, so there is no guarantee that successively created objects will be in adjacent locations on the heap. Given that C# programs run in a managed environment, they are not able to determine the precise position of objects in memory.

8. Most types will require at least one constructor, so that your application can ensure that the object has a valid initial state and can feed information into the type via the constructor to set it up. The construction of the objects in your system is something that should be planned at the time the system is designed.

9. A class that only contains static members does not need to be constructed. You find static classes like this that contain service methods.

10. A static member of a type exists as part of the type, not a given instance of the type. It is accessed via the name of the class. Static members are great for storing things like limits (largest and smallest) and default values (default age for a customer) as these only need to be stored for an entire class, not for each object.

11. A program can provide default values for method parameters. This can be useful, because it can simplify the use of the methods. It also, however, provides a form of information hiding, in that users of the method may not know what the default values are. I restrict default values to parameters that specify "optional" rather than "core" behaviors.

12. A method that is marked as virtual can be overridden in a class hierarchy. When an overridden method is called on a reference the runtime system must search up the class hierarchy for the version of the method to use. The deeper the class hierarchy the longer it will take for this search to find the method. This means that extensive use of overrid-

den methods in a class hierarchy may have an impact on program performance, but it is unlikely to be noticeable unless the class hierarchy is very deep. I usually try to avoid a hierarchy more than five or so levels deep, but this is as much in respect of organizational complexity as it is program performance.

2 Consuming types

1. Boxing is the name given to the action of converting a value type (which is most likely stored on a local stack) into a reference type (which will be stored on the heap). It is performed when we need to work with a value as an object, perhaps to allow the value to be inserted in a data structure that is managed by reference. Some programming languages have no value types at all and manage everything by reference. This simplifies some aspects of the way that programs will execute, but it does this at the expense of performance. A program will spend a lot of its time just manipulating values, and the use of reference types will significantly slow down this process. You could write a C# program that uses nothing but the interface types that provide the object implementations of value types, but this would run a lot more slowly than one that used value types.

2. Widening is the situation when a value is being moved from one type to another with a wide range of possible values, for example from int to double. In this situation there is no possibility of data being lost, and so casting is not required. However, you can add it for clarity if you wish.

3. Casting between value types may be something that the Central Processor Unit (cpu) of the computer can perform very quickly. However, if the casting process involves calling a type conversion method this will take longer.

4. A type conversion method is added to an object to generate a value to be used when an object is cast into a particular type. Each type conversion method is assigned a "target" type, and so it would be possible for an object to have a type conversion that produces an integer result and another that produces a floating-point result. However, I would suggest that in these situations it may be clearer to make use of properties to return a value from a type, rather than using casting and type conversion methods, which are not something that all programmers will have come across.

5. You can write a program that uses entirely dynamic types. It should always compile, since the compiler will not perform any static error checking. However, it would probably fail quite frequently too, as mistakes that would normally produce compilation errors would not be spotted and would manifest themselves as run time errors. Using dynamic types also makes development more difficult in another way. Dynamic types acquire their types at runtime and so the Intellisense feature of Visual Studio cannot provide any useful information about a variable of dynamic type as it doesn't know what that type of information the variable is holding.

6. Many applications, for example the Microsoft Office Suite, provide automation features that are accessed via COM interfaces. This is also true of some of the lower level elements of the Windows operating system. It is unlikely that you will have to interact

with lots of COM objects during your programming career, but it is important to be able to work with them, and the dynamic type removes a lot of effort from this.

3 Enforce encapsulation

1. There are two ways that an object can encapsulate data values. It can provide properties, or it can provide getter and setter methods (sometimes called accessors and mutators respectively). Properties are very easy to use from the point of view of code that has to interact with the encapsulated values, they be assigned and read in the same way as public data values. From a performance perspective there is no difference between properties and get/set methods. We have seen that the compiler actually generates get and set methods when properties are compiled. However, get and set methods are slightly more flexible, in that a set method can perform validation on an input value and return a result that indicates whether an input value has been set correctly. The set behavior of a property could also perform validation, but the set behavior cannot return a status value.

2. There is no reason why a structure should not contain private members and properties. Although most people consider encapsulation as something that is performed on classes, structures can be encapsulated objects. An extreme form of encapsulation is the creation of immutable objects. These contain data that is set when they are created and cannot be modified. An immutable object will provide read-only properties and accessor methods to allow other programs to view the contents of the object.

3. Using properties will slightly slow down a program, in that a property behavior will take longer to complete than just getting a value directly from an object. However, the property access code will be *inlined* in that rather than calling a function to perform the property behavior the compiler will just output the code required. This makes a program slightly larger (there may be multiple copies of the code that uses the property) but it also means that accessing properties in objects is almost as fast as accessing the values directly.

4. A member of a class with the access modifier protected is visible in that class and in any classes that are children of that class. A member of a class with the access modifier internal is visible to any class that is declared in the same assembly. This means that an internal item has the potential to be seen by more classes in an application.

5. The only reason that an object would not use an explicit implementation of interface methods is if the programmer wants to "share" some methods between several interfaces. This is not the kind of thing that sensible programmers should do.

4 Create and implement a class hierarchy

1. The behaviors that are required by an object are best expressed in the form of an interface. You might create a proof of concept application and then create interfaces based

on the behaviors of the objects in that application, but you should make sure that the interfaces are established right at the start of the development process.

2. A C# interface can also contain the definition of properties that should be created any class that implements the interface.

3. Yes. A C# interface can be extended. We actually did this when we extended the IComparable interface. Take a look at Listing 2-40 for how this was done.

4. Yes. All the methods in a C# interface must be made public. However, an interface can be made internal, which means that it is only visible within a given assembly.

5. No. A class must contain implementations of all the methods in an interface if we want to create instances of that class. A class in a class hierarchy could implement some methods in an interface and a child method of the class could implement the rest. In this situation it would not be possible to create an instance of the base class as this does not contain implementations of all the interfaces. Note that this design approach is not something I would encourage.

6. No. Interfaces do not contain constructors. If you want to go down the route of having interface methods that construct instances you will have to put factory methods (methods which return references to instances that they have created) in the interface.

7. It can be. For example an Employee record that must be printed could expose an IEmployee interface and an IPrintable interface.

8. No. Interfaces can be implemented at any level of a class hierarchy. If the base class implements the interface, this has the effect of forcing any children of the base class to implement the interfaces too, but child classes can implement further interfaces. However, this is not something that I would encourage.

9. Yes. Very slightly. A non-virtual method can be called directly, since there will only ever be one copy of that method. When a virtual method is called the .NET runtime must search for the most appropriate method to call, starting with the type of the object and then looking up the class hierarchy to find the method in base classes.

10. Yes. A method that is virtual can be overridden and replaced with one that has a different behavior in the child. You should only do this for methods for which you have a definite need for the ability to override their behavior.

11. An interface specifies a set of behaviors that an object must provide so that it can be referred to by a reference of the interface type. This provides a great deal of flexibility, for example a list of interface references could contain any type of object, as long as that type implemented the interface. By contrast, an abstract type is more restrictive. It contains a set of behaviors that an object must provide, but the object can only then be regarded in terms of the abstract type, not in any other way.

12. No. If there is no need for an object to be extended then it does not need to be part of a hierarchy.

13. Yes it can. However, if a method is going to be overridden (replaced in a child class) then I would be wary of providing too many overloaded forms of the method in the base

class, as the child class will have to provide overriding implementations of all the over-loaded versions, otherwise the behavior of the child objects may not be correct.

14. No. Structures are value types and cannot be used in class hierarchies.

15. Yes. Although structures cannot be used in class hierarchies they can be declared as implementing interfaces. A structure value will be boxed (turned from a value to a reference type – see Skill 2-2 for details) if it is to be accessed via an interface reference, but this will happen automatically.

16. A class that has been sealed cannot be used as the base of a child class that extends it.

17. Yes. Any object can implement IEnumerable. However, it is only meaning for items that contain or deal with enumerable collections to implement this interface.

18. No. It causes an enumerator to return the value specified by the yield return. When the next enumeration is requested from the enumerator the enumerator will continue from the statement following the yield.

19. No. The object will still exist in memory after it has been disposed. However, any attempt to use the object will result in an exception being thrown.

20. Yes. The C# system will not call Dispose automatically. However, if you use the using construction this will call Dispose for you.

21. Not necessarily. The use of using means that the system can be absolutely clear when an object is no longer required, but this will not invoke a garbage collection action to remove that object.

5 Find, execute, and create types at runtime by using reflection

1. The values of attributes are stored in the assembly file that is created when a program is compiled.

2. When a class is loaded the attribute class instances are created and the values in them are initialized. A program can change a value in an attribute, but this will not be persisted when the program ends. This is because programs are not allowed to change the contents of the assembly files from which they are loaded.

3. Yes it can, in fact the AttributeUseage class is an example of an attribute that is applied to attributes.

4. The type information for a class is stored in the assembly file where the code for that class is stored.

5. You can use GetType to get the type of any object in your program. GetType is provided by all objects. The typeof method is used to get the type object that represents a particular type. It is used if you don't have (or need) an instance of the object but you want to use the type data in your program.

6. The GetType method will return the reference to the type of any object; whether the object contents are managed by value or reference. You can even call GetType on a literal

value in a program, in which case the value will be boxed (converted to a reference type) before the GetType runs.

7. No. You can create brand new types by using CodeDOM or expression trees, but you can't modify the behavior of a class by changing elements in its type description. This would be very dangerous if it was possible.

8. Yes. The GetProperty method provided by a Type object can be given Binding flags that specify NonPublic items. But you really shouldn't do this.

9. There is no difference between the speed of code produced "normally" and that produced by a provider that parses a CodeDOM document and generates a program that way.

10. Yes. A programmer given the assemblies for an application could extract all the class names and member names from the assembly. They can also view the actual code of the methods and there are even tools that will reconstruct a C# source file from an .exe or .dll file. If you are planning to release your code into the wild you should investigate technology which "obfuscates" your assembly files, changing the names of items and adding extra code that makes it much harder to understand what your program does.

11. Yes you could. This would be an interesting application of reflection (looking at code to find out what it does) and code generation. A program can add elements to a class being built in CodeDOM document that match those that it has discovered when parsing an interface. Visual Studio does something similar to this when you use the built in support that implements an interface for you in the code editor.

12. Yes you can. The compiled output of a CodeDOM object is an assembly like any other and will contain all the metadata.

6 Manage the object life cycle

1. Value types are normally stored on the stack (unless the type is part of a closure – see the Closures section in Skill 1.4, "Create and implement events and callbacks"). When a program exits from a block the variables on the stack are automatically removed. This means creating and destroying types such as integer, float, and double will not make any work for the garbage collector. However, if the value type is a struct, and the struct contains reference types, it will create work for the garbage collector, as the objects inside the structure will need to be managed.

2. Arrays of value types are implemented as objects. For example, an array of 100 integers will be managed as an object that contains 100 integers and an array reference to that object. This means that such arrays will be implemented on the heap and their removal from memory will involve the garbage collector.

3. No. The stack grows and contracts as a program runs. It is not managed by the garbage collector.

4. Yes. It is the application developer's responsibility to make sure that the Dispose method is called to request that the object release any resources that it is using, but if this does

not happen, and the object is deleted from memory, the finalize method will be called first. The dispose pattern has been designed to ensure that an object would release resources in a sensible way in this situation.

5. No. It would not be meaningful for the finalizer method in a class does to accept any parameters, so overloading the method (providing versions with different numbers of parameters) is not possible.

6. No. There is no need for a finalizer in a child class to make any calls to the finalizer in a parent class. Each class in a class hierarchy can have its own finalizer and each of them will be called in turn when the object is finalized.

7. When the Dispose method in an instance is called is down to the application itself. It may call Dispose multiple times. The dispose pattern uses a flag to ensure that this does not cause problems.

8. A long running finalizer will seriously impact on the performance of the garbage collection process. In an extreme situation this may result in the application running out of memory as the garbage collector cannot recover memory faster than it is being used.

9. It is bad practice for a finalizer to create a new reference to itself. This results in the object not being deleted from memory. Remember that the garbage collector makes another pass through the heap after the finalizers have been called. Any object that has a reference to it will be retained.

10. Security should be designed into an application very carefully from the start. However, in regard to performance and memory use, I advise that you don't do much more than avoid obviously stupid solutions that impact on these factors, and then just focus on creating an application that is easy to understand and test. If you subsequently discover that you have performance or memory issues, that is the point that you use your diagnostics tools to identify resource hungry elements of your program and then optimize those. A lot of developers (including me) have spent a lot of time making programs smaller and quicker when there is no need to do this, particularly with modern hardware.

7 Manipulate strings

1. The novel "War and Peace" by Tolstoy is generally accepted to be a long book. It contains around half a million words. However, even if each word was 20 characters long, this would only equate to around ten million characters. Strings are indexed using a 32-bit integer, which makes the theoretical limit on string size at around two thousand million characters. So you can say that all novels will fit into a single string.

2. The contents of a string object cannot be changed. However; a string variable can be made to refer to a different string instance. In other words, don't change the contents of a string variable called name from "Rob" to "Robert". Instead, make the string variable name refer to a new string instance that contains "Robert."

3. Interning of strings takes place when the compiler notices the same string literal is assigned to multiple variables in the program source. The compiler makes a single

"interned" variable that contains the string literal and all the variables assigned that literal are made to refer to this single value. At run time this has the advantage that the program may be able to compare strings more quickly because two string variables will be equal if they both refer to the same interned object. The only disadvantage of interning is that it slows down the compilation process.

4. The `StringBuilder` type is not based on string. The `StringBuilder` will use one or more arrays of characters to build a string.

5. If a program does a lot of string addition to assemble an output string it may be that using `StringBuilder` to assemble the string will improve performance and perhaps reduce the number of intermediate objects that will be created.

6. You can't store binary data in a `StringWriter` because a `StringWriter` implements the `TextWriter` interface, which can only accept strings of text.

7. The `Trim` method is used to remove whitespace from an input string and return a new string with the whitespace removed. It does not change the contents of a string value because strings are immutable.

8. An object that implements the `iFormattable` interface contains a `ToString` method that accepts a format string and a format provider that can be used to provide culture specific information about the culture for which the string is being formatted. Objects that implement `iFormattable` can be used with formatted output which contains formatting instructions that are given the `ToString` methods.

9. A `CultureInfo` instance contains information describing the formatting of output for use by a particular culture. The `CultureInfo` instance contains references to the `NumberFormatInfo` and `DateTimeFormatInfo` objects for the culture. These specify such things as the ordering of dates when printed, the character to be used to mean currency and the separators between digits in large numbers. A formatter can use those parts of a `CultureInfo` instances as it needs to produce output that reflects different regions of the world.

10. String interpolation takes place when the compiler works on literal string values in the program source. A string that is identified as an interpolated string by having a dollar character ($) added before the start of the string will be parsed and the names of variables to be printed extracted. This all happens at compile time, so it is not possible to use interpolation on strings that are generated when the program runs.

Chapter summary

- Objects in a solution can be managed by value or by reference. A struct is a value type, which means that during assignment the contents of the struct (the value) is copied from one variable to another. A class is a reference type, which means that during assignment the destination of the assignment is made to refer to the same object as the source of the assignment.

- An immutable object is one that cannot be changed. Immutable objects, for example DateTime, provide methods that can be used to provide new, mutated copies of the original. For example, the DateTime structure provides a method that can be used to return a new DateTime structure that represents a given number of days into the future.

- A generic type can be used as a "placeholder" in a type design, so that the type of object that a type works on can be established dynamically. A good example of a situation where generic types are used is in the creation of lists and dictionaries.

- Types can be given a constructor method that is called when a new instance of the type is created. A constructor can be given parameters that can be used to initialize the object. If the constructor detects that the initialization data is invalid it must interrupt the construction process by throwing an exception, as the object will be created when the constructor completes. Constructors can be overloaded to provide different ways in which a given type can be instantiated. By use of the "this" syntax one constructor in type can call another constructor, to allow the creation of a master constructor and avoid code duplication in objects. Classes can contain a static constructor, which is called once when the first instance of the class is created.

- Types can contain methods that allow an object to perform behaviors. A method accepts a number of parameters and has a particular type. A method of type void does not return a value, whereas a method with any other type must return a result of that type.

- An extension method can be added to a class to add to the functionality of the class. The extension method does not have access to any of the private data members of the class it is added to.

- Parameters to a method can be identified by their names when called. This improves the readability of programs and also reduces the likelihood of errors which may be caused by parameters being entered in the wrong sequence.

- Parameters to a method can be made optional by providing a default value for the parameter. If the parameter is left out of the method call the default value is used instead.

- Objects can provide indexed properties which can be used to provide an index value (usually an integer) to identify the item to be returned.

- Methods in a single type can be overloaded. This means that the type will contain multiple versions of the same method, each of which has a different signature. Method overloading is used in situations where there are multiple ways of performing a given task from different data inputs.

- Methods in a class hierarchy can be overridden. To be overridden a method must be marked as virtual. When a virtual method is called on an instance of a class in the hierarchy the system will search up the class hierarchy for an implementation of the method, stating at the class of the object. The first implementation that is found is called. Method overriding is used in situations where objects in a class hierarchy need to be able to perform a given action in their own particular way. The base keyword allows a method to call the method it has overridden.

- Every item in an application is of a particular type. The C# type system will automatically convert between reference and value types and automatically convert (widen) values when it is sensible to do so and no data will be lost.

- If a type conversion will result in data loss (narrowing) the programmer must use casting to explicitly request the conversion of the values.

- Dynamic types are provided so that a C# application can interact with languages and services which are not statically typed. They allow the compiler to be told to ignore the type of an object and build the program even if the typing information indicates errors.

- When a dynamic type is used the type of the variable that is created is inferred from the context of the use. This means that what mistakes that would have been detected as compilation errors are now changed into run-time errors.

- Dynamic types are especially useful when interacting with Component Object Model (COM) based services as they can be automatically mapped onto the correct types from the context of their use.

- The C# access modifiers allow members of a class to be hidden from code outside the class. Unless you specify otherwise, class members are private to a class and not visible outside it. Making a data member public will allow uncontrolled access to that data member in the class, which may not be a good idea.

- C# properties allow get and set behaviors to get control when an external code wishes to interact with a member of a class. The property can control access to private member of the class that holds a *backing value* for the data that is being managed by the class. Properties can provide only get behaviors for read only properties, and only set behaviors for write-only properties. The get and set behaviors can have different access modifiers so that the get behavior for a property can be made public and the set behavior private.

- Generally speaking, methods that a class exposes for other classes to use should be made public, and data contained within the class should be made private.

- The protected access modifier allows a class member to be made visible within classes in a class hierarchy and the internal access modifier allows a class member to be made visible to code in the same assembly as the class member.

- Methods in a class that implement the behaviors of an interface can be identified as explicitly implementing this interface. This improves encapsulation as it means that the only context in which those methods can be used is via a reference to the interface, not a reference to the object. Explicit implementation of behaviors also removes the potential for confusion if a class implements multiple interfaces and the same method appears in some of the interfaces.

- A C# class can implement an interface that contains a set of method signatures. Implementing an interface involves providing a method that matches each of the methods described in the interface. A class that implements an interface can be referred to by references of the interface type.

- A C# class can serve as the base class for a child class that extends it. A child class inherits all of the members of the base class and use C# the override mechanism to provide overridden versions of methods in the base class which have a behavior more specific to child class. For a method in a base class to be overridden it must be declared as virtual. An overriding method can use the base keyword to call overridden methods in the base class.

- A programmer can create replacement methods for those in a base class. This is not to be encouraged.

- A class can be declared as sealed to prevent it from being used as the basis of child classes. Methods in a class that extend those in a base class can also be declared as sealed, preventing them from being overridden.

- To construct a child class a program needs to create an instance of the base class. If a base class has a constructor the child class must call this and supply any required parameters. The base keyword is used in the constructor for this purpose.

- A class can be declared as abstract, in which case it will contain signatures of methods which are to be implemented in child classes. Abstract classes can serve as templates for classes.

- A reference to a base class can refer to any objects that are created from classes that extend the base class. However, the reverse is not true. A reference to a child class is not able to be made to refer to an instance of the parent.

- A class can implement the IComparable interface. This means that it contains a method called CompareTo which can be used to determine the ordering of objects of that type. The IComparable behavior can be used by methods such as the Sort method provided by the List type, which can place objects in order.

- A class can implement the IEnumerable interface, which means that it can provides a method GetEnumerator which will supply an enumerator which can be used by a consumer of the enumeration (for example a foreach construction) to work through the class.

- The C# yield keyword provides an easy way for a programmer to create enumerators. It retains the state of the enumerator method until the next items is requested from the enumeration by the consumer of the enumeration.

- A class can implement the IDisposable interface. The class will contain a Dispose method that can be called to instruct an instance of the class to release critical resources that it is using. The Dispose method is not called automatically by the garbage collection process, but it can be called automatically if the instance of the object is created and used within a C# using construction.

- The IUnknown interface can be used when creating .NET code that must interact directly with Component Object Model (COM) objects.

- Metadata is data about data. In the context of a C# program, the metadata for the code would be expressed in the form of one or more attribute instances that are attached to code elements. This metadata is stored in the assembly file that is created when the program is built and loaded into attribute class instances when the assembly is loaded.

- Attribute classes extend the Attribute class and have names that end with the text "Attribute". An attribute class can be empty, in which case it just indicates that a particular attribute is applied to an item, or an attribute can contain data elements which can be accessed programmatically. Attributes can be applied to many different elements in a program; an `AttributeUseage` attribute can be added to an attribute declaration to specify objects and classes that can have the attribute applied.

- Reflection allows a program to investigate the contents of a type and programmatically interact with it.

- Reflection can be used on an assembly to allow a program determine the characteristics of types in the assembly. This can be used to allow a component-based system to automatically select and load the components that it needs.

- Programs code can be created programmatically by using the CodeDOM document model which allows namespaces, classes, properties and class members to be specified. A CodeDom object can be output as a binary assembly file or as a source file in C# or Visual Basic.

- Another way to programmatically create code behaviors is to create lambda expression trees which contain lambda expressions that give the actions to be performed, along with a range of expression node types that specify other program actions. Expression trees are used to express programmatic behavior for such things as LINQ queries and the implementation of dynamic languages.

- Garbage collection of objects makes program creation much easier. The garbage collection system in C# runs automatically and will delete unused objects (those that are not referred to by any reference).

- Application threads are paused while the garbage collection process runs.

- The garbage collector recognizes persistent objects (those which are present after a garbage collection) and omits those from the garbage collection process.

- The garbage collection process can be initiated manually, although this is not recommended.

- Unused objects that contain references to resources that need to be released when the object is deleted can contain a finalizer method that is executed during the garbage collection process. The finalizer method can release resources allocated to the object.

- In preference to a finalizer method, an object can implement the `IDisposable` interface and contain a `Dispose` method that can be used by the application to instruct the object to release any resources. The using statement can be used to ensure that the `Dispose` method is called on an object which is used in only one part of a program.

- By using the dispose pattern, an object can combine the use of finalizer and Dispose to ensure that resources held by the object are released correctly.

- A string is collection of characters of arbitrary length.

- String variables are immutable (they cannot be changed) but they are managed by reference. This combination means that they can be treated as value types.

- During compilation multiple copies of string literals for a particular string are mapped onto a single string instance in memory. In other words, if a program assigns the string literal "cheese" to several different string variables this would result in a single string value containing the text "cheese" being created to which all the variables would be made to refer.

- Building up a large string by adding many strings together will result in the creation of a large number of substrings. The StringBuilder type provides a string implementation which is mutable. A program can modify the contents in a StringBuilder instance. StringBuilders provide a more efficient means of assembling large strings.

- The StringReader and StringWriter classes allow strings to be used by programs that work with TextReader and TextWriter streams.

- The string type provides a range of methods for working with strings. It is possible to establish the location of substrings within the string, extract them and match the start and the end of a string.

- The contents of a string cannot be changed (strings are immutable) but the Replace string method can be used to create a new string instance with updated contents.

- String matching can be performed using the character codes or according to particular culture where multiple spellings of the same word may be matched.

- Strings can be enumerated, for example by using foreach construction.

- Strings can implement the IFormattable interface, which means that they will contain an additional ToString method that accepts formatting and culture information.

- String interpolation allows a program to use string literals (preceded by a $ character) that combine formatting information and the names of variables to be formatted and incorporated into the string. Interpolated strings are processed at compile time to produce composite format strings.

CHAPTER 3

Debug applications and implement security

Security in an application must be considered at the start of the development process. While it is possible to use performance analysis tools to take an application that is running slowly, identify the slow running elements, and optimize them, it is virtually impossible to add security to an application that has not been designed and constructed with security in mind.

Security must be implemented at all levels of a solution; starting with ensuring that the input values received by an application are in the expected range, then ensuring that the application stores and manages the data correctly.

In this chapter we will look at data validation techniques at a variety of levels; from the tools that you can use to convert raw user input into values for use in your application, through to those that are required to ensure the validity of incoming structured data. We'll also discover how to use encryption to ensure that communication between different applications, or different elements of the same application, can be performed in a highly secure manner.

Security doesn't end once a solution has been installed. You must also consider how to protect and manage the code assemblies that make up the application itself. We'll discover how to use the assembly versioning and management features of .NET when deploying and maintaining a solution.

Bugs in your programs are a natural consequence of software development. I have a theory that any system complex enough to be useful will have bugs in it. Dealing with faults in your code is part of the process of writing software. We'll take a look at debugging techniques that you can use when writing C#. And we'll finish with a look at diagnostics, tools, and language features that let you track the behavior of your application.

Skills in this chapter:

- Skill 3.1: Validate application input
- Skill 3.2: Perform symmetric and asymmetric encryption
- Skill 3.3: Manage assemblies
- Skill 3.4: Debug an application
- Skill 3.5: Implement diagnostics in an application

Skill 3.1: Validate application input

The first step in creating a secure application is ensuring that incoming data is valid. Data in your applications must come from somewhere; whether it is items entered into the application user interface, or packets of formatted values received from another application. In every case you need to make sure that your application is resilient in its response to invalid data. You also need to keep in mind that invalid data may have been entered with malicious intent. It is important that a poorly thought out response to invalid data doesn't expose your systems to attack.

We're going to start with a look at validating a JSON formatted data object, then move on to considering the management of data collections in your applications. This leads to considerations of data integrity; such as how do you make sure that operations on data don't invalidate it. Finally, we'll take a look at some C# techniques that underpin data integrity, examining the use of regular expressions to validate the format of incoming data and the C# functions that can be used to validate incoming data.

> **This section covers how to:**
> - Validate JSON data
> - Choose the appropriate data collection type
> - Manage data integrity
> - Evaluate a regular expression to validate the input format
> - Use built-in functions to validate data type and content

Using JSON

JSON, or JavaScript Object Notation, is a very popular means by which applications can exchange data. It is easy for both people and computers to understand. The JSON standard is defined at *https://www.json.org/*. Before discussing the security implications of using JSON, let's first consider what it is, and how to use it in a C# program.

The JSON document

A JSON document contains a number of name/value pairs that represent the data in an application. A JSON document can also contain arrays of JSON objects. JSON documents map very well onto objects in an object-oriented language, although JSON itself is not tied to any one programming language. JSON is therefore very useful if you want to share data between programs written in different languages.

Start learning about JSON by taking a look at some C# objects and the JSON documents that represent the values in these objects. The code shown next illustrates the MusicTrack class used in previous examples to store the artist and title of a music track. I've added an integer property called Length that holds the length of a track in seconds.

```
class MusicTrack
{
    public string Artist { get; set; }
    public string Title { get; set; }
    public int Length { get; set; }

    // ToString that overrides the behavior in the base class
    public override string ToString()
    {
        return Artist + " " + Title + " " + Length.ToString() + "seconds long" ;
    }

    public MusicTrack(string artist, string title, int length)
    {
        Artist = artist;
        Title = title;
        Length = length;
    }
}
```

You can create an instance of a music track as follows:

```
MusicTrack track = new MusicTrack(artist: "Rob Miles", title: "My Way", length:150);
```

A JSON document is enclosed in braces and contains a series of name and value pairs. The JSON encoded data that represents this instance of MusicTrack looks as follows:

```
{"Artist":"Rob Miles","Title":"My Way","Length":150}
```

Note that the type of data (the fact that it is an instance of the MusicTrack class) is not stored as part of the document. The JSON document only contains the names and values of the data members of the MusicTrack instance. Note also that there is no type information added to the Length property. This is stored as a string of text and it is up to the recipient of the JSON document to understand this and act appropriately.

JSON documents can contain lists of items. The following C# code creates a list called album, which contains a number of MusicTrack values.

```
List<MusicTrack> album = new List<MusicTrack>();

string[] trackNames = new[] { "My Way", "Your Way", "Their Way", "The Wrong Way" };

foreach (string trackName in trackNames)
{
    MusicTrack newTrack = new MusicTrack(artist: "Rob Miles", title: trackName,
                            length:150);
    album.Add(newTrack);
}
```

Any value in a JSON document can be expressed as a comma separated list of name and value pairs, enclosed in square brackets. The JSON encoded data for the album list looks as follows:

```
[{"Artist":"Rob Miles","Title":"My Way","Length":150},
  {"Artist":"Rob Miles","Title":"Your Way","Length":150},
```

```
{"Artist":"Rob Miles","Title":"Their Way","Length":150},
{"Artist":"Rob Miles","Title":"The Wrong Way","Length":150}]
```

The best thing about JSON is that once you have learned the syntax, you know all there is to know about JSON. It is a very lightweight design, but it can also be used to represent highly structured data; particularly when you consider that a list can contain values that represent another list, and so on.

JSON and C#

I was surprised to discover that the most popular way of converting C# classes to and from C# objects was not a library built into .NET, but a library of routines created by the programmer James Newton-King. You can find out more about the library at his web site at *https://www. newtonsoft.com/json*. The library is free to use and the best way to obtain it is to use the NuGet package manager to add them to a Visual Studio project. The NuGet library mechanism built into Visual Studio is a great source of very useful code. It is also very easy to publish your own packages using NuGet.

The first thing you need to do is open the NuGet package manager console. Figure 3.1 shows where you can find this in Visual Studio 2017.

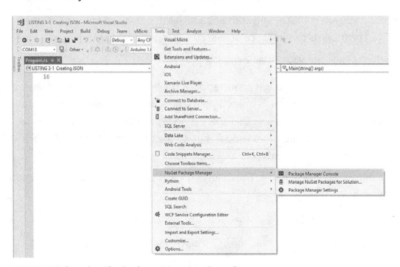

FIGURE 3-1 Opening the Package Manager Console

Once the package manager console is open you can use the `Install-Package` command to add the library to your solution using the command shown in Figure 3.2.

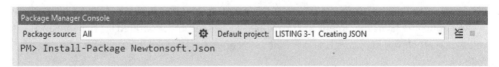

FIGURE 3-2 Installing JSON

Once the library has been installed you will find it in the references for your project, as shown in the References tab in Solution Explorer.

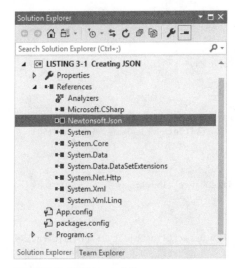

FIGURE 3-3 JSON in a solution

You can also use the visual interface to NuGet to manage the NuGet packages in a solution and browse the NuGet library. This interface is accessed via the Manage NuGet Packages For This Solution option in the menu shown in Figure 3.1.

Once you have added the `Newtonsoft.Json` library to the solution you can use the classes in it to create JSON descriptions of object contents and retrieve them. The program in Listing 3-1 shows how this is done. The program creates the sample JSON that you've already seen in this section. The program uses the `SerializeObject` and `DeserializeObject` methods exposed by the `JsonConvert` object to create and parse strings of JSON.

LISTING 3-1 Creating JSON

```
using Newtonsoft.Json;
using System;
using System.Collections.Generic;

namespace LISTING_3_1_Creating_JSON

    class Program
    {
        static void Main(string[] args)
        {
            MusicTrack track = new MusicTrack(artist: "Rob Miles", title: "My Way",
                                          length: 150);
            string json = JsonConvert.SerializeObject(track);
            Console.Write("JSON: ");
            Console.WriteLine(json);
```

```
        MusicTrack trackRead = JsonConvert.DeserializeObject<MusicTrack>(json);
        Console.Write("Read back: ");
        Console.WriteLine(trackRead);

        List<MusicTrack> album = new List<MusicTrack>();

        string[] trackNames = new[] { "My Way", "Your Way", "Their Way",
                                    "The Wrong Way" };

        foreach (string trackName in trackNames)
        {
            MusicTrack newTrack = new MusicTrack(artist: "Rob Miles",
                                            title:  trackName, length: 150);
            album.Add(newTrack);
        }

        string jsonArray = JsonConvert.SerializeObject(album);
        Console.Write("JSON: ");
        Console.WriteLine(jsonArray);

        List<MusicTrack> albumRead = JsonConvert.DeserializeObject<List<MusicTrack>>
        (jsonArray);

        Console.WriteLine("Read back: ");
        foreach (MusicTrack readTrack in albumRead)
        {
            Console.WriteLine(readTrack);
        }
        Console.ReadKey();
    }
  }
}
```

When you start to use JSON in your programs there are a few things that you need to be aware of from a security and class design point of view:

- If you want to save and load private properties in a class you need to mark these items with the [JsonProperty] attribute.

- If you want to serialize a class using JSON you don't have to add the [Serializable] attribute to the class. You can find out more about serialization in Skill 2.5 in "The Serializable attribute" section.

- When loading a class back using JSON you need to provide the type into which the result is to be stored. No type information is stored in the file that is stored. The Length property of the MusicTrack is automatically converted into an integer upon reloading because the JSON deserializer determines the type of each property in the destination object and then performs type conversion automatically. This is a nice example of the use of the reflection techniques shown in Skill 2.5.

- There is absolutely nothing to prevent changes to the content of the text in a JSON document. If you wish to detect modification of a document transferred by JSON you can add a checksum or hash property to the type that is validated by the recipient of the data. In the next section we will look at encryption techniques you can use to securely send data.

JSON and XML

XML (eXtensible Markup Language) is another way of expressing the content of an object in a portable and human readable form. This is a slightly more *heavyweight* standard, in that an XML document contains more metadata (data about data) than a JSON document. The code shown next is an XML description of the MusicTrack object we saw earlier.

```
<?xml version="1.0" encoding="utf-16"?>
<MusicTrack xmlns:xsi=http://www.w3.org/2001/XMLSchema-instance
 xmlns:xsd="http://www.w3.org/2001/XMLSchema">
  <Artist>Rob Miles</Artist>
  <Title>My Way</Title>
  <Length>150</Length>
</MusicTrack>
```

Note that the XML document is versioned, and also contains encoding details. Note also that each element of the document also contains a name, and that the MusicTrack description includes two namespace documents.

Listing 3-2 shows how a program can create and load XML documents using the XmlSerializer class.

LISTING 3-2 Creating XML

```
using System;
using System.IO;
using System.Xml.Serialization;

namespace LISTING_3_2_Creating_XML
{
    public class MusicTrack
    {
        // MusicTrack body from LISTING 3.1
        // Parameterless constructor required by the XML serializer
        // Does not need to set any property values, these are public.
        public MusicTrack()
        {
        }
    }

    class Program
    {
        static void Main(string[] args)
        {
            MusicTrack track = new MusicTrack(artist: "Rob Miles", title: "My Way",
                                              length: 150);
            XmlSerializer musicTrackSerializer = new XmlSerializer(typeof(MusicTrack));

            TextWriter serWriter = new StringWriter();
```

```
musicTrackSerializer.Serialize(textWriter:serWriter, o:track);
serWriter.Close();

string trackXML = serWriter.ToString();

Console.WriteLine("Track XML");
Console.WriteLine(trackXML);

TextReader serReader = new StringReader(trackXML);

MusicTrack trackRead =
        musicTrackSerializer.Deserialize(serReader) as MusicTrack;

Console.Write("Read back: ");
Console.WriteLine(trackRead);

Console.ReadKey();
        }
    }
}
```

There are a few things you need to be aware of when considering JSON and XML:

- XML serialization can only save and load the public data elements in a type. If you want to save the private elements in a class you should use the Data Contract serializer described in Chapter 4.

- For XML serialization to work the class being serialized must contain a parameterless constructor (a constructor that accepts no parameters).

- The XML deserialization process returns a reference to an object. In Listing 3-2 this reference is cast into a MusicTrack

- XML documents can have a *schema* attached to them. A schema formally sets out the items that a document must contain to be valid. For example, for the MusicTrack type the schema can require that MusicTrack elements in the document must contain Artist, Title, and Length elements. Schemas can be used to automatically validate the structure of incoming documents. You can learn more about schemas at *https://docs. microsoft.com/en-us/dotnet/standard/data/xml/reading-and-writing-xml-schemas*

- Elements in an XML document can also be given attributes to provide more information about them. For example, the Length attribute of a MusicTrack can be given attributes to indicate that it is an integer and the units of the value are in seconds.

- An XML document is no less vulnerable to tampering than a JSON document. However, the attribute mechanism can be used to add validation information to data fields.

XML is explored in more detail in Skill 4.4 later in this book.

Validate JSON data

You can perform simple text-based checks on a JSON file to get some level of confidence about the validity of its contents. For example, a program can check that the text starts and ends with a matching pair of brace characters (curly brackets), contains the same number of open square brackets as close square brackets, and an even number of double quote characters. The exceptions thrown by the JSON parser, however, can also give good information about the content.

The program in Listing 3-3 catches and displays the exception thrown by the JSON deserializer.

LISTING 3-3 Validating JSON

```
using Newtonsoft.Json;
using System;

namespace LISTING_3_3_Validating_JSON
{
    class Program
    {
        static void Main(string[] args)
        {
            string invalidJson =
"{\"Artist\":\"Rob Miles\",\"Title\":\"My  Way\",\"Length\":150\"}";

            try
            {
                MusicTrack trackRead = JsonConvert.DeserializeObject<MusicTrack>(
invalidJson );
                Console.Write("Read back: ");
                Console.WriteLine(trackRead);
            }
            catch (JsonReaderException e)
            {
                Console.WriteLine(e.Message);
            }
            Console.ReadKey();
        }
    }
}
```

The JSON text in Listing 3-3 contains a missing double quote character before the value of the Length property. If you run this program you will see the following output message. Note that the exception also contains integer versions of the line and position values identified in the output text.

```
Unexpected character encountered while parsing number: ". Path 'Length', line 1,
position 51.
```

Choose the appropriate data collection type

During the implementation of an application you will need to decide how collections of the data are to be organized. There are a large number of different options available. In this section we are going to take a look at each option, identifying appropriate situations in which they should be used. There are further details on collection type choice in Chapter 4 in the section "Choose a collection type."

Use typed collection classes

From a program security point of view, it is advisable to use the typed versions of the C# collection classes. The System.Collections namespace provides *untyped* collection classes such as ArrayList. These are regarded as untyped because the data in them is managed in terms of a reference to an object. Since object is the base type of all C# types; this means that such collections can hold any type of object, in any arrangement.

In other words, a single ArrayList collection can hold references to Person, MusicTrack, and BankAccount objects. This can lead to problems at runtime, if an application extracts a MusicTrack reference from the ArrayList and tries to use it as a BankAccount the application will fail with a type exception. The List class in the Systems.Collections.Generic namespace uses generic typing, which allows the programmer to specify that a given list can only contain BankAccount references. Any attempts to store MusicTrack references in such a list will fail at compile time.

Consider threading

In Skill 1.1,"Implement multithreading," we considered the issues that arise when using collections in multi-threaded applications. The standard C# collection classes are not "thread safe." If several processes attempt to interact with a non-thread safe object, it can lead to data being lost or duplicated in ways that can be very hard to debug, because the nature of the error and when it occurs may be dependent on system loading and timing conditions that will be hard to replicate. Consult the section, "Using concurrent collections," in Skill 1.1 for details of the concurrent collection types available in C#.

Use the correct kind of collection

If your application is processing a stream of incoming messages and then discarding them you should consider using a Queue class if you want first-in, first-out (FIFO) behavior and a Stack if you want last-in, first out (LIFO) behavior.

If your application is going to use an index to access elements and you know in advance how many elements there are, you can use a simple array. This is very useful for lookup tables. If the number of items being stored is not known in advance you can use a List<T> type, which allows your program indexed access to given elements (starting at element zero).

If your application will perform frequent insertions and deletions of data items, and also needs to work through a large list of items, you can use the LinkedList<T> class. This will be more efficient than using an index to access elements in sequence.

If you want to store your data sorted in a particular order you can add a CompareTo behavior to your data objects, make them implement the IComparable interface and then use the Sort method in the List type to perform the sorting. You can find more details on how to do this in the section on the IComparable interface in Skill 2.4.

If you want to index your information on a key value, for example search for a bank account object which has a particular account number, then the `Dictionary<TKey,TValue>` collection class will do this. If you are storing only strings you can use the `StringCollection` and `String-List` classes.

Plan to work with LINQ on your collections

Any object that implements the `IEnumerable` or the `IQueryable<T>` interface can be acted on by a LINQ query. For details of `IEnumerable` you can find a description in Skill 2.4 in the section titled "`IEnumerable`." LINQ queries are compiled into expression trees and execute very quickly. It is easy to create LINQ queries and process their results, and the queries can produce sorted results. `IQueryable<T>` is more efficient than `IEnumerable`, because it performs data filtering on the source database, rather than loading all data and then filtering it to produce the result.

In keeping with my previously expressed opinions on premature optimization; I advise you to start by using LINQ for any searching and sorting operations, rather than trying to create custom data high performance storage elements.

Use the Entity Framework to design your data storage

The Entity Framework is part of ADO.NET (Active Data Objects) that you can use to create data storage for your applications. Objects in your application can be mapped onto tables in a database that is automatically created. The objects are created as C# classes and the Entity Framework tools migrate these into a database design.

The object and database design can be updated by performing successive migrations as the application evolves over time. This is a great way to create and deploy line of business applications and web applications. Start by making a simple ASP (Active Server Pages) application to store music track information. You can use Visual Studio Community 2017 to do this. Before building the application, make sure that the ASP.NET and web development toolchain is installed in Visual Studio. Open Visual Studio and select **Get Tools and Features** from the **Tools menu.** Ensure that the tools shown in Figure 3-4 are installed.

ASP.NET and web development
Build web applications using ASP.NET, ASP.NET Core,
HTML/JavaScript, and Containers including Docker support.

FIGURE 3-4 ASP.NET and web development

Once you have the tools installed, make your solution. Select **New Project** from the File menu in Visual Studio. Open the **Web** tab and select ASP.NET Core Web Application as shown in Figure 3-5. Set the name of the project to **MusicTracks** and click **OK**.

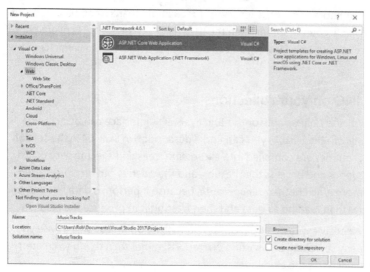

FIGURE 3-5 Create an ASP.NET project

The next dialog lets you select the type of application to be selected. We are going to make a *Model View Controller* application, so select this option from the dialog that appears and click **OK**.

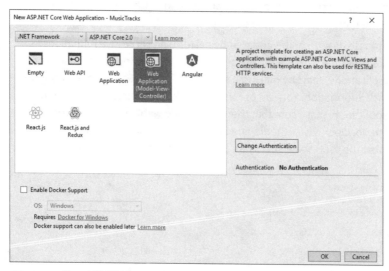

FIGURE 3-6 New ASP.NET Core Web Application

You should now have an empty ASP.NET project, so you can add the data class to this project. Data classes form the Model element of the Model View Controller pattern. This pattern is covered in more detail later in this section. To create the data class, right-click the Model folder in the Solution Explorer, select **Add** from the context menu that appears, and select **Class** as the item being added, as shown in Figure 3-7.

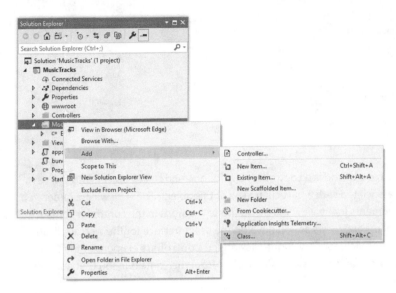

FIGURE 3-7 Create a new class

When you create a class you need to state the kind of class. We are going to create an ASP. NET Core class, so select this from the menu that appears, as shown in Figure 3-8. Give the class the name **MusicTrack** and click **Add**.

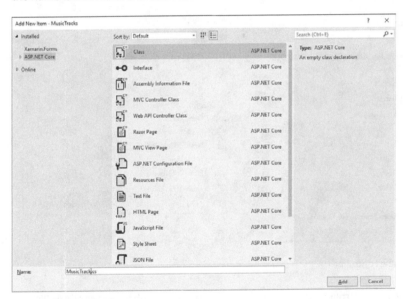

FIGURE 3-8 New class item

You can now add the MusicTrack class description into that class. The code for this class is shown in Listing 3-4. Note that the class contains an integer ID property that will be used as the primary key for the database. This allows each track to be uniquely identified.

LISTING 3-4 ASP MusicTracks

```
namespace MusicTracks.Models
{
    public class MusicTrack
    {
        public int ID { get; set; }
        public string Artist { get; set; }
        public string Title { get; set; }
        public int Length { get; set; }
    }
}
```

The next thing we have to add is a controller class for our `MusicTrack` object. This will perform the behaviors associated with a particular view of this object. The view will be generated
automatically, and elements in the view will be bound to methods in the controller class. You
can add more controllers and views as you develop the user interface for the web application.
Let's create a very simple view for now. Right-click on the **Controllers** element of the **Solution Explorer**, select **Add**, and then select **Controller** from the context menu that appears, as
shown in Figure 3-9.

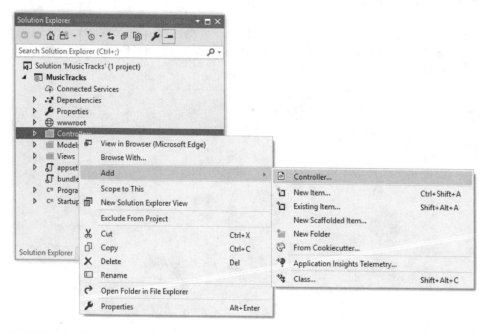

FIGURE 3-9 Create a new controller

We want to create a Controller with Views, which will create the web views for our ASP
application. Select this option from the **Add Scaffold** menu that appears next, as shown in
Figure 3-10.

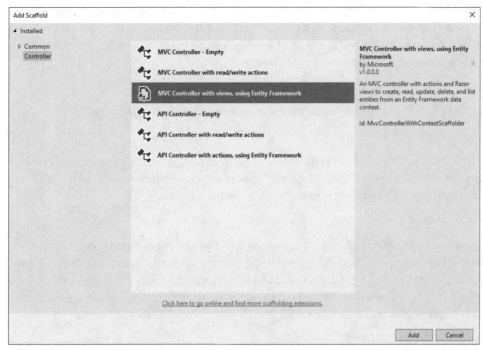

FIGURE 3-10 Add scaffold

Now, specify the source model for this controller, and the data context class. The source model is the `MusicTrack` class, and you want to create a data context class that will serve as the connection between the data and the controller class. The Add MVC Controller dialog should appear as shown in Figure 3-11 when you have finished.

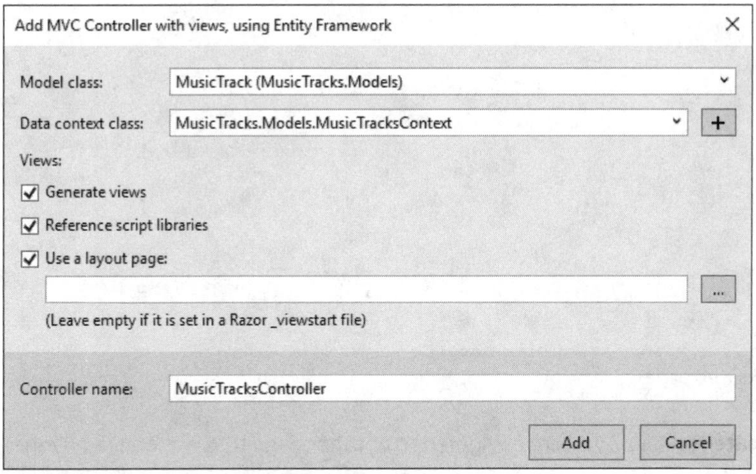

Add MVC Controller with views, using Entity Framework ✕

Model class: MusicTrack (MusicTracks.Models) ⌄

Data context class: MusicTracks.Models.MusicTracksContext ⌄ ＋

Views:

☑ Generate views

☑ Reference script libraries

☑ Use a layout page:

[   ] ...

(Leave empty if it is set in a Razor _viewstart file)

Controller name: MusicTracksController

Add   Cancel

FIGURE 3-11 Add MVC Controller

Now that you have built the code for the application, the next step is to use the class design to create a database to store the music tracks. To do this, use the Package Manager from NuGet, which was used to install the JSON serializer earlier. Start this as shown in Figure 3.1. Now enter the following command to load the tools.

```
Install-Package Microsoft.EntityFrameworkCore.Tools
```

Once the tools are loaded, create the database by performing the first migration:

```
Add-Migration Initial
```

Now that the database has been created, perform an update to create the tables that will store the class data in the application. When you issue this command, you will see the SQL commands that are performed to create the table in the database.

```
Update-Database
```

You now have a real application that exposes data as a web page. Run the program by pressing the green arrow, and the application homepage will appear in your browser. You want to view the page made for the data, so append MusicTracks (the name of the view page) on the end of the site that Visual Studio has created for you, as shown here. Note that the address 52071 might be different on your system.

```
http://localhost:52071/MusicTracks
```

This should result in the web page shown in Figure 3-12. This web page was created for the application when you earlier made the controller class.

FIGURE 3-12 Music Tracks web page

If you click the **Create New** link, you are navigated to another page that was created by the scaffolding process. It allows you to enter new track information as shown in Figure 3-13. You can enter **Artist, Title,** and **Length** items into this page and click the **Create** button to create the entry.

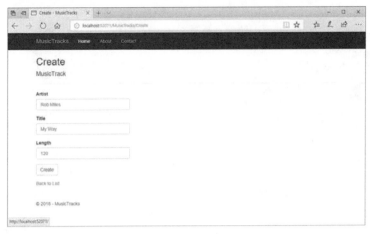

FIGURE 3-13 Music track entry

When you create a new track it will appear in the list, as shown in Figure 3-14.

FIGURE 3-14 Music track in list

Note that the application is surprisingly complete. There are links that can be used to edit, view details, and delete the track entry. You can experiment with these to prove that they work. Furthermore, if you exit the application and return to it, you will find that the data is persisted in a local database. During the deployment phase you migrate this onto a production database server.

Model View Controller and ASP web pages

The application we've created uses the *Model View Controller* (MVC) pattern. The MVC pattern makes it simpler to create complex applications by separating out the activities required to build an application with a rich user interface. Figure 3-15 shows how these entities are related, and how they are realized in the ASP.NET (MVC) application.

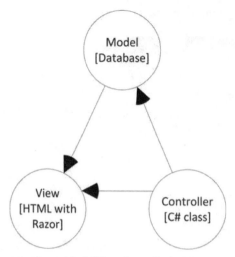

FIGURE 3-15 Model View Controller in ASP

The Model contains the data and any business logic for the application. The model also contains the state of the application. In ASP, a given item in the model is exposed as an instance of a *context*, which provides methods that can be used to interact with the data. In the case of the Music Track application, the model provides a reference to a `MusicTracksContext` object.

The Controller responds to events that are generated by the view and selects which view to render. It also initiates any changes to the Model in response to user action. For example, when we were creating a new `MusicTrack`, the Controller class contained a method that runs when the user presses the Create button in the user interface. The method in the controller class is bound to the Post action that is performed when the user presses Create. This is the method that instructs the model context to create a new item.

The View displays what the user sees on the screen. In the case of our application it is implemented by a web page for each view. A given ASP controller class can be associated with a number of views. The HTML that describes the web page also contains embedded C# code (using an ASP.NET feature called the Razor view engine) that can be used to aid with the presentation of the data.

Manage data integrity

Ensuring that your data has integrity falls directly out of the need to consider security at all points in the creation of your application. You need to actively consider how changes are made to your data and how these might fail or be subverted and cause the data to be corrupted.

When discussing classes in the previous chapter, you saw how to improve the integrity of an object by making use of the public and private access modifiers. Data that is managed by an object should be private to that object, and the object should provide the bare minimum number of public interactions with the data. You can now go beyond this and consider how object interactions can be designed to ensure that the data in the objects has integrity.

Integrity in method calls

Parameters to method calls should be range checked to ensure that their behavior cannot be subverted to corrupt data. For example, a method to withdraw a specified amount from a bank account must ensure that the withdrawal amount specified is always positive, otherwise a withdrawal of a negative amount could be used to actually increase the balance on the account.

When passing parameters into a method call, be aware of the way that passing a method a reference to an object as a parameter raises the possibility that the method may make changes to the object. For example, consider the method PrintTrack shown next. This was written by a programmer called Fred Blogs. This method is supposed to print a MusicTrack object. However, the PrintTrack method also changes the Artist property of the track to the name of the programmer, corrupting the data in the object that it has been called to print.

```
static void PrintTrack(MusicTrack track)
{
    // Print the track
    // Change the artist name for no good reason
    track.Artist = "Fred Blogs";
}
```

An action of a method that changes data outside the method is called a "side effect" of that method. The "side effect" of the above PrintTrack method is that the Artist property of the track provided as a parameter is changed.

If you want to be sure that a method can't change the contents of an object that it is given a reference to, you will have to copy the object and pass the method a reference to the copy. You can make it easy to do this by create a method called a *copy constructor for the* MusicTrack class. The code in Listing 3-5 shows how this works. The MusicTrack class contains a constructor that accepts a MusicTrack as a parameter. It creates a new MusicTrack instance with the same contents as the source. If you are concerned about a method changing the contents of a MusicTrack object that the method is given as a parameter, you can now send that method a copy of the MusicTrack.

LISTING 3-5 Copy constructor

```
using System;

namespace LISTING_3_5_Copy_constructor
{
    class MusicTrack
    {
        public string Artist { get; set; }
        public string Title { get; set; }
        public int Length { get; set; }

        // Copy constructor for MusicTrack
        public MusicTrack(MusicTrack source)
        {
            Artist = source.Artist;
            Title = source.Title;
            Length = source.Length;
```

```
        }

        public MusicTrack(string artist, string title, int length)
        {
            Artist = artist;
            Title = title;
            Length = length;
        }
    }

    class Program
    {
        // Naughty PrintTrack method that changes the Artist property of the
        // track being printed.
        static void PrintTrack(MusicTrack track)
        {
            track.Artist = "Fred Bloggs";
        }

        static void Main(string[] args)
        {
            // Create a new music track instance

            MusicTrack track = new MusicTrack(artist: "Rob Miles", title: "My Way",
                                              length: 120);

            // Use the copy constructor to send a copy of the track to be printed
            // Changes made by the PrintTrack method will have no effect on the original
            PrintTrack(new MusicTrack(track));

            Console.WriteLine(track.Artist);
            Console.ReadKey();
        }
    }
}
```

Note that the use of copies of objects is also a good idea when creating multi-threaded applications. If you are concerned about other threads making changes to a MusicTrack while it is being printed; creating a copy of the MusicTrack to be printed removes this possibility.

Remember, however, that you don't need to do this if the parameter being supplied to the method is a value type. In other words, if the MusicTrack parameter in the previous example was a structure rather than a class, the method would automatically receive a copy of the value, not a reference to a MusicTrack object. Note that this does not mean that you should use structures in preference to classes to improve security. By giving a method a reference to an object, you may be giving that method the ability to do things to the object that you might not want.

When creating copies of objects, you have to be aware of the implications of copying objects that contain references to other objects. In the case of the copy constructor in the MusicTrack class, the three properties of the MusicTrack are either value types (Length is an integer) or immutable (Artist and Title are strings). Changes to these items in the copy will not affect anything else.

However, if the MusicTrack class contained a reference to a Publisher object describing the company that publishes the music track, you would have to decide whether to copy the Publisher object in the copy constructor for MusicTrack, or to just copy the Publisher reference. If you copied the Publisher object in the MusicTrack copy constructor, you would be performing what is called a "deep copy" of a MusicTrack object, which is the name given to a copy process that also copies all of the objects referred to by an object being copied.

Performing a deep copy of the MusicTrack means that a method receiving the MusicTrack would not be able to change the properties of the Publisher for that MusicTrack. However, this would also mean that copying a MusicTrack would now be much slower, particularly if the Publisher object is large and contains references to other objects.

At this point you need to consider whether you "shallow copy" an object and run the risk that methods may able to change the object in ways that you don't want, or put in extra effort to make the object totally secure and "deep copy" it.

Risk and impact

This topic really ends up being a discussion of *risk* and *impact*, as do all security considerations. You need to decide how much risk you can tolerate at every point in your design. You also need to consider the impact of any failure of the security you have implemented to protect your objects.

It is unlikely that anyone would really want to change the artist name of a MusicTrack item (the risk is low), and the effect of a change would not be particularly dangerous (the impact is low too). However, if the MusicTrack item contained a price property, this would need to be regarded differently.

There is the potential for financial loss if someone, maliciously or inadvertently, changes the Price property of a MusicTrack, which means that this would have impact on the business. Furthermore, the risk that this could happen is high, because people might stand to benefit by a price change. This means that you have to put more effort into protecting the Price property than you put into protecting the Artist property, and you should make these decisions at the *start* of the development process.

Atomic actions

An action on a data item should be *atomic*. The word atomic in this context means "indivisible." For example, if you are creating a new MusicTrack item, don't perform this by setting the artist name of the new MusicTrack in one method, followed by the title of the MusicTrack in a second call. This would raise the possibility of the second method not running, and leaving the new MusicTrack object with incomplete data. You should have a single "atomic" action to add a new MusicTrack that will either succeed or fail. There should be no possibility of the action half-completing and leaving the object in an invalid state.

Evaluate a regular expression to validate the input format

Validation of strings of data coming into your program can be hard work. You know that the C# string type can provides methods that can be used to search a string for particular substrings;

take a look at Skill 2.7 for details of how you can do this. However, it would be hard to use just these methods to do things like validate dates, times, email addresses and telephone numbers.

Fortunately, C# contains an implementation of *regular expressions* that can be used to perform data validation. A regular expression is a means of expressing a string of characters that need to be matched in a target string. You can start by investigating how to use a regular expression to search for and replace elements in a text string.

String editing using regular expressions

A regular expression can be as simple as just a single character to match. Listing 3-6 shows how a single space can be used as a regular expression. The `Regex` object (which is in the `System.Text.RegularExpressions` namespace) provides a method called `Replace` that can be used to replace regular expressions in a source string. The `Replace` method is supplied with parameters that specify an input string, a regular expression to match, and a replacement string. When the program runs, all of the spaces in the input string are replaced with commas.

LISTING 3-6 Simple regular expression

```
string input = "Rob Mary David Jenny Chris Imogen Rodney";

string regularExpressionToMatch = " ";
string patternToReplace = ",";

string replaced = Regex.Replace(input, regularExpressionToMatch, patternToReplace);
```

The output of the program in Listing 3-6 is exactly what you'd expect. This means that if you need to perform any text replacement or editing, you will find it much easier to use a regular expression than to write the code yourself.

```
Rob,Mary,David,Jenny,Chris,Imogen,Rodney
```

You can use regular expressions to match more complex input strings. Perhaps you want to match a number of spaces, rather than just one space. In other words, you might have an input string as shown in Listing 3-7, where the names are separated by more than one space.

Listing 3-7 shows how to modify an expression to match one or more spaces in a string of names. The + character after an element is used as a *quantifier* in the regular expression. It creates an expression that matches that element one or more times. The regular expression can be used to replace any number of spaces in an element with a single comma.

LISTING 3-7 Match multiple spaces

```
string input = "Rob    Mary David   Jenny  Chris    Imogen       Rodney";

string regularExpressionToMatch = " +";

string patternToReplace = ",";

string replaced = Regex.Replace(input, regularExpressionToMatch, patternToReplace);
```

You can add other control characters that will allow the expression to match ranges of characters in complex combinations. You can also add repetition to allow the matching process to repeat over elements in a string. You can have a lot of fun creating regular expressions that match particular sequences of characters in the input string. This is how you can use them to validate incoming data.

Data validation using regular expressions

You can see how regular expressions can be made to validate incoming data by using a regular expression to perform validation of an incoming music track description. We could ask users to enter a music track as a single string, with the artist, title and length elements separated by colon characters, as shown in the following statement, which describes the input with the artist Rob Miles, title My Way, and length 120 seconds.

```
string input = "Rob Miles:My Way:120";
```

You can consider that a music track description is valid if it contains three items of text, with colon characters separating them. The regular expression matching such a description string looks as follows:

```
string regexToMatch = ".+:.+:.+";
```

The character . (period) in a regular expression means "match any character." The character + means "one or more of the previous item." So, the character sequence ".+" means "match one or more characters." The previous expression is made up of three "match any one or more character" items separated by colon characters. Listing 3-8 shows how this would be used in a program to validate a music track string. The method IsMatch accepts two strings. The first is the string being tested, and the second is the regular expression being used to test it. The IsMatch method returns True if the regular expression matches a substring in the string being tested.

LISTING 3-8 Validate a music track

```
string input = "Rob Miles:My Way:120";

string regexToMatch = ".+:.+:.+";

if (Regex.IsMatch(input, regexToMatch))
    Console.WriteLine("Valid music track description");
```

You can improve on the validation by ensuring that the string at the end of the music track description is numeric digits, as shown by the match string in Listing 3-9. The sequence [ch-ch] will match any character in that range, so the sequence [0-9] will match any digit, and the sequence [0-9]+ will match one or more digits. The character $ (dollar) means "anchor this character at the end of the string." It is there so that the music track description can't contain any non-digit characters after the track length.

LISTING 3-9 Validate track length

```
string regexToMatch = @".+:.+:[0-9]+$";
```

Note that we've used the @ prefix to the regular expression string. The @ prefix means that the string should be processed by the compiler as a *verbatim* string. In other words, the compiler will make no attempt to process any escape sequences in the string. This is a good idea because regular expressions frequently contain characters that may be regarded by the compiler as escape sequences.

We have still not achieved the perfect validation. Let's be sure that the Artist and Title items in the string contain only alphabetic characters. At the moment, they can contain any character, including the colon character, which will allow invalid track descriptions to be entered that contain multiple colon characters.

You can do this, creating our final, perfect validation as shown in Listing 3-10. This uses some more regular expression features. The ∧(circumflex) character means "the start of a line." The | (vertical bar) character means "or." It is used between alternative match values. It is how you create a validation string to match upper and lower-case letters, along with a space. This selection is enclosed in brackets so that it can be repeated using the + character.

LISTING 3-10 Perfect validation

```
string regexToMatch = @"^([a-z]|[A-Z]| )+:([a-z]|[A-Z]| )+:[0-9]+$";
```

Regular expressions can be very hard to read, because they contain a mix of commands and text to be matched. It is worth spending some time examining the previous expression. Regular expressions get more powerful when you discover that you can use count values, so you can match exact numbers of items. For full details of how to create regular expressions you can refer to *https://docs.microsoft.com/en-us/dotnet/standard/base-types/regular-expressions*.

Use built-in functions to validate data type and content

Defensive programming is a design approach which views an application as a castle that must be protected by a moat and a drawbridge and has guards that say "Halt. Who goes there?" to anyone trying to get inside. Anything coming towards the program is viewed as potentially malicious.

You should design input processing in such a way as to make sure that invalid values are detected and rejected. Regular expressions are a great way to ensure that data has a valid form, but there are also some built-in functions that are provided by C# to help with data validation.

Reading values

The simplest form of conversion is that of a string of digits into a numeric value. The C# numeric types all provide a Parse method that will convert a string into a number. The Parse method will not allow invalid strings to be converted into numbers, but it rejects invalid values by throwing an exception, which seems a little extreme. I reserve exceptions for events, which are more unexpected than a user typing 'o' instead of '0'. All numeric types also provide a TryParse method that will attempt to parse a string and return False if the parse fails. Listing 3-11 shows how TryParse can be used to read a number. The first parameter to TryParse is the string to be parsed. The second parameter is the variable that will receive the value. Note that the second parameter has been specified as an "out" parameter, which means that the `TryParse` method will be able to change the contents of the `result` variable, delivering the parsed value.

LISTING 3-11 Using TryParse

```
int result;

if (int.TryParse("99", out result))
    Console.WriteLine("This is a valid number");
else
    Console.WriteLine("This is not a valid number");
```

The C# library also contains a `Convert` class that can be used to convert between various types. Listing 3-12 shows how this can be used to convert strings into different types. Note that you can even convert strings into Boolean types. The `Convert` method will throw an exception if the conversion fails, but not if the input value is null.

LISTING 3-12 Using Convert

```
string stringValue = "99";

int intValue = Convert.ToInt32(stringValue);
Console.WriteLine("intValue: {0}", intValue);

stringValue = "True";
bool boolValue = Convert.ToBoolean(stringValue);
Console.WriteLine("boolValue: {0}", boolValue);
```

Here are some items to keep in mind whenconsidering the three different ways of converting values:

- `int.Parse` will throw an exception if the supplied argument is `null` or if a string does not contain text that represents a valid value.

- `int.TryParse` will return false if the supplied argument is null or if a string does not contain text that represents a valid value.

- `Convert.ToInt32` will throw an exception if the supplied string argument does not contain text that represents a valid value. It will not, however, throw an exception if the supplied argument is `null`. It instead returns the default value for that type. If the supplied argument is null the `ToInt32` method returns 0.

Validation in ASP.NET

The ASP.NET application created earlier in this chapter has some validation behaviors. The track length property in the `MusicTrack` class has been declared as an integer type, and the user interface that was generated by the scaffolding process contains validation that prevents the user from entering a track length that is not a number. However, we can improve the validation of the data by adding attributes to the model class. Listing 3-13 shows how to restrict the values of the track length property to between 20 and 600 seconds.

LISTING 3-13 ASP validation

```
public class MusicTrack
{
    public int ID { get; set; }
    public string Artist { get; set; }
    public string Title { get; set; }
    [Range(20,600)]
    public int Length { get; set; }
}
```

This attribute is used to provide the correct validation behaviors, as shown in Figure 3-16.

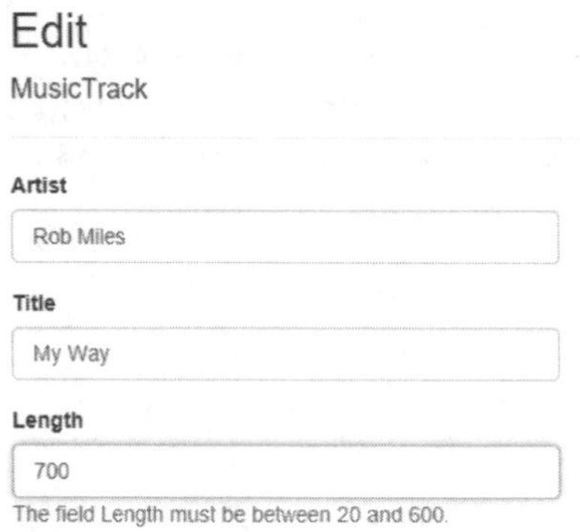

Edit

MusicTrack

Artist

Rob Miles

Title

My Way

Length

700

The field Length must be between 20 and 600.

FIGURE 3-16 Length property validation

Skill 3.2: Perform symmetric and asymmetric encryption

Secrets are a necessary part of life. Computers have been involved in the making and breaking of coded messages since the very start of computing. In this section we consider the fundamentals of modern encryption and how to use the encryption libraries that are part of .NET.

When you create a new application, you need to consider how much effort you need to put into ensuring that the transfer and storage of the data in the application is performed in a secure way. It is important that you identify situations where data security is required.

For example, if you were writing a game, you might think that performance considerations would be paramount, and because it is only a game there is no need to worry about secure communications and data storage. As long as the game works reliably, it doesn't seem worth spending a lot of time to ensure that the data is protected in any way.

This, however, would be very wrong. There have been numerous examples of unscrupulous players tampering with saved data and messages exchanged during large multi-player games. This allows the players to cheat, acquiring skills and game items that they would otherwise have had to earn through many hours of gameplay. You should consider the impact of data security breaches as another part of the risk management you perform on a project.

There are two other things you should remember when considering how to implement security in your applications. The first is that you should never, ever, try to implement your own security using code that you have written. The .NET framework contains "battle hardened" routines that have "industrial strength." Your code will never be as good as this, and it will in fact be highly vulnerable to attack. The second thing to consider is that you should never try to implement "security through obscurity." Using names of files that you don't think anyone would guess or hiding security information in out of the way pieces of code or data does not add any security to your application, it just adds the illusion of security.

This section covers how to:

- Choose an appropriate encryption algorithm
- Manage and create certificates
- Implement key management
- Implement the System.Security namespace
- Hashing data
- Encrypt streams

Cryptography and cryptoanalysis

Cryptography is the business of rending a message unreadable to anyone except for the proper recipient of the message. Cryptoanalysis is the business of code breaking.

Cryptography involves taking the original message and *encrypting* it to generate a version that can be safely transferred over an open network. The recipient will perform *decryption* of the message to recover the original contents. Anyone else who gets a copy of the encrypted message will be unable to make any sense of it. Early encryption techniques involved letter substitution (perhaps changing every letter for a different one agreed upon between sender and recipient) or re-arranging the order of the letters according to a sequence agreed between sender and recipient.

Cryptoanalysis involves examining an encrypted message and looking for statistical patterns in it that reflect the language and conventions of the sender. Once these patterns have been detected they can be used as the basis of attempts to "break" a code by performing repeated guesses as to the encryption method until the original message is retrieved. It turns out that computers are very good at cryptoanalysis. Fortunately, they are quite good at encrypting data as well.

Symmetric and asymmetric encryption

One of my favorite encryption techniques is a very secure one that uses nothing more than a printed book. The sender and the recipient each have a copy of the book and they encrypt their messages by sending each letter in a message as two numbers, a page number in the book and a letter number on that page. The recipient just has to look up the letters in their copy of the book to decrypt the message.

Unless an eavesdropper has exactly the same copy of the book, they will be unable to break the code. Statistical cryptoanalysis doesn't work on our messages because we can encrypt the same letter in many different ways. This technique has been used by real spies and works well. The only way to break it is to perform a thorough search of the suspect's house and look for well-thumbed copies of books.

The book is the *key* to the encryption and decryption process. This is called *symmetric* encryption, because the key at each side of the conversation is exactly the same—the book. The only problem with this technique is that if you want to talk securely to someone new you have to send them a copy of the book you are using as the key. If someone sees the book arrive and gets their own copy, they can easily break the code.

Computers can also use *symmetric* keys to encrypt and decrypt data. The sender uses a key (which in this case is a package of numbers) to encrypt the data, and the recipient uses the same key to decrypt it. However, the computer has the same problem with its digital key that we have with a book key. Before you can send any messages, you need to make sure that both ends of the conversation have the same key.

It turns out that by the use of clever mathematics you can perform encryption and decryption using two different keys. Messages encrypted by one key can be decrypted using the other one. They are called *asymmetric* keys because the keys at each end of the conversation are different.

The only problem is that encrypting and decrypting messages using asymmetric keys is hard work for a computer. Sending very long messages using asymmetric keys requires a lot of computer processing power and very long keys. Using symmetric keys is far easier. You can, however, get around this issue by combining the use of symmetric and asymmetric keys to send messages.

Start by making one of your asymmetric key pairs a *public* key. You can give your public key to anyone that you want to have a secure conversation with. The other key you keep *private*. Anyone with the public key can decrypt messages that have been encrypted with the private key. And, anyone with the public key can encrypt messages that only you can read, because you're using the private key to decrypt them.

Conversing using asymmetric keys

When explaining how an encrypted conversation works, it is the convention to use the names Alice and Bob as the two people who want to have a private conversation, and Eve as the eavesdropper trying to listen in. With that in mind; Let's consider how Alice and Bob can use asymmetric keys to talk in private.

1. At the start of the conversation Alice and Bob each make an asymmetric pair of keys. They nominate one of their keys public and the other private.

2. Alice and Bob then exchange their public keys over an open network. Eve, of course, obtains copies of these.

3. Alice and Bob now each create a symmetric key. Alice uses Bob's public key to encrypt her symmetric key and send it to Bob. Eve, of course, gets a copy of this encrypted message but, because she doesn't have Bob's private key, she can't decrypt it and obtain the symmetric key.

4. Bob uses his private key to decrypt the message containing Alice's symmetric key and can then use this to efficiently encrypt a long message to Alice. Alice can do the same if Bob uses her public key to send her an encrypted symmetric key.

5. Eve, in the middle, can only see encrypted messages. The conversation between Alice and Bob is private.

This combination of asymmetric keys to set up the conversation, and symmetric keys to transfer the data, underpins secure conversations on the Internet.

Using asymmetric keys to "sign" messages

Another use for asymmetric keys is for "signing" messages. A message encoded by a private key can only be decoded by the matching public key. Consider how this can be used to allow Bob to send Alice a "signed" document.

1. Bob creates a document and also a signature or "message digest" that describes the message. The signature is a tiny piece of data that can be used to authenticate the document. The simplest form can be a "checksum," which is a number calculated by adding together the codes of all the characters in the message. (Note that a checksum is a very poor message digest, but we will consider much better ones later).

2. Bob sends Alice three things: his signed document, the signature encrypted using his private key, and his public key.

3. Alice can use the public key she receives from Bob to decrypt the message digest and compare it with one that she has calculated for the document she received. If the two match she can be sure that the document came from Bob. She can also be sure that the document she received has not been tampered with, as any changes would cause her calculated message digest to differ from the one she received in the message digest.

The signing of documents can be extended to cover items such as software downloads and system updates. It is how you can be sure that messages that you receive are actually from the correct person.

Now that you have an understanding of the issues surrounding the use of cryptography you can consider how this all works on .NET. The choice of which encryption algorithm you use depends on what you want to do with it. Let's take a look at a few encryption scenarios and consider how to encrypt them.

Data encryption using AES symmetric encryption

The Advanced Encryption Standard (AES) is used worldwide to encrypt data. It supersedes the Data Encryption Standard (DES). It is a symmetric encryption system. You use the same key to encrypt and decrypt the data. Listing 3-14 shows how to encrypt a string of text using the Aes class in the System.Security.Cryptography namespace. The encryption process is implemented as a stream. The program below creates an encryption stream and writes the super-secret message to that stream. The stream is created from an instance of the Aes class. Plenty of comments have been added so you can better understand what is happening. If you're unsure of how streams work, take a look at Skill 4.1, "Perform I/O operations."

LISTING 3-14 AES encryption

```
using System;
using System.IO;
using System.Security.Cryptography;

namespace LISTING_3_14_AES_encryption
{
    class Program
    {
        static void DumpBytes(string title, byte [] bytes)
        {
            Console.Write(title);
            foreach (byte b in bytes)
            {
                Console.Write("{0:X} ", b);
            }
            Console.WriteLine();
        }

        static void Main(string[] args)
        {
            string plainText = "This is my super secret data";

            // byte array to hold the encrypted message
            byte[] cipherText;

            // byte array to hold the key that was used for encryption
            byte[] key;

            // byte array to hold the initialization vector that was used for encryption
            byte[] initializationVector;

            // Create an Aes instance
            // This creates a random key and initialization vector

            using (Aes aes = Aes.Create())
            {
                // copy the key and the initialization vector
                key = aes.Key;
                initializationVector = aes.IV;

                // create an encryptor to encrypt some data
                // should be wrapped in using for production code
                ICryptoTransform encryptor = aes.CreateEncryptor();

                // Create a new memory stream to receive the
```

```
            // encrypted data.

            using (MemoryStream encryptMemoryStream = new MemoryStream())
            {
                // create a CryptoStream, tell it the stream to write to
                // and the encryptor to use. Also set the mode
                using (CryptoStream encryptCryptoStream =
                        new CryptoStream(encryptMemoryStream,
                                encryptor, CryptoStreamMode.Write))
                {
                    // make a stream writer from the cryptostream
                    using (StreamWriter swEncrypt =
                            new StreamWriter(encryptCryptoStream))
                    {
                        //Write the secret message to the stream.
                        swEncrypt.Write(plainText);
                    }
                    // get the encrypted message from the stream
                    cipherText= encryptMemoryStream.ToArray();
                }
            }

            // Dump out our data
            Console.WriteLine("String to encrypt: {0}", plainText);
            dumpBytes("Key: ", key);
            dumpBytes("Initialization Vector: ", initializationVector);
            dumpBytes("Encrypted: ", cipherText);

            Console.ReadKey();
        }
    }
}
```

The encrypted messages (and the keys that are used to perform the encryption) are stored in arrays of bytes. The program in Listing 3-14 contains the method dumpBytes, which it calls to dump the contents of these arrays. When running the program, the following output is created. The top line is the original message string, followed by the key that was automatically created for the new Aes instance. The next line is the *initialization vector* for the encryption. And the final line is the encrypted data. Note that I've only shown the first few bytes of the values in the output below.

```
String to encrypt: This is my super secret data
Key: 93 47 98 6F 67 10 B0 20 4A 90 9C FC 6 2F 36 71 A7 BB 63 4C
Initialization Vector: CB CA 76 D6 A5 F4 3E 21 29 5 95 8 67 26 E 26
Encrypted: AD BC A9 E4 71 3F  A6 51 F1 F8 85 D6 80 1A 26 D3 A8
```

The initialization vector adds security to a particular key value by specifying a random start point in the stream of encryption values that will be produced to encrypt the input. If every encryption stars at the beginning of the encryption stream, there is a chance that the repeated use of a particular encryption key provides a large enough set of encrypted messages for an eavesdropper to break the code. By using a different initialization vector for each message, you can remove this possibility. The receiver of the message will need both the key and the initialization vector value to decrypt the code.

Listing 3-15 shows how to use an Aes instance to decrypt an array of bytes. It is the reverse of the process shown in Listing 3-14. It creates a stream from the array of bytes that contain the encrypted data. The listing shows the decryption part of the process; the first half of the example is the same code as you can see in Listing 3-14.

LISTING 3-15 AES decryption

```
// Now do the decryption
string decryptedText;

using (Aes aes = Aes.Create())
{
    // Configure the aes instances with the key and
    // initialization vector to use for the decryption
    aes.Key = key;
    aes.IV = initializationVector;

    // Create a decryptor from aes
    // should be wrapped in using for production code
    ICryptoTransform decryptor = aes.CreateDecryptor();

    using (MemoryStream decryptStream = new MemoryStream(cipherText))
    {
        using (CryptoStream decryptCryptoStream =
            new CryptoStream(decryptStream, decryptor, CryptoStreamMode.Read))
        {
            using (StreamReader srDecrypt = new StreamReader(decryptCryptoStream))
            {
                // Read the decrypted bytes from the decrypting stream
                // and place them in a string.
                decryptedText = srDecrypt.ReadToEnd();
            }
        }
    }
}
```

The Aes class provides options that allow you to set the length of the key to use. If you want greater security you can use longer keys, but this will slow down the encryption and decryption process.

Encrypting data using other symmetric standards

The encryption process in .NET is an example of good class design. All of the encryption classes, including Aes, are extensions of the base class SymmetricAlgorithm, which is in the System.Security.Cryptography namespace. There are a number of other encryption implementations that you can use in your program including the Data Encryption Standard (DES), RC2, Rijndael, and Triple DES.

The Data Encryption Standard (DES) was developed in the 1970s. Advances in computer power and cryptoanalysis (code cracking) mean that this standard is now regarded as insecure.

There are libraries available for the use of DES in .NET and the encryption process is performed in exactly the same way as with the AES standard described next. You should only use DES encryption for compatibility with legacy systems. Any new systems requiring data encryption should use AES.

RC2 is another encryption technology that is supported by .NET, but is now regarded as insecure. Again, you should only use this in your applications if you are working with an existing system that uses this encryption.

Rijndael is the cypher on which AES was based. AES is implemented as a subset of Rijndael. If you want to access all the features of Rijndael you can use this class.

TripleDES improves on the security of the DES standard by encrypting the incoming data three times in succession using three different keys. The electronic payment industry makes use of TripleDES.

Use RSA asymmetric encryption to create public and private keys

RSA (Rivest–Shamir–Adleman) is a very popular asymmetric encryption standard. The RSACryptoServiceProvider class in the System.Security.Cryptography namespace will perform encryption and decryption of data using this standard.

Listing 3-16 shows encryption and decryption of data using this class. The RSACryptoServiceProvider instance provides Encrypt and Decrypt methods to encrypt and decrypt byte arrays. In Listing 3-16 the public key from a newly created RSACryptoServiceProvider instance is used to perform encryption. The program then uses the private key from the key pair to encrypt the encrypted message.

LISTING 3-16 RSA encryption

```
using System;
using System.Security.Cryptography;
using System.Text;

namespace LISTING_3_16_RSA_encryption
{
    class Program
    {
        static void Main(string[] args)
        {
            string plainText = "This is my super secret data";
            Console.WriteLine("Plain text: {0}", plainText);

            // RSA works on byte arrays, not strings of text
            // This will convert our input string into bytes and back
            ASCIIEncoding converter = new ASCIIEncoding();

            // Convert the plain text into a byte array
            byte[] plainBytes = converter.GetBytes(plainText);

            dumpBytes("Plain bytes: ", plainBytes);

            byte[] encryptedBytes;
```

```
            byte[] decryptedBytes;

            // Create a new RSA to encrypt the data
            // should be wrapped in using for production code
            RSACryptoServiceProvider rsaEncrypt = new RSACryptoServiceProvider();

            // get the keys out of the encryptor
            string publicKey = rsaEncrypt.ToXmlString(includePrivateParameters: false);
            Console.WriteLine("Public key: {0}", publicKey);
            string privateKey = rsaEncrypt.ToXmlString(includePrivateParameters: true);
            Console.WriteLine("Private key: {0}", privateKey);

            // Now tell the encyryptor to use the public key to encrypt the data
            rsaEncrypt.FromXmlString(privateKey);

            // Use the encryptor to encrypt the data. The fOAEP parameter
            // specifies how the output is "padded" with extra bytes
            // For maximum compatibility with receiving systems, set this as
            // false
            encryptedBytes = rsaEncrypt.Encrypt(plainBytes, fOAEP:false);

            dumpBytes("Encrypted bytes: ", encryptedBytes);

            // Now do the decode - use the private key for this
            // We have sent someone our public key and they
            // have used this to encrypt data that they are sending to us

            // Create a new RSA to decrypt the data
            // should be wrapped in using for production code
            RSACryptoServiceProvider rsaDecrypt = new RSACryptoServiceProvider();

            // Configure the decryptor from the XML in the private key
            rsaDecrypt.FromXmlString(privateKey);

            decryptedBytes = rsaDecrypt.Decrypt(encryptedBytes, fOAEP: false);

            dumpBytes("Decrypted bytes: ", decryptedBytes);
            Console.WriteLine("Decrypted string: {0}",
                            converter.GetString(decryptedBytes));

            Console.ReadKey();
        }
    }
}
```

Implementing public and private key management

The RSACryptoServiceProvider class provides methods that can be used to extract the public and private keys from an instance. These can then be sent to a recipient who can use them to encrypt and decrypt messages. The ToXmlString method will return either the public or the public and private keys, depending on the value of a Boolean argument. This statement used in Listing 3-16, gets the key information out of the variable rsaEncrypt.

```
string privateKey = rsaEncrypt.ToXmlString(includePrivateParameters: true);
```

Once the XML has been sent to the recipient it can be used to configure an RSACryptoSer-viceProvider instance by using the FromXmlString method. This statement used in Listing 3-16, configures the rsaDecript instance of RSACryptoServiceProvider using the private key that was created.

```
rsaDecrypt.FromXmlString(privateKey);
```

This works well, but it means that the user of the encryption service has to find a secure place to store the key file. It is important that this is stored somewhere safe, because it contains the private key.

User level key storage

There is a secure key storage facility provided for each user of a computer. When you create a new RSACryptoServiceProvider instance you can tell the instance to use a particular loca-tion in this storage to save and load keys. The CspParameters class from the System.Security.Cryptography can be used to specify the storage location. Listing 3-17 shows how this is used. The ContainerName property of the CsParameters instance is set to the name of this container.

LISTING 3-17 RSA key management

```
using System;
using System.Security.Cryptography;


namespace LISTING_3_17_RSA_key_management
{
    class Program
    {
        static void Main(string[] args)
        {
            string containerName = "MyKeyStore";

            CspParameters csp = new CspParameters();
            csp.KeyContainerName = containerName;

            // Create a new RSA to encrypt the data
            RSACryptoServiceProvider rsaStore = new RSACryptoServiceProvider(csp);
            Console.WriteLine("Stored keys: {0}",
                            rsaStore.ToXmlString(includePrivateParameters: true));

            RSACryptoServiceProvider rsaLoad = new RSACryptoServiceProvider(csp);
            Console.WriteLine("Loaded keys: {0}",
                            rsaLoad.ToXmlString(includePrivateParameters: true));

            Console.ReadKey();
        }
    }
}
```

When you run this program, you will see that it prints out the same set of key values. Note that we've only printed out the public keys in this example to save space.

```
Stored keys: <RSAKeyValue><Modulus>xiqNeO5Tgjaj+Q9aToJ4VLOSTW/
nKGHcAbpHYafAxOUgoD8pdcyHXU
5dhlOWmv+3+u2GMO3yKDrF6SEMQc7lR38FcPRNGFEV+3ZiAQqtTFbtNa7cdLer+QwVBnP3KOMNLz3
xedBtpQflr1JHfmT653tdusYo/JUSOIRzcDrcewE=</Modulus><Exponent>AQAB</Exponent>
</RSAKeyValue> Loaded keys: <RSAKeyValue><Modulus>xiqNeO5Tgjaj+Q9aToJ4VLOSTW/
nKGHcAbpHYafAxOUgoD8pdcyHXU5dhlOWmv+3+u2GMO3yKDrF6SEMQc7lR38FcPRNGFEV+3ZiAQq
tTFbtNa7cdLer+QwVBnP3KOMNLz3xedBtpQflr1JHfmT653tdusYo/JUSOIRzcDrcewE=
</Modulus><Exponent>AQAB</Exponent></RSAKeyValue>
```

If you want to delete a stored key you can set the PersistKeyInCsP property of the RSACryptoServiceProvider instance to False and then clear the service as shown in Listing 3-18.

LISTING 3-18 RSA stored key clear

```
rsaStore.PersistKeyInCsp = false;
rsaStore.Clear();
```

Machine level key storage

User level key storage is fine if a machine only has one user, but if keys are to be shared among many users, they should be stored at a machine level. Windows implements machine level key storage in a folder that contains a file for each key. The path to this folder on Windows 10 is usually C:\ProgramData\Microsoft\Crypto\RSA\MachineKeys. The program in Listing 3-19 creates a machine level key. If you run it you'll notice a new file appears in the key folder.

LISTING 3-19 Machine level keys

```
CspParameters cspParams = new CspParameters();
cspParams.KeyContainerName = "Machine Level Key";

// Specify that the key is to be stored in the machine level key store
cspParams.Flags = CspProviderFlags.UseMachineKeyStore;

// Create a crypto service provider
RSACryptoServiceProvider rsa = new RSACryptoServiceProvider(cspParams);

Console.WriteLine(rsa.ToXmlString(includePrivateParameters: false));

// Make sure that it is persisting keys
rsa.PersistKeyInCsp = true;
// Clear the provider to make sure it saves the key
rsa.Clear();
```

Once the keys have been saved, they will be loaded from the store the next time the program runs. A machine level key is removed in just the same way as a user key, by setting the PersistKeyInCsp property to false.

Digital signatures and certificates

You may have noticed a significant flaw in our use of public and private keys to provide secure communication. The flaw concerns identity validation. Consider that one day Alice receives a message that is supposed to be from Bob. It contains a public key that she can use to encrypt messages to Bob and use to validate messages from Bob that have been signed by him.

But how does Alice know that this message actually came from Bob? Eve could be pretending to be Bob and trying to get Alice to have an encrypted conversation with her. Or, worse still, a really sneaky Eve could intercept a message from Bob to start a conversation and reply to the message instead of Alice. Alice could be receiving a public key that is being sent by Eve pretending to be Bob. Eve could be sitting in the middle, using the "real" public key she received from Bob and then re-encrypting the messages and passing them on to Alice.

Without some form of identity validation, Alice has no way of knowing whether the sender of a message is who they claim to be. What you need is an authority that can be used to validate the identity of the sender of a message. There are a number of *Certification Authorities* that do this for the Internet. Certification authorities produce *digital certificates* for use when signing messages. Bob can register with a certification authority, providing his details upon request. Alice can ask the relevant authority for the public portion of Bob's certificate and use this to validate a message claiming to come from him. This process is used every time your computer contacts a web site. Your computer contains a list of certification authorities and also provides a certificate store.

Signing documents using certificates

You can test code that uses certificates to sign documents. The first thing you need to do is create a test certificate. This can't be used for real identity validation because it was created by us, and not a trusted certification authority, but it is good enough to show how the process works.

The Visual Studio developer command prompt provides access to a program called makecert, which will make an X.509 certificate. To create a single certificate file, open the developer prompt and issue the following command:

```
makecert democert.cer
```

Note that you will need to create this certificate in a folder where you have write permissions. The certificate is stored in a file. You can also put our certificates into the certificate store on your machine. The following command creates a certificate with the name "RobMiles" in a certificate store called "demoCertStore."

```
makecert -n "CN=RobMiles" -sr currentuser -ss demoCertStore
```

Once you've created your certificate, you can use it to perform encryption and also sign documents. You can think of the certificate store as very similar to the machine key storage used earlier, but the certificate store contains trusted items. Of course, in this case the certificate is not backed by any certification authority, but you can still demonstrate your code using it. The program in Listing 3-20 uses the certificate that you just created to sign a message. It uses the SHA1 hashing algorithm, which we'll cover more later in this chapter.

LISTING 3-20 Signing data

```
using System;
using System.Security.Cryptography.X509Certificates;
using System.Security.Cryptography;
using System.Text;

namespace LISTING_3_20_Signing_data
{
    class Program
    {
        static void Main(string[] args)
        {
            // This will convert our input string into bytes and back
            ASCIIEncoding converter = new ASCIIEncoding();

            // Get a crypto provider out of the certificate store
            // should be wrapped in using for production code
            X509Store store = new X509Store("demoCertStore", StoreLocation.CurrentUser);

            store.Open(OpenFlags.ReadOnly);

            // should be wrapped in using for production code
            X509Certificate2 certificate = store.Certificates[0];

            // should be wrapped in using for production code
            RSACryptoServiceProvider encryptProvider =
                        certificate.PrivateKey as RSACryptoServiceProvider;

            string messageToSign = "This is the message I want to sign";
            Console.WriteLine("Message: {0}", messageToSign);

            byte[] messageToSignBytes = converter.GetBytes(messageToSign);
            dumpBytes("Message to sign in bytes: ", messageToSignBytes);

            // need to calculate a hash for this message - this will go into the
            // signature and be used to verify the message
            // Create an implementation of the hashing algorithm we are going to use
            // should be wrapped in using for production code
            HashAlgorithm hasher = new SHA1Managed();
            // Use the hasher to hash the message
            byte[] hash = hasher.ComputeHash(messageToSignBytes);
            dumpBytes("Hash for message: ", hash);

            // Now sign the hash to create a signature
            byte[] signature = encryptProvider.SignHash(hash,CryptoConfig.
            MapNameToOID("SHA1"));
            dumpBytes("Signature: ", messageToSignBytes);

            // We can send the signature along with the message to authenticate it
            // Create a decryptor that uses the public key
            // should be wrapped in using for production code
```

```
                RSACryptoServiceProvider decryptProvider =
                                certificate.PublicKey.Key as RSACryptoServiceProvider;

                // Now use the signature to perform a successful validation of the message
                bool validSignature = decryptProvider.VerifyHash(hash,
                    CryptoConfig.MapNameToOID("SHA1"), signature);
                Console.WriteLine("Correct signature validated OK: {0}", validSignature);

                // Change one byte of the signature
                signature[0] = 99;
                // Now try the using the incorrect signature to validate the message
                bool invalidSignature = decryptProvider.VerifyHash(hash,
                                    CryptoConfig.MapNameToOID("SHA1"), signature);
                Console.WriteLine("Incorrect signature validated OK: {0}",
                                    invalidSignature);

                Console.ReadKey();
            }
        }
    }
```

When running the program in Listing 3-20 we receive the following output. Your output will differ slightly because your encryption will use different key values, but you should see that the signature validation fails if the content of the signature is changed in any way.

```
Message: This is the message I want to sign Message to sign in bytes: 54 68 69 73
 20 69 73 20 74 68 65 20 6D 65 73 73 61 67 65 20 49 20 77 61 6E 74 20 74 6F 20 73
 69 67 6E Hash for message: 26 6D C4 45 37 CC 44 B1 C2 3D 3B 86 29 92 B7 5C BF 4D
 1C E9 Signature: 54 68 69 73 20 69 73 20 74 68 65 20 6D 65 73 73 61 67 65 20 49
 20 77 61 6E 74 20 74 6F 20 73 69 67 6E
Correct signature validated OK: True
Incorrect signature validated OK: False
```

The recipient of a signed message uses the hash algorithm and the public key of the sender to calculate the hash of the message and then compare it with the hash value received in the signature. If they are different, the message has been changed or does not come from the expected sender.

Implement the System.Security namespace

The System.Security namespace contains the cryptography classes that can be used to en-crypt and decrypt data. As you have already seen, all the encryption classes are extensions of the abstract base class SymmetricAlgorithm. If you want to implement your own encryption technology you can create an encryption class that extends the SymmetricAlgorithm class and implements its own encryption and decryption. Your class can then be used interchangeably with other encryption classes on your machine. As previously mentioned, you are strongly encouraged not to do this.

This namespace also contains classes that underpin file access permissions as well as the cryptography namespace that contains the algorithms we've already been using.

Data integrity by hashing data

Hashing has been previously covered, when it was used to create a hash code in the signature of a document. Now we are going to take a look at hashing in more detail. You "hash" a large lump of data to create a, hopefully small, lump of data that is distinctive for the large lump. Earlier in this document we considered that the checksum of a data item might be a good start for a hash code. We can calculate the checksum of a string very easily. The method calculateChecksum in Listing 3-21 accepts a string and calculates an integer, which is the checksum of that string.

LISTING 3-21 Checksums

```
using System;

namespace LISTING_3_21_Checksums
{
    class Program
    {
        static int calculateChecksum(string source)
        {
            int total = 0;
            foreach (char ch in source)
                total = total + (int)ch;
            return total;
        }

        static void showChecksum(string source)
        {
            Console.WriteLine("Checksum for {0} is {1}",
                source, calculateChecksum(source));
        }

        static void Main(string[] args)
        {
            showChecksum("Hello world");
            showChecksum("world Hello");
            showChecksum("Hemmm world");

            Console.ReadKey();
        }
    }
}
```

The problem is that a checksum calculation does not take into account the order of the characters in a string. The strings "Hello world" and "world Hello" have exactly the same checksum. Also, it is easy to change the characters in the string without affecting the checksum. "Hemmm world" has exactly the same checksum as "Hello world" because we've added one to the character code for the letters "l" in the text and removed two from the character code for the letter "o." The output from the program in Listing 3-12 shows that all of the strings have the same checksum.

```
Checksum for Hello world is 1084
Checksum for world Hello is 1084
Checksum for Hemmm world is 1084
```

A hashing algorithm will weight the values in the source data according to their positions in the data, so that these kinds of changes result in different hash codes being calculated. All C# objects provide a GetHash() method that will return an integer hash value for that object.

The object type provides a GetHash() method that returns a hash value based on the location of that object in memory. When you create a new class you should consider adding a GetHash() method that returns a hash value based on the contents of that object. The string type provides a GetHash() method that uses the contents of the string to calculate a hash value. The showHash method in Listing 3-22 calculates and shows the hash values for the three strings.

LISTING 3-22 Hashing

```
static void showHash(object source)
{
    Console.WriteLine("Hash for {0} is: {1:X}", source, source.GetHashCode());
}
```

The hash values for the three strings are printed out as shown next. Note that these are the values for my machine. If you run the program on your machine you might see different values, depending on the version of the .NET library you're using.

```
Hash for Hello world is: 9D031388
Hash for world Hello is: FC27011E
Hash for Hemmm world is: 1446FEC7
```

The hash value provided by the GetHash() method is a single integer value, which is held in four bytes of memory. The hash value is therefore going to be smaller than the data being hashed. In fact, in the case of a large object, the size of the hash value will be a tiny fraction of the size of the data being hashed. This means that a given hash value will correspond to more than one source file. The hashing algorithm provided by GetHash() is good enough for use in programs so that you only want to use the hash value of an object for indexing and searching, but for cryptographic applications you need a hashing algorithm that produces a larger hash value.

MD5 hashing

The MD (Message Digest) 5 algorithm was created in 1991 to replace MD4. It produces a hash code that is 16 bytes (128) bits in size. It has been shown that it is possible to create different documents that both have the same MD5 hash code, which means that the algorithm should not be used for cryptographic purposes such as document signing.

MD5 can, however, be used to detect data corruption. Corruption due to failure of a storage medium or bit errors during transmission of data is an example. The main advantage MD5 has over other hashing algorithms is that it is fast.

SHA1 hashing

Secure Hash Algorithm (SHA) 1 is a hash algorithm that produces a 20 byte (160 bit) hash code value. While it is better than MD5 (and used it in Listing 3-20) it has been shown to be vulnerable to brute force attack (where an attacker tries to replicate a given hash code by trying many different data files).

SHA2 hashing

SHA2 improves on SHA1 and is actually a family of six hash functions that can produce outputs that are 224, 256, 384 or 512 bits in size. The code in Listing 3-23 uses the SHA2 algorithm to produce a 256-bit hash value.

LISTING 3-23 SHA2

```
using System;
using System.Security.Cryptography;
using System.Text;

namespace LISTING_3_23_SHA2
{
    class Program
    {
        static byte[] calculateHash(string source)
        {
            // This will convert our input string into bytes and back
            ASCIIEncoding converter = new ASCIIEncoding();
            byte[] sourceBytes = converter.GetBytes(source);

            HashAlgorithm hasher = SHA256.Create();
            byte[] hash = hasher.ComputeHash(sourceBytes);
            return hash;
        }

        static void showHash(string source)
        {
            Console.Write("Hash for {0} is: ", source);

            byte[] hash = calculateHash(source);

            foreach (byte b in hash)
                Console.Write("{0:X} ", b);
            Console.WriteLine();
        }

        static void Main(string[] args)
        {
            showHash("Hello world");
            showHash("world Hello");
            showHash("Hemmm world");

            Console.ReadKey();
        }
    }
}
```

The output of this program is as follows. Note that in this case the key is much longer than the document, so you would normally apply the hashing to a much larger dataset.

```
Hash for Hello world is: 64 EC 88 CA 0 B2 68 E5 BA 1A 35 67 8A 1B 53 16 D2
 12 F4 F3 66 B2 47 72 32 53 4A 8A EC A3 7F 3C Hash for world Hello is: E9
 70 A EE E8 36 FD A3 6 9D A4 D1 E1 6D 1B 4C 3C 60 D0 55 C4 A2 E6 8D DF 6A
 C9 A9 D0 D6 71 B2 Hash for Hemmm world is: A1 FB 33 49 44 B 34 28 A4 44 32
 72 A5 2B 8D 87 63 54 10 92 DE D6 EA 28 4C A9 78 48 4E 5E D9 86
```

The SHA2 algorithm is vulnerable to "length extension attacks," where a malicious person can add to the end of an existing document without changing the hash code. The SHA3 standard addresses this, but it is not presently available from the Security.Cryptography namespace. If you need to use SHA3, there are implementations available on GitHub.

Encrypting streams

The symmetric encryption shown in Listing 3-14 uses a CryptoStream object that acts as a Stream object and can be chained together with other objects that implement the behavior of a stream. If you are unsure of the use of streams, you can find out more in Skill 4-1, "Perform I/O operations."

In the case of the example in Listing 3-14 we used MemoryStream instances to connect to the CryptoStream, but you can connect a stream type to any other stream type. You can even chain CryptoStream instances together so that you can implement additional security by "double encrypting" data. Listing 3-24 shows how to perform double encryption using two Aes instances, two symmetric keys, and two initialization vectors. I've not included the decryption, but it is in the example source file that you can download.

LISTING 3-24 Encrypt a stream

```
string plainText = "This is my super super secret data";

// byte array to hold the encrypted message
byte[] encryptedText;

// byte arrays to hold the key that was used for encryption
byte[] key1;
byte[] key2;

// byte array to hold the initialization vector that was used for encryption
byte[] initializationVector1;
byte[] initializationVector2;

using (Aes aes1 = Aes.Create())
{
    // copy the key and the initialization vector
    key1 = aes1.Key;
    initializationVector1 = aes1.IV;

    // create an encryptor to encrypt some data
    ICryptoTransform encryptor1 = aes1.CreateEncryptor();
```

```csharp
// Create a new memory stream to receive the
// encrypted data.

using (MemoryStream encryptMemoryStream = new MemoryStream())
{
    // create a CryptoStream, tell it the stream to write to
    // and the encryptor to use. Also set the mode
    using (CryptoStream cryptoStream1 = new CryptoStream(encryptMemoryStream,
        encryptor1, CryptoStreamMode.Write))
    {
        // Add another layer of encryption
        using (Aes aes2 = Aes.Create())
        {
            // copy the key and the initialization vector
            key2 = aes2.Key;
            initializationVector2 = aes2.IV;

            ICryptoTransform encryptor2 = aes2.CreateEncryptor();

            using (CryptoStream cryptoStream2 = new CryptoStream(cryptoStream1,
                                                encryptor2, CryptoStreamMode.Write))
            {
                using (StreamWriter swEncrypt = new StreamWriter(cryptoStream2))
                {
                    //Write the secret message to the stream.
                    swEncrypt.Write(plainText);
                }
                // get the encrypted message from the stream
                encryptedText = encryptMemoryStream.ToArray();
            }
        }
    }
}
```

Skill 3.3: Manage assemblies

An assembly is an individual component of an application. It can be either an executable program (in which case it will have the language extension ".exe") or it will be a dynamically loaded library (in which case it will have the language extension ".dll").

Figure 3-17 shows the role played by assembly files in running applications within .NET. The programmer creates the source code for the program, along with assets that are required by the application, and are combined by the Visual Studio compiler to produce assembly file outputs. These assembly files contain programs expressed in Microsoft Intermediate Language (MSIL), along with the assets. When an application is executed by the .NET runtime, a Just In Time (JIT) compiler converts the intermediate language files into machine code that can be obeyed by the underlying computer hardware.

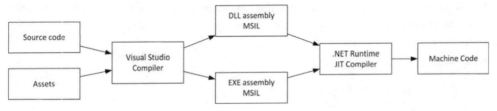

FIGURE 3-17 Assemblies in .NET

There are two very important things to remember about assembly files. The first is that the contents of an assembly file are independent of the language that was used to create it. A single application can be made up of assemblies that have been compiled from C#, F#, and Visual Basic source code files.

The second thing to remember is that the intermediate language is independent of the particular hardware that will actually be running the program. There is an additional compilation stage that converts the MSIL code stored in the assembly into the machine code that runs on the host computer. This takes place just before a method in an assembly is executed and is called *Just in Time* (JIT) compilation.

These two features of .NET are very powerful. You can write applications that contain elements written in different languages (because each source file is compiled into an assembly that contains MSIL). You can run the assembly on a Windows PC, an Xbox, or a mobile device (because the MSIL code in the assembly is compiled into machine code on the target device).

You can see how to use assemblies in a C# application by creating an application that uses a dynamically loaded library. You can regard an assembly as the output of a Visual Studio project. A Visual Studio solution can contain multiple projects. Figure 3-18 shows a solution that contains two projects; one is an application and the other is a library.

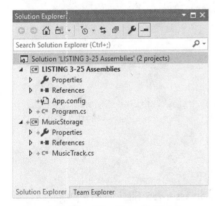

FIGURE 3-18 Visual Studio projects

The project MusicStorage contains a library of classes that can be used to store music information. This library is used by the application. When you want to use a library in an application, you have to add the library to the references specified for that application. Figure 3-19 shows how to do this using the Reference Manager in Visual Studio.

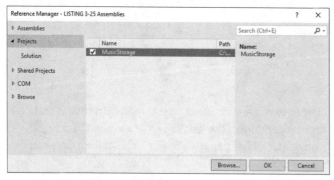

FIGURE 3-19 Visual Studio projects

Note that this creates a dependency relationship between the two projects. The project adding the reference (in this case our sample application) is now dependent on the MusicStorage library. In other words, changes to the behavior of the library might affect the behavior of the application. Note also that this dependency is one-way, in that changes to the user interface will not affect the behavior of the library. Visual Studio will not allow you to create circular dependencies, so it is not possible to make two libraries depend on each other.

Once you have added a library to a project you can use the classes contained in the library. Listing 3-25 shows how this works.

LISTING 3-25 Assemblies

```
using System;
using MusicStorage;

namespace LISTING_3_25_Assemblies
{
    class Program
    {
        static void Main(string[] args)
        {
            MusicTrack m = new MusicTrack(artist: "Rob Miles", title: "My Way",
                                                              length: 150);
            Console.WriteLine(m);
            Console.ReadKey();
        }
    }
}
```

When you build this solution, Visual Studio will create an assembly file for each project in the solution. Figure 3-20 shows the folder where Visual Studio has placed the output. Note that it contains an application file and the file MusicStorage.dll. These files can be copied onto another PC and they will work. The other files are not required. In this section we take a look the management of assemblies in our applications.

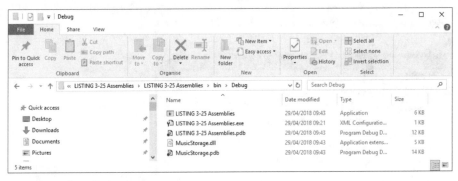

FIGURE 3-20 Compiled output

It is impossible to create and distribute applications without some understanding of how to manage the assemblies that they are made of.

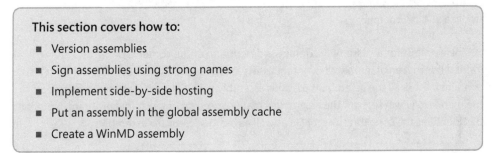

This section covers how to:

- Version assemblies
- Sign assemblies using strong names
- Implement side-by-side hosting
- Put an assembly in the global assembly cache
- Create a WinMD assembly

Version assemblies

Earlier versions of Windows also used dynamically loaded libraries to build large applications. The library files were loaded when required and some library files were shared between multiple applications running on a machine. This was a good idea at the time, because it saved memory, allowing a system to simultaneously host a larger number of applications.

However, sharing libraries causes problems when applications become dependent on particular versions of shared library files. It was frequently the case that installing a new application would break applications already on a machine because the installation process replaced one of the shared libraries with a version incompatible with the other programs on the machine. This problem was referred as "DLL Hell." I got quite good at finding and replacing DLL files with different versions to get all of my applications to work. One of the design aims of .NET was to get rid of "DLL Hell."

You can investigate how the assembly files work by using the ildasm program that you first saw in Chapter 2 when we discussed Boxing and Unboxing. This program can be used to examine the code and the content of an assembly. If we use it to open the application file created in Listing 3-25, we see the dialog displayed in Figure 3-21. You can navigate this interface to view elements of the assembly, including the manifest for the assembly.

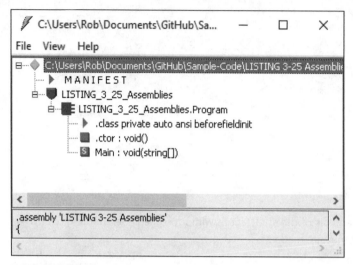

FIGURE 3-21 Ildasm output

The manifest for an assembly contains a description of the contents of the assembly (remember that an assembly can contain assets as well as program code). The manifest also contains a list of all the assemblies that this assembly uses. Figure 3-22 shows the top part of the manifest, which sets out the assemblies that are used by our example program. Note that this identifies the core library mscorlib as well as the MusicStorage assembly.

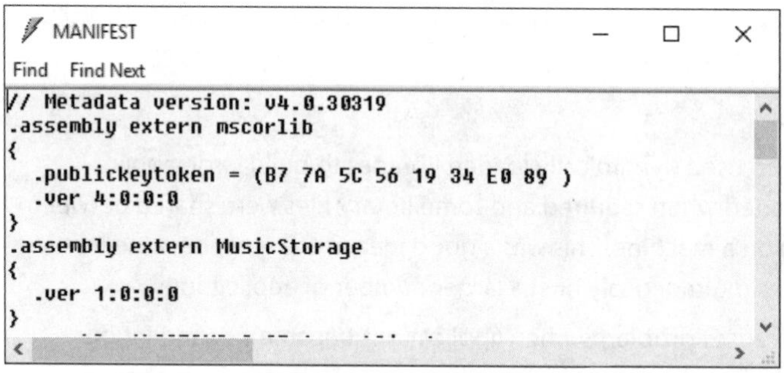

```
// Metadata version: v4.0.30319
.assembly extern mscorlib
{
  .publickeytoken = (B7 7A 5C 56 19 34 E0 89 )
  .ver 4:0:0:0
}
.assembly extern MusicStorage
{
  .ver 1:0:0:0
}
```

FIGURE 3-22 Manifest contents

The version information is added by Visual Studio when the application is built. When the application runs, the .NET runtime environment can ensure that the version of the library that is loaded matches the one that is required. If the version numbers don't match, the application will not run.

We can set the version number in the Properties for a project by selecting the Assembly Information item for the project. This opens the dialog as shown in Figure 3-23. Note that you can also enter other information about the application.

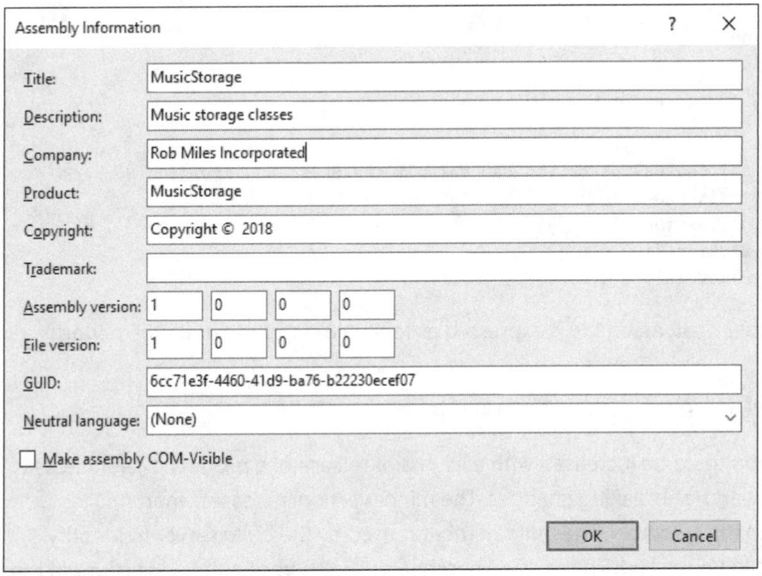

FIGURE 3-23 Editing assembly information

This information is stored in a file called `AssemblyInfo.cs`, which is held in the properties folder for the Visual Studio solution. The code here shows the contents of this file for the `MusicStorage` assembly.

```
using System.Reflection;
using System.Runtime.CompilerServices;
using System.Runtime.InteropServices;

// General Information about an assembly is controlled through the following
// set of attributes. Change these attribute values to modify the information
// associated with an assembly.
[assembly: AssemblyTitle("MusicStorage")]
[assembly: AssemblyDescription("Music storage classes")]
[assembly: AssemblyConfiguration("")]
[assembly: AssemblyCompany("Rob Miles Incorporated")]
[assembly: AssemblyProduct("MusicStorage")]
[assembly: AssemblyCopyright("Copyright ©  2018")]
[assembly: AssemblyTrademark("")]
[assembly: AssemblyCulture("")]

// Setting ComVisible to false makes the types in this assembly not visible
// to COM components.  If you need to access a type in this assembly from
// COM, set the ComVisible attribute to true on that type.
[assembly: ComVisible(false)]

// The following GUID is for the ID of the typelib if this project is exposed to COM
[assembly: Guid("6cc71e3f-4460-41d9-ba76-b22230ecef07")]

// Version information for an assembly consists of the following four values:
```

```
//
//        Major Version
//        Minor Version
//        Build Number
//        Revision
//
// You can specify all the values or you can default the Build and Revision Numbers
// by using the '*' as shown below:
// [assembly: AssemblyVersion("1.0.*")]
[assembly: AssemblyVersion("1.0.0.0")]
[assembly: AssemblyFileVersion("1.0.0.0")]
```

The version number of an assembly is expressed as four values separated by the period character:

```
{Major version}.{Minor version}.{Build Number}.{Revision}
```

The major version should be increased with each major release of a product. Major releases contain new features and/or breaking changes. The minor version increases when smaller changes are made to the assembly. The build number is used by the build server to identify builds so that they can be tracked. The revision number is used to track patched versions in the production environment.

Sign assemblies using strong names

In the previous section we discussed how a document can be signed by the author using their private key so that people receiving the document can use a public key to verify the author, and also that the content of the document has not been changed. A strong-named assembly is signed and validated using the same public/private key arrangement. There are a number of advantages to using strong-named assemblies.

- Version checking of assemblies only takes place when they are signed with *strong names*.

- A strong-named assembly can only be used in an application with other strong-named assemblies. This ensures that an entire application has integrity.

- A strong-named assembly can be loaded into the Global Assembly Cache (GAC), which allows provides performance improvements and allows assemblies to be shared among applications, which will be detailed later.

- A strong-named assembly has a unique name that is generated using the private key when the assembly is signed. This allows multiple versions of the same assembly to exist side-by-side on a system. Because the manifest of an assembly contains the strong name of the other assemblies that it wishes to use; there is no possibility of name confusion leading to "DLL Hell."

The command line tool "sn" can be used to generate public and private keys that can be used to sign an assembly. You can also generate key files by selecting the Sign tab in the properties for an assembly project. Figure 3-24 shows how an assembly can be signed. In the figure we are creating a new key file that will be added to the project.

FIGURE 3-24 The Signing tab in the Properties

Visual Studio provides a dialog to create the key file. Figure 3-25 shows the dialog that is used to create a strong-name key file. Note that the file can be protected with a password.

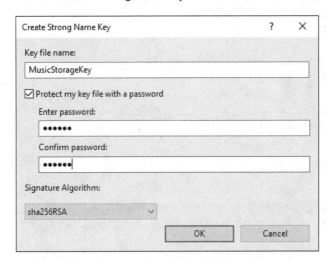

FIGURE 3-25 Creating a strong-name key file

An assembly that has been given a strong-name contains the public key that can be used to validate its signature. The public key is placed in the manifest of the assembly. We can view it using the `ildasm` program as shown in Figure 3-26, which shows part of the manifest for Listing 3-26 Strong names, an example that contains strongly named assemblies. The command line program `sn` can also be used to view this information.

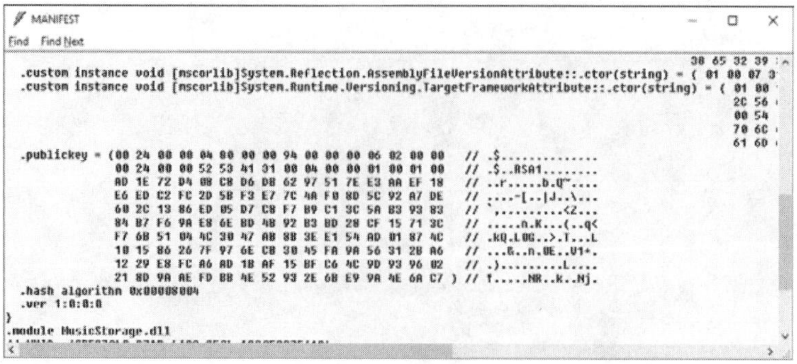

FIGURE 3-26 The public key in a signed assembly

Fully qualified assembly name and public key token

A strong-named assembly has a *fully qualified name* that is made up of the assembly's name, the culture of the assembly, the public key token, and a version number. The public key token is a 64-bit (8 byte) hash of the public key in the strong-name. This ensures that every fully qualified assembly name is unique. You can use reflection to obtain the fully qualified name of an assembly from the `FullName` property as shown in Listing 3-26.

LISTING 3-26 Strong names

```
using System;
using MusicStorage;

namespace LISTING_3_26_Strong_names
{
    class Program
    {
        static void Main(string[] args)
        {
            string assemblyName = typeof(MusicTrack).Assembly.FullName;
            Console.WriteLine(assemblyName);
            Console.ReadKey();
        }
    }
}
```

The output from this program gives the fully qualified name from the strongly named `MusicStorage` assembly as shown below. Note that assemblies without a strong-name have a `PublicKeyToken` value of null.

`MusicStorage, Version=1.0.0.0, Culture=neutral, PublicKeyToken=9aa4095193e2d7b8`

The public key token is used in the manifest of an assembly to specify exactly which assemblies it should work with. Figure 3-27 shows part of the manifest for an application that uses the `MusicStorage` assembly. Note that the public key token value for this matches the public key token printed by the program in Listing 3-26. This means that this program will only work with that specific version of `MusicStorage`.

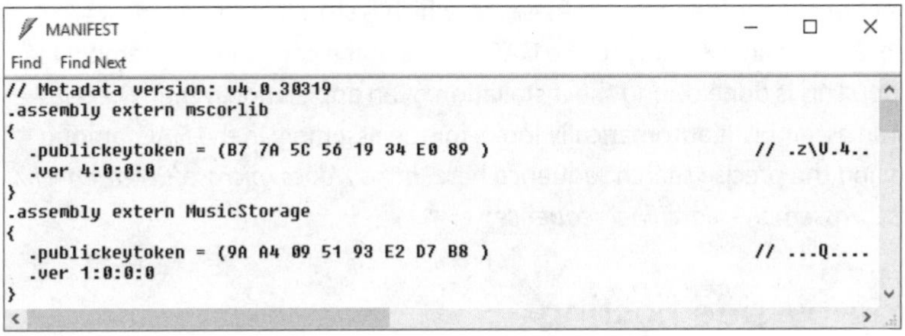

FIGURE 3-27 The public key in a signed assembly

Delay Signing

The key file that is used to sign the assembly contains the private key that is used to sign assemblies. This should be kept securely (for example it should not be uploaded to GitHub) as it allows anyone to create strong-named assemblies signed with that key. An organization using signed assemblies can use "Delay Signing" of assemblies to reduce the chances of the private key falling into the wrong hands. You can see the option to use this on Figure 3-24 above.

In the case of Delay Signing the key that is used to sign the assemblies during production is the public key of the key pair and attributes are added to the assembly to indicate that Delay Signing is being used. During the final build process before distributing the application, the assemblies can be signed with the private key.

Limitations of strong-names

Strong-names prevent "DLL Hell" by giving every assembly a unique name. They prevent tampering with the contents of an assembly and they also prevent the substitution of one assembly for another. However, giving an assembly a strong-name does not in any way protect the contents of the assembly, nor does it prove the identity of the person who created the assembly.

Anyone can use ildasm to view the contents of an assembly with a strong-name; including the actual program code in the applications and the fact that an assembly has been signed does not identify the person who signed it.

If you create and distribute applications you can use Authenticode to identify yourself as the publisher of the code. You use a digital certificate provided by Authenticode to sign code that you create. If you publish applications in Windows Store, this certification process happens automatically and a certificate is created that identifies you as the publisher of the application.

The Global Assembly Cache (GAC)

You have seen that you can just distribute applications to users as folders containing assembly files. When the .EXE assembly is executed it will load the other assemblies as required. This works well as a deployment model for individual applications. However, you might want to share a particular assembly among a number of different applications that you have created. If you want to do this you can put the assembly in the Global Assembly Cache (GAC).

The GAC is implemented as a folder named `assembly`, which is stored in the Windows folder on the machine. Adding an assembly to the GAC means that a copy of the assembly file is placed into this folder. This is done during the installation of an application. When the .NET Runtime searches for an assembly it automatically looks for the assembly in the GAC, among other places. You can find the precise search sequence here: *https://docs.microsoft.com/en-gb/ windows/desktop/SbsCs/assembly-searching-sequence.*

Implement side-by-side hosting

All of the assemblies in the GAC are strong-named and so each assembly in the GAC can be uniquely identified via its fully qualified name. This makes it possible for the GAC to contain multiple versions of the same assembly. This is called *side-by-side* hosting of assemblies.

The manifest of an assembly contains references to the specific assembly version it works with. This removes the possibility of "DLL Hell" in .NET applications; a new "side hosted" version of an assembly that has a different fully qualified name is only associated with assemblies that specify that they want to use the new version of the assembly.

Assembly binding redirection

Side-by-side hosting works because the assemblies used by a particular application are explicitly specified in the manifest for the application. However, this can lead to problems during the lifecycle of an application. If you fix a bug in a shared assembly you can deploy a new version of the assembly into the Global Assembly Cache alongside the original, but it will not be used because all of the existing applications contain references to the original.

This problem can be addressed by creating *assembly binding redirection*, which modifies the behavior of the GAC so that when a module asks for the faulty assembly the request is redirected to the assembly that contains the fixed code.

The redirection can be specified at three levels: at the application level, the publisher level and the machine level. In each you can add a *policy file* to specify that an application requests a particular assembly it should be redirected to the replacement.

The policy file for an application has the same name as the application executable file with the language extension ".*config.*" It is an XML formatted file that contains application configuration options for a specific application. The listing next shows an example of a configuration file that can be used to request an application to use a new version of the `MusicStorage` library.

```
<configuration>
    <runtime>
        <assemblyBinding xmlns="urn:schemas-microsoft-com:asm.v1">

            <dependentAssembly>
                <assemblyIdentity name=" MusicStorage "
                                    publicKeyToken="9aa4095193e2d7b8" />
                <bindingRedirect oldVersion="1.0.0.0-1.2.0.0" newVersion="2.0.0.0"/>
            </dependentAssembly>
```

```
        </assemblyBinding>
      </runtime>
</configuration>
```

Any requests for assembly versions in the range 1.0.0.0 to 1.2.0.0 will be redirected to the new version of the assembly. Note that the replacement assembly must have the same publicKeyToken value. This ensures that only the original publisher of an assembly can release replacement versions.

Rather than modifying all of their applications to use a replacement assembly file, a publisher can instead create a policy file, bind it to an assembly, and then install this in the GAC to redirect all users of an assembly to a replacement version. This is applied during the installation of a service pack or an update to an application.

Finally, a configuration can be applied at the machine level. By adding entries into the system wide machine.config file, a system administrator can redirect all of the applications on a machine to use particular versions of assemblies.

Put an assembly in the global assembly cache

Before you put an assembly into the GAC, you should really consider whether you really need to do this. The primary reason for placing assemblies in the GAC is to allow them to be shared between applications. You might also place assemblies in the GAC to prevent them from being removed from the system; only system administrators can remove assemblies from the GAC. The final reason why you might load an assembly into the GAC is that you want to take advantage of the ability to implement side by side versions of assemblies and perform assembly binding redirection.

There are two ways that developers can add assemblies into the GAC. The files can be added as part of a setup process, or the gacutil, the Global Assembly Cache tool, can be used during development.

Create a WinMD assembly

All of the discussion we have had so far have focused on .NET assemblies. A .NET assembly contains metadata (data about data) that describes the assembly. The assembly also contains the MSIL code that implements the behaviors of the assembly. The MSIL code can be produced by compiling one of a number of languages (for example C# or Visual Basic) and the MSIL will be Just In Time compiled for the target platform when the assembly is loaded and methods in the assembly are called. The MSIL code runs inside a managed code environment.

The runtime element of an operating system starts programs running and manages their execution. When a C# program is started, the .NET runtime opens the starting assembly (the one with the language extension .exe), finds the entry point in the assembly, and begins running the program.

When Windows 8 was released, Microsoft introduced a new WinRT runtime, which is written in C++. Note that the WinRT runtime is completely different from Windows 8 RT, which was a version of Windows developed for use with ARM processors. WinRT was created to provide the same level of support for C++ application components provided by .NET assemblies.

The information about a WinRT component is held in a WinMD file. WinMD stands for "Windows Metadata." A WinMD file might contain both metadata and executable code, or it might just contain metadata and serve as a "wrapper" for an existing block of compiled code.

WinRT has evolved into one of the technologies that underpins the Universal Windows Platform. This allows Windows applications to be created and deployed across a wide range of different devices. WinRT allows programmers to create portable C++ applications that can run on the wide range of devices now supported by the Windows operating system. WinRT applications interact with the operating system via WinMD files that expose all of the API elements of Windows.

If you want to create a C# Windows Runtime Component (a program element that exposes its behaviors via a WinMD file), you can specify this in the type of project that you create within Visual Studio as shown in Figure 3-28.

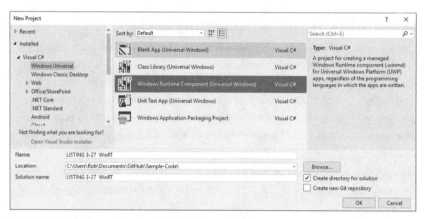

FIGURE 3-28 Creating a Windows Runtime Component

An implementation of the MusicTrack class is created in Listing 3-37.

LISTING 3-27 WinRT

```
namespace LISTING_3_27_WinRT
{
    public sealed class MusicTrack
    {
        public string Artist { get; set; }
        public string Title { get; set; }
        public int Length { get; set; }

        // ToString that overrides the behavior in the base class
        public override string ToString()
        {
            return Artist + " " + Title + " " + Length.ToString() + " seconds long";
        }
    }
```

```
        public MusicTrack(string artist, string title, int length)
        {
            Artist = artist;
            Title = title;
            Length = length;
        }
    }
}
```

When this code is built it generates a WinMD file that can be inspected using the ildasm program that we have previously used to inspect .NET assemblies. Figure 3-29 shows that the metadata generated for this class is quite different to the one that would be produced for a .NET assembly. This reflects the difference in design that is required to interact with the C++ based interface provided by WinRT.

FIGURE 3-29 Using ildasm to view a WinMD file

C# classes that are used in Windows Runtime Components are subject to a few limitations, so that their behaviors conform with the C++ origins of WinRT:

- You must use Windows Runtime types for all the member variables, fields, and return values in your classes.

- It is not possible to use generics in your programs.

- A class can only implement Windows Runtime interfaces.

- A class can only derive from classes from the Windows Runtime.

- Public classes must be sealed (i.e. nothing can derive from them).

- Public structures must contain only public members, which must be strings or value types.

- The namespace of a public type must match the name of the assembly.

- Public member types must not have names that start with the word "Windows".

Skill 3.4: Debug an application

As you become a more skilled programmer you will find that you don't create as many bugs when you create software, but you may also discover that the bugs you do create are harder to track down and fix. As you become more experienced you will also notice that one of the more common causes of a software bug is a fix for a previous bug. Debugging is a necessary part of the development process and in this section we are going to explore techniques that we can use to make debugging easier.

However, my most important tip for debugging may surprise you. If you get completely stuck with a bug you should walk away from the code for a while and go and do something completely different. Sometimes the act of disengaging from a problem frees the brain up to work on it in "background" mode. And then the answer just pops into your mind.

The other tip is that if you are completely stuck you should find a way of generating more data about the bad behavior you're seeing. Add diagnostic code to prove all the assumptions that you have made about things in your program. Never mind if you can't think of a way that the variable PersonNo can ever be zero; add some code to prove that this is not happening.

The good news is that the design of the C# language makes it easier to spot issues with your code before they turn into bugs and Visual Studio make it much easier to find out what your program is doing when it goes wrong. In this section we are going to investigate how we can use these features to find out what happens when our programs don't do what you expect them to.

> **This section covers how to:**
> - Create and manage preprocessor compiler directives
> - Choose an appropriate build type
> - Manage programming program database files and (debug symbols)

Create and manage preprocessor compiler directives

The C# compiler is the program that takes the C# source code and converts it into the Micro-soft Intermediate Language (MSIL) code that will be stored in the assembly file output. You can modify the behavior of the compiler by giving it compiler directives. These are commands that are pre-ceded by the # character.

These commands may also be called *preprocessor directives*. The C and C++ languages have an explicit part of the compilation process in which the program source file is scanned and pre-processor directives are acted on. The C and C++ pre-processor understands a wide range of commands that allow programmers to create and trigger pre-built macros, swap one symbol in a program for another, and even include the contents of one source file in another.

The C# compiler directives are more limited in scope, but they are still very useful. In this section we are going to consider how they are used.

Use the #if directive to control code compilation

One way to investigate the behavior of a program is to add code that produces diagnostic messages that can be used to work out what the program is doing. This is sometimes called *code instrumentation*. You can use Boolean flags to determine whether or not to produce diagnostic output, as in the program shown in Listing 3-28. The MusicTrack class contains a Boolean member called DebugMode, which can be set to true to request that the class produced diagnostic output.

LISTING 3-28 Adding diagnostics

```
using System;

namespace LISTING_3_28_Adding_diagnostics
{
    public class MusicTrack
    {
        public static bool DebugMode = false;

        public string Artist { get; set; }
        public string Title { get; set; }
        public int Length { get; set; }

        // ToString that overrides the behavior in the base class
        public override string ToString()
        {
            return Artist + " " + Title + " " + Length.ToString() + " seconds long";
        }

        public MusicTrack(string artist, string title, int length)
        {
            Artist = artist;
            Title = title;
            Length = length;
            if (DebugMode)
            {
                Console.WriteLine("Music track created: {0}", this.ToString());
            }
        }
    }

    class Program
    {
        static void Main(string[] args)
        {
            MusicTrack.DebugMode = true;

            MusicTrack m = new MusicTrack(artist: "Rob Miles", title: "My Way",
                                            length: 150);
            Console.ReadKey();
        }
    }
}
```

This will work, but it means that when the application is finally shipped to the customer it will also contain all of the code that prints the diagnostic output. This increases the size of the assembly file and makes it run more slowly because it performs the tests to control diagnostic output. It also might make it easier for someone to work out how the code works by turning on diagnostics. It is useful if there is a way that you can leave out the diagnostic code, rather than have the program decide at runtime whether or not to run it.

The #if compiler directive can be used to control whether or not a particular set of statements in a program are actually processed by the compiler. It is used with the #define directive that lets us define a symbol that controls the behavior of #if.

The code in Listing 3-29 shows how this works. The DIAGNOSTICS symbol is defined at the top of the program and the #if directive identifies the code to be compiled if the symbol has been defined. The #endif directive marks the end of the statements that are to be conditionally compiled.

LISTING 3-29 Conditional compilation

```
#define DIAGNOSTICS

using System;

namespace LISTING_3_29_Conditional_compilation
{
    public class MusicTrack
    {
        public static bool DebugMode = false;

        public string Artist { get; set; }
        public string Title { get; set; }
        public int Length { get; set; }

        // ToString that overrides the behavior in the base class
        public override string ToString()
        {
            return Artist + " " + Title + " " + Length.ToString() + " seconds long";
        }

        public MusicTrack(string artist, string title, int length)
        {
            Artist = artist;
            Title = title;
            Length = length;
#if DIAGNOSTICS
            Console.WriteLine("Music track created: {0}", this.ToString());
#endif
        }
    }
}
```

The most important thing to remember about conditional compilation is that if the condition is not fulfilled the code controlled by conditional compilation is never included in the assembly file output. The Visual Studio editor is aware of this and will show conditionally compiled elements as "grayed out" if they are not active. Figure 3-30 shows how this works. It is a screen shot of code being displayed by Visual Studio. The DIAGNOSTICS symbol is not defined, so the code that is controlled by it is shown in gray.

```
        public MusicTrack(string artist, string title, int length)
        {
            Artist = artist;
            Title = title;
            Length = length;
#if DIAGNOSTICS
                Console.WriteLine("Music track created: {0}", this.ToString());
#endif
        }
```

FIGURE 3-30 Greyed out code in Visual Studio

The condition that is tested can be a logical expression that combines tests for multiple symbols. The symbols can only be declared right at the start of a source file.

Conditional compilation symbols can also be defined in the properties of an application. Figure 3-31 shows how this is done. The DIAGNOSTICS symbol has been defined. If you want to set multiple properties, you can enter them separated by the semicolon character.

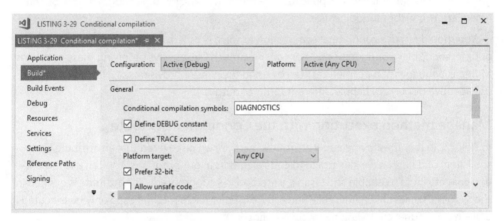

FIGURE 3-31 Defining conditional compilation symbols in the Properties dialog

Note that the dialog in Figure 3-31 also shows tick boxes that indicate that the DEBUG and TRACE constants are defined. The DEBUG constant is only defined if your program is built using the debug build type. You can use the DEBUG symbol rather than the DIAGNOSTICS symbol to control diagnostic output from your program. This ensures that when you build the release version of your program, the debug code will not be included.

An #if directive can have an accompanying #else element that identifies statements to be compiled if the symbol is not defined. You can use the #elif directive to create a chain of conditions as shown in the code here, which selects an appropriate statement depending on whether the TERSE, NORMAL or CHATTTY symbols has been defined.

```
#if TERSE
            Console.WriteLine("Hello");
#elif NORMAL
```

```
                Console.WriteLine("Hello Rob");
#elif CHATTY
                Console.WriteLine("Hello Rob. And how are you");
#endif
```

You can also use the #undef directive to undefine any symbols that might have been defined outside your program source. Note that the #undef directive can only be used at the very start of the program file. You can use it to remove the DEBUG symbol so that elements of code that you are debugging can be made to run in release mode, without DEBUG defined.

```
#undef DEBUG
```

You might think that conditional compilation is very powerful. And you would be right. However, you should use it with care. It makes code much harder to understand. The reader of the program has to be aware which symbols are defined when they read the program text.

Conditional compilation might be useful if you are trying to create a single version of a program that is intended to operate on multiple platforms. Platform specific behaviors can be selected using symbols that are set for each different configuration. The need for this is now greatly reduced for a Universal Application, because this type of application will work on multiple platforms without modification.

You should not use conditional compilation to solve problems such as multiple languages or different display configurations. There are now much better ways of solving these problems. Multiple languages can be implemented by using the culture provisions of .NET, and you can use adaptive displays to handle different forms of output.

Manage method execution with the Conditional attribute

In Skill 2.5, in the "Create and apply attributes" section, we discovered that an attribute is a small item of data that we can attach to code elements in our programs. You can use the Conditional attribute to enable and disable a method in your program. The attribute is defined in the System.Diagnostics namespace and can be used to flag a method as to only be executed if a given conditional compilation symbol is defined.

Listing 3-30 shows how this works. The method display has had a Conditional attribute applied so that it will only be obeyed when the DEBUG symbol is defined. The statement at the top of the listing can be used to undefine the DEBUG symbol and "switch off" the display method.

LISTING 3-30 Conditional attribute

```
//#undef DEBUG

using System;
using System.Diagnostics;

namespace LISTING_3_30_Conditional_attribute
{
    class Program
    {
```

```
    [Conditional("DEBUG")]
    static void display(string message)
    {
        Console.WriteLine(message);
    }
    static void Main(string[] args)
    {
        display("Message for the user");
        Console.ReadKey();
    }
  }
}
```

Note that the use of the Conditional attribute does not control whether or not the method is included in the compiled assembly file output by the compiler. The method is always included in the assembly output. However, the Conditional output will prevent the method from being called.

Mark code as obsolete using the Obsolete directive

You can mark classes, interfaces, methods and properties with the Obsolete attribute to indicate that they have been superseded by new versions. The Obsolete attribute is applied to the superseded element and given a message and a Boolean value that indicates whether a compiler warning (false) or an error (true) should be produced if the element with the attribute is used by a program. The code below would cause compiler warnings to be produced if a program contains a call to OldMethod.

```
[Obsolete ("This method is obsolete. Call  NewMethod instead.", false)]
public string OldMethod()
```

Control compilation with warning and error directives

The #warning and #error directives allow you to produce a compiler warning or even prevent compilation of a source code file. The statement below would produce a compilation warning and display the message when the source code is compiled.

```
#warning This version of the library is no longer maintained. Use Version 2.5
```

The #error directive causes a compilation error to be produced. It is used to prevent the compilation of a source code file with an invalid combination of conditional configuration options. The statements next prevent a program from being compiled if both the DIAGNOSTICS and DEBUG symbols have been defined.

```
#if DIAGNOSTICS && DEBUG
#error Cannot run with both diagnostics and debug enabled
#endif
```

Manage compiler warning reporting with the pragma directive

When writing programs, it is best to see no warnings reported at the end of the build process. However, sometimes you can use code constructions that trigger warnings from the compiler even though the code is correct in the context it is being used. In this situation the `#pragma warning` directive can be used to disable warning reporting for a region of code.

The code next, which is part of an ASP controller class, normally generates a warning, because the method has been declared as asynchronous, but does not contain any await instructions. (For more details of async and await you can look at the section "Using async and await" in Section 1.1) This is perfectly legitimate code. The `#pragma warning disable` directive turns off any warning reporting. Warning reporting can be turned back on with a `#pragma warning restore` statement.

```
#pragma warning disable

        public async Task<IActionResult> Resume()
        {
            return View();
        }
#pragma warning restore
```

The problem with disabling all warnings is that this would cause all other warnings to be disabled, as well as the one that I know to ignore. You can improve on a warning filtering by just specifying the warning that you want the compiler to ignore. The pragma next will ignore just the warning CS1998, which is the warning about async methods. If you want to ignore multiple warnings you can supply them as a comma separated list.

```
#pragma warning disable CS1998
```

To create the statement above I had to look up the warning number and then create the pragma by hand. You can also generate the pragma to suppress a warning directly from the Visual Studio user interface. Figure 3-32 below shows how this is done. If you right-click the warning in the error list you can select Suppress from the menu to have the #pragma construction inserted automatically for that particular warning.

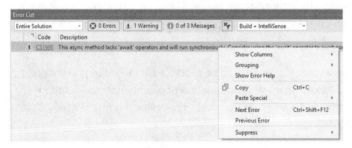

FIGURE 3-32 Suppressing a warning from within Visual Studio

Identify error positions with #line

Some of the code that you work with may contain auto-generated elements. These code components may be inserted into your program files. This happens with systems such as ASP.NET.

These can lead to confusion navigating error reports, where the line number that is reported doesn't match the one you see in the Visual Studio editor. The #line directive can be used to set the reported line numbers of statements in your code. You can also use the #line directive to specify the file name delivered by error reporting.

Listing 3-31 shows how this works. The method Exploder throws an exception. The #line directive in the listing sets the line number to one, at the point of the throw and also sets the reported filename to "kapow.ninja". The **#line default** statement resumes normal line number and source file name reporting.

LISTING 3-31 Line numbers

```
using System;

namespace LISTING_3_31_Line_numbers
{
    class Program
    {
        static void Exploder()
        {
#line 1 "kapow.ninja"
            throw new Exception("Bang");
#line default
        }
        static void Main(string[] args)
        {
            try
            {
                Exploder();
            }
            catch (Exception e)
            {
                Console.WriteLine(e.StackTrace);
            }
            Console.ReadKey();
        }
    }
}
```

When this program runs, it displays the stacktrace for the exception that includes the filename and line number set using the #line directive as shown next. The report of the location of the throw has been modified by the #line directive.

```
    at LISTING_3_31_Line_numbers.Program.Exploder() in C:\Users\Rob\Documents\GitHub\
Sample-Code\LISTING 3-31 Line numbers\LISTING 3-31 Line numbers\kapow.ninja:line 1
    at LISTING_3_31_Line_numbers.Program.Main(String[] args) in C:\Users\Rob\Documents\
GitHub\Sample-Code\LISTING 3-31 Line numbers\LISTING 3-31 Line numbers\Program.cs:
line 17
```

Note that changing the filename in this way will cause problems when debugging, because the run time system will look for a program database file (more in a moment), which corresponds to the filename of the executable. If this filename has been changed by using the #line directive the system will not be able to display any debugging information. Note also that the #line directive will change the filename and line number reported by the compiler if an error or warning is discovered during compilation.

Hide code using #line

Another use for the #line directive is to hide code statements from the debugger. This can be very useful if your source code contains programmatically generated elements. You don't want to have to step through all the programmatically generated statements when debugging, because you are only interested in the code that you have written yourself.

In the code next the program will step past the WriteLine statement because it is in a sequence of statements after a #line hidden statement. The stepping will resume after the #line default statement, which resumes line numbering and file name reporting.

```
#line hidden
// The debugger will not step through these statements
Console.WriteLine("You haven't seen me");
#line default
```

Use DebuggerStepThrough to prevent debugger stepping

You can use the [DebuggerStepThrough] attribute to mark a method or class so that the debugger will not debug each statement in turn when single stepping through the code in that method or class. This is also useful when a program contains programmatically generated elements that you don't want to step through. The attribute is used before the declaration of the element:

```
[DebuggerStepThrough]
public void Update()
{
    ….
}
```

Note that if you apply the attribute to a class, it will mean that the debugger will not step through any of the methods in the class. Note also that the program will not hit any breakpoints that are set in elements marked with this attribute.

Choose an appropriate build configuration

The *build configuration* of your program controls the settings that are applied to the build process. A new Visual Studio project is created with two preset build configurations available; one for Debug and the other for Release. It's important that you understand the difference between these two build types and also how to create additional build configurations for specific projects.

Listing 3-32 is a program that creates two variables, but only uses one of them. The variable i is declared and set to the value 99, but it is never actually used within the program.

LISTING 3-32 Code optimization

```
using System;

namespace LISTING_3_32_Code_optimisation
{
    class Program
    {
        static void Main(string[] args)
        {
            int i = 99;
            int j = 100;
            Console.WriteLine("The value in j is {0}", j);
        }
    }
}
```

I used the ildasm program to take a look at the Microsoft Intermediate Language (MSIL) files that were produced in Debug and Release mode. Figure 3-33 shows the views of each. The Debug file contains statements that declare and initialize the unused variables, whereas the Release file does not.

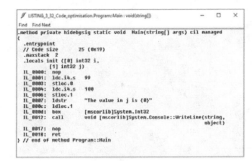 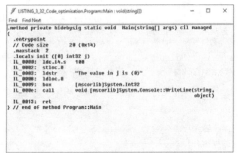

Debug   Release

FIGURE 3-33 Comparing debug and release versions

The Debug file also contains nop statements. The word nop is an abbreviation of "no opera-tion". When the program runs, these statements don't do anything. They are only present to serve as locations in the program that can be used as the position of breakpoints. We only tend to use breakpoints when debugging, so these are omitted in the release build.

Figure 3-34 shows a breakpoint set at the statement that initializes the variable i. This vari-able is never used in the program, but the breakpoint can still be set if the program is in debug mode, because all of the statements in the program are compiled into the output file.

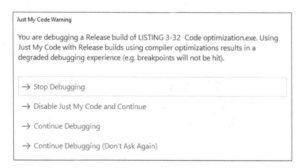

```
LISTING 3-32  Code optimization                                          _  □  ×
Program.cs  + ×
 LISTING 3-32  Code optimization    ▾  LISTING_3_32_Code_optimization.Progra ▾  Main(string[] args)
   1       using System;                                                      ✛
   2
   3     ⊟namespace LISTING_3_32_Code_optimization
   4      {
   5     ⊟   class Program
   6          {
   7     ⊟       static void Main(string[] args)
   8             {
 ● 9                 int i = 99;
  10                 int j = 100;
  11                 Console.WriteLine("The value in j is {0}", j);
  12             }
  13          }
  14      }
  15
132 %  ▾ ◂
```

FIGURE 3-34 Setting a breakpoint

If you run a program that contains breakpoints in a Release build, you get a warning as shown in Figure 3-35. The "Just My Code" feature of Visual Studio allows developers to skip over library functions when they are debugging. Without "Just My Code" you might find your-selves single stepping through the statements in the WriteLine method. The feature raises an alarm when a release build program is debugged because breakpoints will not be hit.

```
Just My Code Warning

You are debugging a Release build of LISTING 3-32  Code optimization.exe. Using
Just My Code with Release builds using compiler optimizations results in a
degraded debugging experience (e.g. breakpoints will not be hit).

→ Stop Debugging

→ Disable Just My Code and Continue

→ Continue Debugging

→ Continue Debugging (Don't Ask Again)
```

FIGURE 3-35 Breakpoints in Release builds

The release build of a program may differ from the debug build in other ways too. The re-lease version may contain "inline" implementations of short methods. If a method body is very short the compiler may decide that the program runs faster if the method body was copied "inline" each time the method is called, rather than generating the instructions that manage a method call.

A release version may also be more aggressive about the removal of objects as it runs, meaning that finalizer methods (see Chapter 2, Skill 6) are more likely to be called on objects. Most of the time the debug and release versions of a program will behave in exactly the same way, but there are situations where they can behave differently, and you should be aware of this possibility.

If you want custom build configurations, for example to configure a build that targets a particular processor platform, you use the build options. Configuration Manager can be used to configure a custom build. Figure 3-36 shows how to access the Configuration Manager in the Visual Studio interface.

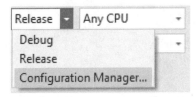

FIGURE 3-36 Opening Configuration Manager

As the name suggests, the Configuration Manager lets you select the configuration of the output file that will be produced when the program is built. Figure 3-37 shows the dialog in use.

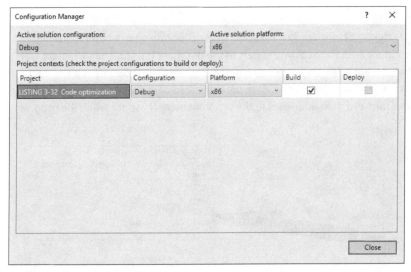

FIGURE 3-37 Configuration Manager

You can create a new configuration using this dialog. Visual Studio creates a separate folder for each configuration that holds the complied output and any program database files that are produced. If you take a look at the Debug version of the ildasm output in Figure 3-33 you can work out that the statement.

Manage programming program database files and (debug symbols)

When Visual Studio builds a program, it produces more than just the executable assembly. Figure 3-39 shows the content of the Debug folder for the program in Listing 3-32. This section is concerned with the Program Debug Database file, which is produced when the program is compiled. This file has the language extension pdb.

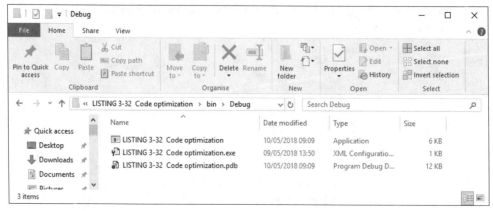

FIGURE 3-38 Code folder

The program debug database file is sometimes called the *symbol* file. The file contains information for the debugger, including a mapping of the program source code to the compiled statements. Figure 3-39 shows how this part of the database is used. The statement with a breakpoint actually maps to the indicated statement in the compiled output. It is the debug database that contains this mapping. The debug database also contains the names of all the symbols in the program and their addresses in the program memory space when the program runs.

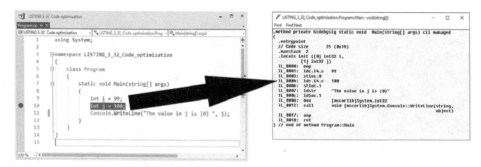

FIGURE 3-39 Debugging a program

A new program debug database is generated each time a program is compiled. A database file contains a Globally Unique Identifier (GUID), which is also held in the executable file with which the debug database is associated. When the debug database is opened this value is checked, and only the database with the matching GUID can be used. In other words, it is not possible to use an "old" debug database file with a newly compiled executable.

You can use the command `Debug > Windows > Modules` in Visual Studio to view the modules associated with a given debugging session. Figure 3-40 shows the debug modules display for Listing 3-32. Only the Listing 3-32 element can be debugged as the symbols are not normally loaded for Microsoft code.

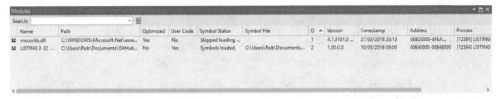

FIGURE 3-40 Debug modules

Symbol servers

A symbol server provides debug database information to a program in place of a local debug database file. If you really want to step through the Microsoft elements of our program you can connect Visual Studio to a Symbol Server that provides the information that would normally be in the debug database. To do this, and to manage the use of other symbol servers, you can use the Debugging element of Visual Studio options. The management of debugging symbols is shown in Figure 3-41. You can add new locations for symbol files that are to be used with debugging, and you can also request that the application connect to the Microsoft Symbol Servers when the program runs.

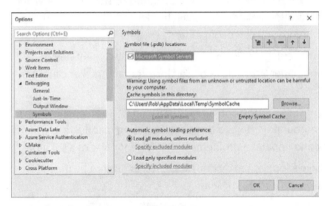

FIGURE 3-41 Symbol server configuration

The dialog also shows where program debug symbols should be cached on this machine. Visual Studio will keep local copies of debug database information to reduce the amount of network traffic that is generated during debugging. When you select "Microsoft Symbol Servers" in the dialog in Figure 3-41, you will be warned that downloading debug information may slow down the loading of assemblies.

If you use Team Foundation Server (TFS) to manage your projects, you have the option of saving all debug data files to a central server from which they can be accessed as required.

Public and private symbols

A program debug file will contain two kinds of symbol information: public and private. The public information contains descriptions of elements that are public in that assembly. The private information also contains descriptions of things like private methods and local variables.

Visual Studio creates debug files that contain both private and public components. You might not want other people to be able to see information about private elements in your solution. The tool pdbcopy can be used to make a copy of a pdb file and remove all the private elements. You can also provide pdbcopy with a list of symbols to be removed.

Note that the output from pdbcopy has the same identifying GUID as an incoming file, so it can be used with the same executable file. The pdbcopy program is not provided as part of a Visual Studio installation. It is part of the set of Debugging Tools for Windows.

Skill 3.5: Implement diagnostics in an application

The previous section has shown how to use debugging techniques to discover the reasons behind program failure. Programs built using the debug build configuration can be stepped through and their operations examined in detail to try and discover the reason for the failure.

A "good" bug is one that causes the entire program to fail in a very recognizable and re-peatable way. If you're told that your code crashes every time the "Print" button is pressed, you can be confident that the fix will be easy. If you're told that the program crashes every now and then when the "Print" button is pressed, you will find this much harder to fix because you need to figure out what causes the crash before you can begin to fix it.

In this situation diagnostic output is crucial. If I know the size of each document being printed, along with the language and paper sizes selected I can look for factors that cause the problem.

Note that, as with security, diagnostics support should be "designed in" to an application at the start of the development. The amount of effort to be applied creating diagnostic elements should be weighed against the risk and impact of problems with different parts of a solution.

In this section we are going to take a look at the diagnostics features offered by the .NET framework and how we incorporate them into our programs.

> **This section covers how to:**
> - Implement logging and tracing
> - Profiling applications
> - Create and monitor performance counters
> - Write to the event log

Implement logging and tracing

Frequently you don't have the luxury of having a local debug build of a failing program and all the data that it is using. Sometimes a failure occurs on a distant server behind a firewall that prevents direct access to the broken code. In this situation diagnostics information in the form of logs and traces of program execution will be crucial in discovering what went wrong.

You can also use information generated by logging and tracing to investigate performance issues with systems out in the field. If is very useful to be able to determine the loading levels and the nature of transactions being performed on the customer site.

You use logging to find out what your program is doing and what happened when it failed. You use tracing to discover the path followed by the program to perform a particular action.

Trace execution using Debug and Trace

The System.Diagnostics namespace contains Debug and Trace classes that can be used to trace execution of a program. The classes contain methods that can be used to generate tracing output from a program when it runs. Listing 3-33 shows how this is used. The WriteLineIf method can be used to write a debug message if a given condition is true.

LISTING 3-33 Debug code tracing

```
using System.Diagnostics;

namespace LISTING_3_33_Debug_code_tracing
{
    class Program
    {
        static void Main(string[] args)
        {
            Debug.WriteLine("Starting the program");
            Debug.Indent();
            Debug.WriteLine("Inside a function");
            Debug.Unindent();
            Debug.WriteLine("Outside a function");
            string customerName = "Rob";
            Debug.WriteLineIf(string.IsNullOrEmpty(customerName), "The name is empty");
        }
    }
}
```

By default, the output from the Debug statements is directed to the Output window in Visual Studio. Listing 3-42 shows the output from the program.

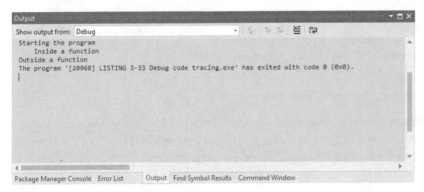

FIGURE 3-42 Debug tracing output

Note, that if the program is not compiled for debug, the debug statements are not included in the program that is produced. The debug code uses a conditional attribute (see the section "Manage method execution with the Conditional attribute," in Skill 3.4) to disable these methods when the debug symbol is not defined.

If you want to add this form of tracing output to production code you can use the Trace object, which can be used in the same way as the Debug object, as shown in Listing 3-34. The Trace symbol is usually defined for release code, which means that these statements will produce output in production code. The Trace object provides additional messages; the TraceInformation, TraceWarning, and TraceError methods can be used to specify the importance of the message. Later you will see how to filter these messages so that, for instance, you can only see error information.

LISTING 3-34 Trace code tracing

```
Trace.WriteLine("Starting the program");
Trace.TraceInformation("This is an information message");
Trace.TraceWarning("This is a warning message");
Trace.TraceError("This is an error message");
```

Use assertions in Debug and Trace

An assertion is a statement that you make, believing it to be true. For example, in the application design you might assert that "the name of a customer is never an empty string." When my program fails, the first thing to do is make sure that all of the assertions about the state of the program are actually true. In the case of the customer name you will add code to display the customer name so that you can check it, or you will add code to test the assertion.

Listing 3-35 shows how the Debug.Assert method can be used to perform this test when the program is running. There are the same methods available in the Trace class. The Debug.Assert method is provided with a Boolean parameter. If the parameter is true, the assertion is correct and the program continues. If the parameter is false, the assertion fails and the program will display a message offering the developer the option to continue the program.

LISTING 3-35 Assertions in debug

```
string customerName = "Rob";
Debug.Assert(!string.IsNullOrWhiteSpace(customerName));

customerName = "";
Debug.Assert(!string.IsNullOrWhiteSpace(customerName));
```

The first assertion succeeds because the name is not null or white space. However, the second assertion fails, leading to the output shown in Figure 3-43. If **Abort** is clicked the program displays a stack trace and stops. If **Retry** is clicked the program opens the debugger at this point in the code. If the **Ignore** is clicked, the program will continue.

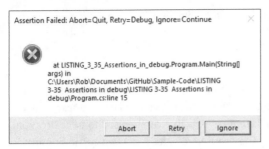

FIGURE 3-43 Assertion failure

Use listeners to gather tracing information

By default (unless specified otherwise) the output from the Debug and Trace classes is sent to the output window in Visual Studio. This will work during development, but once the program has been deployed this will not be useful. A program can attach *listener* objects to Debug and Trace, which will serve as destinations for tracing information.

Listing 3-36 shows how this is used. It attaches a ConsoleTraceListener instance to the collection of listener objects that are accepting output from the Trace class. When this program runs, the message produced by the Trace object are also displayed on the console.

LISTING 3-36 Trace listener

```
TraceListener consoleListener = new ConsoleTraceListener();
Trace.Listeners.Add(consoleListener);
Trace.TraceInformation("This is an information message");
Trace.TraceWarning("This is a warning message");
Trace.TraceError("This is an error message");
```

There are a number of different TraceListener objects that can be created. Table 3-1 shows them all. You can also create your own custom listener class based on the TraceListener class.

TABLE 3-1 Types of TraceListener

Class Name	Output
ConsoleTraceListener	Sends the output to the console.
DelimitedTextTraceListener	Sends the output to a TextWriter
EventLogTraceListener	Sends the output to the Event log
EventSchemaTraceListener	Sends the output to an XML encoded file compliant with the Event log schema
TextWriterTraceListener	Sends the output to a given TextWriter
XMLWriterTraceListener	Sends XML formatted output to an XML writer

You can add multiple listeners to a given tracing source so that tracing information can be sent to both the console, and an XML log file if you wish. To stop the output of tracing information you can remove listeners from the Listeners collection. You can use listeners with the Debug and the Trace classes.

Trace using the TraceSource class

The Trace and Debug classes provide tracing for a program in the form of simple messages. If you want to take a more managed approach to program tracing, you can use the TraceSource class. An instance of the TraceSource class will create events that can be used to trace program execution. Listing 3-37 shows how this works. The program creates four events. The simplest event contains event type information and an event number. You can also add a text string to an event, and the TraceData method also allows information to be added to an event in the form of a collection of object references.

LISTING 3-37 Simple TraceSource

```
TraceSource trace = new TraceSource("Tracer",SourceLevels.All);
trace.TraceEvent(TraceEventType.Start, 10000);
trace.TraceEvent(TraceEventType.Warning, 10001);
trace.TraceEvent(TraceEventType.Verbose, 10002, "At the end of the program");
trace.TraceData(TraceEventType.Information, 1003, new object[] { "Note 1", "Message 2" });
trace.Flush();
trace.Close();
```

Each event is given a particular event type and an event number. The event number element of an event is just an integer value that identifies the particular event. When you design the tracing in the application, you can define values that will be used to represent particular events, such as events 0 to 999 can mean user interface, and 1,000 to 1,999 databases, and so on.

There are a range of event types that are specified by a value of type TraceEventType. The event types, in increasing order of significance, are as follows:

- **Stop**, **Start**, **Suspend**, **Resume**, **Transfer** These are *activity* event types. You can use these events to indicate events that occur in the normal operation of your application. They don't reflect any error conditions.

- **Verbose** This indicates events that provide detailed information about the application activity during normal operation. This may include messages that are produced when methods are entered and exited, or objects created and destroyed. There may be a lot of verbose information generated when this level of tracing is active.

- **Information** This indicates events that provide significant information about application activity during normal operation; perhaps that transaction has started or ended.

- **Warning** This indicates a warning event. Perhaps a login has failed, an operation took longer to complete than expected or a resource such as memory is becoming low.

- **Error** This indicates that an error has been detected and dealt with by the application. Perhaps some incoming data was provided in the wrong format, or an operation did not complete and was re-tried.

- **Critical** This indicates that the application has reached a point where it cannot continue. Perhaps an exception has been raised which the exception handler does not recognize, or a required resource or connection is no longer available.

Unless you specify otherwise, the events are delivered to the Output window in Visual Studio, but you can also add a TraceListener as for the Debug and Trace classes.

Use TraceSwitch to control tracing output

The TraceSwitch object is provided to help manage tracing output from a program. The TraceSwitch object contains a Level property that can be set to determine the level of tracing output to be produced.

Listing 3-38 shows how it is used. A TraceSwitch instance with the name control is created and set to the Warning level. This variable is then used to control tracing output, first to the console, and then to the Trace class. Note that, as with the levels above, the control level sets the base value for messages. In other words, setting a trace level of Warning will also cause Error events to be generated.

LISTING 3-38 TRACESWITCH

```
TraceSwitch control = new TraceSwitch("Control", "Control the trace output");
control.Level = TraceLevel.Warning;

if(control.TraceError)
{
    Console.WriteLine("An error has occurred");
}

Trace.WriteLineIf(control.TraceWarning, "A warning message");
```

Use SourceSwitch to control tracing

The SourceSwitch can be used to directly control the behavior of a TraceSource object. It works in the same way as the TraceSwitch described above. Listing 3-39 shows how it is used. A SourceSwitch instance is created with the name control. It is then assigned to the Switch property of the TraceSource object.

LISTING 3-39 SourceSwitch

```
TraceSource trace = new TraceSource("Tracer", SourceLevels.All);

SourceSwitch control = new SourceSwitch("control", "Controls the tracing");
control.Level = SourceLevels.Information;
trace.Switch = control;

trace.TraceEvent(TraceEventType.Start, 10000);
trace.TraceEvent(TraceEventType.Warning, 10001);
trace.TraceEvent(TraceEventType.Verbose, 10002, "At the end of the program");
trace.TraceEvent(TraceEventType.Information, 10003, "Some information",
new object[] { "line1", "line2" });
trace.Flush();
trace.Close();
```

Configure tracing using application config files

The examples earlier show how a program can configure tracing output when it runs. However, it is also possible to configure tracing output using the application configuration file that you first saw in the section "Assembly binding redirection," in Skill 3.3. In that section you saw how to use an assembly configuration file to tell the .NET runtime that a given assembly should be used in place of an earlier version.

You can configure tracing by using the configuration file for the application. If you then want to change the tracing behavior of an application you just need to supply a new configuration file. Listing 3-40 shows how a switch should be set up in a config file. A switch with the name configControl is created that will cause all tracing events to be produced.

LISTING 3-40 Config file

```xml
<?xml version="1.0" encoding="utf-8" ?>
<configuration>
    <startup>
        <supportedRuntime version="v4.0" sku=".NETFramework,Version=v4.6.1" />
    </startup>
  <system.diagnostics>
    <switches>
      <add name="configControl" value="All" />
    </switches>
  </system.diagnostics>
</configuration>
```

When the application runs, it can locate this switch by name. The statement next creates a TraceSource that is configured using the switch options in the config file.

```
TraceSource trace = new TraceSource("configControl");
```

Note that if switch information with the given name is not found in the application configuration file, a trace is created that will not output any events.

Advanced tracing

You can add more complex behaviors to the configuration file, including the creation and assignment of listeners to TraceSource objects. You can also apply filters to listeners, so that a given listener will only receive particular levels of tracing information. This gives you a lot of flexibility in the tracing and logging that your application can perform.

Profiling applications

One of the most common developer mistakes is to spend too much time optimizing a solution during development. It turns out that there are usually much more important issues than performance, especially considering the power of modern computers. However, there are occasions where performance can become a problem, and in this section we consider the tools that can be used to address this.

The StopWatch class

Before you can speed up your application you need to know where it is spending most of its time. The StopWatch class can be used to measure elapsed time as shown in Listing 3-41. The program compares the performance of two algorithms that create thumbnail images. One uses a parallel for loop and the other works sequentially. The full solution is in the example programs for this book, along with a set of images for the program to work on. The StopWatch class provides Start, Stop, Reset, and Restart methods. The Restart method resets the stopwatch and starts it running again.

LISTING 3-41 Stopwatch class

```
Stopwatch stopwatch = new Stopwatch();

stopwatch.Start();
sequentialTest();
stopwatch.Stop();
Console.WriteLine("Sequential time in milliseconds: {0}",
                  stopwatch.ElapsedMilliseconds);
stopwatch.Restart();
parallelTest();
stopwatch.Stop();
Console.WriteLine("Parallel loop time in milliseconds: {0}",
                  stopwatch.ElapsedMilliseconds);
```

Profiling in Visual Studio

The Diagnostics display in Visual Studio gives a very good overview of the performance of an application. Figure 3-44 below shows the Diagnostic Tools in use.

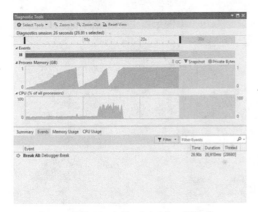

FIGURE 3-44 Diagnostic Tools in Visual Studio

If you require more detail than you can get from the Diagnostic Tools, Visual Studio 2017 contains powerful profiling tools that you can use to discover where your application is spending most of its time. Once you know this, you can focus on optimizing that particular method. The profiling tools can be found on the Analyze menu, as show in Figure 3-45.

FIGURE 3-45 Performance profiler

The Performance Profiler provides a range of profiling tools, as shown in Figure 3-46.

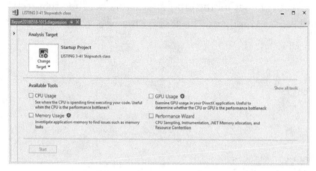

FIGURE 3-46 Performance profiler tools

A detailed look at all the performance profilers is beyond the scope of this text; we are going to focus on the use of the Performance Wizard you can see at the bottom right of Figure 3-46. This provides a good starting point for application profiling. If you select the checkbox for this tool and then click the **Start** button, the profiling process produces a dialog that lets you select the profiling method as shown in Figure 3-47.

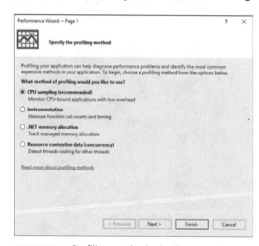

FIGURE 3-47 Profiling method selection

There are four profiling options available:

- **CPU sampling** This is a good place to start. The profiling process does not impose much loading on the processor and generates enough information to indicate where you should investigate further.

- **Instrumentation** This method works by adding extra code into methods to capture detailed timing information. It can be used to focus on methods identified by CPU sampling.

- **.NET memory allocation** Logs the creation and destruction of objects in the program, including the activity of the garbage collector. It can be used to determine whether you should create pools that allow you to reuse objects.

- **Resource contention data** If you are creating a multi-threaded application, this will allow you to discover which methods are being blocked when working with a shared resource. It can be used to identify bottlenecks in performance.

If you use the default CPU sampling option, your application will be executed and a report generated. Figure 3-48 shows a report generated by profiling the Stopwatch demonstration program in Listing 3-41, which compares sequential and parallel execution of an image scaling application.

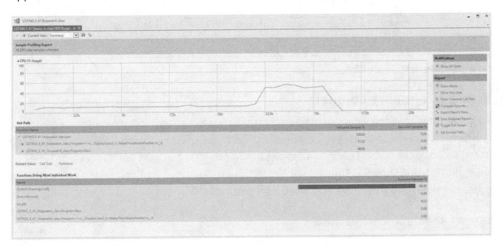

FIGURE 3-48 Profiling report

The output in Figure 3-48 is what you would expect. The increased CPU usage is caused by the multi-threaded version of the rescaling algorithm; this will make use of more processor cores. The System.Drawing library contains the method that is being used to perform the rescaling of the image, which is being used for most of the time the program is running. By navigating down the functions in the Hot Path, you can find your way to the call of the resize method.

Create and monitor performance counters

Windows maintains a large number of performance counters that can be used to monitor your computer. These counters can be viewed using the Performance Monitor (perfmon) tool. You can start this tool from the Windows Powershell or Command prompt by issuing the command perfmon. You can read the existing performance counters to enable your program to monitor the system it is running on. Figure 3-49 shows the Performance Monitor displaying the % Processor time for all the processors on a computer.

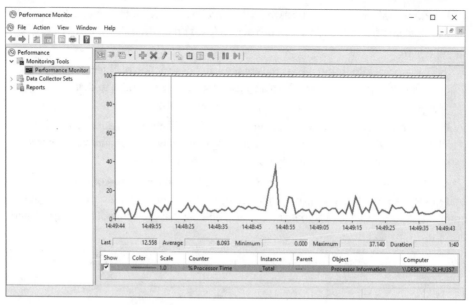

FIGURE 3-49 Performance monitor

Read performance counters

A program can read the values of the performance counters so that it can monitor the system in which it is running. A given performance counter is identified by its category name, counter name and instance name. Listing 3-42 shows how a program can read the %Processor Time value that is being shown in Figure 3-49. When this program runs it prints out the percentage processor time for the machine every half a second.

LISTING 3-42 Read performance counters

```
using System;
using System.Diagnostics;
using System.Threading;

namespace LISTING_3_42_Read_performance_counters
{
    class Program
    {
        static void Main(string[] args)
        {
            PerformanceCounter processor = new PerformanceCounter(
                categoryName:"Processor Information",
                counterName: "% Processor Time",
                instanceName:"_Total");
            Console.WriteLine("Press any key to stop");

            while (true)
            {
                Console.WriteLine("Processor time {0}", processor.NextValue());
                Thread.Sleep(500);
```

```
                if (Console.KeyAvailable)
                    break;
            }
        }
    }
}
```

Create your own performance counters

You can also create your own performance counters too. These are added to the performance counters on the host machine and can be accessed by other programs and viewed using the Performance Monitor program.

Listing 3-43 shows how performance counters are created. Two counters are created for use by the image processing program you have seen earlier. One counter tracks the total number of images processed by the computer, and the other the average number of images processed per second by the computer. The SetupPerformanceCounters method checks that the counters exist before it tries to load them. If the counters don't exist they are created. Counters are organized in categories. Each counter also has a name and can be applied to one or more instances. For example, the system has multiple instances of counters for each processor.

LISTING 3-43 Create performance counters

```
static PerformanceCounter TotalImageCounter;
static PerformanceCounter ImagesPerSecondCounter;

enum CreationResult
{
    CreatedCounters,
    LoadedCounters
};

static CreationResult SetupPerformanceCounters()
{
    string categoryName = "Image Processing";

    if (PerformanceCounterCategory.Exists(categoryName))
    {
        // production code should use using
        TotalImageCounter = new PerformanceCounter(categoryName:categoryName,
            counterName:"# of images processed",
        readOnly:false);
        // production code should use using
        ImagesPerSecondCounter = new PerformanceCounter(categoryName:categoryName,
            counterName: "# images processed per second",
        readOnly:false);
    return CreationResult.LoadedCounters;
    }

    CounterCreationData[] counters = new CounterCreationData[] {
        new CounterCreationData(counterName:"# of images processed",
        counterHelp:"number of images resized",
        counterType:PerformanceCounterType.NumberOfItems64),
```

```
    new CounterCreationData(counterName: "# images processed per second",
    counterHelp:"number of images processed per second",
    counterType:PerformanceCounterType.RateOfCountsPerSecond32)
};

CounterCreationDataCollection counterCollection =
new CounterCreationDataCollection(counters);

PerformanceCounterCategory.Create(categoryName:categoryName,
    categoryHelp:"Image processing information",
    categoryType: PerformanceCounterCategoryType.SingleInstance,
    counterData:counterCollection);

return CreationResult.CreatedCounters;
}
```

There are a number of different types of counter that can be created. The program above uses two types of counter. The counter that counts the number of images processed is the NumberOfItems64 type, which counts using a 64 bit integer. The counter that counts the number of images being processed per second is a RateOfCountsPerSecond32 that averages the number of updates per second to the counter.

The first time that the program is run it creates the counters and then ends. The second time the program is run it will update the counters during image processing. The code next shows how this works. If the SetupPerformanceCounters method returns the value that indicates that it created the counters, the program displays an appropriate prompt and then ends.

```
if(SetupPerformanceCounters() == CreationResult.CreatedCounters)
{
    Console.WriteLine("Performance counters created");
    Console.WriteLine("Restart the program");
    Console.ReadKey();
    return;
}
```

The counters are updated in the method that processes each image as shown next in the code. A program can increment a counter or an update by any value.

```
public static void MakeThumbnail(string sourceFile, string destDir,
int width, int height)
{
    TotalImageCounter.Increment();

    ImagesPerSecondCounter.Increment();
    // image processing code goes here
}
```

Once the counters have been created on a machine, they can be browsed for and viewed as any other counter. Figure 3-50 shows the output from Performance Monitor as the image processing program runs. The upper trace shows the number of images resized increasing, while the profile of the lower trace shows how image processing speeds up when the program performs image resizing across multiple processors.

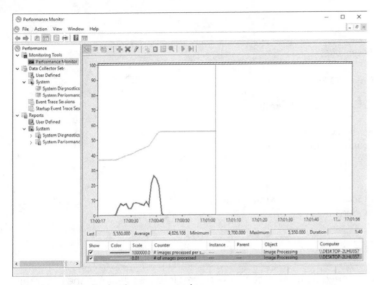

FIGURE 3-50 Monitoring image processing

Note that for a program to create performance monitors, it must be running with Administrator privileges.

Write to the event log

You have already seen how an application can write tracing information to an output file. It is also possible to send tracing output to the Windows Event Log. The Event Log is used by Windows system components and applications to log the operation of your computer. The EventLog class in the System.Diagnostics can be used to add events to the event log in a similar manner to that adding performance counters.

As with using performance counters, an application can only write to the event log if it has appropriate permissions. When using Visual Studio you need to make sure that you are running the program as an administrator. To run Visual Studio as an administrator you right-click on the program in the Start menu, select More from the menu that appears, and then select "Run as Administrator."

The process of writing to an event log is very similar to that of creating and updating a counter. Before a log can be written, it must be created. Then, once the log has been created it can accept log events. The code in Listing 3-44 will either open an existing log or create a new one.

LISTING 3-44 Write to the event log

```
static EventLog imageEventLog;

enum CreationResult
{
    CreatedLog,
```

```
        LoadedLog
    };

    static CreationResult SetupLog()
    {
        string categoryName = "Image Processing";

        if(EventLog.SourceExists(categoryName))
        {
            imageEventLog = new EventLog();
            imageEventLog.Source = categoryName;
            return CreationResult.LoadedLog;
        }

        EventLog.CreateEventSource(source: categoryName,
            logName: categoryName + " log");

        return CreationResult.CreatedLog;
    }
```

Once the log has been opened a program can write entries into it as shown in the program code here.

```
    static void Main(string[] args)
    {
        if (SetupLog() == CreationResult.CreatedLog)
        {
            Console.WriteLine("Log created");
            Console.WriteLine("Restart the program");
            Console.ReadKey();
            return;
        }

        Console.WriteLine("Processing started");

        imageEventLog.WriteEntry("Image processing started");

        // process images

        imageEventLog.WriteEntry("Image processing ended");

        Console.WriteLine("Processing complete. Press any key to exit.");
        Console.ReadKey();
    }
```

Reading from the event log

A program can also read from the event log. Listing 3-45 shows how this is performed. The program reads the image processing event log and prints out every entry in it. If the log has not been created (or none of the earlier example programs have been run on the computer) the program prints a warning message and ends.

LISTING 3-45 Read from the event log

```csharp
using System;
using System.Diagnostics;

namespace LISTING_3_45_Read_from_the_event_log
{
    class Program
    {
        static void Main(string[] args)
        {
            string categoryName = "Image Processing";

            if (!EventLog.SourceExists(categoryName))
            {
                Console.WriteLine("Event log not present");
            }
            else
            {
                EventLog imageEventLog = new EventLog();
                imageEventLog.Source = categoryName;
                foreach(EventLogEntry entry in imageEventLog.Entries)
                {
                    Console.WriteLine("Source: {0} Type: {1} Time: {2} Message: {3}",
                        entry.Source, entry.EntryType, entry.TimeWritten, entry.
Message);
                }
            }

            Console.WriteLine("Press any key");
            Console.ReadKey();
        }
    }
}
```

Binding to log events

A program can bind to an event log and receive notification events when the log is written to. You can use this to create a dashboard that displays the activity of your applications. The dashboard binds to log events that your application generates. Listing 3-46 shows how this is done. The program binds a handler to the Image Processing log events and then waits for events to arrive. To see this in action, run Listing 3-46 and then run Listing 3-44. You will see event messages printed out as they are written into the log.

LISTING 3-46 Bind to the event log

```
using System;
using System.Diagnostics;

namespace LISTING_3_46_Bind_to_the_event_log
{
    class Program
    {
        static void Main(string[] args)
        {
            string categoryName = "Image Processing";

            EventLog imageEventLog = new EventLog();
            imageEventLog.Source = categoryName;
            imageEventLog.EntryWritten += ImageEventLog_EntryWritten;
            imageEventLog.EnableRaisingEvents = true;

            Console.WriteLine("Listening for log events");
            Console.WriteLine("Press any key to exit");
            Console.ReadKey();
        }

        private static void ImageEventLog_EntryWritten(object sender,
        EntryWrittenEventArgs e)
        {
            Console.WriteLine(e.Entry.Message);
        }
    }
}
```

Thought experiments

In these thought experiments, demonstrate your skills and knowledge of the topics covered in this chapter. You can find the answers to these thought experiments in the next section.

1 Validate application input

Unfortunately, programs will fail in response to invalid data. It is a situation where the user of the program looks clever and the developer looks stupid. However, there is more to validation than looking stupid; a failure to pay attention to this issue can lead to the creation of applications that are vulnerable to exploits that can be initiated just by entering some invalid values.

Here are some questions to consider:

1. Can a JSON document contain binary data?
2. Can a JSON document contain a structure?
3. Does a program run faster if it uses untyped collection classes?
4. You want to count the number of occurrences of different words in a document. What data structure should you use?

5. What is the difference between model, view, and controller? Why do we have them?

6. What would you do if you wanted to add publisher information to the MusicTracks application that were implemented using ASP.NET.

7. What would you do if you wanted to view all the tracks recorded by a particular artist in the MusicTracks application that you implemented using ASP.NET.

8. Are there any situations in which a data variable in a class should be made public?

9. Is it always bad for a method to have "side effects"?

10. What is the difference between a "deep" and a "shallow" copy of an object?

11. Why do you never have to create a copy constructor for a structure?

12. When should you consider risk in software development?

13. What is a regular expression?

14. Can you only use regular expressions in C# programs?

2 Perform symmetric and asymmetric encryption

Secure storage and transfer of data is a vital aspect of application development. It is important to understand the principles that underpin the process, in particular the differences between symmetric and asymmetric encryption, and how asymmetric encryption enables public/private keys.

Here are some questions to consider:

1. When in a project should you consider the use of encryption?

2. What is the difference between encoding and encryption?

3. Is it really impossible to encrypt data without using a key?

4. Can you encrypt using a private key?

5. What happens if you lose your private key?

6. Can you encrypt a large document using asymmetric encryption? If not, how do you securely send a large document to someone you've never met?

7. Does signing a document keep it secret?

8. What is "padding"?

9. Is it hard to add encryption to an existing .NET application?

10. Is it hard to change from one encryption algorithm to another in a .NET program?

11. Can you prove your identity without using a certification authority?

12. Why can't you use asymmetric encryption to encrypt a stream?

13. What does it mean when a hashing algorithm is considered compromised?

14. How would you write your own hashing algorithm for your own data types?

3 Manage assemblies

Assemblies are the fundamental building blocks of .NET applications. Classes allow you to break your applications down into cooperating elements. Assemblies let you bring your classes together into the files that will be deployed to users of your application. It goes without saying that the contents of each assembly need to be considered during the design phase of your application.

Here are some questions to consider:

1. How should you organize the elements in my assemblies?
2. What is there a difference between an assembly written in C# and one written in Visual Basic .NET?
3. Can a library assembly contain a main method?
4. Why does the manifest for an assembly contain a reference to the mscorelib as well as any other assembly libraries that it uses?
5. Why does Microsoft bother with the intermediate language? Surely a program would start up more quickly if it didn't have to be compiled before it can be run?
6. Can two strong-named assemblies ever have the same fully qualified name?
7. Does the use of .NET assemblies mean that the computer might have multiple versions of the same library dll loaded at the same time?
8. Why don't we put all of our assemblies in the Global Assembly Cache?

4 Debug an application

Debugging is a fact of life. Good design and test-driven development will expose errors that can lead to bugs, but debugging is something that every developer has to do. The good news is that the tools provided in Visual Studio, and the way that they are integrated into the C# language, provide a really good place to debug programs.

Here are some questions to consider:

1. When does the C# pre-processor run?
2. Can you use the #if conditional compilation directive to test the value of a variable?
3. Some of the lines in the Visual Studio editor are gray. Why is this?
4. Visual Studio is telling you that none of the breakpoints will be hit. Why is this?
5. What type of data is a symbol defined by the #define directive?
6. Do you always have to #define my symbols in my program source files?
7. Can a program create a #define symbol when it runs?
8. Can you use the #pragma pre-processor directive to ignore compilation errors?
9. Do you need to copy the program debug database to the customer when you ship the product?

10. A fellow programmer wants to discard all their program database files. Why is this a bad idea?

11. What is the effect on performance of using a symbol server when debugging?

5 Implement diagnostics in an application

The true value of diagnostics only becomes apparent once you hit a problem with an application that has been deployed to users. In this situation it is incredibly useful to have detailed descriptive output and the ability to view the path followed by your code. Adding tracing and logging elements to your applications has other benefits too, in that it makes debugging significantly easier, and the tracing outputs can be incorporated into a test-driven design. And, as you have seen, the use of different build options means that code elements for tracing and debugging can be completely omitted from the final program if required.

Here are some questions to consider:

1. When should you plan the logging and tracing in your application?

2. What is the difference between logging and tracing?

3. What is the difference between the Debug and Trace classes?

4. Does adding Debug and Trace elements to a program slow it down appreciably?

5. Do you have to modify the program to add tracing to it?

6. What is the difference between the TraceSwitch and SourceSwitch classes?

7. Where does the program store its performance counter information?

8. What is a log event?

9. A fellow programmer is complaining that their program is not creating and updating its performance counters. Can you think of any reason why this would happen?

10. Does the operating system generate events when performance counter values are updated?

11. How could an application monitor the amount of free memory that is available as the application runs?

Thought experiment answers

This section provides the solutions for the tasks included in the thought experiments.

1 Validate application input

1. Binary data includes things like images and sounds, which are comprised of a large number of values. A JSON document can only contain elements that can be represented

by text, so binary values are converted into text (using an encoding called base64) by Json.NET before they are added to the document.

2. A JSON document can contain class or struct types.

3. An untyped collection manages all of the elements that it stores in terms of references to objects. It is arguable that this might slightly increase the speed of adding and removing objects from the collection, because the collection will not be performing any type validation as the program runs. However, the speed increase will be barely measurable. The benefits of using typed collections and discovering type errors at compile time, rather than when the program runs, far outweigh any performance gains that might accrue from using untyped collections.

4. The best way to do this is to use a dictionary of integers indexed on a string. The integer in the dictionary holds the count of that word, and the index is the word itself. When the document is being processed, each word is isolated in turn. If the word is not present in the dictionary, it is added to the dictionary, and the count for that word is set to 1. If the word is present in the dictionary, the count for that word is incremented.

5. The model holds the data; the view is generated to show the user some information about the model (there may be multiple views), and the controller generates the information to populate the view and responds to messages from the views. In ASP.NET terms, the model is the database connection. The view is the HTML web endpoints, and the controllers are C# classes bound to events produced by the views. You have this separation so that the different elements provide a "separation of concerns." The creator of the data store doesn't have to consider how the information will be presented, and the view doesn't have to contain any of the programmatic behaviors of the application. The controller can focus on the actions to be performed to generate the user interface and update the data store.

6. If the publisher is a simple string that gives the publisher name, it can be added as another property in the MusicTrack class. It makes sense to create a new Publisher class that is added to the models for the application. A MusicTrack instance contains a "foreign key" that identifies the particular Publisher record associated with the track. Once the changes have been made, the new class can migrate into the Entity Framework model for the application, and the web page views updated to show the new publisher information.

7. This requires the creation of an additional view of the document that takes the form of an additional web page that allows the artist to be selected and the tracks displayed. The behavior to obtain the information is added to an existing controller class, or a new controller class can be created.

8. The only situation in which I consider it to be acceptable for data in a class to be made public is if you are highly concerned about performance, and the effect of damage to the object is not critical. For example, when writing a game I would make public the positions of the objects on the screen and the images that are displayed when they are drawn on the screen. This improves performance, and if the values are corrupted, the

game may not behave as it should, but I consider that the effect of any error will not be expensive or dangerous.

9. A side effect of a method is some change it makes in the environment around it. Using side-effects can improve performance, and a method might have an effect on an object that is passed as a parameter, but try to avoid side effects because they can be confusing for anyone trying to understand a program that they haven't seen before.

10. An object may contain references to other objects. If you make a shallow copy of the object, the references themselves are copied. If you make a deep copy of the object, each of the objects that the references refer to is also copied.

11. A structure may not need a copy constructor, because whenever you assign a structure value, the values in the structure are already copied. In other words, assigning one struct variable to another performs a "shallow" copy of the data in the source structure. However, if the source structure contains references to other objects, you will need to create a copy constructor to perform a "deep copy" of the structure.

12. You should consider risk at all stages of development. It is not enough to perform a risk analysis at the start of the project and then assume that all risks have been addressed. Risks should be monitored and the search for new risks should continue during the project development.

13. A regular expression can be used to match the contents of a string. A simple regular expression, such as the string "Rob," matches the string "Rob." You can add elements to the expression to identify ranges of characters to match and give alternatives to match. They can be used to identify elements to be edited, but also to determine if an input string matches the expression. In this second role, they are very useful for data validation.

14. Regular expressions can be used in a wide range of operating systems and programming languages.

2 Perform symmetric and asymmetric encryption

1. You should consider which elements in an application require encryption right at the start of the development process. This is a return to the risk-based approach to design, where you consider the chances of an exploit and the impact that such an exploit should have.

2. Encoding is a process which takes data and represents it in some way. The UNICODE standard is a way of encoding character data into particular numeric values, for example the letter A could be encoded into the UNICODE value 65. Encryption is a process that takes data and converts it into a form where it must be decrypted before it can be read. In other words, encoding keeps the meaning of the data, whereas encryption tries to hide it.

3. Encryption without using a key is very dangerous, and very open to attack. This technology is more often called "obfuscation," which is the process of making something hard

to read. Obfuscation has its place in application development. If you are distributing compiled code and you don't want other developers to be able to decompile and read your source you can pass the assemblies through an "obfuscator," which will remove all of the meaningful variable names and introduce extra constructions to confuse the meaning of the source.

4. You can encrypt using your private key, but since the public key is public, there is not a lot of point in doing this for data protection, as anyone can obtain your public key and use it to decrypt the data. However, encrypting with a private key is useful if you want to prove the origins of a document. It is the basis of document signing.

5. If you lose your private key you will be unable to read any messages that have been encoded with your public key. There is no "back door" that will allow you to recover your key from your public key. This is why computers have key stores and certificate stores built into them, so that the user doesn't need to worry about this.

6. Asymmetric encryption is not suitable for encrypting large documents. There are two reasons for this. First, the process is quite processor intensive. Second, the larger the encrypted message the more vulnerable that message is to a "brute force" attack to determine the keys used to encrypt it. If you want to send someone a large, secret, document you should do this by using asymmetric encryption to securely obtain a symmetric key from the document recipient and then use this key to send the document using asymmetric encryption.

7. Signing a document is a way of proving that the document is authentic. It allows the recipient to be confident that they know who sent the document and that the contents of the document have not been tampered with. However, signing a document does not protect the contents of the document from being read.

8. The same message encrypted using RAS always produces the same output. Padding adds randomness to a message so that the same text always appears different. It is added and removed by the encryption and decryption process.

9. Adding encryption to the movement of data is easy because the encryption process for symmetric encryption is implemented as a stream that can be inserted into the data movement process. The hardest aspect of adding encryption will be the management of the keys.

10. All the encryption classes in the `System.Security.Cryptography` namespace are child classes of the `SymmetricAlgorithm` class, so switching to another encryption method is easy. However, you may have to handle existing data that has been encoded using the previous algorithm.

11. Proving your identity to someone without a certification authority means physically meeting them and showing them your drivers ID or some other physical proof of identity. If you do this and give them a USB memory key with your key files on it, that might work.

12. You should not use asymmetric encryption to encrypt large amounts of data, because it might be passed through a stream. Asymmetric encryption is demanding on the processor and vulnerable to attack if used for large amounts of data.

13. If a hashing algorithm is described as compromised, it means that techniques have been discovered that allow the contents of a document to be changed without the hash value (manifest) changing.

14. The object class contains a virtual method called GetHash(), which is used within .NET to calculate a value that represents the content of the object. You can overload this method in your types so that it uses the contents of the object to generate a value that represents those contents. However, it is not possible to create a cryptographically secure hash value this way as the result of the GetHash method is only a single integer. An integer value is useful in a data management context, but for document signing we need a bigger hash code. You therefore have to create your own hashing technology. One way is to combine elements in the object into a block of bytes and then use an SHA2 method to create a manifest from this block.

3 Manage assemblies

1. It makes sense to organize the elements in an assembly on the basis of function. The data access elements can be placed in one assembly, the business model behaviors in another and the user interface in a third. You should be mindful of dependencies when you design your assemblies, so ideally you should not have two assemblies that each contain classes that are dependent on each other.

2. Because the assembly contains the compiled code there should be no difference in the MSIL produced for the different languages. I've actually done tests where I've written the same code in both languages and then compared the MSIL files and they are essentially the same.

3. A library assembly should not have an entry point. An assembly is always loaded by a program that is already executing.

4. An assembly is not just dependent on components that we have written. It can also be dependent on the behavior of system routines. If an assembly specifies the particular version of a system library that it will use this means that it will not be affected by changes to that library?

5. The Microsoft Intermediate Language (MSIL) adds a great deal of flexibility. A system can support multiple programming languages and can also execute on a range of systems. The use of MSIL also makes it easy to create an application out of several different programming languages.

6. The fully qualified name of an assembly uses a hash of the public key of the assembly as part of the name. As we saw when we discussed encryption in the previous section, it is not guaranteed that two different key values can create the same hash value, but this is so unlikely as to be impossible. We can say that it is sufficiently unlikely for two names to be different for us not to have to worry about it.

7. A machine might have multiple versions of a particular library in the Global Assembly Cache (GAC). This might sound like a waste of space but remember that the GAC is just

file storage. The libraries are only loaded into memory when they are required by an application. Fortunately, .NET came along at a time when the price and capacity of storage space meant that storing multiple versions of libraries is not a problem for modern systems.

8. The Global Assembly Cache (GAC) is intended to provide a means by which applications can share assemblies. The word cache implies that elements in it will somehow be loaded more quickly, but this is not the case with the GAC.

4 Debug an application

1. The C# pre-processor runs when the compiler starts running. It opens the file and reads lines looking for pre-processor directives; these are statements that start with a # character.

2. The #if conditional compilation directive performs a test when the program is compiled, not when it runs. So, it cannot test the contents of any variable because at this point the variables have not been given any values.

3. Visual Studio is aware of pre-processor directives. In fact, you can regard the Visual Studio text editor as having a pre-processor built-in. This means that it is able to identify which lines will not be compiled because of pre-processor directives. It draws these lines grayed out.

4. If your breakpoints suddenly become unusable, this is usually because the build type for the project is now release rather than debug. The release version of a program contains optimizations that mean the running code may not perform actions in the same sequence as the compiled source. This makes it impossible to set breakpoints and step through the code. The other reason for breakpoints being unavailable is if the program debug database is not accessible.

5. The #defined directive creates a symbol. The symbol itself does not hold any data. The fact that the symbol exists is what we are interested in, not what the symbol contains. This is different behavior from the languages C and C++, where defined symbols can contain values.

6. You can #define symbols at the top of source files, but you can also define symbols in the Visual Studio project for an application.

7. By the time a program runs the pre-processor is long gone. The pre-processor just controls what code statements are processed by the C# compiler, so there is no way that a running program can create #define symbols.

8. The #pragma directive tells the compiler to ignore all, or nominated, warnings. It is not possible to make the compiler ignore compilation errors. This would be a very dangerous thing to do.

9. The user of your program has no particular use for a program debug database, but it can be a good idea to provide the file to them. For one thing, the error reports pro-

duced by the program can contain more detail. For another, if you want to try remote debugging of the application it is useful to have the file on the machine.

10. It would be a very bad idea to delete the program database files. While they are not needed to run the application, they are vital for debugging. If a pdb file is lost, it cannot be recreated because any new file will not have the same GUID as the original and will not be recognized by the debugger. It is possible to send a compiled application to a customer without the pdb files, but the files themselves should be retained.

11. A symbol server provides program debug database information to a program in place of a local program debug database file. The symbols are accessed via a network connection. This means that loading an assembly might take longer as the debug symbols are loaded. This can result in a slowdown of the application.

5 Implement diagnostics in an application

1. The logging and tracing elements of an application should be planned at the very start of the design process. The more important a component is, the more carefully you should consider how to determine the proper operation of that component and the ease with which you can investigate failures.

2. Logging is the production of output every time your program does something interesting. For example, each time a bank application processes a transaction, it can write an entry into a log file. Tracing is the production of output that shows the path followed by the program. For example, methods could generate messages when they are entered and when they are completed.

3. The Debug and Trace classes provide a similar set of behaviors. Both can be used to generate events, and both support assertions and can support listeners that receive the events they generate. The difference is that Debug behaviors are not present in release builds, and the Trace class supports levels of tracing output (information, warning and error) alongside simple messages.

4. The Debug elements of a program are not active in an application when the application is compiled in Release mode. However, the Trace elements will always be performed when the program runs, although this may only take the form of a single test to determine if a given TraceSource object has any listeners assigned to it. The performance impact of inactive tracing is trivial, compared with the benefits of having trace data in the event of problems.

5. If you want to add tracing to a program that contains no trace code at all, you will have to modify the program. However, you can create a program that contains tracing elements that you can then control by modification of the application configuration file. So, rather than modifying the application, you can instead add a section to the application configuration file and even create listeners and specify where their output is to be sent.

6. The TraceSwitch class allows a program to create an object that a program can use to control any tracing activities it may perform. The program can set the required tracing

level on the `TraceSwitch` instance, and then test the instance to decide what tracing output to produce. The `SourceSwitch` class is used with the `TraceSource` class to specify the level of tracing to be produced by a `TraceSource` instance.

7. A program doesn't have to store any of the performance counter information that it works with. Performance counters are managed by the operating system on the computer.

8. A log event is a packet of data that describes a particular event. It will typically contain the date and time the event occurred, an event status, and some text.

9. A program is only permitted to create performance counters and log events if it is running with Administrator permissions. It might be that the failing program is not running with these permissions enabled.

10. A "dashboard" application can read performance counters that are set by the system being monitored. It can also read event log entries produced by the system, and also binds to log events so that the dashboard display can be updated as the status of the application changes.

11. An application can read the appropriate performance counter. There are several that deal with memory use.

Chapter summary

- Data validation is a crucial component of a secure application. It must be designed into an application at the start.

- JavaScript Object Notation (JSON) provides a way of converting a C# class structure into a document string that contains a series of name values pairs that match the elements in the class. Private elements in a type are not automatically stored, but can be.

- The Newtonsoft JSON library can be used to convert classes to and from JSON strings. It will throw exceptions if given an invalid JSON string to decode. The exceptions contain information that describe the position in the source text of the error.

- XML (eXtensible Markup Language) is another means by which classes can be converted into text documents. XML documents can be validated by XML schemas that describe a particular document structure.

- A program should use typed collection classes so that errors with the use of types will be detected at compile time, rather than causing exceptions when the program runs.

- If there is any prospect of an application making use of multiple threads it should use the concurrent collection classes.

- Selecting the correct form of collection (queue, stack, indexed storage, linked list or dictionary) will improve performance and ease of coding.

- An ASP.NET (Active Server Pages) application can be built on an Entity Framework data store that provides the Model element of a Model View Controller (MVC) pattern. In this mapping the Views of the data are provided by HTML web pages and the Controllers (which respond to inputs from the views and update the data model) are created as C# classes.

- When deciding how much effort to put into retaining object integrity, it is important to consider the risk of an integrity failure and the impact that such a failure will have. The allocation of effort to mitigate risk should be made at the start of a project once the risks have been identified and their impact assessed.

- Actions that are performed on data should be "atomic," in that they should not be made up of a number of smaller actions that are performed independently. A non-atomic (or made up of a number of other parts) action may fail part way through, leading to an object being left in an invalid state.

- Regular expressions can be used to edit data and also to match against a given data element to validate its structure and contents.

- C# provides built-in Parse and TryParse behaviors that can be used to convert data from string values into a destination type. The Parse method will throw an exception if the conversion fails. The TryParse method will return True or False, which is easier to manage than creating exception handlers to deal with what should be regarded as a fairly common issue.

- C# provides a Convert class that contains a number of methods that will perform data conversion.

- The data classes in an Entity Framework application can be given extra attributes to indicate validation actions.

- Cryptography is sending messages that cannot be read by eavesdroppers. Crypto-analysis is reading messages that you're not supposed to be able to read. Encryption is the process of converting plain text (the message) into encrypted data that has to be decrypted so that it can be read. Decryption is the reverse of encryption.

- A key is an item that is used in the encryption and decryption processes. Encryption that does not involve the use of a key is vulnerable to statistical techniques that can reveal the encryption technique through patterns in the language and conventions of the conversing parties.

- Symmetric encryption uses the same key at each end of an encrypted conversation. This can provide high levels of security and is easy for computers to perform; but requires that both sides of a conversation have copies of the key.

- There are .NET libraries that will perform symmetric encryption. The encryption algorithms are exposed in the form of child classes of the SymmetricAlgorithm abstract class, making it easy to change encryption algorithms. The encryption process itself is provided as a stream, making it easy to integrate encryption into data transfer. The preferred encryption mechanism is AES (Advanced Encryption Standard).

- Asymmetric encryption uses different keys for sender and receiver. Data encrypted by one key can be read by the other key. The mathematical techniques used to generate the keys make it very computationally difficult to deduce one key given the other, or to determine either key from encrypted data.

- Asymmetric encryption requires more computer processing power to perform and is only suitable for comparatively small packets of data. It is used for transferring symmetric key values and for signing digital documents to validate them and prove their origin.

- In a public/private encryption a party (perhaps called Alice) will make one asymmetric key public and keep the other private. Other parties can use this public key to encrypt messages that can only be read by Alice. This is how you can send Alice a symmetric key that you can then use to have an encrypted conversation with her.

- The `RSACryptoServiceProvider` class provides RSA encryption for blocks of bytes. It does not encrypt streams. It is possible to generate XML that describes key values, public or private. It is also possible to store key values in a key store on a computer, either on a user or a machine basis.

- The public/private key mechanism is a convenient way to establish secure communications, but it does not provide any form of identify validation. Anyone could make a public key and claim to be Alice. Certification Authorities are trusted parties who can validate the identity of a given party. The party, (perhaps called Bob) can send Alice a public key that has been signed by a certificate that is hosted by a Certification Authority.

- The `makecert` program can be used to generate test certificates to be used during development. These can be stored in files, or in the certificate store of a given machine.

- Signing a document allows the receiver to determine who sent the document, and that the contents have not been altered. To achieve this, a program must calculate a "hash" of the document. A hash function is applied to a block of data to generate a much smaller value (tens of bytes) that are unique to that block. This is called the "block manifest."

- Hash functions can be vulnerable to attack, in that it may be possible to change the contents of a document without the hash function changing, raising the possibility of undetectable tampering. The longer the block manifest, the better. The SHA1 (Secure Hash Algorithm 1) has been compromised and is not recommended for use. SHA2 is better, but SHA3 will become the standard in the future. SHA3 is not presently supported by a .NET library although implementations are available via GitHub.

- An assembly is the basic building block of .NET applications. It can have an entry point and serve as the starting point of an application, in which case it will have the language extension .EXE or an assembly can contain a library of classes, which will be dynamically loaded as required, in which case the assembly file will have the extension .DLL.

- The assembly file contains a manifest that describes the contents of the assembly and identifies any other assemblies that are used by code in that assembly.

- The program code in an assembly is written in Microsoft Intermediate Language (MSIL), which is produced by compiling the original program source code that can be written in any .NET compatible language.

- An assembly contains version information. Assemblies with strong-names are signed using a private key that allows each assembly to be uniquely identified via its corresponding public key. This also protects against changes to the content of the assembly file.

- The code in a strong-named assembly is not protected in any way by the strong-name, and code signing does not prove the authenticity of the originator of the assembly. Services such as Authenticode, which are used by the Windows Store, can provide digital certificates that can be used to sign strong-named assemblies and identify the author.

- Assemblies can be stored in the Global Assembly Cache (GAC). This allows the assembly to be shared among applications on a machine. Multiple versions of the same assembly can be stored "side-by-side" in the GAC and each will be used appropriately by different applications on the machine.

- A faulty assembly in the GAC can be replaced by a fixed one and assembly binding redirection used to cause applications to target the new version. Redirection can be specified at application, publisher, and machine level by the use of policy files.

- WinRT is a runtime system that is based on compiled C++ code. It uses the same metadata fundamentals of .NET assemblies to express the behavior of an object. The behaviors are expressed in a file of type WinMD (Windows MetaData). This can be a wrapper around existing C++ (in the case of the Windows API) or the WinMD file can contain code. It is possible to create Windows Runtime Components (elements that express their behavior in WinMD files) from C# classes, although there are some restrictions on the behaviors of the C# objects that can be used in WinRT.

- The C# compiler understands preprocessor directives. A directive is a command preceded by a # character. The #if directive can be used to control, which code elements of a program are actually compiled into code. It tests to see if a given symbol has been defined using the #define directive. The #if directive can be used to switch on and off diagnostic elements of a program and to create custom versions of programs. However, it should not be overused because it can lead to confusing code.

- The DEBUG symbol is defined if the program is compiled with the debug option. It can be used to activate code that will run when the program is being debugged.

- The Conditional attribute can be used to control the execution of a method based on a particular symbol. If the symbol is not defined the statements that would call the method are omitted from a program when it is built.

- The #warning directive produces a warning message when a program is built.

- The #error directive produces a compilation error with the specified message when the program is built. It can be used to prevent a program from being compiled if it contains an incompatible selection of conditional options.

- The #pragma directive allows a programmer to identify blocks of source code were some, or specified, compiler warnings will be ignored.

- The #line directive lets the developer set the line numbers reported by Visual Studio during compiling and tracing through the source file. It is useful if a source code file has automatically generated code inserted during the build process. A #line directive can also be used to hide source code lines from the debugging process. A #line directive can also be used to set the name for the source file that will be displayed by diagnostic messages.

- A Visual Studio project can have a number of build configurations that specify debug options and target platforms. A newly created project will have debug and release build configurations. We can use the Configuration Manager in Visual Studio to configure build configurations and create new ones.

- The assemblies produced by a debug build will contain code that implements unused variables and methods that are not called. A release build will discard unused elements and will also perform optimizations that may change the order in which statements are performed when the program runs. For this reason, debug breakpoints cannot be set in release builds.

- When a program is built Visual Studio creates a Program Debug Database file, which contains the names of the symbols used in the program and the locations where their values are stored. The file also contains mappings of source code statements to the MSIL that implements them. A given database file is mapped to a particular source code file using a GUID that is stored in both files. A program will run if the program database file, but it cannot be debugged without one.

- Program database information can be shared from a symbol server. The Microsoft symbol server provides symbols that allow developers to step through Microsoft libraries. Development teams can create their own symbol servers to share symbol information within a project.

- A program database file can contain public and private elements. Public elements are those that are visible in the assemblies themselves, for example public methods. Private elements include things like local variables. Access to a database containing private elements could give insights into how the code works, which might be a potential security issue. The pdbcopy program, part of the Debugging Tools for Windows, can be used to copy a database file and remove public elements.

- The Debug and Trace classes in System.Diagnostics can be used to generate messages as a program runs. They can also be used to test assertions.

- When a program is built using the Debug option, the Debug code will be executed when it runs. Trace code is executed if the program is built using the Debug or Release options.

- The Trace object provides information, warning and error levels of output.

- Listeners can be bound to the Debug and Trace classes. There are different forms of listener that can be used to display output, log output as comma separated lists, and as XML formatted data.

- The TraceSource class manages the production of tracing events. There are several types of events, from informational events that are produced during normal operation, through to warning, error, and critical events. One or more TraceListener instances can be bound to a TraceScource instance to receive notifications of events.

- The TraceSwitch class can be used to determine the level of tracing to be performed by a program. The program code can test the value of a TraceSwitch instance to determine what level of tracing output to produce.

- The SourceSwitch class is used to control the tracing messages produced by a TraceSource instance. An instance of the SourceSwitch class can be associated with a TraceSource to determine the tracing events to be produced.

- The level of tracing output can also be defined by the creation of SourceSwitch values in the config file of an application. This allows the tracing behavior of a program to be changed without changing the actual program code of the application.

- Profiling of an application is used to determine the elements that are using up the most processor time when the program runs. These elements can then be specifically optimized to improve performance, if required. The simplest form of profiling is to use the Stopwatch class to measure elapsed time as the program runs.

- Visual Studio provides a range of Profiling tools. The default profiler allows a number of profiling options. The simplest, CPU sampling, is usually sufficient to determine where a program is spending most of its time. This option profiles the loading on the computer and shows the "Hot Path," which identifies the methods consuming most of the processor time.

- Performance counters are maintained by the operating system and can be used to view many different items of information about the host computer, including memory and processor use.

- An application can create and update its own performance counters. Their values will be held by the operating system. There are a range of different counter types including ones that just count values, and ones that will evaluate the number of events per second. Programs need Administrator permissions to be able to create their own performance counters.

- The values of performance counters can be viewed using the Performance monitor (perfmon) program. Programs can also read performance counters to create their own dashboard displays.

- The operating system also manages an Event log. Programs can create their own event category and event types and add events to the log. It is also possible for a program to read events and also bind a listener method to a particular event to receive notifications when that event is logged.

CHAPTER 4

Implement data access

A program can use variables to store values as it is running, but it needs a means of persisting data. We have already touched on data storage at several points in this book, in Skill 3.1 in the section "Choose the appropriate data collection type," we considered how best to map information in our application onto the data types that C# offers. Later in the section "Using JSON," we saw how data in objects can be serialized. And finally, in the "Use the Entity Framework to design your data storage" section we created classes that were automatically mapped into database tables for use in an application. Before you read this chapter, it is worth going over those topics so that they are fresh in your mind.

In this chapter we're going to bring all of these different data storage and access abilities together and consider how a C# program can store and manipulate data; starting with the use and management of file storage before moving into databases, and then onto the use of Language Integrated Query (LINQ). Then we'll take a look at serialization in detail and finally explore the data collection facilities offered by the .NET framework.

Skills in this chapter:

- Skill 4.1: Perform I/O operations
- Skill 4.2: Consume data
- Skill 4.3: Query and manipulate data and objects by using LINQ
- Skill 4.4: Serialize and deserialize data
- Skill 4.5: Store data in and retrieve data from collections

Skill 4.1: Perform I/O operations

In this section we will look at the fundamental input/output (I/O) operations that underpin data storage in applications. You will discover how files are managed by the operating system and the .NET Framework libraries that allow programs to store and load data. File access is a very slow activity when compared with the speed of modern processors, so we are also going to investigate the use of asynchronous i/o, which can be used to keep an application responsive even when it is reading or writing large amounts of data.

Read and write files and streams

A stream is a software object that represents a stream of data. The .NET framework provides a Stream class that serves as the parent type for a range of classes that can be used to read and write data. There are three ways that a program can interact with a stream:

- Write a sequence of bytes to a stream
- Read a sequence of bytes from a stream
- Position the "file pointer" in a stream

The file pointer is the position in a stream where the next read or write operation will take place. A program can use the Seek method provided by the stream to set this position. For example, a program can search through a file stream connected to formatted records for one that has a particular name.

The Stream class is abstract and serves as a template for streams that connect to actual storage resources. It is a very good example of how C# classes can be used to deploy resources. Any object that can work with a Stream can work with any of the objects that behave like a stream. In Chapter 3 in Listing 3-24 we used a MemoryStream to capture the output of an encryption process into a byte array. It would be very easy to redirect the encrypted data produced in that program to a file or a network connection by using a different type of stream object. Figure 4-2 shows how the System.IO.Stream type is the base type for a large number of classes that provide different forms of stream connections.

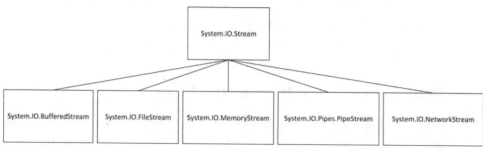

FIGURE 4-1 Some of the Stream types

The child classes all contain the stream behaviors that allow data to be transferred, for example the Stream method Write can be used on any of them to write bytes to that stream. However, how each type of stream created is dependent on that stream type. For example, to create a `FileStream` a program must specify the path to the file and how the file is going to be used. To create a `MemoryStream` a program must specify the buffer in memory to be used.

Use FileStream

The `FileStream` object provides a stream instance connected to a file. The stream object instance converts calls into the stream into commands for the filesystem on the computer running the program. The file system provides the interface to the physical device performing the data storage for the computer. Figure 4-2 shows how this works. A call of the `Write` method in a stream object will generate a request to the file system to write the data to the storage device.

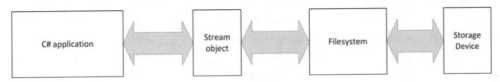

FIGURE 4-2 The Stream object

Listing 4-1 shows how a program can use a `FileStream` to create an output stream connected to a new or existing file. The program writes a block of byes to that stream. It then creates a new stream that is used to read the bytes from the file. The bytes to be written are obtained by encoding a text string.

LISTING 4-1 Using a FileStream

```
using System;
using System.IO;
using System.Text;

namespace LISTING_4_1_Using_a_FileStream
{
    class Program
    {
        static void Main(string[] args)
        {
            // Writing to a file
            FileStream outputStream = new FileStream("OutputText.txt", FileMode.
            OpenOrCreate, FileAccess.Write);
            string outputMessageString = "Hello world";
            byte[] outputMessageBytes = Encoding.UTF8.GetBytes(outputMessageString);
            outputStream.Write(outputMessageBytes, 0, outputMessageBytes.Length);
            outputStream.Close();

            FileStream inputStream = new FileStream("OutputText.txt", FileMode.Open,
            FileAccess.Read)
            long fileLength = inputStream.Length;
            byte[] readBytes = new byte[fileLength];
            inputStream.Read(readBytes, 0, (int)fileLength);
            string readString = Encoding.UTF8.GetString(readBytes);
            inputStream.Close();
            Console.WriteLine("Read message: {0}", readString);
```

```
            Console.ReadKey();
        }
    }
}
```

Control file use with FileMode and FileAccess

A stream can be associated with reading, writing, or updating a file. The base `Stream` class provides properties that a program can use to determine the abilities of a given stream instance (whether a program can read, write, or seek on this stream).

The `FileMode` enumeration is used in the constructor of a `FileStream` to indicate how the file is to be opened. The following modes are available:

- **FileMode.Append**   Open a file for appending to the end. If the file exists, move the seek position to the end of this file. If the file does not exist; create it. This mode can only be used if the file is being opened for writing.

- **FileMode.Create**   Create a file for writing. If the file already exists, it is overwritten. Note that this means the existing contents of the file are lost.

- **FileMode.CreateNew**   Create a file for writing. If the file already exists, an exception is thrown.

- **FileMode.Open**   Open an existing file. An exception is thrown if the file does not exist. This mode can be used for reading or writing.

- **FileMode.OpenOrCreate**   Open a file for reading or writing. If the file does not exist, an empty file is created. This mode can be used for reading or writing.

- **FileMode.Truncate**   Open a file for writing and remove any existing contents.

The `FileAccess` enumeration is used to indicate how the file is to be used. The following access types are available:

- **FileAccess.Read**   Open a file for reading.
- **FileAccess.ReadWrite**   Open a file for reading or writing.
- **FileAccess.Write**   Open a file for writing.

You can see these used in Listing 4-1. If a file stream is used in a manner that is incompatible with how it is opened, the action will fail with an exception.

Convert text to binary data with Unicode

A stream can only transfer arrays of bytes to and from the storage device, so the program in Listing 4-1 uses the `Encoding` class from the `System.Text` namespace. The `UTF8` property of this class provides methods that will encode and decode Unicode text. We looked at Unicode in the section "String comparison and cultures," in Skill 2.7.

Unicode is a mapping of character symbols to numeric values. The `UTF8` encoding maps Unicode characters onto 8-bit values that can be stored in arrays of bytes. Most text files are encoded using UTF8. The Encoding class also provides support for other encoding standards including UTF32 (Unicode encoding to 32-bit values) and ASCII.

The `GetBytes` encoding method takes a C# string and returns the bytes that represent that string in the specified encoding. The `GetString` decoding method takes an array of bytes and returns the string that a buffer full of bytes represents.

IDispose and FileStream objects

The `Stream` class implements the `IDisposable` interface shown in Skill 2.4. This means that any objects derived from the `Stream` type must also implement the interface. This means that we can use the C# `using` construction to ensure that files are closed when they are no longer required. Listing 4-2 shows how this works.

LISTING 4-2 FileStream and IDisposable

```
using (FileStream outputStream = new FileStream("OutputText.txt", FileMode.OpenOrCreate,
FileAccess.Write))
{
    string outputMessageString = "Hello world";
    byte[] outputMessageBytes = Encoding.UTF8.GetBytes(outputMessageString);
    outputStream.Write(outputMessageBytes, 0, outputMessageBytes.Length);
}
```

Work with text files

The filesystem makes no particular distinction between *text* files and *binary* files. We have already seen how we can use the `Encoding` class to convert Unicode text into an array of bytes that can be written into a binary file. However, the C# language provides stream classes that make it much easier to work with text. The `TextWriter` and `TextReader` classes are abstract classes that define a set of methods that can be used with text.

The `StreamWriter` class extends the `TextWriter` class to provide a class that we can us to write text into streams. Listing 4-3 shows how the `StreamWriter` and `StreamReader` classes can be used work with text files. It performs the same task as the program in Listing 4-1, but it is much more compact.

LISTING 4-3 StreamWriter and StreamReader

```
using (StreamWriter writeStream = new StreamWriter("OutputText.txt"))
{
    writeStream.Write("Hello world");
}

using (StreamReader readStream = new StreamReader("OutputText.txt"))
{
    string readSTring = readStream.ReadToEnd();
    Console.WriteLine("Text read: {0}", readSTring);
}
```

Chain streams together

The Stream class has a constructor that will accept another stream as a parameter, allowing the creation of chains of streams. Listing 4-4 shows how to use the GZipStream from the System. IO.Compression namespace in a chain of streams that will save and load compressed text.

LISTING 4-4 Storing compressed files

```
using (FileStream writeFile = new FileStream("CompText.zip", FileMode.OpenOrCreate,
 FileAccess.Write))
{
    using (GZipStream writeFileZip = new GZipStream(writeFile,
    CompressionMode.Compress))
    {
        using (StreamWriter writeFileText = new StreamWriter(writeFileZip))
        {
            writeFileText.Write("Hello world");
        }
    }
}

using (FileStream readFile = new FileStream("CompText.zip", FileMode.Open,
 FileAccess.Read))
{
    using (GZipStream readFileZip = new GZipStream(readFile,
    CompressionMode.Decompress))
    {
        using (StreamReader readFileText = new StreamReader(readFileZip))
        {
            string message = readFileText.ReadToEnd();
            Console.WriteLine("Read text: {0}", message);
        }
    }
}
```

Use the File class

The File class is a "helper" class that makes it easier to work with files. It contains a set of static methods that can be used to append text to a file, copy a file, create a file, delete a file, move a file, open a file, read a file, and manage file security. Listing 4-5 shows some of the features of the File class in action.

LISTING 4-5 The File class

```
File.WriteAllText(path: "TextFile.txt",   contents: "This text goes in the file");

File.AppendAllText(path: "TextFile.txt",   contents: " - This goes on the end");

if (File.Exists("TextFile.txt"))
    Console.WriteLine("Text File exists");

string contents = File.ReadAllText(path:"TextFile.txt");
Console.WriteLine("File contents: {0}", contents);
```

```
File.Copy(sourceFileName: "TextFile.txt", destFileName: "CopyTextFile.txt");

using (TextReader reader = File.OpenText(path: "CopyTextFile.txt"))
{
    string text = reader.ReadToEnd();
    Console.WriteLine("Copied text: {0}", text);
}
```

Handle stream exceptions

Exceptions are situations where it is not meaningful for a given thread of execution to continue. The thread can raise an exception and pass control to a handler that will attempt to resolve the situation in a sensible way. You first saw exceptions in Skill 1.5, "Implement exception handling." When creating applications that use streams you need to ensure that your code can deal with any exceptions that might be thrown by the stream. These can happen at any time during the use of a stream. Our application may try to open a file that does not exist, or a given storage device may become full during writing. It is also possible that threads in a multi-threaded application can "fight" over files. If one thread attempts to access a file already in use by another, this will lead to exceptions being thrown.

With this in mind you should ensure that production code that opens and interacts with streams is protected by try–catch constructions. There are a set of file exceptions that are used to indicate different error conditions. Listing 4-6 shows how a program can detect the FileNotFoundException and respond to that in a different way to other file exceptions.

LISTING 4-6 Stream exceptions

```
try
{
    string contents = File.ReadAllText(path: "Testfile.txt");
    Console.WriteLine(contents);
}
catch(FileNotFoundException notFoundEx)
{
    // File not found
    Console.WriteLine(notFoundEx.Message);
}
catch(Exception ex)
{
    // Any other exception
    Console.WriteLine(ex.Message);
}
```

Files storage

A given storage device, perhaps a disk drive or USB portable disk, can be divided into *partitions*. Each partition represents an area on the storage device that can be used to store data. A partition on a storage device is exposed as a *drive* which, on the Windows operating system, is represented by a *drive letter*. The drive letter is assigned by the operating system and is used as the root of an *absolute path* to a file on the computer.

The Disk Management application allows administrators to re-assign drive letters, combine multiple physical drives into a single logical drive, and attach virtual hard drives (VHD) created from drive images. Figure 4-3 below shows this program in use.

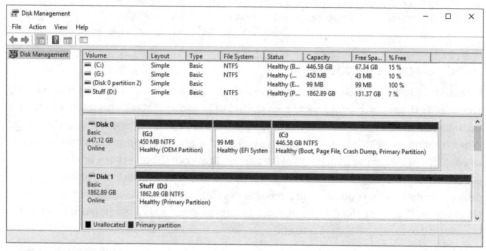

FIGURE 4-3 The Disk Management program

Each of the partitions on a physical storage device is *formatted* using a particular *filing system* that manages the storage of file. The program in Listing 4-7 shows how the DriveInfo class in the System.IO namespace can be used to obtain information about the drives attached to a system.

LISTING 4-7 Drive information

```
DriveInfo[] drives = DriveInfo.GetDrives();
foreach (DriveInfo drive in drives)
{
    Console.Write("Name:{0} ", drive.Name);
    if (drive.IsReady)
    {
        Console.Write("  Type:{0}", drive.DriveType);
        Console.Write("  Format:{0}", drive.DriveFormat);
        Console.Write("  Free space:{0}", drive.TotalFreeSpace);
    }
    else
    {
        Console.Write("  Drive not ready");
    }
    Console.WriteLine();
}
```

When I ran the program the following output was created:

```
Name:C:\   Type:Fixed  Format:NTFS  Free space:69709230080
Name:D:\   Type:Fixed  Format:NTFS  Free space:133386022912
Name:E:\   Drive not ready
```

```
Name:F:\    Type:Removable  Format:exFAT  Free space:41937928192
Name:G:\    Type:Fixed  Format:NTFS  Free space:44650496
Name:K:\    Drive not ready
Name:L:\    Drive not ready
```

Note that some of the drive letters have been allocated to removable devices. Drive F is a memory card from a camera. The drives that are shown as not ready do not presently have devices physically connected.

Use FileInfo

A file system maintains information about each file it stores. This includes the name of the file, permissions associated with the file, dates associated with the creation, modification of the file, and the physical location of the file on the storage device. The filesystem also maintains attribute information about each file. The attribute information is held as a single value with different bits in the value indicating different attributes. We can use logical operators to work with these values and assign different attributes to a file. The available attributes are as follows:

- **FileAttributes.Archive** The file has not been backed up yet. The attribute will be cleared when/if the file is backed up.

- **FileAttributes.Compressed** The file is compressed. This is not something that our program should change.

- **FileAttributes.**Directory The file is a directory. This is not something our program should change.

- **FileAttributes.Hidden** The file will not appear in an ordinary directory listing.

- **FileAttributes.Normal** This is a normal file with no special attributes. This attribute is only valid when there are no other attributes assigned to the file.

- **FileAttributes.ReadOnly** The file cannot be written.

- **FileAttributes.System** The file is part of the operating system and is used by it.

- **FileAttributes.Temporary** The file is a temporary file that will not be required when the application has finished. The file system will attempt to keep this file in memory to improve performance.

This information is exposed to C# programs by means of the FileInfo class. Listing 4-8 shows how a program can obtain the FileInfo information about a file and then work with the attribute information. The program creates a new file and then obtains the FileInfo object that represents the file. It uses the Attributes property of the FileInfo object to make the file readOnly and then removes the readOnly attribute.

LISTING 4-8 Using FileInfo

```
string filePath = "TextFile.txt";

File.WriteAllText(path: filePath, contents: "This text goes in the file");
FileInfo info = new FileInfo(filePath);
Console.WriteLine("Name: {0}", info.Name);
```

```
Console.WriteLine("Full Path: {0}", info.FullName);
Console.WriteLine("Last Access: {0}", info.LastAccessTime);
Console.WriteLine("Length: {0}", info.Length);
Console.WriteLine("Attributes: {0}", info.Attributes);
Console.WriteLine("Make the file read only");
info.Attributes |= FileAttributes.ReadOnly;
Console.WriteLine("Attributes: {0}", info.Attributes);
Console.WriteLine("Remove the read only attribute");
info.Attributes &= ~FileAttributes.ReadOnly;
Console.WriteLine("Attributes: {0}", info.Attributes);
```

You can use a `FileInfo` instance to open a file for reading and writing, moving a file, renaming a file, and also modifying the security settings on a file. Some of the functions provided by a `FileInfo` instance duplicate those provided by the `File` class. The `File` class is most useful when you want to perform an action on a single file. The `FileInfo` class is most useful when you want to work with a large number of files. In the next section you will discover how to get a collection of `FileInfo` items from a directory and work through them.

Use the Directory and DirectoryInfo classes

A file system can create files that contain collections of file information items. These are called *directories* or *folders*. Directories can contain directory information about directories, which allows a user to *nest* directories to create tree structures.

As with files, there are two ways to work with directories: the `Directory` class and the `DirectoryInfo` class. The `Directory` class is like the `File` class. It is a static class that provides methods that can enumerate the contents of directories and create and manipulate directories. Listing 4-9 shows how a program can use the `Directory` class to create a directory, prove that it exists, and then delete it. Note that if a program attempts to delete a directory that is not empty an exception will be thrown.

LISTING 4-9 The Directory class

```
Directory.CreateDirectory("TestDir");

if (Directory.Exists("TestDir"))
    Console.WriteLine("Directory created successfully");

Directory.Delete("TestDir");

Console.WriteLine("Directory deleted successfully");
```

An instance of the `DirectoryInfo` class describes the contents of one directory. The class also provides methods that can be used to create and manipulate directories. Listing 4-10 performs the same functions as Listing 4-9 using the `DirectoryInfo` class.

LISTING 4-10 The DirectoryInfo class

```
DirectoryInfo localDir = new DirectoryInfo("TestDir");

localDir.Create();
```

```
if(localDir.Exists)
    Console.WriteLine("Directory created successfully");

localDir.Delete();

Console.WriteLine("Directory deleted successfully");
```

Files and paths

A *path* defines the location of a file on a storage device. In all the example programs above we have simply given the path as a string of text. In this case the file or directory being created will be located in the same directory as the program that is running and will have the name given. If you want to store files in different places on the computer you need to create more complex paths.

Paths can be *relative* or *absolute*. A relative path specifies the location of a file relative to the folder in which the program is presently running. Up until now all the paths that we have specified have been relative to the current directory. When expressing paths, the character "." (period) has a special significance. A single period "." means the current directory. A double period ".." means the directory above the present one. You can use relative paths to specify a file in a parent directory, or a file in a directory in another part of the tree. Next you can see the path used to locate the image directory that is provided with the sample programs for this text. The @ character at the start of the string literal marks the string as a *verbatim* string. This means that any escape characters in the string will be ignored. This is useful because otherwise the backslash characters in the string might be interpreted as escape characters.

```
string imagePath = @"..\..\..\..\images");
```

The program is running in the debug directory. The path must "climb" up through four parent directories to find the images directory. The diagram in Figure 4-4 shows how the directories are structured.

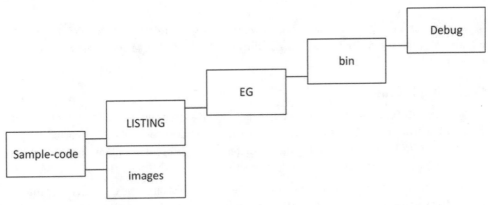

FIGURE 4-4 Navigating a relative path

An absolute path includes the drive letter and identifies all the sub-directories in the path to the file. The statement here gives the path to the document test.txt in the Documents folder on a machine.

```
string absPath = @"c:\users\rob\Documents\test.txt"
```

The path to a file contains two elements: the directories in the path and the name of the file in the directory. The Path class provides a lot of very helpful methods that can be used to work with paths in programs. It provides methods to remove filenames from full paths, change the extension on a filename, and combine filenames and directory paths. Listing 4-11 shows some of the ways that Path can be used.

LISTING 4-11 Using Path

```
string fullName = @"c:\users\rob\Documents\test.txt";

string dirName = Path.GetDirectoryName(fullName);
string fileName = Path.GetFileName(fullName);
string fileExtension = Path.GetExtension(fullName);
string lisName = Path.ChangeExtension(fullName, ".lis");
string newTest = Path.Combine(dirName, "newtest.txt");

Console.WriteLine("Full name: {0}", fullName);
Console.WriteLine("File directory: {0}", dirName);
Console.WriteLine("File name: {0}", fileName);
Console.WriteLine("File extension: {0}", fileExtension);
Console.WriteLine("File with lis extension: {0}", lisName);
Console.WriteLine("New test: {0}", newTest);
```

When you run the program in Listing 4-11 it produces the following output:

```
Full name: c:\users\rob\Documents\test.txt
File directory: c:\users\rob\Documents
File name: test.txt
File extension: .txt
File with lis extension: c:\users\rob\Documents\test.lis
New test: c:\users\rob\Documents\newtest.txt
```

The Path class is very useful and should **always** be used in preference to manually working with the path strings. The Path class also provides methods that can generate temporary filenames.

Searching for files

The DirectoryInfo class provides a method called GetFiles that can be used to get a collection of FileInfo items that describe the files in a directory. One overload of GetFiles can accept a search string. Within the search string the character * can represent any number of characters and the character ? can represent a single character.

The program in Listing 4-12 uses this form of GetFiles to list all of the C# source files that are in the example programs. Note that this program also provides a good demonstration of the use of recursion, in that the FindFiles method calls itself to deal with any directories found inside a given directory.

LISTING 4-12 C sharp programs

```
static void FindFiles(DirectoryInfo dir, string searchPattern)
{
    foreach (DirectoryInfo directory in dir.GetDirectories())
    {
        FindFiles(directory, searchPattern);
    }

    FileInfo[] matchingFiles = dir.GetFiles(searchPattern);
    foreach(FileInfo fileInfo in matchingFiles)
    {
        Console.WriteLine(fileInfo.FullName);
    }
}
static void Main(string[] args)
{
    DirectoryInfo startDir = new DirectoryInfo(@"..\..\..\..\..");
    string searchString = "*.cs";

    FindFiles(startDir, searchString);

    Console.ReadKey();
}
```

The `Directory` class provides a method called `EnumerateFiles` that can also be used to enumerate files in this way.

Read and write from the network by using classes in the System.Net namespace

The .NET Framework provides a range of application programming interfaces that can interact with a TCP/IP (Transmission Control Protocol/Internet Protocol) network. C# programs can create network *socket* objects that can communicate over the network by sending unacknowledged *datagrams* using UDP (User Datagram Protocol) or creating managed connections using TCP (Transmission Control Protocol).

In this section we are going to focus on the classes in the `System.Net` namespace that allow a program to communicate with servers using the HTTP (HyperText Transport Protocol). This protocol operates on top of a TCP/IP connection. In other words, TCP/IP provides the connection between the server and client systems and HTTP defines the format of the messages that are exchanged over that connection.

An HTTP client, for example a web browser, creates a TCP connection to a server and makes a request for data by sending the HTTP GET command. The server will then respond with a page of information. After the response has been returned to the client the TCP connection is closed.

The information returned by the server is formatted using HTML (HyperText Markup Language) and rendered by the browser. In the case of an ASP (Active Server Pages) application (for example the one that we created at the beginning of Chapter 3) the HTML document may be produced dynamically by software, rather than being loaded from a file stored on the server.

HTTP was originally used for the sharing of human-readable web pages. However, now an HTTP request may return an XML or JSON formatted document that describes data in an application.

The REST (REpresentational State Transfer) architecture uses the GET, PUT, POST and DELETE operations of HTTP to allow a client to request a server to perform functions in a client-server application. The fundamental operation that is used to communicate with these and other servers is the sending of a "web request" to a server to perform an HTML command on the server, and now we are going to discover how to do this. Let's look at three different ways to interact with web servers and consider their advantages and disadvantages. These are WebRequest, WebClient, and HttpClient.

WebRequest

The WebRequest class is an abstract base class that specifies the behaviors of a web request. It exposes a static factory method called Create, which is given a *universal resource identifier* (URI) string that specifies the resource that is to be used. The Create method inspects the URI it is given and returns a child of the WebRequest class that matches that resource. The Create method can create HttpWebRequest, FtpWebRequest, and FileWebRequest objects. In the case of a web site, the URI string will start with "http" or "https" and the Create method will return an HttpWebRequest instance.

The GetResponse method on an HttpWebRequest returns a WebResponse instance that describes the response from the server. Note that this response is not the web page itself, but an object that describes the response from the server. To actually read the text from the webpage a program must use the GetResponseStream method on the response to get a stream from which the webpage text can be read. Listing 4-13 shows how this works.

LISTING 4-13 httpWebRequest

```
WebRequest webRequest = WebRequest.Create("https://www.microsoft.com");
WebResponse webResponse = webRequest.GetResponse();

using (StreamReader responseReader = new StreamReader(webResponse.GetResponseStream()))
{
    string siteText = responseReader.ReadToEnd();
    Console.WriteLine(siteText);
}
```

Note that the use of using around the StreamReader ensures that the input stream is closed when the web page response has been read. It is important that either this stream or the WebResponse instance are explicitly closed after use, as otherwise the connection will not be reused and a program might run out of web connections.

Using WebRequest instances to read web pages works, but it is rather complicated. It does, however, have the advantage that a program can set a wide range of properties on the web and request to tailor it to particular server requirements. This flexibility is not available on some of the other methods we are going to consider.

The code in Listing 4-13 is synchronous, in that the program will wait for the web page response to be generated and the response to be read. It is possible to use the WebRequest in an asynchronous manner so that a program is not paused in this way. However, the programmer has to create event handlers to be called when actions are completed.

WebClient

The WebClient class provides a simpler and quicker way of reading the text from a web server. Listing 4-14 shows how this is achieved. There is now no need to create a stream to read the page contents (although you can do this if you wish) and there is no need to deal with the response to the web request before you can obtain the reply from the server. Listing 4-14 shows how this works.

LISTING 4-14 WebClient

```
WebClient client = new WebClient();
string siteText = client.DownloadString("http://www.microsoft.com");
Console.WriteLine(siteText);
```

The WebClient class also provides methods that can be used to read from the server asynchronously. Listing 4-15 is used in a Windows Presentation Foundation (WPF) application to read the contents of a web page for display in a window.

LISTING 4-15 WebClient async

```
async Task<string> readWebpage(string uri)
{
    WebClient client = new WebClient();
    return await client.DownloadStringTaskAsync(uri);
}
```

HttpClient

The HTTPClient is important because it is the way in which a Windows Universal Application can download the contents of a website. Unlike the WebRequest and the WebClient classes, an HTTPClient only provides asynchronous methods. It can be used in a very similar manner to the WebClient, as shown in Listing 4-16.

LISTING 4-16 HttpClient

```
async Task<string> readWebpage(string uri)
{
    HttpClient client = new HttpClient();
    return await client.GetStringAsync(uri);
}
```

Exception handling

As with file handling, loading information from the Internet is prone to error. Network connections may be broken or servers may be unavailable. This means that web request code should be enclosed in appropriate exception handlers. The code next is part of the program in Listing 4-16; it catches exceptions thrown by the asynchronous loading method and displays a MessageDialog containing error information.

```
try
{
    string webText = await readWebpage(PageUriTextBox.Text);
    ResultTextBlock.Text = webText;
}
catch (Exception ex)
{
    var dialog = new MessageDialog(ex.Message, "Request failed");
    await dialog.ShowAsync();
}
```

Implement asynchronous I/O operations

Up until now all the file input/output in our example programs has been *synchronous*. A program calling a method to perform a file operation must wait for the method to complete before it can move onto the next statement. A user of the program has to wait for the file action to complete before they can do anything else, which might lead to a very poor user experience.

In Chapter 1, in the Skill "Using async and await," you saw that a program can use tasks to perform asynchronous background execution of methods. It is worth taking a look at that section to refresh your understanding of these elements before reading further.

The file operations provided by the File class do not have any asynchronous versions, so the FileStream class should be used instead. Listing 4-17 shows a function that writes an array of bytes to a specified file using asynchronous writing.

LISTING 4-17 Asynchronous file writing

```
async Task WriteBytesAsync(string filename, byte [] items)
{
    using (FileStream outStream = new FileStream(filename, FileMode.OpenOrCreate,
FileAccess.Write))
    {
        await outStream.WriteAsync(items, 0, items.Length);
    }
}
```

The demonstration program is a Windows Presentation Foundation application that contains both synchronous and asynchronous file writing methods. Figure 4-5 shows the program display. The user can write a large number of values to a file either synchronously or asynchronously depending on which start button they select. They can also test the responsiveness of the application by selecting the Get Time button, which will display the current time. When the synchronous version of the writer is running, they should note that the user interface becomes unresponsive for a short while.

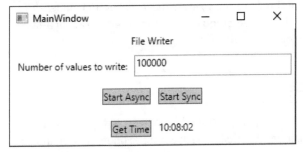

FIGURE 4-5 Async File Writer demo

Handling exceptions in asynchronous methods

If any exceptions are thrown by the asynchronous file write method they must be caught and a message displayed for the user. This will only happen if the WriteBytesAsync method returns a Task object that is awaited when the WriteBytesAsync method is called. Listing 4-18 shows a button event handler that does this correctly and catches exceptions that may be thrown by the file write action.

LISTING 4-18 File exceptions

```
private async void StartTaskButton_Click(object sender, RoutedEventArgs e)
{
    byte[] data = new byte[100];

    try
    {
        // note that the filename contains an invalid character await
            WriteBytesAsyncTask("demo:.dat", data);
    }
    catch (Exception writeException)
    {
        MessageBox.Show(writeException.Message, "File write failed");
    }
}
```

When you run the example program for Listing 4-18 the program displays a menu that lets you select between two write methods; one which returns a Task and the other of which is void. Both writes will throw an exception, but only the write that returns a Task will catch the exception correctly (see Figure 4-6) and display a message box. The other exception will not be handled correctly.

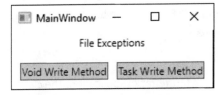

FIGURE 4-6 Catching file exceptions

The only asynchronous methods that should return void are the actual event handlers for the windows controls. Every other asynchronous method must return either a result or a Task, so that any exceptions thrown by the method can be dealt with correctly.

Skill 4.2: Consume data

In the previous section we saw how to create files and store data in them. In this section you are going to look at data storage techniques that build on a file store to underpin working applications. Initially you will look at how a database engine can expose information to applications. Then you're going to take a look at how to use XML and JSON to impose structure on a file of stored data. Finally, you are going to investigate web services, which allow a program to expose data to other programs over a network in a portable manner.

> **This section covers how to:**
> - Retrieve data from a database
> - Update data in a database
> - Consume JSON and XML data
> - Retrieve data by using web services

Retrieve data from a database

In Skill 3.2, in the "Use the Entity Framework to design your data storage" section you saw how to use a class-based design to express the data storage needs of an application to store information about music tracks. We designed a class called MusicTrack and then used the Entity Framework toolchain in Visual Studio to automatically create the underlying database.

Before you read any further you might like to revisit that section to remind yourself of what we were trying to do, and how we did it. If you want to use the database samples in this section you can perform the steps in Skill 3.2 to create your own local database file.

A single SQL database server can provide data storage to be shared between a large number of clients. The server can run on the same machine as the program that is using the database or the server can be accessed via a network connection. Developers can work with development version of the database server running on their machine, before creating a dedicated server for the published application. The MusicTracks application that we worked with in Skill 3.2 used a local database running on a machine in development mode. Later in this section we will consider how to manage the environment of an ASP application to allow it to use a remote database server when it runs on a production server.

Data in a database

The code next shows the MusicTrack class that is used in the MusicTracks application. The class contains data members that store the Artist, Title, and Length of a music track. The class also contains an integer ID value, which will be used by the database to allow it to uniquely identify each music track that is stored.

```
public class MusicTrack
{
    public int ID { get; set; }
    public string Artist { get; set; }
    public string Title { get; set; }
    public int Length { get; set; }
}
```

The Entity Framework toolchain uses the class definition to produce a table in a database that has the required data storage. Table 4.1 shows the database table that was created for the MusicTrack class. Each row in the table equates to an instance of the MusicTrack class. The table contains three songs. Each song has a different ID value. The database has been configured to automatically create ID values when a new MusicTrack entry is created.

TABLE 4-1 MusicTrack table

ID	Artist	Title	Length
1	Rob Miles	My Way	150
2	Fred Bloggs	His Way	150
3	The Bloggs Singers	Their Way	200

From a data design point of view a table in a database can be considered as a collection of objects. In other words, the table in Table 4-1 can be thought of as a list of references to MusicTrack objects in a C# program. Creating a program to read the data in a database table, however, is the same as accessing an element in a C# list. A program has to make a connection with the database and then send the database a command to request the MusicTrack information.

Read with SQL

The database in the MusicTracks application is managed by a server process that accepts commands and acts on them. The commands are given in a format called *Structured Query Language* (SQL). SQL dates back to the 1970's. It is called a *domain specific language* because it is used solely for expressing commands to tell a database what to do.

SQL is very useful. For example, one day the user of your music track program might ask you to make the program produce a list of all the tracks by a particular artist. This would be easy to do if all the music tracks are held in a list. You can write a for loop that works through the list looking for tracks with a particular name. Then, the next day the user might ask for a list of tracks ordered by track length, and on the next day you might get asked for all the artists who have recorded a track called "My Way" that is longer than 120 seconds. Each time you are asked for a new view of the data you have to write some more C# to search through the list of tracks and produce the result. However, if the music track information is held in a database, each of these requests can be satisfied by creating an SQL query to obtain the data.

The first SQL query that we are going to perform on the MusicTracks database has the form shown next. The * character is a "wildcard" that matches all of the entries in the table.

This command tells the database server that our program wants to read all of the elements in the MusicTrack table.

```
SELECT * FROM MusicTrack
```

Now that we have our SQL command, let's discover how to present the command to the database. A program uses an SQL database in a similar way to a stream. The program creates an object that represents a connection to the database and then sends SQL commands to this object. The database connection mechanism is also organized in the same way as the input/output stream classes. The DbConnection class that represents a connection to a database is an abstract class that describes the behaviors of the connection in the same way that the Stream class is also abstract and describes the behaviors of streams. The SqlConnection class is a child of the DbConnection class and represents the implementation of a connection to an SQL database.

To make a connection to a database a program must create a SqlConnection object. The constructor for the SqlConnection class is given a *connection string* that identifies the database that is to be opened. Before we can begin to read from the database we need to consider how the connection string is used to manage the connection.

The connection string contains a number of items expressed as name-value pairs. For a server on a remote machine the connection string will contain the address of the server, the port on which the server is listening and a username/password pair that can authenticate the connection.

In the case of the MusicTracks application that we created earlier, this connection string was created automatically and describes a connection to a local database file held on the computer in the folder for the user. If you followed the steps in Chapter 3 to build your own application, the database file will be created on your machine.

The program in Listing 4-19 shows how a C# program can make a connection to a database, create an SQL query, and then execute this query on the database to read and print out information from the MusicTrack table. The program prints the Artist and Title of each music track in the database.

LISTING 4-19 Read with SQL

```
using System;
using System.Data.SqlClient;

namespace LISTING_4_19_Read_with_SQL
{
    class Program
    {
        static void Main(string[] args)
        {
            string connectionString = "Server=(localdb)\\mssqllocaldb;" +
                "Database=MusicTracksContext-e0f0cd0d-38fe-44a4-add2-359310ff8b5d;" +
                "Trusted_Connection=True;MultipleActiveResultSets=true";

            using (SqlConnection connection = new SqlConnection(connectionString))
            {
                connection.Open();
                SqlCommand command = new SqlCommand("SELECT * FROM MusicTrack",
                connection);
```

```
            SqlDataReader reader = command.ExecuteReader();

            while (reader.Read())
            {
                string artist = reader["Artist"].ToString();
                string title = reader["Title"].ToString();

                Console.WriteLine("Artist: {0} Title: {1}", artist, title);
            }
        }
        Console.ReadKey();
    }
}
```

The connection string in the program makes a connection to the MusicTracks database. Note that is important that the connection string is **not** "hard wired" into program source code. The program in Listing 4-19 is just an example, not how you should create production code. Anyone obtaining the source code of this program can view the connection string and get access to the database and anyone obtaining the compiled version of the program can use a tool such as ildasm to view the MSIL code and extract the connection. You would also have to change the code of the program each time you want to use a different database.

Connection string management in ASP.NET

The database connection string to be used by an ASP.NET application is held in the configuration information for the solution. This is stored in the file appsettings.json in the solution. The location of this file is shown in Figure 4-7, which shows the solution files for the MusicTracks application.

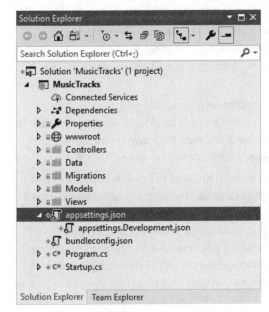

FIGURE 4-7 The appsetting.json file

The solution in Figure 4-7 has a setting file `appsettings.Development.json` that contains custom settings for use during development. If you add an `appsettings.Production.json` file to the solution, you can create settings information that will be used when the program is running on a production server. The `appsettings.json` file for the MusicTracks application on my machinecontains the following:

```
{
  "Logging": {
    "IncludeScopes": false,
    "LogLevel": {
      "Default": "Warning"
    }
  },
  "ConnectionStrings": {
    "MusicTracksContext": "Server=(localdb)\\mssqllocaldb;Database=MusicTracksContext-
e0f0cd0d-38fe-44a4-add2-359310ff8b5d;Trusted_Connection=True;MultipleActiveResultSets=true"
  }
}
```

The `ConnectionStrings` element in the settings file contains the connection string for the MusicTracks database context. The database name that is created when the solution is created has a globally unique identifier (GUID) appended, so the name of the database on your machine will be different from mine. If you want to run the database samples that follow in this text you will have to copy your connection string into the example programs.

The setting information in a solution can contain the descriptions of *environments* that are to be used for development and production deployments of an application. The environments used for application deployment set out the database connection string and any other options that you would like to customize. For example, the development environment can use a local database server and the production environment can use a distant server.

The setting information to be used is when a server is started and determined by an environment variable on the computer that is tested when the program starts running. The word environment is being used in two different contexts in this situation, which can be confusing.

- An *ASP application environment* determines the settings for logging, tracing, and debugging, and the database connection string that will be in force when the ASP application runs on a machine. A developer can also create their own settings values that can be used to give then more control over a particular environment.

- An *environment variable* is a value that is maintained by the operating system and can be used by processes running on the machine. Environment variables managed by Windows 10 include the name of the computer and the file paths to be used to search for programs. The system environment variable `ASPNETCORE_ENVIRONMENT` can be set to values that will determine which environment an ASP application will select when it starts running. You can manage the setting of this variable in Visual Studio, in the **Debug** tab of the **Properties** page for an ASP application, as shown in Figure 4-8.

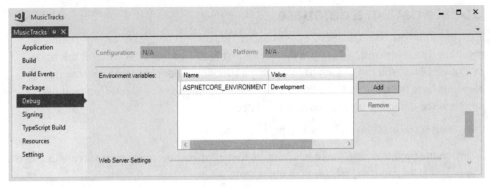

FIGURE 4-8 Setting the ASPNETCORE_ENVIRONMENT variable

In older ASP.NET applications the SQL settings are held in the web.config file, which is part of the solution. Developers then use XML transformations to override settings in the file to allow different SQL servers to be selected.

SQL query operation

A program can make a query of a database by creating an SqlCommand instance. The constructor for an SqlCommand is given a string, which is the SQL query and the database connection, as shown in the statement from Listing 4-19.

```
SqlCommand command = new SqlCommand("SELECT * FROM MusicTrack", connection);
```

The query is then executed as a reader command (because it is reading from the database). This operation returns an SqlReader instance as shown in the following statement.

```
SqlDataReader reader = command.ExecuteReader();
```

The SqlReader provides methods that can be used to move through the results returned by the query. Note that it is only possible to move forward through the results. The Read method moves the reader on to the next entry in the results. The Read method returns False when there are no more results. The individual items in the element can be accessed using their name, as shown here.

```
while (reader.Read())
{
    string artist = reader["Artist"].ToString();
    string title = reader["Title"].ToString();

    Console.WriteLine("Artist: {0} Title: {0}", artist, title);
}
```

The first SQL command selected all of the elements in a table. You can change this so that you can filter the contents of the table using a query. Listing 4-20 shows a query that selects only music tracks from the artist "Rob Miles."

LISTING 4-20 Filter with SQL

```
SELECT * FROM MusicTrack WHERE Artist='Rob Miles'
```

Update data in a database

A program can use the SQL UPDATE command to update the contents of an entry in the database. The command below finds the track with the ID 1 and sets the artist for this track to 'Robert Miles.' You can use the ID to identify a specific element in a table because no two elements have the same ID. If the WHERE component of the command selected multiple entries in the database, they would all be updated.

```
UPDATE MusicTrack SET Artist='Robert Miles' WHERE ID='1'
```

When the update is performed it is possible to determine how many elements are updated. The program in Listing 4-21 shows how this is done.

LISTING 4-21 Update with SQL

```
using (SqlConnection connection = new SqlConnection(connectionString))
{
    connection.Open();
    dumpDatabase(connection);
    SqlCommand command = new SqlCommand(
        "UPDATE MusicTrack SET Artist='Robert Miles' WHERE ID='1'", connection);
    int result = command.ExecuteNonQuery();
    Console.WriteLine("Number of entries updated: {0}", result);
    dumpDatabase(connection);
}
```

SQL injection and database commands

Suppose you want to allow the user of your program to update the name of a particular track. Your program can read the information from the user and then construct an SQL command to perform the update. Listing 4-22 shows how this can be done:

LISTING 4-22 SQL injection

```
Console.Write("Enter the title of the track to update: ");
string searchTitle = Console.ReadLine();
Console.Write("Enter the new artist name: ");
string newArtist = Console.ReadLine();
string SqlCommandText =
    "UPDATE MusicTrack SET Artist='" + newArtist + "' WHERE Title='" + searchTitle + "'";
```

If you run the program in Listing 4-22, you will find that it does work. You can select a track by title and then change the artist for that track. However, this is very dangerous code. Consider the effect of a user running the program and then typing in the following information.

```
Enter the title of the track to update: My Way
Enter the new artist name: Fred'); DELETE FROM MusicTrack; --
```

The track title is fine, but the new artist name looks rather strange. What the user of the program has done is *injected* another SQL command after the UPDATE command. The command would set the new artist name to Fred and then perform an SQL DELETE command. The DELETE command does exactly what you would expect. It deletes the entire contents of the table.

This works because there is nothing to stop the user of the program from typing in the delimiter ' (single quote) to mark the end of a string and then adding new SQL statements after that. A malicious user can use SQL injection to take control of a database.

For this reason, you should never construct SQL commands directly from user input. You must use parameterized SQL statements instead. Listing 4-23 shows how they work. The SQL command contains markers that identify the points in the query where text is to be inserted. The program then adds the parameter values that correspond to the marker points. The SQL server now knows exactly where each element starts and ends, making SQL injection impossible.

LISTING 4-23 Parameterized query

```
string SqlCommandText = "UPDATE MusicTrack SET Artist=@artist WHERE Title=@searchTitle";

SqlCommand command = new SqlCommand(SqlCommandText, connection);
command.Parameters.AddWithValue("@artist", newArtist);
command.Parameters.AddWithValue("@searchTitle", searchTitle);
```

Asynchronous database access

The SQL commands that we have used have all used synchronous methods to evaluate queries and work through results. There are also asynchronous versions of the methods. A program can use the async/await mechanism with these versions of the methods so that database queries can run asynchronously. This is particularly important if your program is interacting with the user via a windowed interface.

The dumpDatabase method in Listing 4-24 uses asynchronous database commands to create a listing of the contents of the MusicTrack database. This method is part of a WPF (Windows Presentation Foundation) application that also allows database editing. Note that to use this example on your machine you will have to set the database connection string to make a connection to a database on your machine.

LISTING 4-24 Asynchronous access

```
async Task<string> dumpDatabase(SqlConnection connection)
{
    SqlCommand command = new SqlCommand("SELECT * FROM MusicTrack", connection);
    SqlDataReader reader = await command.ExecuteReaderAsync();
    StringBuilder databaseList = new StringBuilder();
    while (await reader.ReadAsync())
    {
        string id = reader["ID"].ToString();
        string artist = reader["Artist"].ToString();
        string title = reader["Title"].ToString();

        string row = string.Format("ID: {0} Artist: {1} Title: {2}", id, artist, title);
        databaseList.AppendLine(row);
    }
    return databaseList.ToString();
}
```

Using SQL in ASP applications

If you examine the ASP MusicTracks application that we created at the start of Skill 3.2, you will not find any SQL commands in the code that implement the controller classes for this application. This is because database updates in an ASP application are performed using an Update method that accepts a modified instance of the class to be updated.

You can see this behavior in action by taking a look at the code in the Edit method in the MusicTrackController.cs source file, as shown next. The variable musicTrack contains the modified music track instance, as received from the web form. The variable _context contains the database context for this page. The code updates the database and catches any exceptions that may be thrown by this operation.

```
try
{
    _context.Update(musicTrack);      // update the database context with the edited track
    await _context.SaveChangesAsync(); // save all the changes
}
catch (DbUpdateConcurrencyException)
{
    // deal with exceptions

}
```

The ASP application uses embedded C# code in the web page (using a feature called Razor), which iterates through the database contents and presents a view of the data. The code shown next is part of the index.cshtml file for the MusicTracks application. Razor enables C# statements to be inserted into the HTML page description to programmatically generate some of the content. The C# elements on the page are preceded by an @ character. In the following code you can see how a foreach loop is used to iterate through the items in the database and call the DisplayFor method for each item.

```
@foreach (var item in Model) {
        <tr>
            <td>
                @Html.DisplayFor(modelItem => item.Artist)
            </td>
            <td>
                @Html.DisplayFor(modelItem => item.Title)
            </td>
            <td>
                @Html.DisplayFor(modelItem => item.Length)
            </td>
            <td>
                <a asp-action="Edit" asp-route-id="@item.ID">Edit</a> |
                <a asp-action="Details" asp-route-id="@item.ID">Details</a> |
                <a asp-action="Delete" asp-route-id="@item.ID">Delete</a>
            </td>
        </tr>
}
```

Figure 4-9 shows the web output generated by this code. Note that for each item that is displayed there are also links to the behaviors to edit, view the details, or delete the item. If you look at the earlier code you can see that the routing information for each link contains the ID of that item, which is how the server will know which item has been selected.

Rob Miles	My Way	150	Edit | Details | Delete
Fred Bloggs	His Way	150	Edit | Details | Delete
The Bloggs Singers	Their Way	200	Edit | Details | Delete

FIGURE 4-9 Track list in MusicTracks

Consume JSON and XML data

You have seen that it is very easy for a program to load the contents of a web page. In Listing 4-14 you found that the WebClient class can do this with a single method call. A lot of data resources are now provided to applications via a structured data documents that can be obtained in this way. There are two popular formats for such data, JavaScript Object Notation (JSON) and eXtensible Markup Language (XML). In this section you are going to see examples of each in use.

Consume JSON data

In Skill 3.1 in the "Using JSON" section, you saw that JSON (JavaScript Object Notation) is a means by which applications can exchange data. A JSON document is a plain text file that contains a structured collection of name and value pairs. You also discovered how to read and write JSON files using the Newtonsoft.Json library. Read that section again to refresh your memory about JSON before continuing with this section.

The program in Listing 4-25 consumes a JSON feed provided by the National Aeronautics and Space Administration (NASA). The feed is updated every day with a new picture or video from the NASA archives. The method getImageOfDay returns an object describing the image of the day for a particular address on the NASA site. It uses the Newtonsoft libraries described in Skill 3.1 to convert the text loaded from the NASA web page into an instance of the ImageOfDay class with all of the fields initialized.

LISTING 4-25 NASA JSON

```
public class ImageOfDay
{
    public string date { get; set; }
    public string explanation { get; set; }
    public string hdurl { get; set; }
    public string media_type { get; set; }
    public string service_version { get; set; }
    public string title { get; set; }
```

```
        public string url { get; set; }
}

async Task<ImageOfDay> GetImageOfDay(string imageURL)
{
    string NASAJson = await readWebpage(imageURL);

    ImageOfDay result = JsonConvert.DeserializeObject< ImageOfDay>(NASAJson);

    return result;
}
```

For this to work I had to create an `ImageOfDay` class that exactly matches the object described by the JSON feed from NASA. One way to do this is to use the website *http://json2csharp.com*. which will accept a web address that returns a JSON document and then automatically generates a C# class as described in the document.

The code that displays the image when the user clicks a button to perform the load is shown next. The method `displayUrl` asynchronously loads the image and displays it on the screen. The code also gets the descriptive text for the image and displays it in a text box.

```
private async void LoadButtonClicked(object sender, RoutedEventArgs e)
{
    try
    {
        ImageOfDay imageOfDay = await getImageOfDay(
                "https://api.nasa.gov/planetary/apod?api_key=DEMO_KEY&date=2018-05-29");

        if (imageOfDay.media_type != "image")
        {
            MessageBox.Show("It is not an image today");
            return;
        }

        DescriptionTextBlock.Text = imageOfDay.explanation;

        await displayUrl(imageOfDay.url);
    }
    catch (Exception ex)
    {
        MessageBox.Show("Fetch failed: {0}", ex.Message);
    }
}
```

The program works well, although at the moment it always shows the same image, which is specified in the address in the previous code. It would be easy to modify the program to display the image for a particular day. Note, that the program uses a demo API key to gain access to the NASA site. This can only be used for a few downloads an hour. If you want to use this service for your application you can apply for a free API key from NASA. Figure 4-10 shows the output from the program.

FIGURE 4-10 NASA image display

Consume XML data

In Skill 3.1 in the "JSON and XML" section we explored the difference between JSON and XML. The XML language is slightly more expressive than JSON, but XML documents are larger than equivalent JSON documents and this, along with the ease of use of JSON, has led to JSON replacing XML. However, a lot of information is still expressed using XML. In Skill 3.1 we saw an XML document that described a MusicTrack instance.

```xml
<?xml version="1.0" encoding="utf-16"?>
<MusicTrack xmlns:xsi="http://www.w3.org/2001/XMLSchema-instance" xmlns:xsd="http://www.w3.org/2001/XMLSchema">
  <Artist>Rob Miles</Artist>
  <Title>My Way</Title>
  <Length>150</Length>
</MusicTrack>
```

One way to consume such a document is to work through each element in turn. The System.XML namespace contains a set of classes for working with XML documents. One of these classes is the XMLTextReader class. An instance of the XMLTextReader class will work through a stream of text and decode each XML element in turn.

The program in Listing 4-26 shows how this is done. It creates a StringReader stream that is used to construct an XMLTextReader. The program then iterates through each of the XML elements that are read from the stream, printing out the element information.

LISTING 4-26 XML elements

```
string XMLDocument = "<?xml version=\"1.0\" encoding=\"utf-16\"?>" +
    "<MusicTrack xmlns:xsi=\"http://www.w3.org/2001/XMLSchema-instance\" " +
    "xmlns:xsd=\"http://www.w3.org/2001/XMLSchema\"> " +
    "<Artist>Rob Miles</Artist>  " +
    "<Title>My Way</Title>  " +
    "<Length>150</Length>" +
    "</MusicTrack>";

using (StringReader stringReader = new StringReader(XMLDocument))
{
    XmlTextReader reader = new XmlTextReader(stringReader);

    while (reader.Read())
    {
        string description = string.Format("Type:{0} Name:{1} Value:{2}",
            reader.NodeType.ToString(),
            reader.Name,
            reader.Value);
        Console.WriteLine(description);
    }
}
```

The output from this program gives each item in turn as shown next. Note that not all items have both names and values.

```
Type:XmlDeclaration Name:xml Value:version="1.0" encoding="utf-16"
Type:Element Name:MusicTrack Value:
Type:Whitespace Name: Value:
Type:Element Name:Artist Value:
Type:Text Name: Value:Rob Miles
Type:EndElement Name:Artist Value:
Type:Whitespace Name: Value:
Type:Element Name:Title Value:
Type:Text Name: Value:My Way
Type:EndElement Name:Title Value:
Type:Whitespace Name: Value:
Type:Element Name:Length Value:
Type:Text Name: Value:150
Type:EndElement Name:Length Value:
Type:EndElement Name:MusicTrack Value:
```

XML documents

It is possible to read information from an XML document by decoding each individual element, but this can be hard work to code. An easier approach is to use an XMLDocument instance. This creates a Document Object Model (DOM) in memory from which data can be extracted. Another advantage of a DOM is that a program can change elements in the DOM and then write out a modified copy of the document incorporating the changes.

The program in Listing 4-27 creates an XmlDocument instance from a string of XML describing a MusicTrack and then reads the artist and title information from it. The program checks to make sure that the document describes a MusicTrack before writing the information.

LISTING 4-27 XML DOM

```
XmlDocument doc = new XmlDocument();
doc.LoadXml(XMLDocument);

System.Xml.XmlElement rootElement = doc.DocumentElement;
// make sure it is the right element
if (rootElement.Name != "MusicTrack")
{
    Console.WriteLine("Not a music track");
}
else
{
    string artist = rootElement["Artist"].FirstChild.Value;
    Console.WriteLine("", artist);
    string title = rootElement["Title"].FirstChild.Value;
    Console.WriteLine("Artist:{0} Title:{1}", artist, title);
}
```

An XmlDocument contains a hierarchy of items with a rootElement object the top of the hierarchy. A program can access items in an element by using a string indexer that contains the name of the required item. In the next section we will discover how to use Language Integrated Queries (LINQ) to work with XML documents.

Retrieve data by using Windows Communication Foundation (WCF)

You have already seen how an application can consume data from a service by using an HTTP request to download a JSON or XML document. The NASA image reader in Listing 4-25 works by converting a response from a server into an instance of a class that contains a description of the image and the web address from which the image can be downloaded. To use the information provided by the NASA server, a client program contains a C# class that matches the JSON document that is received from the server.

A client of a web service also uses an instance of an object to interact with a server. However, in this case, the client can call methods on the object to read data and also update information on the server. The object that is created is called a "proxy object." A call to a method on the proxy object will cause a request to be created that is sent to the service on the server.

When the server receives the request, it will then call the method code in a server object. The result to be returned by the method will then be packaged up into another network message, which is sent back to the client and then sends the return value back to the calling software. Don't worry about how the messages are constructed and transferred. You just need to create server methods and calls from the client systems.

The service also exposes a description of the methods that it provides. This is used by the development tool (in our case Visual Studio) to actually create the proxy object in the client program. This means that you can easily create a client application.

Create a web service

To discover how all of this works let's create a "Joke of the Day" service. This will return a string containing something suitably rib-tickling on request from the client. The user will be able to select the "strength" of the joke, ranging from 0 to 2 where 0 is mildly amusing and 2 is a guaranteed roll on the floor laughing experience.

The application will be made up of two parts, the server program that exports the service, and the client program that uses it. The server is created as a WCF (Windows Communication Foundation) Service application. The client will be an application that connects to the service and requests a joke.

The code next shows the single method that is provided by the service. This is part of the code in the server application. The GetJoke method accepts an integer and returns a string of text. The attributes [ServiceContract] and [OperationContract] denote that the interface and method are to be exposed as services.

```
using System.ServiceModel;

namespace JokeOfTheDay
{
    [ServiceContract]
    public interface IJokeOfTheDayService
    {
        [OperationContract]
        string GetJoke(int jokeStrength);
    }
}
```

Once you have the interface you now need a class that implements the method. This method will provide the service that the interface describes. As you can see from the code next, the method is quite simple, and so are the jokes. The input parameter is used to select one of three joke strings and return it. If there is no match to the input the string "Invalid strength" is returned.

```
public class JokeOfTheDayService : IJokeOfTheDayService
{
    public string GetJoke(int jokeStrength)
    {
        string result = "Invalid strength";
```

```
        switch (jokeStrength)
        {
            case 0:
                result =
"Knock Knock. Who's there? Oh, you've heard it";
                break;
            case 1:
                result =
"What's green and hairy and goes up and down? A gooseberry in a lift";
                break;
            case 2:
                result =
"A horse walks into a bar and the barman asks 'Why the long face?";
                break;
        }
        return result;
    }
}
```

If you create a service you can use the WCF Test Client to invoke the methods and view the results. This tool allows you to call methods in the service and view the results that they return. Figure 4-11 shows the test client in use. You can see the results of a call to the method with a parameter of 1.

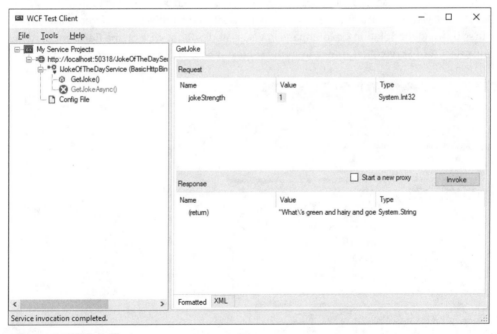

FIGURE 4-11 WCF Test Client

You can also view the service description in a browser as shown in Figure 4-12. This gives a link to the service description, as well some sample code that shows how to use it.

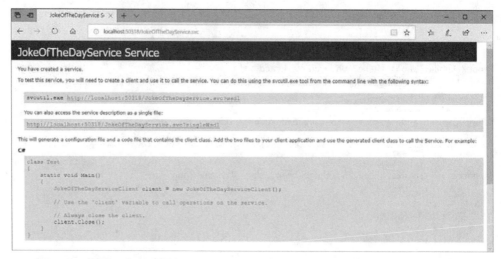

FIGURE 4-12 Service description in a browser

Joke of the Day Client

The client application can run on any machine that has a network connection and wants to consume the service. The client application needs to contain a connection to the JokeOfTheDayService. This is added to the client Visual Studio project as a reference like any other, by using the Solution Explorer pane in Visual Studio. Right-click on the **References** item and select **Add Service Reference** from the context menu, as shown in Figure 4-13.

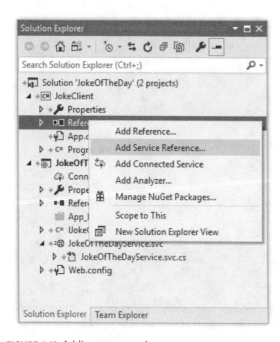

FIGURE 4-13 Adding a new service

At this point Visual Studio needs to find the description of the service that is to be used. The Add Service Reference dialog allows you to type in the network address of a service, and Visual Studio will then read the service description provided by the service. Figure 4-14 shows the dialog used to set up the client. You can see that the JokeOfTheDay service only provides one method. At the bottom of this dialog you can see the namespace that you want the service to have in the client application. Change this name to JokeOfTheDayService.

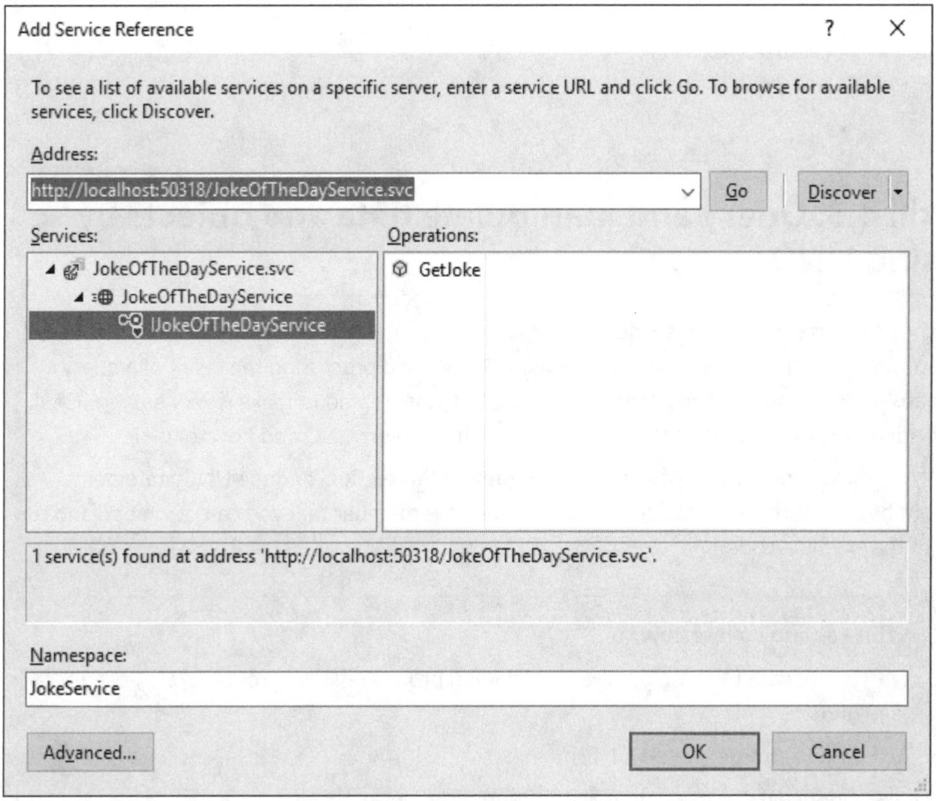

FIGURE 4-14 Adding a new service

Once the service has been added it now takes its place in the solution. Our application must now create a proxy object that will be used to invoke the methods in the service. The code next creates a service instance and calls the GetJoke method to get a joke from the service. Note that the example solution for Listing 4-28 contains two Visual Studio projects. One implements the server and the other the client.

LISTING 4-28 Web Service

```
using System;
using JokeClient.JokeService;

namespace JokeClient
{
```

```
class Program
{
    static void Main(string[] args)
    {
        using (JokeOfTheDayServiceClient jokeClient =
                new JokeOfTheDayServiceClient())
        {
            Console.WriteLine(jokeClient.GetJoke(1));
        }

        Console.ReadKey();
    }
}
}
```

Skill 4.3: Query and manipulate data and objects by using LINQ

In the previous section you saw how a program can work with stored data by using SQL commands. SQL commands are time consuming to create and processing the result of a query is hard work. Language INtegrated Query, or LINQ, was created to make it very easy for C# programmers to work with data sources. This section covers LINQ and how to use it.

Note that there are a lot of example programs in this section, and the LINQ statements might be a bit hard to understand at first. However, remember that you can download and run all of the example code.

> **This section covers how to:**
> - Query data by using operators, including projection, join, group, take, skip, aggregate
> - Create method-based LINQ queries
> - Query data by using query comprehension syntax
> - Select data by using anonymous types
> - Force execution of a query
> - Read, filter, create, and modify data structures by using LINQ to XML

Sample application

In order to provide a good context for the exploration of LINQ we are going to develop the MusicTracks application used earlier in this book. This application allows the storage of music track data. Figure 4-15 shows the classes in the system. Note that at the moment we are not using a database to store the class information. Later we will consider how to map this design onto a database.

350 **CHAPTER 4** Implement data access

In previous versions of the application, the MusicTrack class contained a string that gave the name of the artist that recorded the track. In the new design, a MusicTrack contains a reference to an Artist object that describes the artist that recorded the track. Figure 4-15 shows how this works. If an artist records more than one track (which is very likely), the artist details will only be stored once and referred to by many MusicTrack instances.

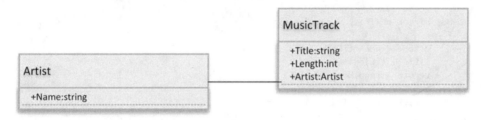

FIGURE 4-15 Music tracks class design

The code next shows the C# code for the classes.

```csharp
class Artist
{
    public string Name { get; set; }
}
class MusicTrack
{
    public Artist Artist { get; set; }
    public string Title { get; set; }
    public int Length { get; set; }
}
```

Now that you have the class design for the application, the next thing to do is create some sample data. This *must* be done programmatically. Testing a system by entering data by hand is a bad idea for a number of reasons. First, it is very time-consuming. Second, any changes to the data store design will mean that you will probably have to enter all the data again. And third, the act of creating the test data can give useful insights into your class design.

Listing 4-29 shows code that creates some artists and tracks. You can increase the amount of test data by adding more artists and titles. In this version all of the artists recorded all of the tracks. A random number generator provides each track a random length in the range of 20 to 600 seconds. Note that because the random number generator has a fixed seed value the lengths of each track will be the same each time you run the program.

LISTING 4-29 Musictrack classes

```csharp
string[] artistNames = new string[] { "Rob Miles", "Fred Bloggs",
                                      "The Bloggs Singers", "Immy Brown" };
string[] titleNames = new string[] { "My Way", "Your Way", "His Way", "Her Way",
                                     "Milky Way" };

List<Artist> artists = new List<Artist>();
List<MusicTrack> musicTracks = new List<MusicTrack>();
```

```
Random rand = new Random(1);

foreach (string artistName in artistNames)
{
    Artist newArtist = new Artist { Name = artistName };
    artists.Add(newArtist);
    foreach (string titleName in titleNames)
    {
        MusicTrack newTrack = new MusicTrack
        {
            Artist = newArtist,
            Title = titleName,
            Length = rand.Next(20, 600)
        };
        musicTracks.Add(newTrack);
    }
}

foreach (MusicTrack track in musicTracks)
{
    Console.WriteLine("Artist:{0} Title:{1} Length:{2}",
        track.Artist.Name, track.Title, track.Length);
}
```

Use an object initializer

If you look at the code in Listing 4-29 you will see that we are using *object initializer* syntax to create new instances of the music objects and initialize their values at the same time. This is a very useful C# feature that allows you to initialize objects when they are created without the need to create a constructor method in the class being initialized.

The code next shows how it works. The statement creates and initializes a new MusicTrack instance. Note the use of braces ({and}) to delimit the items that initialize the instance and commas to separate each value being used to initialize the object.

```
MusicTrack newTrack = new MusicTrack
{
    Artist = "Rob Miles",
    Title = "My Way",
    Length = 150
};
```

You don't have to initialize all of the elements of the instance; any properties not initialized are set to their default values (zero for a numeric value and null for a string). The properties to be initialized in this way must all be public members of the class.

Use a LINQ operator

Now that you have some data can use LINQ operators to build queries and extract results from the data. The code in Listing 4-30 prints out the titles of all the tracks that were recorded by the artist with the name "Rob Miles." The first statement uses a LINQ query to create an enumerable collection of MusicTrack references called selectedTracks that is then enumerated by the foreach construction to print out the results.

LISTING 4-30 LINQ operators

```
IEnumerable<MusicTrack> selectedTracks = from track in musicTracks where track.Artist.
Name == "Rob Miles" select track;

foreach (MusicTrack track in selectedTracks)
{
    Console.WriteLine("Artist:{0} Title:{1}", track.Artist.Name, track.Title);
}
```

The LINQ query returns an `IEnumerable` result that is enumerated by a foreach construc-tion. You can find an explanation of `IEnumerable` in Skill 2.4 in the "IEnumerable" section. The "Create method-based LINQ queries" section has more detail on how a query is actually implemented by C# code.

Use the var keyword with LINQ

The C# language is "statically typed." The type of objects in a program is determined at compile time and the compiler rejects any actions that are not valid. For example, the follow-ing code fails to compile because the compiler will not allow a string to be subtracted from a number.

```
string name = "Rob Miles";
int age = 21;
int silly = age  - name;
```

This provides more confidence that our programs are correct before they run. The downside is that you have to put in the effort of giving each variable a type when you declare it. Most of the time, however, the compiler can infer the type to be used for any given variable. The `name` variable in the previous example must be of type `string`, since a `string` is being assigned to it. By the same logic, the age variable must be an `int`.

You can simplify code by using the `var` keyword to tell the compiler to infer the type of the variable being created from the context in which the variable is used. The compiler will define a string variable called `namev` in response to the following statement:

```
var namev = "Rob Miles";
```

Note. that this does not mean that the compiler cannot detect compilation errors. The statements in Listing 4-31 still fails to compile:

LISTING 4-31 var errors

```
var namev = "Rob Miles";
var agev = 21;
var sillyv = agev - namev;
```

The `var` keyword is especially useful when using LINQ. The result of a simple LINQ query is an enumerable collection of the type of data element held in the data source. The statement next shows the query from Listing 4-30.

```
IEnumerable<MusicTrack> selectedTracks =
    from track in musicTracks where track.Artist.Name == "Rob Miles" select track;
```

To write this statement you must find out the type of data in the musicTracks collection, and then use this type with IEnumerable. The var keyword makes this code much easier to write (see Listing 4-32).

LISTING 4-32 var and LINQ

```
var selectedTracks =
    from track in musicTracks where track.Artist.Name == "Rob Miles" select track;
```

There are some situations where you won't know the type of a variable when writing the code. Later in this section you will discover objects that are created dynamically as the program runs and have no type at all. These are called anonymous types. The only way code can refer to these is by use of variables of type var.

You can use the var type everywhere in your code if you like, but please be careful. A statement such as the following will not make you very popular with fellow programmers because it is impossible for them to infer the type of variable v without digging into the code and finding out what type is returned by the DoRead method.

```
var v = DoRead();
```

If you really want to use var in these situations you should make sure that you select variable names that are suitably informative, or you can infer the type of the item from the code, as in the following statements.

```
var nextPerson = DoReadPerson();
var newPerson = new Person();
```

LINQ projection

You can use the select operation in LINQ to produce a filtered version of a data source. In previous examples you discovered all of the tracks recorded by a particular artist. You can create other search criteria, for example by selecting the tracks with a certain title, or tracks longer than a certain length.

The result of a select is a collection of references to objects in the source data collection. There are a couple of reasons why a program might not want to work like this. First, you might not want to provide references to the actual data objects in the data source. Second, you might want the result of a query to contain a subset of the original data.

You can use *projection* to ask a query to "project" the data in the class onto new instances of a class created just to hold the data returned by the query. Let's start by creating the class called TrackDetails that will hold just the artist name and the title of a track. You will use this to hold the result of the search query.

```
class TrackDetails
{
    public string ArtistName;
    public string Title;
}
```

The query can now be asked to create a new instance of this class to hold the result of each query. Listing 4-33 shows how this works.

LISTING 4-33 LINQ projection

```
var selectedTracks = from track in musicTracks
                     where track.Artist.Name == "Rob Miles"
                     select new TrackDetails
                     {
                         ArtistName = track.Artist.Name,
                         Title = track.Title
                     };
```

Projection results like this are particularly useful when you are using *data binding* to display the results to the user. Values in the query result can be bound to items to be displayed.

Anonymous types

You can remove the need to create a class to hold the result of a search query by making the query return results of an *anonymous type*. You can see how this works in Listing 4-34. Note that the name of the type is now missing from the end of the select new statement.

LISTING 4-34 Anonymous type

```
var selectedTracks = from track in musicTracks
                     where track.Artist.Name == "Rob Miles"
                     select new // projection type name missing from here
                     {
                         ArtistName = track.Artist.Name,
                         track.Title
                     };
```

The query in Listing 4-34 creates new instances of an anonymous type that contain just the data items needed from the query. Instances of the new type are initialized using the object initializer syntax. In this case the first property in the type is the name of the artist recording the track, and the second is the title of the track. For the first property you actually supply the name of the field to be created in the new type. For the second property the property is created with same name as the source property, in this case the property name will be Title.

The item that is returned by this query is an enumerable collection of instances of a type that has no name. It is an anonymous type. This means you *have* to use a var reference to refer to the query result. You can iterate through the collection in this result as you would any other. Note that each item in the selectedTracks collection must now be referred to using var because its type has no name. The code next shows how var is used for each item when printing out the results of the query in Listing 4-34.

```
foreach (var item in selectedTracks)
{
    Console.WriteLine("Artist:{0} Title:{1}", item.ArtistName,item.Title);
}
```

Note that the use of an anonymous type doesn't mean that the compiler is any less rigorous when checking the correctness of the code. If the program tries to use a property that is not present in the item, for example if it tries to obtain the Length property from the result of the query, this generates an error at compile time.

LINQ join

The class design used up to this point uses C# references to implement the associations between the objects in the system. In other words, a MusicTrack object contains a reference to the Artist object that represents the artist that recorded that track. If you store your data in a database however, you will not be able to store the associations in this way.

Instead, each item in the database will have a unique id (its *primary key*) and objects referring to this object will contain this ID value (a *foreign key*). Rather than a reference to an Artist instance, the MusicTrack now contains an ArtistID field that identifies the artist associated with that track. Figure 4-16 shows how this association is implemented.

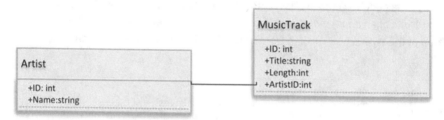

FIGURE 4-16 Music tracks and Artist ID

This design makes it slightly more difficult to search for tracks by a particular artist. The program needs to find the ID value for the artist with the name being searched for and then search for any tracks with that value of artist id. Fortunately, LINQ provides a join operator that can be used to join the output of one LINQ query to the input of another.

Listing 4-35 shows how this works. The first query selects the artist with the name "Rob Miles." The results of that query are joined to the second query that searches the musicTracks collection for tracks with an ArtistID property that matches that of the artist found by the first query.

LISTING 4-35 LINQ join

```
var artistTracks = from artist in artists where artist.Name == "Rob Miles"
                   join track in musicTracks on artist.ID equals track.ArtistID
                   select new
{
    ArtistName = artist.Name,
    track.Title
};
```

LINQ group

Another useful LINQ feature is the ability to group the results of a query to create a summary output. For example, you may want to create a query to tell how many tracks there are by each artist in the music collection.

Listing 4-36 shows how to do this. The group action is given the data item to group by and the property by which it is to be grouped. The artistTrackSummary contains an entry for each different artist. Each of the items in the summary has a Key property, which is the value that item is "grouped" around. You want to create a group around artists, so the key is the ArtistID value of each track. The Key property of the artistTrackSummary gives the value of this key. You can use behaviors provided by a summary object to find out about the contents of the summary, and the Count method returns the number of items in the summary. You will discover more summary commands in the discussion about the aggregate commands later in this section.

LISTING 4-36 LINQ group

```
var artistSummary = from track in musicTracks
                    group track by track.ArtistID
                    into artistTrackSummary
                    select new
                    {
                        ID = artistTrackSummary.Key,
                        Count = artistTrackSummary.Count()
                    };
```

You can print out the contents of the anonymous classes produced by this query by using a foreach loop as shown next.

```
foreach (var item in artistSummary)
{
    Console.WriteLine("Artist:{0} Tracks recorded:{1}",
        item.ID, item.Count);
}
```

The problem with this query is that when run it produces the results as shown next. Rather than generating the name of the artist, the program displays the ArtistID values.

```
Artist:0 Tracks recorded:5
Artist:6 Tracks recorded:5
Artist:12 Tracks recorded:5
Artist:18 Tracks recorded:5
```

You can fix this by making use of a join operation that will extract the artist name for use in the query. The needed join is shown next. You can then create the group keyed on the artist name rather than the ID to get the desired output.

```
var artistSummaryName = from track in musicTracks
                    join artist in artists on track.ArtistID equals artist.ID
                    group track by artist.Name
                    into artistTrackSummary
                    select new
                    {
                        ID = artistTrackSummary.Key,
                        Count = artistTrackSummary.Count()
                    };
```

The output from this query is shown here:

```
Artist:Rob Miles Tracks recorded:5
Artist:Fred Bloggs Tracks recorded:5
Artist:The Bloggs Singers Tracks recorded:5
Artist:Immy Brown Tracks recorded:5
```

Note that this is strong LINQ magic. It is worth playing with the sample code a little and examining the structure of the query to see what is going on.

LINQ Take and skip

A LINQ query will normally return all of the items that if finds. However, this might be more items that your program wants. For example, you might want to show the user the output one page at a time. You can use take to tell the query to take a particular number of items and the skip to tell a query to skip a particular number of items in the result before taking the requested number.

The sample program in Listing 4-37 displays all of the music tracks ten items at a time. It uses a loop that uses Skip to move progressively further down the database each time the loop is repeated. The loop ends when the LINQ query returns an empty collection. The user presses a key at the end of each page to move onto the next page.

LISTING 4-37 LINQ take and skip

```
int pageNo = 0;
int pageSize = 10;

while(true)
{
    // Get the track information
    var trackList = from musicTrack in musicTracks.Skip(pageNo*pageSize).Take(pageSize)
                    join artist in artists on musicTrack.ArtistID equals artist.ID
                    select new
                    {
                        ArtistName = artist.Name,
                        musicTrack.Title
                    };

    // Quit if we reached the end of the data
    if (trackList.Count() == 0)
        break;

    // Display the query result
    foreach (var item in trackList)
    {
        Console.WriteLine("Artist:{0} Title:{1}",
            item.ArtistName, item.Title);
    }

    Console.Write("Press any key to continue");
    Console.ReadKey();

    // move on to the next page
    pageNo++;
}
```

LINQ aggregate commands

In the context of LINQ commands, the word *aggregate* means "bring together a number of related values to create a single result." You can use aggregate operators on the results produced by group operations. You have already used one aggregate operator in a LINQ query. You used the Count operator in Listing 4-36 to count the number of tracks in a group extracted by artist. That provided the number of tracks assigned to a particular artist. You may want to get the total length of all the tracks assigned to an artist, and for that you can use the Sum aggregate operator.

The parameter to the Sum operator is a lambda expression that the operator will use on each item in the group to obtain the value to be added to the total sum for that item. To get the sum of MusicTrack lengths, the lambda expression just returns the value of the Length property for the item. Listing 4-38 shows how this works.

LISTING 4-38 LINQ aggregate

```
var artistSummary = from track in musicTracks
        join artist in artists on track.ArtistID equals artist.ID
        group track by artist.Name
        into artistTrackSummary
        select new
        {
            ID = artistTrackSummary.Key,
            Length = artistTrackSummary.Sum(x => x.Length)
        };
```

The result of this query is a collection of anonymous objects that contain the name of the artist and the total length of all the tracks recorded by that artist. The program produces the following output:

```
Name:Rob Miles   Total length:1406
Name:Fred Bloggs   Total length:1533
Name:The Bloggs Singers   Total length:1413
Name:Immy Brown   Total length:1813
```

You can use Average, Max, and Min to generate other items of aggregate information. You can also create your own Aggregate behavior that will be called on each successive item in the group and will generate a single aggregate result.

Create method-based LINQ queries

The first LINQ query that you saw was in Listing 4-30 as shown here.

```
IEnumerable<MusicTrack> selectedTracks =
    from track in musicTracks where track.Artist.Name == "Rob Miles" select track;
```

The query statement uses *query comprehension syntax*, which includes the operators from, in, where, and select. The compiler uses these to generate a call to the Where method on the MusicTracks collection. In other words, the code that is actually created to perform the query is the statement below:

```
IEnumerable<MusicTrack> selectedTracks =
        musicTracks.Where(track => track.Artist.Name == "Rob Miles");
```

The Where method accepts a lambda expression as a parameter. In this case the lambda expression accepts a MusicTrack as a parameter and returns True if the Name property of the Artist element in the MusicTrack matches the name that is being selected.

You first saw lambda expressions in Skill 1.4, "Create and implement events and callbacks." A lambda expression is a piece of behavior that can be regarded as an object. In this situation the Where method is receiving a piece of behavior that the method can use to determine which tracks to select. In this case the behavior is "take a track and see if the artist name is Rob Miles." You can create your own method-based queries instead of using the LINQ operators. Listing 4-39 shows the LINQ query and the matching method-based behavior.

LISTING 4-39 Method based query

```
//IEnumerable<MusicTrack> selectedTracks = from track in musicTracks where
      track.Artist.Name == "Rob Miles" select track;
// Method based implementation of this query
IEnumerable<MusicTrack> selectedTracks = musicTracks.Where(track =>
        track.Artist.Name == "Rob Miles");
```

Programs can use the LINQ query methods (and execute LINQ queries) on data collections, such as lists and arrays, and also on database connections. The methods that implement LINQ query behaviors are not added to the classes that use them. Instead they are implemented as *extension methods*. You can find out more about extension methods in Skill 2.1, in the "Extension methods" section.

Query data by using query comprehension syntax

The phrase "query comprehension syntax" refers to the way that you can build LINQ queries for using the C# operators provided specifically for expressing data queries. The intention is to make the C# statements that strongly resemble the SQL queries that perform the same function. This makes it easier for developers familiar with SQL syntax to use LINQ.

Listing 4-40 shows a complex LINQ query that is based on the LINQ query used in Listing 4-38 to produce a summary giving the length of music by each artist. This uses the orderby operator to order the output by artist name.

LISTING 4-40 Complex query

```
var artistSummary = from track in musicTracks
                    join artist in artists on track.ArtistID equals artist.ID
                    group track by artist.Name
                    into artistTrackSummary
                    select new
                    {
                        ID = artistTrackSummary.Key,
                         Length = artistTrackSummary.Sum(x => x.Length)
                    };
```

The SQL query that matches this LINQ is shown below:

```sql
SELECT SUM([t0].[Length]) AS [Length], [t1].[Name] AS [ID]
FROM [MusicTrack] AS [t0]
INNER JOIN [Artist] AS [t1] ON [t0].[ArtistID] = [t1].[ID]
GROUP BY [t1].[Name]
```

This output was generated using the LINQPad application that allows programmers to create LINQ queries and view the SQL and method-based implementations. The standard edition is a very powerful resource for developers and can be downloaded for free from *http://www.linqpad.net/*.

Select data by using anonymous types

You first saw the use of anonymous types in the "Anonymous types" section earlier in this chapter. The last few sample programs have shown the use of anonymous types moving from creating values that summarize the contents of a source data object (for example extracting just the artist and title information from a MusicTrack value), to creating completely new types that contain data from the database and the results of aggregate operators.

It is important to note that you can also create anonymous type instances in method-based SQL queries. Listing 4-41 shows the method-based implementation of the query from Listing 4-40; anonymous type is shown in bold. Note the use of an intermediate anonymous class that is used to implement the join between the two queries and generate objects that contain artist and track information.

LISTING 4-41 Complex anonymous types

```
var artistSummary = MusicTracks.Join(
                Artists,
                track => track.ArtistID,
                artist => artist.ID,
                (track, artist) =>
                    new
                    {
                        track = track,
                        artist = artist
                    }
            )
            .GroupBy(
                temp0 => temp0.artist.Name,
                temp0 => temp0.track
            )
            .Select(
                artistTrackSummary =>
                    new
                    {
                        ID = artistTrackSummary.Key,
                        Length = artistTrackSummary.Sum(x => x.Length)
                    }
            );
```

Force execution of a query

The result of a LINQ query is an item that can be iterated. We have used the foreach construction to display the results from queries. The actual evaluation of a LINQ query normally only takes place when a program starts to extract results from the query. This is called *deferred execution*. If you want to force the execution of a query you can use the ToArray() method as shown in Listing 4-42. The query is performed and the result returned as an array.

LISTING 4-42 Force query execution

```
var artistTracksQuery = from artist in artists
                   where artist.Name == "Rob Miles"
                   join track in musicTracks on artist.ID equals track.ArtistID
                   select new
                   {
                       ArtistName = artist.Name,
                       track.Title
                   };

var artistTrackResult = artistTracksQuery.ToArray();

foreach (var item in artistTrackResult)
{
    Console.WriteLine("Artist:{0} Title:{1}",
        item.ArtistName, item.Title);
}
```

Note that in the case of this example the result will be an array of anonymous class instances. Figure 4-17 shows the view in Visual Studio of the contents of the result. The program has been paused just after the artistTrackResult variable has been set to the query result, and the debugger is showing the contents of the artistTrackResult.

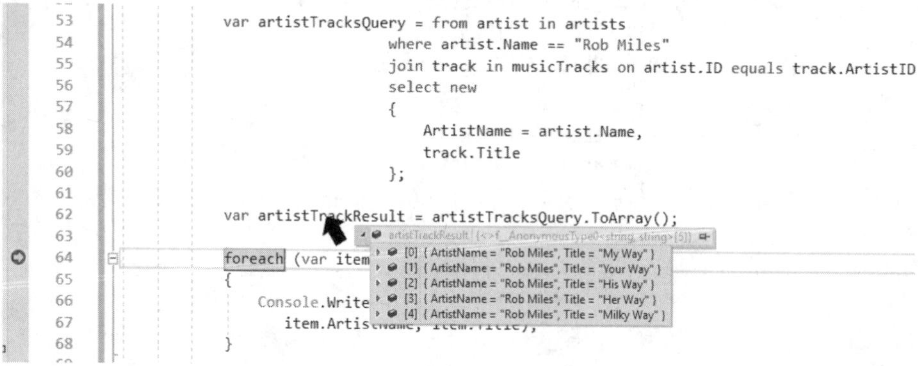

FIGURE 4-17 Immediate query results

A query result also provides ToList and ToDictionary methods that will force the execution of the query and generate an immediate result of that type. If a query returns a singleton value (for example the result of an aggregation operation such as sum or count) it will be immediately evaluated.

Read, filter, create, and modify data structures by using LINQ to XML

In this section we are going to investigate the LINQ to XML features that allow you to use LINQ constructions to parse XML documents. The classes that provide these behaviors are in the `System.XML.Linq` namespace.

Sample XML document

The sample XML document is shown next. It contains two `MusicTrack` items that are held inside a `MusicTracks` element. The text of the sample document is stored in a string variable called `XMLText`.

```
string XMLText =
    "<MusicTracks> " +
        "<MusicTrack> " +
            "<Artist>Rob Miles</Artist>  " +
            "<Title>My Way</Title>  " +
            "<Length>150</Length>" +
        "</MusicTrack>" +

        "<MusicTrack>" +
            "<Artist>Immy Brown</Artist>  " +
            "<Title>Her Way</Title>  " +
            "<Length>200</Length>" +
        "</MusicTrack>" +
    "</MusicTracks>";
```

Read XML with LINQ to XML and XDocument

In the previous section, "Consume XML data" you learned how to consume XML data in a program using the `XMLDocument` class. This class has been superseded in later versions of .NET (version 3.5 onwards) by the `XDocument` class, which allows the use of LINQ queries to parse XML files.

A program can create an `XDocument` instance that represents the earlier document by using the `Parse` method provided by the `XDocument` class as shown here.

```
XDocument musicTracksDocument = XDocument.Parse(XMLText);
```

The format of LINQ queries is slightly different when working with XML. This is because the source of the query is a filtered set of XML entries from the source document. Listing 4-43 shows how this works. The query selects all the "MusicTrack" elements from the source document. The result of the query is an enumeration of `XElement` items that have been extracted from the document. The `XElement` class is a development of the `XMLElement` class that includes XML behaviors. The program uses a `foreach` construction to work through the collection of `XElement` results, extracting the required text values.

LISTING 4-43 Read XML with LINQ

```
IEnumerable<XElement> selectedTracks =
    from track in musicTracksDocument.Descendants("MusicTrack") select track;
```

```
foreach (XElement item in selectedTracks)
{
    Console.WriteLine("Artist:{0} Title:{1}",
        item.Element("Artist").FirstNode,
        item.Element("Title").FirstNode);
}
```

Filter XML data with LINQ to XML

The program in Listing 4-43 displays the entire contents of the XML document. A program can perform filtering in the query by adding a where operator, just as with the LINQ we have seen before. Listing 4-44 shows how this works. Note that the where operation has to extract the data value from the element so that it can perform the comparison.

LISTING 4-44 Filter XML with LINQ

```
IEnumerable<XElement> selectedTracks =
        from track in musicTracksDocument.Descendants("MusicTrack")
                where (string) track.Element("Artist") == "Rob Miles"
                select track;
```

The LINQ queries that we have seen so far have been expressed using query comprehension. It is possible, however, to express the same query in the form of a method-based query. The Descendants method returns an object that provides the Where behavior. The code next shows the query in Listing 4-44 implemented as a method-based query.

```
IEnumerable<XElement> selectedTracks =
  musicTracksDocument.Descendants("MusicTrack").Where(element =>
(string)element.Element("Artist") == "Rob Miles");
```

Create XML with LINQ to XML

The LINQ to XML features include very easy way to create XML documents. The code in Listing 4-45 creates a document exactly like the sample XML for this section. Note that the arrangement of the constructor calls to each XElement item mirror the structure of the document.

LISTING 4-45 Create XML with LINQ

```
XElement MusicTracks = new XElement("MusicTracks",
    new List<XElement>
    {
        new XElement("MusicTrack",
            new XElement("Artist", "Rob Miles"),
            new XElement("Title", "My Way")),
        new XElement("MusicTrack",
            new XElement("Artist", "Immy Brown"),
            new XElement("Title", "Her Way"))
    }
);
```

Modify data with LINQ to XML

The XElement class provides methods that can be used to modify the contents of a given XML element. The program in Listing 4-46 creates a query that identifies all the MusicTrack items that have the title "my Way" and then uses the ReplaceWith method on the title data in the element to change the title to the correct title, which is "My Way."

LISTING 4-46 Modify XML with LINQ

```
IEnumerable<XElement> selectedTracks =
    from track in musicTracksDocument.Descendants("MusicTrack")
        where (string) track.Element("Title") == "my Way"
        select track;

foreach (XElement item in selectedTracks)
{
    item.Element("Title").FirstNode.ReplaceWith("My Way");
}
```

As you saw when creating a new XML document, an XElement can contain a collection of other elements to build the tree structure of an XML document. You can programmatically add and remove elements to change the structure of the XML document.

Suppose that you decide to add a new data element to MusicTrack. You want to store the "style" of the music, whether it is "Pop", "Rock," or "Classical." The code in Listing 4-47 finds all of the items in our sample data that are missing a Style element and then adds the element to the item.

LISTING 4-47 Add XML with LINQ

```
IEnumerable<XElement> selectedTracks =
    from track in musicTracksDocument.Descendants("MusicTrack")
        where track.Element("Style") == null
        select track;

foreach (XElement item in selectedTracks)
{
    item.Add(new XElement("Style", "Pop"));
}
```

Skill 4.4: Serialize and deserialize data by using binary serialization, custom serialization, XML Serializer, JSON Serializer, and Data Contract Serializer

We have already explored the serialization process in Skill 2.5, "The Serializable attribute," Skill 3.1, "JSON and C#," Skill 3.1, "JSON and XML," and Skill 3.1. "Validate JSON data." You should read these sections before continuing with this section.

Serialization does not store any of the active elements in an object. The behaviors (methods) in a class are not stored when it is serialized. This means that the application deserializing the data must have implementations of the classes that can be used to manipulate the data after it has been read.

Serialization is a complex process. If a data structure contains a graph of objects that have a large number of associations between them, the serialization process will have to persist each of these associations in the stored file.

Serialization is best used for transporting data between applications. You can think of it as transferring the "value" of an object from one place to another. Serialization can be used for persisting data, and a serialized stream can be directed into a file, but this is not normally how applications store their state. Using serialization can lead to problems if the structure or behavior of the classes implementing the data storage changes during the lifetime of the application. In this situation developers may find that previously serialized data is not compatible with the new design.

Sample data

We are going to use some sample music track data to illustrate how serialization works. The code shown next is the MusicTrack, Artist, and MusicDataStore objects that you are going to be working with. The MusicDataStore type holds lists of MusicTrack and Artist values. It also holds a method called TestData that creates a test music store that can be used in our examples.

```
class Artist
{
    public string Name { get; set; }
}

[Serializable]
class MusicTrack
{
    public Artist Artist { get; set; }
    public string Title { get; set; }
    public int Length { get; set; }
}

[Serializable]
class MusicDataStore
{
    List<Artist> Artists = new List<Artist>();
    List<MusicTrack> MusicTracks = new List<MusicTrack>();

    public static MusicDataStore TestData()
    {
        MusicDataStore result = new MusicDataStore();
        // create the same test data set as used for the LINQ examples
        return result;
    }
}
```

Use binary serialization

There are essentially two kinds of serialization that a program can use: binary serialization and text serialization. In Skill 4.1, "Convert text to binary data with Unicode," we noted that a file actually contains binary data (a sequence of 8-bit values). A UNICODE text file contains 8-bit values that represent text. Binary serialization imposes its own format on the data that is being serialized, mapping the data onto a stream of 8-bit values. The data in a stream created by a binary serializer can only be read by a corresponding binary de-serializer. Binary serialization can provide a complete "snapshot" of the source data. Both public and private data in an object will be serialized, and the type of each data item is preserved.

Classes to be serialized by the binary serializer must be marked with the [Serializable] attribute as shown below for the Artist class.

```
[Serializable]
class Artist
{
    public string Name { get; set; }
}
```

The binary serialization classes are held in the System.Runtime.Serialization.Formatters.Binary namespace. The code next shows how binary serialization is performed. It creates a test MusicDataStore object and then saves it to a binary file. An instance of the BinaryFormatter class provides a Serialize behavior that accepts an object and a stream as parameters. The Serialize behavior serializes the object to a stream.

```
MusicDataStore musicData = MusicDataStore.TestData();

BinaryFormatter formatter = new BinaryFormatter();
using (FileStream outputStream =
    new FileStream("MusicTracks.bin", FileMode.OpenOrCreate, FileAccess.Write))
{
    formatter.Serialize(outputStream, musicData);
}
```

An instance of the BinaryFormatter class also provides a behavior called Deserialize that accepts a stream and returns an object that it has deserialized from that stream. Listing 4-48 shows how to serialize an object into a binary file. The code uses a cast to convert the object returned by the Deserialize method into a MusicDataStore. This sample file for this listing also contains the previously shown serialize code.

LISTING 4-48 Binary serialization

```
MusicDataStore inputData;

using (FileStream inputStream =
    new FileStream("MusicTracks.bin", FileMode.Open, FileAccess.Read))
{
    inputData = (MusicDataStore)formatter.Deserialize(inputStream);
}
```

If there are data elements in a class that should not be stored, they can be marked with the NonSerialized attribute as shown next. The tempData property will not be serialized.

```
[Serializable]
class Artist
{
    public string Name { get; set; }
    [NonSerialized]
    int tempData;
}
```

Binary serialization is the only serialization technique that serializes private data members by default (i.e. without the developer asking). A file created by a binary serializer can contain private data members from the object being serialized. Note, however, that once an object has serialized there is nothing to stop a devious programmer from working with serialized data, perhaps viewing and tampering with the values inside it. This means that a program should treat deserialized inputs with suspicion. Furthermore, any security sensitive information in a class should be explicitly marked NonSerialized. One way to improve security of a binary serialized file is to encrypt the stream before it is stored, and decrypt it before deserialization.

Use custom serialization

Sometimes it might be necessary for code in a class to get control during the serialization process. You might want to add checking information or encryption to data elements, or you might want to perform some custom compression of the data. There are two ways that to do this. The first way is to create our own implementation of the serialization process by making a data class implement the ISerializable interface.

A class that implements the ISerializable interface must contain a GetObjectData method. This method will be called when an object is serialized. It must take data out of the object and place it in the output stream. The class must also contain a constructor that will initialize an instance of the class from the serialized data source.

The code in Listing 4-49 is an implementation of custom serialization for the Artist class in our example application. The GetObjectData method has two parameters. The SerializationInfo parameter info provides AddValue methods that can be used to store named items in the serialization stream. The StreamingContext parameter provides the serialization method with context about the serialization. The GetObjetData method for the Artist just stores the Name value in the Artist as a value that is called "name."

LISTING 4-49 Custom serialization

```
[Serializable]
class Artist : ISerializable
{
    public string Name { get; set; }

    protected Artist(SerializationInfo info, StreamingContext context)
    {
        Name = info.GetString("name");
    }
```

```
    protected Artist ()
    {
    }

    [SecurityPermissionAttribute(SecurityAction.Demand,  SerializationFormatter = true)]
    public void GetObjectData(SerializationInfo info, StreamingContext context)
    {
        info.AddValue("name", Name);
    }
}
```

The constructor for the Artist type accepts info and context parameters and uses the GetString method on the info parameter to obtain the name information from the serialization stream and use it to set the value of the Name property of the new instance.

The GetObjectData method must access private data in an object in order to store it. This can be used to read the contents of private data in serialized objects. For this reason, the GetObjectData method definition should be preceded by the security permission attribute you can see in Listing 4-49 to control access to this method.

The second way of customizing the serialization process is to add methods that will be called during serialization. These are identified by attributes as shown in Listing 4-50. The OnSerializing method is called before the serialization is performed and the OnSerialized method is called when the serialization is completed. The same format of attributes is used for the deserialize methods. These methods allow code in a class to customize the serialization process, but they don't have access to the serialization stream, only the streaming context information. If you run the example program in Listing 4-50 you will see messages displayed as each stage of serialization is performed on the data.

LISTING 4-50 Customization methods

```
[Serializable]
class Artist
{
    [OnSerializing()]
    internal void OnSerializingMethod(StreamingContext context)
    {
        Console.WriteLine("Called before the artist is serialized");
    }

    [OnSerialized()]
    internal void OnSerializedMethod(StreamingContext context)
    {
        Console.WriteLine("Called after the artist is serialized");
    }

    [OnDeserializing()]
    internal void OnDeserializingMethod(StreamingContext context)
    {
        Console.WriteLine("Called before the artist is deserialized");
    }
```

```
[OnDeserialized()]
internal void OnDeserializedMethod(StreamingContext context)
{
    Console.WriteLine("Called after the artist is deserialized");
}
}
```

Manage versions with binary serialization

The `OnDeserializing` method can be used to set values of fields that might not be present in data that is being read from a serialized document. You can use this to manage versions. In Skill 4.3, in the "Modify data with LINQ to XML" section you added a new data element to `MusicTrack`. You added the "style" of the music, whether it is "Pop", "Rock," or "Classical." This causes a problem when the program tries to deserialize old `MusicTrack` data without this information.

You can address this by marking the new field with the `[OptionalField]` attribute and then setting a default value for this element in the `OnDeserializing` method as shown in Listing 4-51. The `OnDeserializing` method is performed during deserialization. The method is called before the data for the object is deserialized and can set default values for data fields. If the input stream contains a value for a field, this will overwrite the default set by `OnDeserializing`.

LISTING 4-51 Binary versions

```
[Serializable]
class MusicTrack
{
    public Artist Artist { get; set; }
    public string Title { get; set; }
    public int Length { get; set; }

    [OptionalField]
    public string Style;

    [OnDeserializing()]
    internal void OnDeserializingMethod(StreamingContext context)
    {
        Style = "unknown";
    }
}
```

Use XML serializer

You have already seen the XML serializer in use in Skill 3.1, in the "JSON and XML" section. A program can serialize data into an XML steam in much the same way as a binary formatter. Note, however, that when an `XmlSerializer` instance is created to perform the serialization, the constructor must be given the type of the data being stored. Listing 4-52 shows how this works.

LISTING 4-52 XML Serialization

```
MusicDataStore musicData = MusicDataStore.TestData();
```

```
XmlSerializer formatter = new XmlSerializer(typeof(MusicDataStore));
using (FileStream outputStream =
    new FileStream("MusicTracks.xml", FileMode.OpenOrCreate, FileAccess.Write))
{
    formatter.Serialize(outputStream, musicData);
}

MusicDataStore inputData;

using (FileStream inputStream =
    new FileStream("MusicTracks.xml", FileMode.Open, FileAccess.Read))
{
    inputData = (MusicDataStore)formatter.Deserialize(inputStream);
}
```

XML serialization is called a *text* serializer, because the serialization process creates text documents.

The serialization process handles references to objects differently from binary serialization. Consider the class in Listing 4-53. The MusicTrack type contains a reference to the Artist describing the artist that recorded the track.

LISTING 4-53 XML References

```
class MusicTrack
{
    public Artist Artist { get; set; }
    public string Title { get; set; }
    public int Length { get; set; }
}
```

If this is track is serialized using binary serialization, the Artist reference is preserved, with a single Artist instance being referred to by all the tracks that were recorded by that artist. However, if this type of track is serialized using XML serialization, a copy of the Artist value is stored in each track. In other words, a MusicTrack value is represented as follows, with the contents of the artist information copied into the XML that is produced as shown.

```
<MusicTrack>
  <ID>1</ID>
  <Artist>
    <Name>Rob Miles</Name>
  <Title>My Way</Title>
  <Length>164</Length>
</MusicTrack>
```

When the XML data is deserialized each MusicTrack instance will contain a reference to its own Artist instance, which might not be what you expect. In other words, all of the data serialized using a text serializer is serialized by value. If you want to preserve references you must use binary serialization.

Note that the sample program in Listing 4-51 uses an ArtistID value to connect a given MusicTrack with the artist that recorded it.

Use JSON Serializer

The JSON serializer uses the JavaScript Object Notation to store serialized data in a text file. Note that we have already discussed this serializer in detail in Skill 3.1, "JSON and XML," and Skill 3.1, "Validate JSON data."

Use Data Contract Serializer

The data contract serializer is provided as part of the Windows Communication Framework (WCF). It is located in the `System.Runtime.Serialization` library. Note that this library is not included in a project by default. It can be used to serialize objects to XML files. It differs from the XML serializer in the following ways:

- Data to be serialized is selected using an "opt in" mechanism, so only items marked with the `[DataMember]` attribute will be serialized.

- It is possible to serialize private class elements (although of course they will be public in the XML text produced by the serializer).

- The XML serializer provides options that allow programmers to specify the order in which items are serialized into the data file. These options are not present in the `DataContract` serializer.

The classes here have been given the data contract attributes that are used to serialize the data in them.

```
[DataContract]
public class Artist
{
    [DataMember]
    public int ID { get; set; }
    [DataMember]
    public string Name { get; set; }
}

[DataContract]
public class MusicTrack
{
    [DataMember]
    public int ID { get; set; }
    [DataMember]
    public int ArtistID { get; set; }
    [DataMember]
    public string Title { get; set; }
    [DataMember]
    public int Length { get; set; }
}
```

Once the fields to be serialized have been specified they can be serialized using a `DataContractSerializer`. Listing 4-54 shows how this is done. Note that the methods to serialize and deserialize are called `WriteObject` and `ReadObject` respectively.

LISTING 4-54 Data contract serializer

```
MusicDataStore musicData = MusicDataStore.TestData();

DataContractSerializer formatter = new DataContractSerializer(typeof(MusicDataStore));

using (FileStream outputStream =
    new FileStream("MusicTracks.xml", FileMode.OpenOrCreate, FileAccess.Write))
{
    formatter.WriteObject(outputStream, musicData);
}

MusicDataStore inputData;

using (FileStream inputStream =
    new FileStream("MusicTracks.xml", FileMode.Open, FileAccess.Read))
{
    inputData = (MusicDataStore)formatter.ReadObject(inputStream);
}
```

Skill 4.5: Store data in and retrieve data from collections

C# programs can create variables that can store single data values, but there are many situations in which data values need to be grouped together. Objects provide one form of grouping. You can create types that describe a particular item, for example the MusicTrack type that has been used throughout the preceding examples.

Collections are a different way of grouping data. Collections are how to store a large number of objects that are usually all the same type, such as a list of MusicTrack instances. Unlike a database, which can be regarded as a service that provides data storage for an application, a collection is a structure that is stored in computer memory, alongside the program text and other variables.

You have used collections throughout the text so far. Now it is time to bring together your knowledge of how they work, the different collection types, and most importantly, how to select the right kind of collection for a particular job.

> **This Skill covers how to:**
> - Store and retrieve data by using dictionaries, arrays, lists, sets, and queues
> - Choose a collection type
> - Initialize a collection
> - Add and remove items from a collection
> - Use typed vs. non-typed collections
> - Implement custom collections
> - Implement collection interfaces

Store and retrieve data by using dictionaries, arrays, lists, sets, and queues

Before deciding what kind of data storage to use in your programs, you need an understanding of the collection types available to programs. Let's take a look at each in turn, starting with the simplest.

Use an array

An array is the simplest way to create a collection of items of a particular type. An array is assigned a size when it is created and the *elements* in the array are accessed using an *index* or *subscript* value. An array instance is a C# object that is managed by reference. A program creates an array by declaring the array variable and then making the variable refer to an array instance. Square brackets ([and]) are used to declare the array and also create the array instance. The statements next create an array variable called intArray that can hold arrays of integer values. The array variable intArray is then made to refer to a new array that contains five elements.

```
int [] intArray;
intArray = new int[5];
```

These statements can be combined into a single statement:

```
int [] intArray = new int[5];
```

An array of value types (for example an array of integers) holds the values themselves within the array, whereas for an array of reference types (for example an array of objects) each element in the array holds a reference to the object. When an array is created, each element in the array is initialized to the default value for that type. Numeric elements are initialized to 0, reference elements to null, and Boolean elements to false. Elements in an array can be updated by assigning a new value to the element.

Arrays implement the IEnumerable interface, so they can be enumerated using the foreach construction.

Once created, an array has a fixed length that cannot be changed, but an array reference can be made to refer to a new array object. An array can be initialized when it is created. An array provides a Length property that a program can use to determine the length of the array.

Listing 4-55 creates a new array, puts values into two elements and then uses a for loop to print out the contents of the array. It replaces the existing array with a new one, which is initialized to a four-digit sequence, and then prints out the contents of the new array using a foreach construction.

LISTING 4-55 Array example

```
// Array of integers
int[] intArray = new int[5];

intArray[0] = 99; // put 99 in the first element
intArray[4] = 100; // put 100 in the last element
```

```
// Use an index to work through the array
for (int i = 0; i < intArray.Length; i++)
    Console.WriteLine(intArray[i]);

// Use a foreach to work through the array
foreach (int intValue in intArray)
    Console.WriteLine(intValue);

// Initilaise a new array
intArray = new int [] { 1,2,3,4};

// Use a foreach to work through the array
foreach (int intValue in intArray)
    Console.WriteLine(intValue);
```

Any array that uses a single index to access the elements in the array is called a *one dimensional* array. It is analogous to a list of items. Arrays can have more than one dimension.

Multi-dimensional arrays

An array with two dimensions is analogous to a table of data that is made up of rows and columns. An array with three dimensions is analogous to a book containing a number of pages, with a table on each page. If you find yourself thinking that your program needs an array with more than three dimensions, you should think about arranging your data differently. The code next creates a two-dimensional array called compass, which holds the points of the compass. Elements in the array are accessed using a subscript value for each of the array dimensions. Note the use of the comma between the brackets in the declaration of the array variable. This denotes that the array has multiple dimensions.

```
string [,] compass = new string[3, 3]
{
    { "NW","N","NE" },
    {"W",  "C", "E" },
    { "SW", "S", "SE" }
};

Console.WriteLine(compass[0, 0]);  // prints NW
Console.WriteLine(compass[2, 2]);  // prints SE
```

Jagged arrays

You can view a two-dimensional array as an array of one dimensional arrays. A "jagged array" is a two-dimensional array in which each of the rows are a different length. You can see how to initialize one here:

```
int[][] jaggedArray = new int[][]
{
   new int[] {1,2,3,4 },
   new int[] {5,6,7},
   new int[] {11,12}
}
```

Use an ArrayList

The usefulness of an array is limited by the way you must decide in advance the number of items that are to be stored in the array. The size of an array cannot be changed once it has been created (although you can use a variable to set the dimension of the array if you wish). The ArrayList class was created to address this issue. An ArrayList stores data in a dynamic structure that grows as more items are added to it.

Listing 4-56 shows how it works. An ArrayList is created and three items are added to it. The items in an ArrayList can be accessed with a subscript in exactly the same way as elements in an array. The ArrayList provides a Count property that can be used to count how many items are present.

LISTING 4-56 ArrayList example

```
ArrayList arrayList = new ArrayList();

arrayList.Add(1);
arrayList.Add(2);
arrayList.Add(3);

for (int i = 0; i < arrayList.Count; i++)
    Console.WriteLine(arrayList[i]);
```

The ArrayList provides an Add method that adds items to the end of the list. There is also an Insert method that can be used to insert items in the list and a Remove method that removes items. There is more detail on the operations that can be performed on an ArrayList in the "Add and remove items from a collection" section.

Items in an ArrayList are managed by reference and the reference that is used is of type object. This means that an ArrayList can hold references to any type of object, since the object type is the base type of all of the types in C#. However, this can lead to some programming difficulties. This is discussed later in the "Use typed vs. non-typed collections" section.

Use a List

The List type makes use of the "generics" features of C#. You can find out more about generics in the "Generic types" section in Skill 2.1. When a program creates a List the type of data that the list is to hold is specified using C# generic notation. Only references of the specified type can be added to the list, and values obtained from the list are of the specified type. Listing 4-57 shows how a List is used. It creates a list of names, adds two names, and then prints out the list using a for loop. It then updates one of the names in the list and uses a foreach construction to print out the changed list.

LISTING 4-57 List example

```
List<string> names = new List<string>();

names.Add("Rob Miles");
names.Add("Immy Brown");
```

```
for (int i = 0; i < names.Count; i++)
    Console.WriteLine(names[i]);

names[0] = "Fred Bloggs";
foreach (string name in names)
    Console.WriteLine(name);
```

The List type implements the ICollection and IList interfaces. You can find out more about these interfaces later in the "Implement collection interfaces" section.

Use a dictionary

A Dictionary allows you to access data using a key. The name Dictionary is very appropriate. If you want to look up a definition of a word, you find the word in a dictionary and read the definition. In the case of an application, the key might be an account number or a username. The data can be a bank account or a user record.

Listing 4-58 shows how a Dictionary is used to implement bank account management. Each Account object has a unique AccountNo property that can be used to locate the account. The program creates two accounts and then uses the AccountNo value to find them. You can think of the key as being a *subscript* that identifies the item in the dictionary. The key value is enclosed in square brackets like for an array or a list.

LISTING 4-58 Dictionary example

```
BankAccount a1 = new BankAccount { AccountNo = 1, Name = "Rob Miles" };
BankAccount a2 = new BankAccount { AccountNo = 2, Name = "Immy Brown" };

Dictionary<int, BankAccount> bank = new Dictionary<int, BankAccount>();

bank.Add(a1.AccountNo, a1);
bank.Add(a2.AccountNo, a2);

Console.WriteLine(bank[1]);

if (bank.ContainsKey(2))
    Console.WriteLine("Account located");
```

A dictionary can be used to implement data storage, but it is also useful in very many other contexts. Listing 4-59 shows how to use a dictionary to count the frequency of words in a document. In this case the dictionary is indexed on a word and contains an integer that holds the count of that word. The document is loaded from a file into a string. The program extracts each word from the string. If the word is present in the dictionary the count for that word is incremented. If the word is not present in the dictionary, an entry is created for that word with a count of 1.

LISTING 4-59 Word counter

```
Dictionary<string, int> counters = new Dictionary<string, int>();

string text = File.ReadAllText("input.txt");
```

```
string[] words = text.Split(new char[] { ' ', '.', ',' },
    StringSplitOptions.RemoveEmptyEntries);

foreach (string word in words)
{
    string lowWord = word.ToLower();
    if (counters.ContainsKey(lowWord))
            counters[lowWord]++;
        else
            counters.Add(lowWord, 1);
}
```

Here, you would like the word counter to produce a sorted list of word counts. List and array instances provide a `Sort` method that can be used to sort their contents. Unfortunately, the `Dictionary` class does not provide a sort behavior. However, you can use a LINQ query on a dictionary to produce a sorted iteration of the dictionary contents. This can be used by a `foreach` loop to generate sorted output. The code to do this is shown next. It requires careful study. Items in a `Dictionary` have `Key` and `Value` properties that are used for sorting and output. When trying the code on an early version of this text I found that the word "the" was used around twice as many times as the next most popular word, which was "a."

```
var items = from pair in counters
            orderby pair.Value descending
            select pair;

foreach (var pair in items)
{
    Console.WriteLine("{0}: {1}", pair.Key, pair.Value);
}
```

Use a set

A set is an unordered collection of items. Each of the items in a set will be present only once. You can use a set to contain tags or attributes that might be applied to a data item. For example, information about a `MusicTrack` can include a set of style attributes. A track can be "Electronic," "Disco," and "Fast." Another track can be "Orchestral," "Classical," and "Fast." A given track is associated with a set that contains all of the attributes that apply to it. A music application can use set operations to select all of the music that meets particular criteria, for example you can find tracks that are both "Electronic" and "Disco."

Some programming languages, such as Python and Java, provide a set type that is part of the language. C# doesn't have a built-in set type, but the `HashSet` class can be used to implement sets. Listing 4-60 shows how to create three sets that contain strings that contain the names of style attributes that can be applied to music tracks. The first two, t1Styles and t2Styles, give style information for two tracks. The third set is the search set that contains two style elements that you might want to search for in tracks. The `HashSet` class provides methods that implement set operations. The `IsSubSetOf` method returns true if the given set is a subset of another. The program uses this method to determine which of the two tracks matches the search criteria.

LISTING 4-60 Set example

```
HashSet<string> t1Styles = new HashSet<string>();
t1Styles.Add("Electronic");
t1Styles.Add("Disco");
t1Styles.Add("Fast" );

HashSet<string> t2Styles = new HashSet<string>();
t2Styles.Add("Orchestral");
t2Styles.Add("Classical");
t2Styles.Add("Fast");

HashSet<string> search = new HashSet<string>();
search.Add("Fast");
search.Add("Disco");

if (search.IsSubsetOf(t1Styles))
    Console.WriteLine("All search styles present in T1");

if (search.IsSubsetOf(t2Styles))
    Console.WriteLine("All search styles present in T2");
```

Another set methods can be used to combine set values to produce unions, differences, and to test supersets and subsets.

Use a queue

A queue provides a short term storage for data items. It is organized as a *first-in-first-out* (FIFO) collection. Items can be added to the queue using the Enqueue method and read from the queue using the Dequeue method. There is also a Peek method that allows a program to look at an item at the top of the queue without removing it from the queue. A program can iterate through the items in a queue and a queue also provides a Count property that will give the number of items in the queue. Listing 4-61 shows the usage of a simple queue that contains strings.

LISTING 4-61 Queue example

```
Queue<string> demoQueue = new Queue<string>();

demoQueue.Enqueue("Rob Miles");
demoQueue.Enqueue("Immy Brown");

Console.WriteLine(demoQueue.Dequeue());
Console.WriteLine(demoQueue.Dequeue());
```

The program will print "Rob Miles" first when it runs, because of the FIFO behavior of a queue. One potential use of a queue is for passing work items from one thread to another. If you are going to do this you should take a look at the ConcurrentQueue, which is described in Skill 1.1.

Use a stack

A stack is very similar in use to a queue. The most important difference is that a stack is organized as *last-in-first-out* (LIFO). A program can use the Push method to push items onto the top of the stack and the `Pop` method to remove items from the stack. Listing 4-62 shows simple use of a stack. Note that the program prints out "Immy Brown" first, because that is the item on the top of the stack when the printing is first performed. There is a `ConcurrentStack` implementation that should be used if different Tasks are using the same stack.

LISTING 4-62 Stack example

```
Stack<string> demoStack = new Stack<string>();

demoStack.Push("Rob Miles");
demoStack.Push("Immy Brown");

Console.WriteLine(demoStack.Pop());
Console.WriteLine(demoStack.Pop());
```

Choose a collection type

The type of collection to use normally falls naturally from the demands of the application. If you need to store a list of values, use a `List` in preference to an array or `ArrayList`. An array is fixed in size and an `ArrayList` does not provide type safety. A `List` can only contain objects of the list type and can grow and contract. It is also very easy to remove a value from the middle of a list or insert an extra value.

Use an array if you are concerned about performance and you are holding value types, since the data will be accessed more quickly. The other occasion where arrays are useful is if a program needs to store two-dimensional data (for example a table of values made up of rows and columns). In this situation you can create an object that implements a row (and contains a `List` of elements in the row) and then stores a `List` of these objects.

If there is an obvious value in an object upon which it can be indexed (for example an account number or username), use a dictionary to store the objects and then index on that value. A dictionary is less useful if you need to locate a data value based on different elements, such as needing to find a customer based on their customer ID, name, or address. In that case, put the data in a `List` and then use LINQ queries on the list to locate items.

Sets can be useful when working with tags. Their built-in operations are much easier to use than writing your own code to match elements together. Queues and stacks are used when the needs of the application require FIFO or LIFO behavior.

Initialize a collection

The examples that you have seen have added values to collections by calling the collection methods to add the values. For example, use the `Add` method to add items to a `List`. However, there are quicker ways to initialize each type of object. Listing 4-63 shows the initialization process for each of the collections that we have just discussed.

LISTING 4-63 Collection initialization

```
int[] arrayInit = { 1, 2, 3, 4 };

ArrayList arrayListInit =   new ArrayList { 1, "Rob Miles", new ArrayList() };
```

```
List<int> listInit = new List<int>{ 1, 2, 3, 4 };

Dictionary<int, string> dictionaryInit =  new Dictionary<int, string> {
        {1, "Rob" },
        {2, "Immy" } };

HashSet<string> setInit = new HashSet<string> { "Electronic", "Disco", "Fast" };

Queue<string> queueInit = new Queue<string>( new string [] {"Rob", "Immy" });

Stack <string> stackInit = new Stack<string>(new string[] { "Rob", "Immy" });
```

Add and remove items from a collection

Some of the collection types that we have discussed contain support for adding and removing
elements from the types. Here are the methods for each collection type.

Add and remove items from an array

The array class does not provide any methods that can add or remove elements. The size of an
array is fixed when the array is created. The only way to modify the size of an existing array is
to create a new array of the required type and then copy the elements from one to the other.
The array class provides a CopyTo method that will copy the contents of an array into another
array. The first parameter of CopyTo is the destination array. The second parameter is the start
position in the destination array for the copied values. Listing 4-64 shows how this can be used
to migrate an array into a larger one. The new array has one extra element, but you can make it
much larger than this if required. Note that because arrays are objects managed by reference,
you can make the dataArray reference refer to the newly created array.

LISTING 4-64 Grow an array

```
int[] dataArray= { 1, 2, 3, 4 };
int[] tempArray = new int[5];
dataArray.CopyTo(tempArray, 0);
dataArray= tempArray;
```

Add and remove items in ArrayList and List

There are a number of methods that can be used to modify the contents of the ArrayList and
List collections. Listing 4-65 shows them in action.

LISTING 4-65 List modification

```
List<string> list = new List<string>();
list.Add("add to end of list");     // add to the end of the list
list.Insert(0, "insert at start"); // insert an item at the start
list.Insert(1, "insert new item 1"); // insert at position
list.InsertRange(2, new string[] { "Rob", "Immy" }); // insert a range
list.Remove("Rob");                 // remove first occurrence of "Rob"
list.RemoveAt(0);                   // remove element at the start
```

```
list.RemoveRange(1, 2);          // remove two elements
list.Clear();                    // clear entire list
```

Add and remove items from a Dictionary

The Dictionary type provides Add and Remove methods, as shown in Listing 4-66.

LISTING 4-66 Dictionary modification

```
Dictionary<int, string> dictionary = new Dictionary<int, string>();
dictionary.Add(1, "Rob Miles");  // add an entry
dictionary.Remove(1);            // remove the entry with the given key
```

Add and remove items from a Set

The Set type provides Add, Remove and RemoveWhere methods. Listing 4-67 shows how they are used. The RemoveWhere function is given a *predicate* (a behavior that generates either true or false) to determine which elements are to be removed. In the listing the predicate is a lambda expression that evaluates to true if the element in the set starts with the character 'R.'

LISTING 4-67 Set modification

```
HashSet<string> set = new HashSet<string>();
set.Add("Rob Miles");     // add an item
set.Remove("Rob Miles"); // remove an item
set.RemoveWhere(x => x.StartsWith("R")); // remove all items that start with 'R'
```

Add and remove items in Queue and Stack

The most important aspect of the behavior of queues and stacks is the way that items are added and removed. For this reason, the only actions that allow their contents to be changed are the ones you have seen earlier.

Use typed vs. non-typed collections

When comparing the behavior of the ArrayList collection types we noted that there is nothing to stop a programmer putting any type of object in the same ArrayList. The code next adds an integer, a string, and even an ArrayList to the ArrayList called MessyList. While this may be something you want to do, It is not good programming practice.

```
ArrayList messyList = new ArrayList();
messyList.Add(1); // add an integer to the list
messyList.Add("Rob Miles"); // add a string to the list
messyList.Add(new ArrayList());  //add an ArrayList to the list
```

Another difficultly caused by the untyped storage provided by the ArrayList is that all of the references in the list are references to objects. When a program removes an item from an ArrayList it must cast the item into its proper type before it can be used. In other words, to use the int value at the subscript 0 of the messyList above, cast it to an int before using it, as shown here:

```
int messyInt = (int) messyList[0];
```

Note that if you are confused to see the value type `int` being used in an ArrayList, where the contents are managed by reference, you should read the"Boxing and unboxing" section in Skill 2.2.

These problems occur due to an `ArrayList` existing in an *untyped* collection. For this reason, the `ArrayList` has been superseded by the `List` type, which uses the generics features in later versions of C# to allow a programmer to specify the type of item that the list should hold. It is recommended that you use the `List` type when you want to store collections of items.

Implement custom collections

A custom collection is a collection that you create for a specific purpose that has behaviors that you need in your application. One way to make a custom collection is to create a new type that implements the `ICollection` interface. This can then be used in the same way as any other collection, such as with a program iterating through your collection using a `foreach` construction. We will describe how to implement a collection interface in the next section.

Another way to create a custom collection is to use an existing collection class as the base (parent) class of a new collection type. You can then add new behaviors to your new collection and, because it is based on an existing collection type, your collection can be used in the same way as any other collection.

Listing 4-68 shows how to create a custom `MusicTrack` store, which is based on the `List` collection type. The method `RemoveArtist` has been added to the new type so that a program can easily remove all the tracks by a particular artist. Note how the `RemoveArtist` method creates a list of items to be removed and then removes them. This is to prevent problems that can be caused by removing items in a collection at the same time as iterating through the collection. If you investigate the sample program for Listing 4-68, you will find that the `TrackStore` class also contains a `ToString` method and also a static `GetTestTrackStore` method that can be used to create a store full of sample tracks.

LISTING 4-68 Custom collection

```
class TrackStore : List<MusicTrack>
{
    public int RemoveArtist(string removeName)
    {
        List<MusicTrack> removeList = new List<MusicTrack>();
        foreach (MusicTrack track in this)
            if (track.Artist == removeName)
                removeList.Add(track);

        foreach (MusicTrack track in removeList)
            this.Remove(track);

        return removeList.Count;
    }
}
```

Implement collection interfaces

The behavior of a collection type is expressed by the `ICollection` interface. The `ICollection` interface is a child of the `IEnumerator` interface. Interface hierarchies work in exactly the same way as class hierarchies, in that a child of a parent interface contains all of the methods that are described in the parent. This means that a type that implements the `ICollection` interface is capable of being enumerated. For a more details on the `IEnumerator` interface, consult the "IEnumerable" section in Skill 2.4.

The class in Listing 4-69 implements the methods in the `ICollection` interface. It contains an array of fixed values that give four points of a compass. It can be used in the same way as any other collection, and can be enumerated as it provides a `GetEnumerator` method. Note that the collection interface does not specify any methods that determine how (or indeed whether) a program can add and remove values.

LISTING 4-69 ICollection interface

```
class CompassCollection : ICollection
{
    // Array containing values in this collection
    string[] compassPoints = { "North", "South", "East", "West" };

    // Count property to return the length of the collection
    public int Count
    {
        get { return compassPoints.Length; }
    }

    // Returns an object that can be used to syncrhonise
    // access to this object
    public object SyncRoot
    {
        get { return this; }
    }

    // Returns true if the collection is thread safe
    // This collection is not
    public bool IsSynchronized
    {
        get { return false; }
    }

    // Provide a copyto behavior
    public void CopyTo(Array array, int index)
    {
        foreach (string point in compassPoints)
        {
            array.SetValue(point, index);
            index = index + 1;
        }
    }

    // Required for IEnumerate
```

```
    // Returns the enumerator from the embedded array
    public IEnumerator GetEnumerator()
    {
        return compassPoints.GetEnumerator();
    }
}
```

Note, that if you want the new collection type to be used with LINQ queries it must implement the IEnumerable<type> interface. This means that the type must contain a GetEnumerator<string> () method.

Thought experiments

In these thought experiments, demonstrate your skills and knowledge of the topics covered in this chapter. You can find the answers to these thought experiments in the next section.

1 Perform I/O operations

Class hierarchies are an important element in the design of the data management mechanisms provided by .NET. The Stream class sets out the fundamental data movement commands and is used as the basis of classes that provide data storage on a variety of platforms. Streams can also be chained together so that character encoding, encryption and compression can be performed on data being moved to or from any stream-based store.

Here are some questions to consider:

1. Why can't a program create an instance of the Stream type?

2. When would a program modify the file pointer in a file?

3. What is the difference between UT8 Unicode and UTF32 Unicode?

4. Is there such a thing as a "text file?"

5. Can a program both read from and write to a single file?

6. What is the difference between a TextWriter and a StreamWriter?

7. Why is it useful for a stream class to have a constructor that accepts an object of the stream type?

8. What is the File class for?

9. Will you need to re-compile a program for it to be used on a system with a different file system?

10. What happens to the files in a directory when you delete the directory?

11. How can you tell if a file path is an absolute path to the file?

12. Why should you use the Path class to construct file paths in your programs?

13. What is the difference between HTTP and HTML?

14. When should you use the HttpWebRequest class to contact a web server?

15. Can a program make web requests asynchronously?

16. Why is it a good idea to perform file operations asynchronously?

2 Consume data

Databases are the storage resource that underpins many applications. In this section you've seen how a program can use Structured Query Language (SQL) to interact with a database. You've also discovered more about the use of databases in Active Server Pages (ASP) and considered how JavaScript Object Notation (JSON) and eXtensible Markup Language (XML) documents allow programs to exchange structured data. Finally, you've taken a look at web services; a means by which a server can expose resources in the form of method calls.

Here are some questions to consider:

1. Does each user of a database need their own copy of the data?

2. What would happen if two users of a database updated the same record at the same time?

3. What would happen if two items in a database had the same ID value?

4. Why do you need to protect your database connection string?

5. Do you always have to write SQL queries to interact with a database?

6. What is an SQL injection attack, and how do you protect against one?

7. You can see how to read JSON data from a server, but is it possible to store JSON for-matted data values on a server?

8. What is the difference between a web service and just downloading JSON document from a server?

3 Query and manipulate data and objects by using LINQ

LINQ allows developers to take their SQL skills in building queries and apply them to software objects. By exposing query elements as C# operators using the query comprehension syntax LINQ allows you to create C# statements that closely resemble SQL queries. These queries can be applied to structured data from a database, but they can also be applied to normal col-lections and XML documents. LINQ is useful for filtering data and extracting subsets; it also provides the group operator that can be used to summarize data. LINQ queries are actually implemented as method calls onto objects and can be created that way if preferred.

Here are some questions to consider:

1. What does "Language INtegrated Query" actually mean?

2. Does LINQ add new features for data manipulation?

3. Is it more efficient to build and perform our own SQL queries than to use LINQ?

4. Why would the statement var counter; cause a compilation error?

5. What is an anonymous type?

6. What does "deferred execution" of a LINQ query mean?

7. What does the group behavior do in a LINQ query?

8. What do the `take` and `skip` behaviors do?

9. What is the difference between query comprehension and method-based LINQ queries?

10. What is the difference between the `XDocument` and `XElement` types?

11. What is the difference between the `XmlDocument` and `XDocument` types?

4 Serialize and deserialize data

Serialization is very useful when you want to store or transfer structured data. It is susceptible to problems if the content or arrangement of data items that have been serialized change in later versions of an application. But, as you have seen, it is possible for these to be addressed with sensible data design.

Here are some questions to consider:

1. When should you use serialization in your program?

2. Do you need a copy of the type to read a serialized object?

3. Can any data type be serialized?

4. Can value types and reference types be stored using serialization?

5. Does serialization store all of the elements of a class?

6. When should you use binary serialization and when should you use XML serialization?

7. Why should you be concerned about security when using binary serialization?

8. Can you use a custom serializer when serializing to an XML document?

9. Is it possible to encrypt a serialized class?

10. What is the difference between an XML serializer and a `DataContract` serializer?

5 Store data in and retrieve data from collections

You can think of the collection classes provided by .NET as a set of tools. Each tool is suited for a particular situation. When considering how to store data in a program it is important to consider the whole range of different kinds of collections. Most of the time storage demands tend to be met by the List or Dictionary types, but there have been occasions where you need the FIFO behavior provided by a queue, and a set can save a lot of work because of the behaviors that it provides. There are two things that are important when dealing with collections. The first is that extending a parent collection type is a great way to add custom behaviors. The second is that you should remember that it is possible to perform LINQ queries on collections, which can save you a lot of work writing code to search through them and select items.

Here are some questions to consider:

1. When should you use a collection, and when should you use a database?

2. Can you create an array of arrays?

3. Can you create a twenty-dimensional array?

4. Why does the program keep crashing with an array index error?

5. The array is one element too small. How do you add a new element on the end of the array?

6. Why do you use Length to get the length of an array and Count to get the number of items in an ArrayList?

7. How does a Dictionary actually work?

8. When would you use a set?

9. What is the difference between a stack and a queue?

10. Could you use a List to store every type of data in my program?

Thought experiment answers

This section provides the solutions for the tasks included in the thought experiments.

1 Perform I/O operations

1. It is not possible for a program to create an instance of the Stream type, because the Stream class is defined as abstract and intended to be used as the base class for child classes that contain implementations of the behaviors described by Stream.

2. The file pointer value is managed by a stream and specifies the position at which the next input/output transaction will be performed. When reading a file, the file pointer starts at the beginning of the file. If a program wishes to "skip" some locations in the file the file pointer can be updated to the new location. It is faster to update the file pointer than it is to move down a file by reading form it. When writing into a file the file pointer is updated as the file is written. When a file is opened in the "append" mode the file pointer is moved to the end of the file after the file has been opened.

3. Unicode is a mapping between values and text characters. As an example, the character π has the Unicode value 120587. The UTF8 standard maps Unicode characters onto one or more 8-bit storage locations. The UTF32 standard maps Unicode characters onto one or more 32-bit storage locations.

4. The file system on a computer does not make a distinction between a "text" file and a "binary" file. This distinction is made by the programs using the file system to store files. In the case of C#, a text file is one that contains values that represent text. The values in the text file will be encoded using a standard that maps numeric values onto characters. The Unicode standard is frequently used for this.

5. If a stream is opened for ReadWrite access, the program can both read from and write into the file. The file will usually hold fixed length records, so that a single record in the middle of a file can be changed without affecting any of the other records in the file.

6. The TextWriter class is an abstract class that specifies operations that can be performed to write text into a stream. The StreamWriter class is a child of the TextWriter class that can be instantiated and used to write text into a stream.

7. A program can construct a stream from a stream to allow two streams to be "chained" together. The output of one stream can then be sent to the input of the next. The example used was that we could use a compression stream in conjunction with a file stream to create a stream that would compress data as it was written into a file.

8. The File class provides a set of very useful methods that can be used to create and populate files with only a small number of statements. It also provides a number of very useful file management commands.

9. The precise way in which a given file system works is completely hidden from the programs that are using it. There is need to recompile a program to change to a different files system.

10. If a program tries to delete a directory that is not empty, the delete action will fail with an exception. The program must delete all the files in a directory before the directory itself can be removed.

11. An absolute file path will start with the drive letter on which the file is stored and contain all the directories to be traversed to reach the file. A relative path will not start with a drive letter.

12. Programs frequently have to create filenames by adding drives, directory names, and filenames together. The Path class provides a static Combine method that makes sure that all the path separators are correctly inserted into the path that is created. This is much less prone to error than trying to make sure that the correct number of "backslash" characters has been included in the name.

13. HTTP stands for "Hyper Text Transfer Protocol." It defines the way that a client can give instructions to a web server. HTML stands for "Hyper Text Markup Language." It defines the format of documents that are sent back from the server in response to an HTTP request.

14. The HttpWebRequest class is extremely customizable and provides much more flexibility than the WebClient class when creating requests to be sent to web servers. Some forms of web request can only be sent using an HttpWebRequest.

15. The WebClient and HTTPClient classes support the use of async and await for making asynchronous web requests.

16. It is a good idea to perform file operations asynchronously because they are frequently the slowest actions performed on a computer. Writing to a physical disk takes much longer than calculations, and disk transactions may take much longer if the system is busy.

2 Consume data

1. The idea behind a database server is that it can provide access to a central store of data. It is a bad idea for each user to have their own copy of the data because the copies can become updated in different ways. However, it is possible for a system to keep a local copy of a database for use when the system is not connected to a network and then apply the updates to a database when network connectivity is available.

2. A database server is designed to ensure that the stored data is always consistent. If two users update a particular record at the same time the updates will be performed in sequence and the server will make sure that data is not corrupted. It is possible for a user of a database to flag actions as *atomic* so that they are either completed or the database is "rolled back" to the state it had before the action.

3. If the ID of an item is being used as a "key" to uniquely identify the item, it is impossible to create two items with the same ID. The database will generate ID values for items automatically when they are added to the database.

4. The database connection string is used to create a connection to the database. If the database is not on the same computer as the program using it, the connection string will include the network address of the server and authentication information. Armed with this information anyone can create a connection to the database and send it SQL commands, which would be a bad thing.

5. SQL queries are the lowest level of communication with the database. However, you have seen that in an ASP.NET application you can perform actions on objects in the program and then update the contents of the database with the new objects.

6. An SQL command is a construction that contains command and data elements. An SQL injection attack is performed by "injecting" SQL commands into the data parts of the command. For example, if the user of a database is asked to enter a new name for the customer, they can add malicious SQL commands to the name text. If this text is used to build the command sent to the database, these commands are obeyed by the database. These attacks can be prevented by using parameterized SQL commands, which specifically separate the data from the command elements.

7. If your application needs to be able to upload data to a server application it can use the Representational State Transfer (REST) model. This makes use of the HTTP command set to allow an application to send data between the client and the server. The data can be XML or JSON documents.

8. A web service provides the client application with a "proxy object" that represents a connection to the service. The client can call methods on the proxy to interact with the service. This provides a much richer set of options than simply downloading a file.

3 Query and manipulate data and objects by using LINQ

1. The phrase "Language Integrated Query" refers to the way that a data query can be expressed using language elements in a format called "query comprehension". The LINQ operators (from, show, join, etc.) allow the programmer to express their intent directly, without having to make a chain of method calls to create a query. That said, we know that the compiler actually converts "query comprehension" notation queries into a chain of method calls, and programmers can create "method-based" queries if they prefer.

2. LINQ doesn't create any new data manipulation features, but it does make it much, much easier for a programmer to express what they want to do.

3. Building your own SQL queries is slightly more efficient than using LINQ. The very first time a LINQ query is used it will be compiled into the method sequence that is then called to deliver the result. This is rarely a problem from a performance point of view, however, and LINQ makes programmers more efficient.

4. When you declare a variable of type var you are asking the compiler to infer the type of the variable from the value being assigned to it. If the declaration does not assign an initial value to the variable (as in this case) the compiler will refuse to compile the statement because it has no value from which it can infer the type of the variable.

5. An anonymous type is a type that has no name. This is not a very helpful thing to say, but it is true. Normally a type is defined and then the new keyword is used to make new instances of that type. In the case of an anonymous type the instance is created without the associated type. The object initializer syntax (which allows a programmer to initialize public properties of a class when an instance is created) also allows objects to be created without an associated type. In the case of LINQ these objects can be returned as the results of queries. The objects contain custom result types that exactly match the data requested. Note that these objects must be referred to using the var keyword.

6. A LINQ query will return a result that describes an iteration that can then be processed using a foreach construction. If the query result contains many result values, it takes a long time (and uses up a lot of memory) to actually generate that result when the query is performed. So instead, the iteration is evaluated and each result is generated in turn when it is to be consumed.

7. The group operator creates a new dataset grouped around the value of one item in the input dataset. You used it in the MusicTracks application to take a list of all the tracks (each track containing an ArtistID value) and create a group that contains one entry for each ArtistID value in the dataset. You can then use aggregate operations on the group to do things such as count the number of tracks and sum the total length of the tracks for each artist.

8. The take behavior creates a LINQ query that takes a particular number of items from the source dataset. The skip behavior skips down the dataset a given number of items

before the query starts taking values. Used in combination they allow a program to work through a dataset one "page" at a time.

9. The "query comprehension" and "method-based" LINQ query formats can be used interchangeably in programs. You can use them both in a single solution, depending on which is most convenient at any given point in the program.

10. The XDocument class can hold an XML document, including the elements that can be used to express a "fully formed" XML document, including metadata about the document contents. An XElement can contain an element in an XML document (which can contain a tree of other XElement objects). An XDocument contains XElement objects that contain the data in the document.

11. The XmlDocument implements a Document Object Model (DOM) for XML documents. The XDocument builds on the ability of an XmlDocument to allow it to work with LINQ queries. The same relationship applies between XmlElement and XElement.

4 Serialize and deserialize data

1. Serialization is very useful if you are storing small amounts of structured data. The high score table for a game can be stored as a serialized object. Another use for a small serialized object can be the settings for an application. It would be less sensible to store a large data structure as a serialized object, particularly if the object has to be repeatedly updated.

2. Serialization takes a snapshot of the data elements in a particular type. During the deserialization process a new instance of the serialized type is created. This process requires the type to be deserialized to be available on the receiving machine. In the case of binary serialization, the binary file contains type information that is compared with type information in the destination class. If this information doesn't match, the deserialization fails. Note that in the case of serialization to XML and JSON text files, this matching does not take place. You can regard these two types as being more portable, at the expense of security. The DataContract serialization process allows the serialized object to contain type information that can be checked during deserialization, but the format of the serialized file is still human readable XML.

3. Binary serialization can store any type of data, but XML serialization is restricted to numeric and text types.

4. A binary serializer can store reference types as references, whereas XML, JSON, and DataContract serialization will resolve references to obtain values that are then serialized.

5. Serialization does not store the methods in a class, or any static elements. Binary serialization will store private data members of a type. DataContract serialization can store private data members as XML text.

6. Binary serialization is very useful for taking a complete snapshot of the data content of a class. It forces the serialize and deserialize process to make use of identical classes. It

is very useful for transferring an object from one process to another, where the serialized data stream will not be persisted. I'm not keen on using it to persist data for long periods of time because it is vulnerable to changes in the classes used. Text serialization such as XML is very useful if you want to transfer data from one programming language or host to another. It is highly portable. It is also very useful for storing small amounts of structured data.

7. Binary serialization produces a stream that represents the entire contents of a class, including all private content. However, with an understanding of the content, it is possible that this can be compromised, allowing the private contents of an object to be viewed and changed. Just because you can't view the contents of a binary serialized object with a text editor does not mean that it is not immune to tampering.

8. A custom serializer allows the programmer to get control of the serialization process either by creating their own serialization process or by getting control during the phases of the serialization process. These customizations are only possible when using binary data serialization.

9. All serializers use data streams to transfer data being serialized and deserialized. In Skill 3.2, in the "Encrypting data using AES symmetric encryption," section you saw that it is possible to send a data stream through an encrypting stream, making it possible to encrypt serialized data. It is also possible to compress serialized data in the same way.

10. Both XML and DataContract serializers produce XML output. In the case of XML, if a class is marked as serializable, all of the data elements in the class will be serialized and the programmer must mark as NonSerialized any data members that should not be serialized. In the case of DataContract serialization, the programmer must mark elements to be serialized. The other functional difference is that private data members can be serialized using DataContract serialization.

5 Store data in and retrieve data from collections

1. A database provides storage where database queries are used to manipulate the data stored. The data in the database is moved into the program for processing. A collection is stored in the memory of the computer and can therefore be accessed much more quickly. A database is good for very large amounts of data that won't necessarily fit in memory and have to be shared with multiple users. In-memory collections have performance many times that of data access from a database, but are limited in capacity to the memory of the computer. One major attraction of a database is the ease with which a database query can be used to extract data. However, you should remember that LINQ can be used on in-memory collections.

2. You can create an array of arrays. Each of the arrays in the array can consist of a different length, leading to the creation of what is called a "jagged" array.

3. The C# compiler will not complain if you make a twenty-dimensional array. However, it might use up a lot of computer memory, and it would certainly be very hard to visualize.

Don't confuse adding array dimensions with adding properties to an object. To hold the name, birthday and address of a person you don't need a three-dimensional array, you need a one-dimensional array of Person elements.

4. Remember that C# arrays are indexed starting at 0. This means that if you have an array with 4 elements they are given the indices 0, 1, 2, and 3. In other words there is no element with the index value 4. This can be counter-intuitive, and it is also not how some other languages work, where array indices start at 1.

5. It is impossible to change the size of an array once it has been created. The only way to "add" an element is to create a new, larger, array and then copy the existing one into it.

6. The use of Length for the length of an array and Count for the number of elements in other collection types can be confusing, but the explanation is that an array has the same size at all times, so you can just get the length of it. However, a dynamic collection class such as an ArrayList can change in size at any time, and so the program will actually have to count the number of items to find out the current size.

7. Dictionaries decide where to store an item by using a *hashing* algorithm. You saw hashing in Skill 3.2, where a hashing function reduces a large amount of data to a single, smaller value that represents that data. The Dictionary class uses a hashing algorithm to convert the key value for the item being stored into a number that will give the location of the item. When searching for the location represented by a key, the dictionary doesn't have to search through a list of keys to find the one selected. It just has to hash the supplied key value to calculate exactly there the item is stored.

8. Sets are useful if you want to item properties that may grow and change over time, such as with a tag metadata. A user can generate new tags as the application is used, and the set provides operators that can search for items. The difficulty with tags is that it may be difficult to store them in fixed sized storage such as databases. Furthermore, LINQ operators can be used in place of set operations.

9. The prime difference between a stack and a queue is how the order of items is changed when they are pushed and popped. A queue retains the order, so the first item added to the queue is the first one to be removed from the queue. A stack reverses the order, so the first item to be pushed onto the stack will be the last one to be removed. If you think about it, you can reverse the order of a collection by pushing all of the elements onto a stack and then popping them off.

10. You can use the List type to meet all of your data storage needs, but you must put in substantial extra amounts of work to get a list to perform like a set or a dictionary.

Chapter summary

- A stream is an object that represents a connection to a data source. A stream allows a program to read and write sequences of bytes and set the position of the next stream operation.

- The Stream class is the abstract parent class that defines fundamental stream behaviors. A range of different child classes extend this base class to provide stream interaction with different data sources.

- The FileStream class provides a stream interface to file storage.

- A file contains a sequence of 8-bit values (bytes) that can be encoded into text using a particular character mapping. The Encoding class provides methods for different character mappings.

- The TextWriter and TextReader classes are abstract classes that define operations that can be performed with text in files. The StreamWriter and StreamReader class are implementations of this class that can be used to work with text files in C#.

- Stream classes have constructors that can accept other streams, allowing a program to create a "pipeline" of data processing behaviors that are ultimately connected to a storage device.

- The File class is a "helper" class that contains static methods that can be used to write, read, append, open, copy, rename, and delete files.

- It is important that a program using files deals with any exceptions that are thrown when the files are used. File operations are prone to throwing exceptions.

- The actual file storage on a computer is managed by a file system that interacts with a partition on a disk drive. The file system maintains information on files and directories which can be manipulated by C# programs.

- The FileInfo class holds information about a particular file in a filesystem. It duplicates some functions provided by the File class but is useful if you are working through a large number of files. The File class is to be preferred when working with individual files.

- The DirectoryInfo class holds information about a particular directory in a filesystem. This includes a list of FileInfo items describing the files held in that directory.

- A path describes a file on a filesystem. Paths can be absolute, thus starting at the drive letter, or relative. The Path class provides a set of methods that can be used to work with path strings, including extracting elements of the path and concatenating path strings.

- A C# program can use the HttpWebRequest, WebClient, and HttpClient classes to communicate with an HTTP server via the Internet. HttWebRequest provides the most flexibility when assembling HTTP messages. WebClient is simpler to use and can be used with await and async to perform asynchronously. HttpClient only supports asynchronous use and must be used when writing Universal Windows Applications.

- Programs can (and should) perform file operations asynchronously. The FileStream class provides asynchronous methods. When catching exceptions thrown by file operations, ensure that the methods being awaited do not have a void return type.

- A database provides data storage for applications in the form of tables. A row in a table equates to a class instance. Each row can have a unique ID (called a *primary key*) which allows other objects to refer to that row.

- Programs interact with a database server by creating an instance of a connection object. The connection string is used to configure this connection, to identify the location of the server and to provide authentication details. ASP.NET applications can be configured with different environments for development and production, including the contents of the connection string.

- A database responds to commands expressed in Structured Query Language (SQL). SQL is plain text that contains commands and data elements. Care must be taken when incorporating user entered data elements in SQL queries because a malicious user can inject additional SQL commands into the data.

- When creating ASP.NET applications, the SQL commands to update the database are performed by methods in that act on objects in the application.

- A program can download data from a web server in the form of a JSON or XML document that describes the elements in an object.

- A program can download data from a web server in the form of an XML document. XML documents can be parsed element by element or used to create a Document Object Model (DOM) instance, which provides programmatic access to the elements in the data.

- A web service takes the form of a server and a client. The server exposes a description of the service in the form of method calls that are implemented by a proxy object created by the client. The method calls in the client proxy object are translated into requests sent to the server. The server performs the requested action and then sends the response back to the client, which receives the response in the form of the result from the method call.

- LINQ allows programmers to express SQL-like queries using "query comprehension syntax."

- LINQ queries can be performed against C# collections, database connections, and XML documents.

- A LINQ query generates an iteration. The execution of the query is deferred until the iteration is enumerated, although it is possible to force the execution of a query by requesting the query to generate a List, array, or dictionary as a result.

- LINQ queries are compiled into C# method calls. A programmer can express a query as methods if required.

- A LINQ query generates an iteration as a result. This may be an iteration of data objects or an iteration of anonymous types, which are created dynamically when the query runs.

- A program can work with anonymous types by using the var type, which requests that the compiler infer the type of the data from the context in which it is used. Using var types does not result in any relaxation of type safety because the compiler will ensure that the inferred type is not used incorrectly.

- The output from one query can be joined with a next, to allow data in different sources (C# collections or database tables) to be combined.

- The output from a query can be grouped on a particular property of the incoming data, allowing a query to create summary information that can be evaluated by the aggregate commands, which are sum, average, min, max, and count.

- LINQ to XML can be used to perform LINQ queries against XML documents held in the XDocument and XElement objects. These objects also provide behaviors that make it easy to create new XML documents and edit existing ones.

- Serialization involves sending (serializing) the contents of an object into a stream. The stream can be deserialized to create a copy of the object with all the data intact. The code content (the methods) in an object are not transferred by serialization.

- Classes that are to be serialized by the binary serializer must be marked using the [Serializable] attribute, which will request that all the data items in the class be serialized. It is possible to mark data items in a class with the [NotSerialized] attribute if it is not meaningful for them to be serialized.

- Binary serialization encodes the data into a binary file. Binary serialization serializes public and private data elements and preserves references. Sensitive data should not be serialized without paying attention to the security issues, because a binary serialized file containing private data can be compromised.

- A programmer can write their own serialization behaviors in a class, which save and restore the data items using the serialization stream. Note that customized serialization behaviors may be used to illicitly obtain the contents of private data in a class, and so must be managed in a secure way.

- A programmer can add methods that can modify the contents of a class during the serialization and deserialization process. This allows you to create classes that can create default values for missing attributes when old versions of serialized data are deserialized.

- The XML serializer serializes public elements of a class into XML text. The value of each element is stored in the file. References in objects that are serialized are converted into copies of the value at the end of the reference. There is no need for the [Serializable] attribute to be added to classes to be serialized using XML.

- The JSON serializer uses the JavaScript Object Notation to serialize data into a stream.

- The DataContract serializer can serialize public and private data elements into XML files. Classes to be serialized must be given the [DataContract] attribute and data elements to be serialized must be given the [DataMember] attribute.

- The C# language allows a program to create arrays. An array can contain value or reference types. The size of the array (the number of elements in it) is fixed when the array is created and cannot be changed. Array elements are accessed by the use of a subscript/index value which is 0 for the element at the start of the array. Arrays can have multiple dimensions.

- The ArrayList is a collection class that provides dynamic storage of elements. A program can add and remove elements. Elements in an ArrayList are managed in terms of references to the object type, which is the base type of all types in C#. This means that a program can store any type in an ArrayList.

■ The List type uses generics to allow developers to create lists of a particular type. The list stores elements of the given type. It is used in exactly the same way as an ArrayList, with the difference that there is no requirement to cast elements removed from the List to their proper type.

■ Dictionaries provide storage organized on a key value of a particular type. The key value must be unique for each item in the dictionary.

■ Sets store a collection of unique values. They are useful because of the set functions that they provide. Sets are useful for storing tag values and other kinds of unstructured properties of an item.

■ A Queue is a First-In-First-Out (FIFO) storage device that provides methods that can be used to Enqueue and Dequeue items.

■ A program can customize a collection by extending the base collection type and adding additional behaviors.

■ Programmers can create their own collection types by creating types that implement the ICollection interface.

■ A Stack is a Last-In-First-Out (LIFO) storage device that provides methods that can be used Push items on the stack and Pop them off.

Index

Symbols